A Grateful Heart

Recent Titles in
Contributions in Military Studies

A Grateful Heart

The History of a World War I Field Hospital

Michael E. Shay

Contributions in Military Studies, Number 212

Greenwood Press
Westport, Connecticut • London

Library of Congress Cataloging-in-Publication Data

Shay, Michael E., 1945–
  A grateful heart : the history of a World War I field hospital / Michael E. Shay.
    p. cm. — (Contributions in military studies, ISSN 0883–6884 ; no. 212)
  Includes bibliographical references and index.
  ISBN 0–313–31911–1 (alk. paper)
  1. United States. Army. Field Hospital Company, 103rd—History. 2. World War,
1914–1918—Campaigns—France. 3. World War, 1914–1918—Hospitals—France. 4. World
war, 1914–1918—Medical care—France. I. Title. II. Series.
  D570.354 103rd .S43 2002
  940.4′7644—dc21   2001023324

British Library Cataloguing in Publication Data is available.

Library of Congress Catalog Card Number: 2001023324
ISBN: 0–313–31911–1
ISSN: 0883–6884

First published in 2002

Greenwood Press, 88 Post Road West, Westport, CT 06881
An imprint of Greenwood Publishing Group, Inc.
www.greenwood.com

Printed in the United States of America

The paper used in this book complies with the
Permanent Paper Standard issued by the National
Information Standards Organization (Z39.48–1984).

10 9 8 7 6 5 4 3 2 1

TO MY GRANDFATHER
Cpl. Edward James Shay, Sr. (1893–1961)
103rd Field Hospital, 26th Division

AND TO

GREAT UNCLE
Sgt. Frank Henry "Cy" Shay (1896–1982)
137th & 802nd Aero Squadrons, U.S. Army

GREAT UNCLE
Sgt. Edward J. Acton (1893–1951)
101st Military Police Company, 26th Division

COUSIN
2nd Lt. John William Gleason, DSC. (1893–1982)
Tank Corps, U.S. Army
(Wounded in Action)

COUSIN
Sgt. Fred Stephen Murphy (1894–1918)
Co. L, 101st Inf., 26th Division
(Killed in Action)

AND ALSO TO
All those who served in the Great War—heroes every one!

Epigraph

Greet them ever with grateful hearts.
—Inscription above entry to Flanders Field Memorial
at the American Cemetery, Waregem, Belgium

I first read this quotation on the copyright page of Laurence Stallings's superb tribute to the American fighting man in World War I entitled *The Doughboys*. I was so taken by its poignancy that I sought to find out just who first penned those words. After consulting with the American Battle Monuments Commission as well as several of the University of Pennsylvania libraries, I have concluded that the author was Paul P. Cret (1876–1945). Dr. Cret was a Philadelphia architect of international reputation. He designed not only the Flanders Field American Cemetery and Memorial, as well as several other war memorials in France, but also many significant public buildings throughout the United States, including the Folger Shakespeare Library in Washington, D.C. A native of France, he himself saw action, first with the elite Alpine Chasseurs ("Blue Devils") and later as an interpreter with the AEF. Although the war left him with a partial hearing loss, and a subsequent operation on his larynx left him without the ability to speak, he continued to practice his profession until his death.

Contents

Photographic essay and maps follow page 108.

Preface

It has been known variously as the Great War, the First World War, and World War I. However, it has been largely ignored by modern writers, for a variety of reasons, not the least of which is the fact that the other three major conflicts—World War II, the Korean War, and that interminable quagmire called Vietnam—came one right after the other. So much has been written about these three, in large part by the participants themselves, that the first great war of this century has drifted into near oblivion. Most of the participants of the more recent wars (the sons and grandsons of those doughboys) are still alive and are reaching that age when the initial horror of their own experiences gives way, in part, to a nostalgic return to the days of their youth and the formation of their manhood. Their wars have become, as it were, the ultimate adventures. For the warriors—the "band of brothers," those who suffered through the terrors of combat—there is the sense of intense bonding with both the living and the dead. On the other hand, scarcely any warrior from those heady days of 1917–1918 is yet alive.

There was very little evidence at the house on 53 Maple Street in Framingham, then a quiet Boston suburb, that my grandfather had taken part in the first major overseas war that the United States ever fought. When I asked him about the faded corporal's stripes, with the caduceus on it, that he had tacked to the wall above his basement workbench to hold his pencils, all he would say was, "I used to be a sergeant, but I got busted back to corporal!" He never offered any explanation for the colorful medal with the unpronounceable place-names on it, which he kept in a crude, handmade frame on the bookshelf in the upstairs hall. Yet there were other hints, hints that I was too young to pick up on or appreciate.

There was the time that I fell beside the street in front of his house and picked up some nasty cinders in my knee. Grandma kept trying to calm me down, as

Grandpa removed them and washed the cuts, by telling me, "Your grandfather was *like* a doctor in the Army." I still have the scar on my left knee, but he was gentle and the operation was relatively painless. Later, when my grandfather had been dead for many years and my grandmother's mind was no longer what it had once been, she told me, "Your grandfather was gassed in the war, and when he came back, he was changed. He was never the same."

Since that conversation with my grandmother, I have tried to gather up the bits and pieces of his participation in that great conflict—a picture of him and his brother "Cy" (two doughboys in France), his dog tags, a scrap of a First Army shoulder patch, even the rusted belt buckle of a German soldier. The more I looked, the more interested I became in World War I. Soon I embarked upon a course of self-study to learn more about that time long ago when our country's muscles were flexed and so many young men went to war with enthusiasm and a sense of purpose—my grandfather among them.

Acknowledgments

Every author of a nonfiction work is dependent upon the generosity of many able persons to unlock the mysteries of and find the treasures located in our nation's libraries and archives. First and foremost, I wish to thank Alan C. Aimone, Special Collections, U.S. Military Academy Library, West Point, N.Y. Although he un-doubtedly will not remember it, he was instrumental in getting me to narrow my work to a more manageable scope. Even so, it has taken me more than four years to complete. He also made available to me the fantastic resources of the Cadet Library at West Point, which I have used quite often and extensively. Former director Stephen T. Seames, as well as Kent C. DeGroodt and Dana Essigman, archivists at the Massachusetts National Guard Military Museum and Archives in Worcester, Massachusetts, gave generously of their time in locating otherwise unavailable materials. By the end of each visit, their enthusiasm for my project was clear, as they brought out yet more documents for my perusal. I cannot say enough about Mitchell Yockelson at Old Military and Civil Records at the National Archives in Washington, D.C. Mitch made sure that the mountains of materials that needed to be reviewed were ready and waiting when my wife and I arrived. His persistence in locating some crucial documents is much appreciated.

In addition, the staff at the Still Pictures Branch of the National Archives in College Park, Maryland, was very capable and courteous. They made what would have been the daunting task of sifting through literally hundreds of photographs a pleasure. Lynn Swanson, the Interlibrary Loan Librarian at the Wilton Library, Wilton, Connecticut, permitted me to complete much of the research at home. Her quiet manner belies a dogged determination to obtain even the most obscure, out-of-print tomes. She never failed to find any book that I sought, not one. Michael Winey, John Slonaker, and Randy Hackenberg of the Military History Institute at

Carlisle Barracks, Pennsylvania, provided invaluable assistance in locating photographs and materials. Their quick turnaround time in filling my requests underscores their professionalism and the well-deserved reputation for excellence of their institution. Judith Ellen Johnson of the Connecticut Historical Society in Hartford, was a great help in making manuscript materials available. Barbara Jones and Anne Cowne of Lloyd's Register of Shipping in London, England, and T. Kenneth Anderson of the Ulster Folk and Transport Museum, Northern Ireland, found rare photographs of the ships that carried the 103rd Field Hospital to and from the war.

Laurence Urdang of Old Lyme, Connecticut—friend as well as publisher, author, and editor (to name just a few of his many talents)—has offered me encouragement and sage advice about the world of publishing. Edward MacEwen's many artistic talents are clearly evident in the superb maps that he has drawn for this work. I am sure the reader will agree with me that the clarity of these maps greatly enhances the story. Thanks a million! Charlie Flynn and Kathie Blakeslee, my former law partners, cut me a lot of slack, and I owe them big-time.

My entire family has offered me enthusiasm and encouragement every step of the way. Thanks to my mom and dad. I sure wish both were around to read it. I never mastered algebra, but they left me with a lifelong love of history. Thanks as well as to Pat, Ann, and Paul (splendid sibs) and to Ted and Kevin (peerless progeny). Last, but not least, thanks to my wife Marilyn, my biggest booster (as I am hers). She has been with me through the entire project (including a "near death experience" at the George Washington Bridge) as editor, researcher, critic, and overall boon companion. I hope that she has had as much fun as I have on this journey.

Place Names, Distances, and Abbreviations

If I was bedeviled by one thing in the course of my research, it was the eclectic and sometimes indecipherable spellings of place-names in France, not only in letters and diaries, but also in orders and official reports, where clarity and accuracy were essential. For consistency in this work, wherever possible, I have adopted the spellings or current place-names set forth in the Michelin series of touring maps of France (scale: 1/200000, 1 cm:2 km). Again, for consistency, I have used the distances between towns as shown on those maps, which are expressed in kilometers. In converting to miles, I have multiplied by point 61.

ANC	Arlington National Cemetery, Arlington, Va.
BCL	O'Neill Library, Boston College, Chestnut Hill, Mass.
CHS	The Connecticut Historical Society, Hartford, Conn.
CSL	Connecticut State Library, Hartford, Conn.
FHS	Framingham Historical Society, Framingham, Mass.
FPL	Framingham Public Library, Framingham, Mass.
MHI	Military History Institute, Carlisle Barracks, Carlisle, Penn.
MI	Morse Institute, Natick, Mass.
MNGA	Massachusetts National Guard Archives and Museum, Worcester, Mass.
NA RG120	National Archives and Records Administration, Washington, D.C., Record Group 120.
USMA	Cadet Library, United States Military Academy, West Point, N.Y.
WPL	Worcester Public Library, Worcester, Mass.

Chapter One

"Let's Go!"—The Yankee Division Gears Up

> We are of the blood of all the nations that are at war.
> —Woodrow Wilson (Second Inaugural Address)

THE GREAT WAR—AN OVERVIEW (APRIL 1917–OCTOBER 1917)

Europe

By April 2, 1917, when Woodrow Wilson asked Congress for a declaration of war, the European continent had been in the throes of a bloody conflict without resolution or significant movement for two and one-half years. For America, the Great War was a series of news dispatches from unfamiliar places like Ypres, Gallipoli, and Armentiers. The French army, once the pride of Europe, was experiencing mass mutiny, or as the French euphemistically referred to it, "collective indiscipline."[1] The "great man" of Europe was mired in the sucking mud of Flanders and the misty vales of the Argonne Forest. Defenses in depth, series of interlocking parallel trenches that stretched from the North Sea through the Vosges Mountains and Alsace all the way to the Swiss border, made it virtually impossible for either side to make significant penetrations, much less flank their opponent's positions.[2] Stalemate was the order of the day. Stalemate and stagnation; disease and death; heroes and horror—There were staggering numbers of dead and wounded, of artillery shells fired, of coils of barbed wire. Great Britain had used up the flower of her manhood by early 1915, and only a year later, she was in danger of doing the same with the new "supply of heroes."[3] The year 1916 saw the British incur 50,000 casualties in a single day during the Somme offensive,[4] and 370,000 more by the time that series of battles was done.[5] For most of the same year, the French and German armies were locked in a titanic struggle surrounding a place called Verdun. The city itself never fell, but nearly three-quarters of a million soldiers, both French and German, died or were wounded on that narrow front straddling the Meuse River. Even today the bones of those lost at Verdun are still being recovered as they work their way to the surface, like stones in a New England farm field. This is such a frequent occurrence that the French government maintains a chaplain to see to their reverent interment. The Ossuary, a grimly ostentatious memorial at the site, contains the bones of more than 250,000 men from both sides.[6] Whole villages surrounding the area simply disappeared from the map, with no evidence today that they ever existed save memorial markers where they used to be. The narrow road from Bar-le-Duc winds uphill much as it did then, only now a well-paved road has replaced the muddy lane that was once the lifeline of the French army. Today it is called the Voie Sacrée, in honor of those men who, along with ammunition and supplies, moved slowly forward with resignation to that holy ground, in a pilgrimage toward death.

It is little wonder that during the following year large segments of the French army simply said, "Enough is enough!" American doughboys fighting alongside French troops in 1918 noted that, with certain exceptions, mainly among the colonial regiments, their colleagues just did not have the fire in their bellies and the *élan* that had been the hallmarks of the *poilu* in the preceding years. The French soldier was jaded and cautious. In marked contrast, the Americans advanced quickly toward their objectives, often with their flanks exposed.

United States

For a long time the United States sat on the sideline, an interested observer. Ostensibly we were neutral, but our hearts and minds were with the Entente, in particular, with Great Britain. This fact was not lost upon the Germans, who waged a ruthless U-boat campaign in the Atlantic. That, in turn, only served to further stoke the fires of our Anglophilia, which finally burst into open flame with the sinking of the *Lusitania*, with significant loss of American life.

President Wilson had been reelected with the promise to "keep us out of war." We had no draft and no army to speak of. What we did have was an army that was ill-equipped and ill-prepared, and ranked well behind those of most nations of the civilized world.[7] The Punitive Expedition to Mexico in 1916 was a farce. In response to the unsettled conditions in neighboring Mexico and an unprovoked attack by guerrillas on the citizens of Columbus, New Mexico, the United States dispatched to the border Gen. John Pershing and a military force composed largely of cavalry and many National Guard units, including elements of the Massachusetts National Guard.[8] The soldiers were unable to seize the bandit leader, Pancho Villa. Still, the expedition was a proving ground for many future doughboys, including Pershing and his aide, George S. Patton, Jr.[9]

Pershing became the hands-down choice of President Wilson to head the American Expeditionary Force. Some thought that Gen. Leonard Wood had the inside track, but the signs were all there for people to read. Earlier, in 1906, President Theodore Roosevelt had promoted Captain Pershing to brigadier general, passing over more than 800 more senior officers. Being the son-in-law of Senator Francis E. Warren, chairman of the Senate Military Affairs Committee, did not hurt, and his star was clearly on the rise.

Born John Joseph Pershing on September 13, 1860, in Laclede, Missouri, he entered the U.S. Military Academy in 1882. While his academic performance left something to be desired, his natural capacity for leadership brought about his election as class president and first captain of cadets. He served on the frontier and later taught military science at the University of Nebraska, where he earned a law degree. Pershing also saw active duty in the Spanish-American War, where he earned the nickname "Black Jack," due to his service with black troops. Later service in the Phillippines pitted him against the fierce Moros of Mindinao. When trouble erupted on the border with Mexico, he was the logical choice to lead the expedition. While he was there, tragedy struck when his home at the Presidio in San Francisco caught fire and his wife and three daughters perished in the flames.[10]

War was declared on April 6, 1917. Marshal Joseph-Jacques-Césaire Joffre made a quick trip to Washington following the declaration in order to plead for men.[11] His visit coincided with the British diversionary attacks at Arras and the start of the Aisne offensive by the French.[12] There was a sense of urgency to his visit, as the French attacks soon began to falter as mutiny spread throughout the army.

Congress responded on May 18, 1917, with the Draft Act, which was promptly signed by Wilson. Registration of draft-age men was to commence on June 5, to be followed by the selection process on July 20. On May 28, Pershing, as commander of the American Expeditionary Force, departed for France along with his staff. Just over one month later, elements of the U.S. 1st Division (the "Big Red One") arrived in France.[13] Far too small to be anything but a morale booster, this trickle of men would become a torrent of more than a 1 million within one year.

The U.S. troops proudly paraded through the streets of Paris to the tumultuous cheers of her citizens, but this was only for show, since the real work had yet to begin. As he began to establish his headquarters, it must have seemed to Pershing that politics ruled the day. On a basic level, the British and French took the newly arriving Americans in tow, training and indoctrinating them in the skills and tactics that they had learned from long, bitter experience on the Western Front. However, on a higher level, the allies pressured Pershing and his staff to integrate his forces directly into British and French units. Before Pershing left for France, President Wilson had warned his general that this might happen and ordered him to resist.[14] Pershing could not have agreed more, and he firmly and resolutely rebuffed any and all such pressures. U.S. troops were to fight as an independent American army, led by American officers. If it was to be coalition warfare, we would be a full partner. That is not to say that compromises were not reached. Many U.S. divisions fought bravely and well under British command in Flanders, and under French command in the Aisne-Marne sector, but they fought as Americans and with their own officers to lead them. They received universally high praise for their spirit and fighting qualities. These very attributes only increased the frequency of requests for the doughboys. In addition to infantry, many artillery, medical, and other service units served and trained with distinction with the Allies.

As the buildup continued, Pershing played the game with skill and poise, rarely losing his temper in public. He kept the Allies at bay while building up his army for its eventual debut. He had to put up with the insufferable hubris of his partners, who viewed the brash Americans as a necessary evil. If the truth be told, underlying the fear of a large, independent American army was the fact that it would give the United States, and in particular Woodrow Wilson, a say in the re-creation of postwar Europe. Moreover, we would be entitled to a share in the spoils of victory, not the least of which were the guns and capital ships produced by Germany. However, because three years of total war had resulted in acute manpower shortages among the Allies, and because of the collapse of the Russian state, Germany would shortly begin to transfer men from the eastern front. They knew that they had no choice but to keep up the pressure on America to send men, and to strike the best bargain they could with Pershing. When the American First Army finally came into being. It was Pershing's turn. French divisions, he declared, could now serve with his troops! But that would be a year down the road. Before that could happen, America would have to provide the men, and he would have to form them into a cohesive, effective fighting force.

THE "YANKEE DIVISION"

Beginnings (March 1917 to October 1917)

The 26th Division was not supposed to be the first complete National Guard division dispatched to France. Aside from the regular divisions of the United States Army, it was envisioned that the honor would be accorded a unit composed of men from all over the United States, an all-American division.[15] Colonel Douglas MacArthur would coin the nickname "Rainbow Division,"[16] as an apt symbol of the diversity it represented and for the spirit of unity it would demonstrate. The 42nd Division NG, as it was officially called, would contain such geographically diverse and legendary units as the 69th Regiment of the New York National Guard (the "Fighting 69th"), which traced its ancestry to the famous Irish Brigade of the Union army, and the 4th Alabama Regiment of that state's National Guard. These old adversaries, who had met as enemies during the Civil War, would now fight together in France. No, the honor of being the first National Guard division overseas fell to the New Englanders thanks to the foresight and organizational skills of their commander, Maj. Gen. Clarence Ransom Edwards.[17]

General Edwards graduated from the U.S. Military Academy at West Point as a member of the class of 1883. Born in Cleveland, Ohio, on New Year's Day 1859,[18] of New England stock (a direct descendant of the Reverend Jonathan Edwards),

Edwards served in the regular army in both staff and line duties throughout his long career, which spanned more than forty years. Shortly after his graduation from West Point, he commanded the honor guard at the grave of President James Garfield. He married Bessie Rochester Porter in Niagara Falls, New York, on June 11, 1899. The couple had one daughter, Bessie. Edwards was a veteran of the Spanish-American War (1898–1899) and was thrice awarded the Silver Star for gallantry during the Philippine Insurrection (1899–1901). Edwards commanded a brigade on the Mexican border in 1916, and he was later appointed a major general and commander of the Northeastern Department. He was a straight-talking man of scrupulous honesty, a man who looked after his men, even if it meant a dust up with higher authority.[19] His men, many of whom were tough veterans of the recent expedition to the southwestern United States and the incursion into Mexico, reciprocated the loyalty, and he became affectionately known as "Daddy" to them.[20]

A telegram from the War Department dated August 13, 1917, to Edwards at the Northeastern Department, authorized the creation of a brand-new division for service in France. As a result of Edwards' energetic efforts, on August 22, 1917, a collection of various Guard units from all over New England was melded together and designated the 26th Division NG[21] to signify that it was the first such unit (numbers one through twenty-five had been reserved for regular army divisions). However, the division was nicknamed, appropriately enough, the "Yankee Division," and later in the war it took for its shoulder patch the now-familiar "YD."

American divisions were large by any standard. They contained approximately 28,000 men. Consequently, they were twice as large as their Allied counterparts, sometimes larger due to attrition within the latter, and often three and four times larger than the German divisions that they faced on any given day.[22] They were organized on the principle of a square, with two brigades composed of two regiments each. The regiments, in turn, contained three battalions, with four companies each. There were separate machine gun battalions and artillery units, together with support troops, such as headquarters, service of supply, and sanitary trains.[23] Each division was a self-contained, self-supporting fighting unit of incredible power. What an American division lacked initially in experience was more than offset by the sheer numbers and enthusiasm of its soldiers.

At first, virtually all of the new division was composed of New England men. It was only later, after disease and death had taken their toll, that replacements came from all over the United States. Even then it remained a predominantly New England outfit, which contributed to its *esprit*. Long after the war was over, the men who saw service in the division, especially the New Englanders, would speak of that time with a sense of great pride. In March 1917, even before the formal declaration of war, when the call went out to the New England militias, they were able, much like the Minutemen of the Revolution, to assemble on very short notice. This time, however, the ranks were full of the sons of immigrants, a large proportion of whom were Irish. By early August the various units had been consolidated and redesignated. Thus, the former 5th and 9th Regiments became the 101st Infantry Regiment—again, the very first of the National Guard fighting units.[24] The 51st

Brigade was composed of the 101st Infantry Regiment (mostly Massachusetts men) and the 102nd Infantry Regiment (mostly Connecticut men), while the 52nd Brigade was made up of the 103rd Infantry Regiment (Maine and New Hampshire) and 104th Infantry Regiment (Massachusetts).[25] As it came into being, the 26th Division, along with all the other National Guard divisions now forming across the country, was federalized.

On Tuesday afternoon, August 21, 1917, the New England troops assembled at Camp McGuinness, formerly the Muster Field, in Framingham for a final review before departure for France. During the day the temperature had plunged seventeen degrees, from a sultry 81 degrees at 11 A.M. to a cool 64 degrees at 6 P.M. A strong, cool northeast wind had driven into a warm air mass over New England and produced an enormous line of powerful thunderstorms all throughout the Boston area, lasting four to eight hours in some places. Some locations reported three inches of rain, but the worst damage came from the lightning strikes. In Boston, three fires were blamed on the storm, and telegraph service was interrupted with New York. The towns of Clinton, Hingham, Quincy, Everett, and even New London, Connecticut, all felt the storm's wrath. Numerous reports were received of people struck by bolts lightning, including a postman, a sailor, and, sadly, a woman killed in Marshfield. Many of the tents of the Rhode Island Ambulance Company and others, pitched just the day before at Camp Holcomb in Niantic, Connecticut, were blown over by the violent storm, and the troops were deluged. It was also the day that the 1st New Hampshire Field Hospital Company was ordered to set up camp in Framingham. The men had barely completed the train trip from New Hampshire when they, too, were greeted with driving rain. In spite of the foul weather, they managed to pitch three ward tents and thus slept relatively dry.[26]

Without a doubt, the worst single incident occurred at Camp McGuinness. It was there, shortly before 5 P.M., and just after the consolidation ceremony[27] of the 5th and 9th Massachusetts Infantry (which had been held in a drenching rain, in a bizarre portent of things to come), that the violent storm struck the middle of the encampment. Witnesses described a deluge of rain both before and after the main force of the storm. The lightning came from all sides, and the thunder was continuous. When it was over, two soldiers lay dead, and more than fifty had been flattened by the strike, many rendered unconscious. Of the latter, eleven, three officers and eight enlisted men, were injured seriously enough to be evacuated to either Framingham or regimental hospitals. Many no doubt owed their lives to the quick-acting regimental surgeons present for the review, as well as to the men of the 1st and 2nd Field Hospitals (later the 101st and 103rd Field Hospitals). For some the doctors had to use a Pulmotor, a device for pumping oxygen into an asphyxiated person. The dead were twenty-two-year-old Cpl. Edward Payson Clark, Jr. of Natick, and Pvt. Patrick J. Sullivan of Norwood. Both soldiers were members of Co. L, 9th Infantry, whose company street of tents received the brunt of the blow. Clark, who had been promoted the day before, had had the company tailor sew the stripes on his sleeve just hours before his death. Sullivan, who had been married just two weeks to Mary Crane of Framingham, had been holding a metal tripod while erecting a tent. Needless to say the incident "spread great gloom over the camp."[28] Hardly an auspicious beginning![29]

On August 24, an advance party set sail from New York for France on the SS *Panonia*, stopping first in Liverpool, England.[30] Later, as the 26th Division became fully organized, the troops were transported by rail to New York City and ultimately to Hoboken, New Jersey, or to Montreal, Canada. Camp Merritt at Hoboken would not be completed until October, so the departing troops walked off of the train and literally onto the ship. For the most part, the transport vessels were registered in Allied countries, predominantly Great Britain. Many a doughboy sailed to war on luxurious liners like the *Olympic, Aquitania,* and *Mauritania*,[31] in convoys of between ten and twenty ships.[32] The Yankee Division began the crossing on September 6, 1917, with the last ship sailing about October 9. The convoy method was used, as a precaution against the prowling German U-boats, and the ships assembled at Halifax Harbor to commence the Atlantic journey. The ports of destination were St. Nazaire in France and Liverpool in England.[33]

Upon arrival in France, the men were transported by rail, for the most part in boxcars labeled "40 *Hommes*—8 *Chevaux*," also known as "side-door Pullmans."[34] A typical French troop train consisted of fifty cars and was capable of moving an infantry battalion of one thousand men and their equipment. Such a train was broken down as follows:

17 flatcars for guns or vehicles

30 boxcars for enlisted men or horses ("40/8")

2 coaches for officers

1 baggage van for the train crew

The mix of rolling stock could vary, depending upon the type of unit. At the beginning of the war it took a typical artillery battery about two and one-half hours to load itself onto the train. Later on, an experienced battery could embark in fourteen to twenty-one minutes.[35]

Aside from the doughboy's feet, these freight cars, of "ridiculously light and flimsy construction," became the principal means of transporting large numbers of men and equipment long distances. One doughboy who paced off one of these cars opined that the fourteen feet between the front and rear trucks made them about half as long as their American counterparts. Moreover, he found that:

There are no air brakes, the lack being supplied by shock absorbers at each end—large disks the size of dinner plates, which clash loudly together when the cars bump. . . . These cars were equipped with a diabolical arrangement of heavy plank seats, which were convenient during the day, but made it impossible to get any sleep at night. There was not a spot in the car where a man could stretch himself out flat.[36]

In addition, the floor of the car was often covered with manure.[37]

The destination of the 26th Division was a relatively quiet sector in the Vosges Mountains in the Fourth Training Area, which encompassed Neufchâteau and its environs. They reached it after an uncomfortable ride that took between 36 and 48 hours.[38] In addition to the discomfort, lack of sufficient food was also a problem during the trip. Members of the 101st Engineers described the "English rations" of "tea, hard-tack, bacon, and cheese," which they received at Le Havre, as inadequate to sustain them on their journey, let alone for the work to which they were assigned immediately upon arrival.[39] Still, for many of those young men, most of whom had not traveled outside their native New England, the novelty of seeing the beautiful French countryside passing by the open boxcar door must have, at least temporarily, offset the discomfort.[40] Pfc. Bartlett Bent of Newington, Connecticut, was assigned to the 120th Aero Squadron, stationed near Tours. He described the train that took him there in September 1918 as "frightfully slow" and the trip itself as "aweful tiresome." As he hung his feet over the doorsill of the moving boxcar, he "took in everything seeable," observing that, "the trip altho most uncomfortable was mighty interesting for practically everything I saw was new to me."Aside from the numerous trainloads of wounded and prisoners, as well as the French soldiers at every station, the countryside reminded him of home.[41]

101st Sanitary Trains: "What's in a Name?"

Like their counterparts in the combat units, the men of the medical units came from all over New England. As of July 15, 1917, every state but Maine was represented in one capacity or another. From Massachusetts came the 1st and 2nd Massachusetts Ambulance Companies, as well as the 1st and 2nd Massachusetts Field Hospital Companies. Connecticut supplied the 1st Connecticut Field Hospital Company and the 1st Connecticut Ambulance Company. Rhode Island provided the 1st Rhode Island Ambulance Company, while from New Hampshire came the 1st New Hampshire Field Hospital Company.

In addition to the geographical proximity, these units also had an advantage during the organizational phase, in that they were all placed under the command of the division surgeon. The surgeon general of the United States quickly assigned to the division an administrative unit, originally slated for another division, to be the core of the headquarters staff of the 26th Division surgeon, Lt. Col. James Lung Bevans, MD. What these people lacked in military experience was more than made up for in their enthusiastic energy as they set about the tasks assigned to them.

Initially, all of the field hospital and ambulance companies were understrength in enlisted personnel. In addition, the strengths of the medical detachments assigned to the various line companies were mixed—some units had a surplus, while others were weak. Accordingly, many replacements were transferred from artillery posts in the Northeastern Department and from the Depot Brigade. Some came from the national draft, which was a further blow to local unit pride. In short, the quality of many recruits was very poor. A shortage of experienced noncommissioned officers was to plague the division medical service throughout the war. The selection of medical officers for service overseas also presented problems. Some candidates were overage and were thought unable to handle the stress of a long campaign, while others just did not want to go. Many were simply unqualified. After considerable effort to obtain good personnel and weed out the unfit, the division sailed for France with slightly more medical officers and men than called for in the table of organization.[42]

The division medical personnel were consolidated into a unit designated the 101st Sanitary Trains. In addition to a headquarters section formed on August 20, 1917, all of the units were redesignated as follows:[43]

1st Mass. Ambulance Co.	became	1st Ambulance Co., 26th Div.
2nd Mass. Ambulance Co.	became	2nd Ambulance Co., 26th Div.
1st Mass. Field Hosp. Co.	became	1st Field Hospital, 26th Div.
2nd Mass. Field Hosp. Co.	became	*2nd Field Hospital, 26th Div.*
1st Conn. Field Hosp. Co.	became	3rd Field Hospital, 26th Div.
1st Conn. Ambulance Co.	became	3rd Ambulance Co., 26th Div.
1st R.I. Ambulance Co.	became	4th Ambulance Co., 26th Div.
1st N.H. Field Hosp. Co.	became	4th Field Hospital, 26th Div.

At the time of sailing, medical supplies were inadequate, and there was virtually no motor transport.[44] As an example, the 2nd Field Hospital left Framingham with only four complete hospital tents and two Model J Indian motorcycles with sidecars. Its motor transport was to be delivered at Montreal. Two field hospitals and two ambulance companies, slated to be animal drawn, had no horses or mules.[45] Also, many elements of the division as a whole had few dressings or medicines. The division surgeon and his staff were busy right up to the last minute with organizational issues, and they sailed to France on the last transport.[46]

2nd Massachusetts Field Hospital Company (2nd Field Hospital, 26th Division): Movement at Last

Seventy-two enlisted men and three officers answered "present" at the initial muster at the armory on Dartmouth Street, Boston, on July 28, 1917. Three more officers and nine additional enlisted men were assigned to the company but were not there for roll call that day.[47] According to the table of organization and equipment (TOE), the authorized strength of a motorized field hospital was six officers and eighty-three enlisted men,[48] so the company was just two men short of full strength; as the weeks of preparation and training passed, these numbers would fluctuate. Shortly thereafter, the unit moved to Camp McGuinness.[49] Like every unit scheduled to go to France, the company tried to screen out those men thought unfit to withstand the anticipated rigors of war. During the month of August, three men were honorably discharged for disability, and one man was transferred to the

2nd Ambulance Company. The deficit was offset by the addition of five men that month.[50] Maj. Frederick A. King, MD, of Boston, a National Guard officer, was the first company commander. This was a time of learning, and the duties of the medics were very light. Daily reports showed no patients treated in July, and August was not much more active. On August 14, for example, the company's report lists one patient sick and one remaining for treatment.[51]

September 15, 1917, brought movement. The unit, along with the 2nd Massachusetts Ambulance Company, left Framingham for an overnight journey by train to the docks at Montreal.[52] It was joined there by the 3rd Battalion of the 102nd Infantry Regiment, Connecticut men who had left their camp in Niantic the same day in order to join the medicos for the journey to France. They would all meet again under different circumstances, when the infantrymen would be carried in on litters after fights at places like the Pas Fini and the Toul sector. Now their steps were sprightly as they boarded, with anxious anticipation, the RMS *Canada*.[53] On September 16, the ship pulled away from the dock and headed down the beautiful St. Lawrence River. It paused for a while at Halifax, Nova Scotia, to await the arrival of the other troopships that would make up the convoy for the dangerous North Atlantic passage. In Halifax some of the men were able to exchange cigarettes with, and ask questions of, wounded Canadians returning for recuperation.[54] During the voyage the company reported no patient activity, but training continued with classes and exercise.[55] A member of the 103rd Field Artillery who sailed the North Atlantic about one month later, referred to "monster waves" as high as the ship, so seasickness must have been epidemic.[56] The journey was without incident,[57] and the ship docked at Liverpool, during the night of October 2.[58]

No doubt, the medics shared the experiences of their comrades from the 3rd Battalion. At Liverpool their eyes were opened to the frustrations of army life. There they were greeted at the docks by British officers who summarily ordered them to board trains for a camp in southern England. They were not permitted to take their own rations, nor were they allowed to bring their own baggage. They were told, "It would come later." The baggage never caught up with some of them, and those "lucky souls" who did receive it weeks later in France found to their disgust that their barracks bags and other baggage had been opened and the contents looted, particularly tobacco, cigarettes, shoes, and flannel shirts.[59]

The men boarded trains during the night and the early morning hours of October 3 for their interim destination, a rest camp at Southampton. However, the stay there was hardly restful. More senior officers enjoyed the "comforts" of prefabricated Adrian barracks, while the junior officers and enlisted men were billeted in tents. The fall weather was generally wet and miserable, and the ground was composed of a "black, sticky mud" and cinders. Food was another problem—not enough of it. And when the men were fed, it was tea with jam and bread, or perhaps a half cup of soup.[60] Some groups continued their training with five-mile hikes.

The 2nd Field Hospital spent the better part of two days at Southampton. On the afternoon of the second day, it embarked on another ship, arriving at Le Havre, France, on October 5 after an uneventful passage of the English Channel.[61] The unit marched to Rest Camp No. 2 and then promptly marched back to the railroad station, where, pursuant to verbal orders, it entrained for transport to its assigned duty station at Bazoilles-sur-Meuse, in the Department of Vosges. The unit arrived on October 7 to begin a tour in France that was to span nearly a year and a half.

In October 1917, Bazoilles-sur-Meuse was a small farming village of 150 souls in the narrow valley of the upper Meuse, approximately four miles south of Neufchâteau.[62] One soldier described the town as "dirty, romantic, and interesting." Dr. Harvey Cushing and his colleagues referred to it as "Bacillus on the Mess."[63] The west bank rises steeply to a plateau, while the east bank rises more gradually toward wooded hills and farm fields. The village proper lies on the west bank. National Route 14 (now Route D74) between Neufchâteau to the north and Langres to the south dips down into the valley and crosses the river over a multi-arched stone bridge. The Est rail line traveled along the east bank; the station lay just off the main road. The river widens somewhat at this point, and the shallow waters near its banks are full of reeds and water plants. The narrow main street of the village branched off from the highway and twisted uphill from the river past the *maire* (mayor's office) and the Catholic church, dedicated to Saint Martin. The latter would be nondescript but for a tall and very ornate tower clearly visible for miles around. The street continued its upward climb toward the summit past typical farm dwellings combining house and barn under one roof. The ubiquitous manure piles in front of each dwelling, some of which had low stone retaining walls, spoke of the wealth of those within, but they proved unsightly and offensive to the doughboys. Moreover, when the rains came, the mixture of manure and mud in the street was unspeakable.[64]

At the top of the hill, was the chateau, or hunting lodge, of the Drummond family, the comtes de Melfort. The family had been expatriates from Scotland during the defeat and flight of James II. The main building was situated on a twenty-five-acre parcel of forested land and contained several groups of stone outbuildings. Its view of the Meuse Valley was splendid. Since March of 1916, the French had used the chateau, a lovely stone structure with a tree-lined approach, as a hospital. On July 26, 1917, a hospital unit organized at Johns Hopkins Hospital in Baltimore, Maryland, took over from the French and was designated Base Hospital No. 18; it was then the farthest advanced hospital in the AEF.[65] At that time, the hospital was a one-thousand-bed facility consisting of thirty-six frame barracks and the chateau. The latter was used as an office and administration building.

The barracks were divided into two groups. The first, consisting of twenty-five buildings, was considered the hospital proper. Twenty buildings were used as wards, while the remainder comprised an operating room, receiving office, shower baths, clothing room, linen and supply room, and a sleeping barracks for the hospital staff. The second group of eleven buildings was used for general purposes, such as an officers' barracks, six barracks for enlisted men, a kitchen and mess hall, carpenter shop, fumigation room and plumber's shop, storage building, and a morgue.

Water was piped in from a well five miles away. During the dry season, the pipe supplied one thousand gallons a day, stored in two small reservoirs. The water was tested regularly and was considered safe. Lighting, however, was a definite problem. The source of electricity was a generator driven by a small gasoline motor that could be run only a couple of hours a day. The generator provided light from 8 to 10 P.M. and an additional two hours early in the morning; however, when the X-ray machine was in use, the lights had to be turned off. Each ward had two or three small coal-burning stoves, which were totally inadequate during the winter. Waste water was drained into the ground after exposure to sunlight in putrefication vats. Human waste, however, was collected daily in cans and taken to a collection point where it was burned. The laundry was located on the bank of the Meuse about half a mile from the hospital. It was a moveable steam laundry, run by coal and gasoline. The capacity was minimal, and it was apparently operated by paid civilians. One kitchen served the entire complex, and a moderate-sized mess hall in the same building was used by the enlisted men as well as ambulatory patients. Food for other patients had to be carried into the individual wards, the farthest one being about three city blocks away. Dishes were washed by hand, for which the supply of hot water was inadequate.[66]

Starting with Base Hospital No. 18 at the chateau and its grounds, the small hospital would eventually mushroom into a very large complex on both sides of the Meuse, with seven separate hospitals. Each hospital section would have wooden barracks built to accommodate a thousand beds, to which were eventually added tent wards holding a thousand more patients. All in all, the hospital complex would have about 13,000 beds at its peak.[67] When complete, Base Hospital No. 18 would have a laboratory, with sections for bacteriology, serology, pathology, typhoid-dysentery examinations, and pneumococcus typing.[68] However, none of this would have been possible without the tireless efforts of Companies B and C of the 101st Engineers, which arrived on October 23, 1917. They occupied an old barracks at the edge of town and set to work immediately constructing standard wooden barracks, as well as the familiar Adrian barracks, which required assembly. The engineers became so proficient at their task that by the time their tour at Bazoilles-sur-Meuse was completed, they could fully assemble an entire barracks in one day.[69] Nevertheless, the quality of the construction materials left much to be desired, and while the finished product was a step up for most of the hospital personnel, the barracks and wards were drafty and very poorly heated, due to the small stoves installed. Moreover, wood was in short supply on the west side of the river; it had to be harvested on and transported from the east bank. The green, unseasoned wood did not burn efficiently.[70]

It was to this location that the 2nd Field Hospital was initially assigned. Its duty was to assist in the establishment of the fledgling base hospital and at the same time afford its personnel the opportunity to acquire the art of medical treatment from the somewhat more experienced members of the Hopkins unit, who formed the core of Base Hospital No. 18. However, the first priority for the medics when they debarked from the train on October 7 was to locate housing. The 101st Engineers had not yet arrived to build barracks, wards, and other facilities. Unfortunately for them, the 1st Field Hospital Company had arrived on October 1 and had undoubtedly secured the best accommodations in the town. The usual practice was for a division billeting officer to go through a village beforehand to locate appropriate space—generally lofts, barns, or other outbuildings. Numbers were stenciled on the walls of the dwellings indicating the number of officers, enlisted men, and animals that could be accommodated within.[71] The men of the 2nd Field Hospital had to be somewhat apprehensive as they filed off the train and entered the town. Fanning out, they stopped periodically to look at the numbers on the houses and to occupy their assigned quarters. In most cases their concerns were justified, since the spaces allocated to them were located in dirty and drafty "barns and vacant garrets." Each officer was assigned a room with a bed in a private home.[72]

Recreation during the enlisted men's free time was necessarily limited, due to the unit's being in a small farming town. Their commanding officer limited it even more. On October 8, 1917, Major King posted a guard of two men at the bridge to prevent any man from crossing into the town without a pass. He rescinded the order the very next day (most likely as impractical) and said that from then on, the men could go to Bazoilles-sur-Meuse, reporting to the first sergeant, who also had the responsibility for their returning "condition."[73]

The entire Yankee Division, including the medical units, was like a giant advance party. The infrastructure of the area had to be built from the ground up, including roads, communications, and sanitation. Not only did the soldiers have to learn the ropes themselves, but they also had to pave the way for the millions that would soon follow. Reveille was at 7 A.M. and taps at 10 P.M.[74] Training went on all the time in between. A typical weekday for the medicos began with a hike at 8:30 A.M., followed by two hours of classes, another hike at 1 P.M. and two more hours of classes. The courses were taught by the company officers; they included such medical subjects as anatomy, physiology, and first aid, as well as military subjects like camp sanitation and military discipline. Saturday was set aside for general inspections of quarters and of personal equipment. Sunday was a day of rest and attendance at church.[75] In addition the men of the 2nd Field Hospital had light medical duties. On October 14, the daily log noted that four sick patients were treated.[76] In the week ending October 19, the unit handled a total of fifteen patients, including one case of measles. That patient and five others were transferred to another hospital. During the following two weeks, no patients were seen.[77]

While at Bazoilles-sur-Meuse, the 2nd Field Hospital Company was ordered to provide a detail of three men to assist in the conversion of the old French barracks (originally built by the Germans, about 1871) at Rebeval into a hospital for the division's sick.[78] The site was on the west side of the river across from Neufchâteau; it was later occupied by the 104th Field Hospital.[79] At the same time thirteen men were promoted to private first class.[80] As of October 31, 1917, company records for the end of the month disclosed an effective strength of seventy-nine enlisted men—a slight drop, due in part, no doubt, to the transfer of the work detail. In addition to Major King, four other medical officers were part of the company, all lieutenants: Harold F. Parker, Joseph R. Helff, James Y. Roger, and William S. Schley.[81] First Lt. Roy F. Brown, who had sailed with the company, was transferred.[82]

NOTES

1. Thomas E. Greiss, ed. *The Great War* (Wayne, N.J.: Avery, 1986), 122; Rod Paschall, *The Defeat of Imperial Germany, 1917–1918* (Chapel Hill, N.C.: Algonquin, 1989), 50–51.

2. Paschall, *Defeat of Imperial Germany,* 12–13.

3. Sir Edward Carson, Speech.

4. Martin Gilbert, *The First World War* (New York: Henry Holt, 1994), 260. More than 21,000 men died out of a total of 50,000 casualties. It was the largest single-day total of the war.

5. John Keegan, *The Face of Battle* (London: Penguin, 1976), 285.

6. Alistair Horne, *The Price of Glory: Verdun, 1916* (London: Penguin, 1993), 327–28 and 350.

7. Philip J. Haythornthwaite, *The World War One Source Book* (London: Arms and Armor, 1996), 308–9; Paschall, *Defeat of Imperial Germany,* 27.

8. Edward M. Coffman, *The War to End All Wars: The American Experience in World War I* (Madison, Wis.: Univ. of Wisconsin Press, 1986), 13–14.

9. Carlo D'Este, *Patton: A Genius for War* (New York: HarperCollins, 1995), 172–77.

10. Roger J. Spiller, ed., *Dictionary of American Military Biography* (Westport, Conn.: Greenwood, 1984), vol. 2, 846–50. After the world war, he served briefly as Chief of Staff from 1921 to 1924. His memoirs, *My Experiences in the World War*, won him the Pulitzer Prize. He died in Washington, D.C., on July 15, 1948.

11. Coffman, *War to End All Wars,* 8–9.

12. Gilbert, *First World War,* 320–23.

13. Coffman, *War to End All Wars,* 27–28, 122, and 131–32.

14. Paul Braim, *The Test of Battle: The American Expeditionary Forces in the Meuse–Argonne* (Newark: Univ. of Delaware Press, 1988), 9–13.

15. Frank Sibley, *With the Yankee Division in France* (Boston: Little, Brown, 1919), 19.

16. William Manchester, *American Caesar* (Boston: Little, Brown, 1978), 79; Geoffrey Perret, *Old Soldiers Never Die* (New York: Random House, 1996), 77.

17. Coffman, *War to End All Wars,* 147.

18. Some sources incorrectly list his birth year as 1860. His obituary and gravestone list the year as 1859.

19. "Annual Report," *Assembly,* 10 June 1931, 198–201.

20. James T. Duane, *Dear Old "K"* (Boston: Thomas Todd, 1922), tribute to General Edwards.

21. James Lung Bevans, *Medical History of the 26th Division from Organization to June 24, 1918* (typescript, n.d.), 1. NA RG120

22. Coffman, *War to End All Wars,* 48.

23. Laurence Stallings, *The Doughboys* (New York: Harper and Row, 1963), 32–33.

24. Duane, *Dear Old "K,"* 3.

25. *Immortal Yankee Division 1917–1918* (Boston: Young Men's Christian Association, 1919), 12–13.

26. R. S. Porter, *101st Sanitary Train, 26th Division A.E.F., History, March 20th, 1919,* manuscript, 338. Other units at Camp Holcomb were the 1st Connecticut Field Hospital and the 1st Connecticut Ambulance Company. MNGA See also *Boston Globe, August 22, 1917,* 3. BCL

27. The consolidation of the two regiments did not go smoothly from the beginning. Earlier that day, when a large group of 5th Infantry men, including noncommissioned

officers, then stationed at Camp Darling in South Framingham, learned of the consolidation with the 9th Infantry, they began a protest march to the Statehouse in Boston. Some even commandeered a train. Cooler heads prevailed, including the commanding officer and Chaplain Rollins. Both spoke to the angry men, and the soldiers returned to camp. Thus a full-scale revolt was averted. *Framingham Evening News*, August 21, 1917, 1. FHS

28. *Boston Daily Globe*, 22 August 1917, 1 and 6; see also *Boston Globe*, 22 August 1917, p. 6. BCL.; *Natick Bulletin*, August 24, 1917, 1, and *Framingham Evening News*, August 22, 1917, 1. The seriously injured were Edward Day of Medford, Arthur Kelliher of Cochituate, Malcolm Russell of Melrose, Maurice Mendoza of Everett, Robert H. Dicker of Medford, Lt. Charles Cannon of Dorchester, Maurice Gouldsburg of Revere, Leslie Bennett and Edward Fannon of Natick, and Capt. James D. Weir and Lt. Eli Benway of Charlestown. All but the last two were taken to Framingham Hospital. They were treated at the regimental hospital. MI and FHS.

29. Duane, *Dear Old "K,"* 3–4; See also Horatio Rogers, *World War I through My Sights* (San Raphael, Calif.: Presidio, 1976), 11. There is a reference to fatal lightning strike at the 102nd Field Artillery camp at Boxford, Massachusetts, in August 1917. A bolt of lightning hit a tent, injuring five and killing one. *Framingham Evening News*, August 22, 1917, p. 2 (relates two deaths); *Natick Bulletin*, August 24, 1917, p.1 refers to a lightning strike two weeks before at the Bay State Range at Wakefield, Massachusetts. The same strike in Wakefield is also reported in the *Framingham Evening News*, which refers to several injuries.

30. War Department, *Report of the Surgeon General U.S. Army to the Secretary ow War, 1919* (Washington, D.C.: GPO, 1920), 3293.

31. Albert S. Bowen, ed., *The Medical Department of the United States in the World War, vol. 4, Activities Concerning Mobilization Camps and Ports of Embarkation* (Washington, D.C.: GPO, 1928), 253 and 259–60.

32. *Report of the Surgeon General*, 3293.

33. Sibley, *With the Yankee Division in France*, 31–32.

34. Ibid., photographs between pages 36 and 37.

35. Emerson G. Taylor, *New England in France, 1917–1919: A History of the Twenty-sixth Division U.S.A.* (Boston: Houghton Mifflin, 1920), 67.

36. Frederick A. Pottle, *Stretchers: The Story of a Hospital Unit on the Western Front* (New Haven, Conn: Yale Univ. Press, 1929), 85–86.

37. Rogers, *World War I through My Sights*, 30.

38. *Report of Surgeon General, 1919*, 3293. See also Porter, *History*, 344. MNGA.

39. *History of the 101st United States Engineers American Expeditionary Forces 1917–1918–1919* (Cambridge, Mass.: Harvard Univ. Press, 1926), 74; Rogers, *World War I through My Sights*, 31. Typical fare consisted of cheese, hardtack, canned corned beef, and jam.

40. Pottle, *Stretchers*, 87.

41. Bartlett Bent, *Diary: England 1918–19*, manuscript. CHS

42. Bevans, *Medical History*, 1–3.

43. Eben Putnam, *Report of the Commission on Massachusetts' Part in the World War, vol. 1, History* (Boston: Commonwealth of Massachusetts, 1931), 30; The headquarters as well as the ambulance and field hospital companies were officially consolidated into the 101st Sanitary Train on August 25, 1917. Regimental Return, 101st Sanitary Train, August 1917. NA RG120.

44. Bevans, *Medical History*, 2.

45. Special Report for the Surgeon General, 101st Sanitary Train, 26th Division, September 20, 1917. Later, when the 103rd Field Hospital was stationed in Dijon, Major

King, in response to an inquiry by Lt. Col. Bevans as to tentage on hand, reported that he had no field hospital tentage on hand, just eighty-two shelter halves. What happened to the four complete hospital tents the unit had taken over to France is a mystery. Memorandum from Chief Surgeon to Commanding Officer Headquarters Field Hospital Section, January 10, 1918 and Telegram from Maj. King to John G. Towne. NA RG120.

46. Bevans, *Medical History*, 2–3.

47. Initial Muster, 2nd Field Hospital Company, 28 July 1917. NA RG120.

48. General Headquarters, American Expeditionary Forces, General Staff, First Section, Tables of Organization, Series A, January 14, 1918, Corrected to June 26, 1918, Dated August 1, 1918, Part 1, Infantry Division, table 28.

49. Porter, *History*, 338. He says that the unit moved from Boston on July 27, 1917, but the Initial Muster is dated July 28 and lists Boston as the locus. He was most likely off by a couple of days.

50. Tri-monthly Report of Enlistments for the periods ended August 10 and 31, 1917, which show five men. See also Return of the Hospital Corps, 2nd Field Hospital Company, 26th Division, 31 August 1917 (shows three enlisted since the report dated August 10,1917). NA RG120.

51. Daily Field Report of Patients, 2nd Field Hospital Company, 14 August 1917. NA RG120.

52. Station List, Sheet #1, 103rd Field Hospital. NA RG120. Porter says that the field hospital and ambulance companies left Framingham on September 12, but this would place them in Montreal three days prior to the infantry, and I have found no record to that effect. Porter, *History*, 340; see also Field Return of the 2nd Field Hospital Company, 26th Division, October 31,1918. NA RG120.

53. Station List, Sheet #1, 103rd Field Hospital. NA RG120. According to the records of Lloyd's Register of Shipping, the RMS *Canada* was built in Belfast, Ireland by Harland and Wolff in 1896. She was a "steel screw schooner rigged steamer" (the first twin-screwed steamship built for Canadian service) with an overall length of 500.4 feet, a beam of 58.2 feet, and a depth of 38.9 feet (Emmons lists her overall length as 514'). Her gross registered tonnage fluctuated between 8,806 and 9,413 tons and her speed was 15 knots. The port of registry was Liverpool, and she was owned by the Dominion Line. She carried passengers from England to North America, primarily Boston, Montreal and Quebec. Twice she served as a troopship, the Boer War (1899–1902) and during the First World War (1914–1918). She was scrapped in 1926. See Frederick Emmons, *The Atlantic Liners* (New York: Bonanza, 1972), 31–32; R. J. Cornewall-Jones, *The British Merchant Service* (London: Sampson Low, Marston, 1898), 189–91.

54. Porter, *History*, 341. See also Lawrence B. Neeld, Letter, November 14, 1960; F. J. Gunshannon, Notebook; and John Edgar Reynolds, Letter. Reynolds was a member of Company K, 102nd Infantry (This unit also sailed with 103rd Field Hospital.). CHS.

55. Frederick E. Jones, *Historical Sketch of the Medical Department of the 26th Division*, typescript, n.d. (Contains "Introductory Note" and other comments by R.S. Porter, 8 August 1919), 4. Early reports of patient activity are inconsistent at best. Activity was negligible, but not, as reported by some sources, nonexistent. Nominal Checklists for the months of September and October 1917, which period includes the voyage over, list the names of thirteen patients admitted or treated. This number is confirmed by the Report of Sick and Wounded at 2nd Massachusetts Field Hospital Company on file for each of the months in question. NA RG120.

56. Stanley J. Herzog, *The Fightin' Yanks* (Stamford, Conn.: Cunningham, 1922), 31.

57. John Edgar Reynolds, Letters, September 15 and October 9, 1917. CHS. Corporal Reynolds was a resident of North Haven, Connecticut, and served in K Company, 3rd Battalion, 102nd Infantry. He was gassed, and he died shortly after the war from its effects. In his letter home dated October 9, 1917, he refers to a rumor that the transport ship they were on (RMS *Canada*) had been sunk.

58. Station List, Sheet #1, 103rd Field Hospital. NA RG120.

59. Daniel W. Strickland, *Connecticut Fights: The Story of the 102nd Regiment* (New Haven, Conn.: Quinnipiack Press, 1930), 72–73; see also Sibley, *With the Yankee Division in France*, 35. Horatio Rogers of the 102nd Field Artillery describes a similar loss of barrack bags in France just before they boarded trains for Coetquidon. Rogers, *World War I through My Sights*, 30.

60. Strickland, *Connecticut Fights*, 72. See also Herzog, *Fightin' Yanks*, 32.

61. Station List, Sheet #1, 103rd Field Hospital. NA RG120.

62. Porter, *History*, 342–45; Pottle, *Stretchers*, 92; Lettie Gavin, *American Women in World War I* (Niwot: Univ. Press of Colo., 1997), 56. Referred to as the town as "a village of 412 souls." Other nicknames for it were "Bacillus on Mush" and "Bazwillie Sure Moose." Porter bases his population figure on "pre-war statistics." Gavin may be closer to the mark, since at a minimum the village was required to provide billets for two field hospital companies, containing a total of approximately 175 men.

63. Harvey Cushing, *From a Surgeon's Journal* (Boston: Little, Brown, 1936), 301.

64. *History of the 101st Engineers*, 72–73.

65. Joseph H. Ford, ed., *The Medical Department of the United States Army in the World War*, vol. 2, *Administration American Expeditionary Forces*, (Washington, D.C.: GPO, 1927), 644–45.

66. *Brief History of U.S. Army Hospital No. 2 From the Time of Occupation of Present Quarters to Date*, September 20, 1917, U.S.A. Hospital No. 2, AEF, France. NA RG120.

67. Ford, ed, *The Medical Department of the United States Army in the World War*, vol. 2, 537.

68. Ibid., 543.

69. *History of the 101st Engineers*, 75.

70. Ibid., 74.

71. Sibley, *With the Yankee Division in France*, 38.

72. Porter, *History*, 345.

73. Camp Order 3, October 8, 1917 and Camp Order 5, October 9, 1917, 2nd Field Hospital Company, 26th Division. Some orders are denominated "Company Orders," and the file at the National Archives is labeled as such. NA RG120.

74. Camp Order No. 12, 12 October 1917, 2nd Field Hospital Company, 26th Division. NA RG120.

75. Training Schedule, October 29–November 4, 1917, 103rd Field Hospital Company. NA RG120.

76. Daily Field Report, 14 October 1917, 103rd Field Hospital Company. NA RG120.

77. Weekly Report of Sick and Wounded, 19 October 1917, 103rd Field Hospital Company. NA RG120.

78. Sibley, *With the Yankee Division in France*, 38. See also Special Order #7, par. 2, HQ Twenty-sixth Division, noted in Return of Enlisted Force, 2nd Field Hospital Company, 26th Division, 31 Oct. 1917. NA RG120.

79. Jones, *Historical Sketch*, 8.

80. Return of Enlisted Force, 2nd Field Hospital Company, 26th Division, 31 Oct. 1917. NA RG120.

81. Ibid. See also Company Roster. NA RG120.

82. Special Report for the Surgeon General, 101st Sanitary Train, 26th Division, September 20, 1917. Lieutenant Brown would be temporarily reassigned to the company as "Acting Supply Officer" in April 1918. Lieutenants Rodger, Schley, and Brown all list wives as next of kin on Report from C.O. 2nd Field Hospital Company, 26th Division to Division Surgeon, September 4, 1917. NA RG120.

Chapter Two

Camp Life—Mud, Disease, and Accident

War is declared, gentlemen—on lice!
                                    —Lt. Col. Winston S. Churchill

Only the Choisin Reservoir in Korea was worse.
                                    —Gen. Lemuel Shepherd, Jr., USMC
                                    (of the French winter of 1917–1918)

THE TIDE TURNS (NOVEMBER 1917 THROUGH JANUARY 1918)

France

The British lowlands campaign, which began on July 31, 1917, with such high hopes of a breakthrough, ended on a ridge of ground called Passchendaele with very little to show except for a high cost in life and limb.[1] Wounded and dead alike had simply disappeared into the sucking mud.[2] The difficulty of getting about in this glutenous soil had been demonstrated time and again as gallant, overworked stretcher bearers, sometimes six or eight to a litter, took hours to negotiate the usual several hundred yards to an aid station.[3]

In an on-again-off-again series of attacks, the British wore themselves out in the mud, and they were content to go into winter quarters after the final push on November 10—almost. The last bolt was fired at Cambrai on November 20, 1917, when the British spearheaded an infantry attack with tanks. The effectiveness of the tank was clearly demonstrated. However, like all the previous attempts to break through the German defenses, this failed, because there was not enough strength to exploit the initial advantage. The attack fell short of its objective, and the survivors had to be withdrawn. In fact, in a tragically ironic twist, the unit chosen to exploit the gain was a troop of horse cavalry. Moreover, the Germans, determined to have the last word that season, launched a counterattack at Cambrai on November 30 and negated the minimal British gains. Also, the initial frustration and awe that the German infantryman felt when he first encountered the tank gave way to creativity in the formulation of an effective defense.[4]

With the Russian Revolution, the European situation took on a new character. The Russians and the Germans negotiated the Treaty of Brest-Litovsk, thus permitting the latter to transfer nearly 900,000 men, as well as artillery, to the western front.[5] What had been a war of stalemate for so long would now return to the war of maneuver as it had been in 1914.

Meanwhile, on November 5, 1917, representatives of the four Allied powers, together with Marshall Foch, met at Rapallo, Italy, to discuss the recent setback for Italian troops at Caporetto. At that meeting was born the Supreme War Council.[6] Later Foch would be named supreme commander. His powers, though not absolute, would be sufficient, when combined with his passionately forceful personality, to maintain an effective coalition to prosecute the war. Within days France chose Georges Clemenceau ("The Tiger") as its premier. He had the look of an elderly grandfather, but looks were definitely deceiving. Clemenceau was a blunt, fearless Francophile who worked tirelessly for Allied victory.[7] He was also no friend of Pershing, and from then until the end of the war, he worked just as hard behind the scenes to induce Wilson to replace him.

United States: At Home and at the Front

The woeful state of our unpreparedness soon became quite clear. There were no tanks, there was no artillery to speak of, and there were not enough ships to transport the growing number of men.[8] The draft was in full swing, and training camps had been set up all over the United States. For many, these were mere processing centers; troops were arriving daily in France, some without ever having fired a weapon. Pershing and his staff realized that something had to be done, and thus was born the training schools for officers, noncommissioned officers (NCOs), and soldiers at corps, division, and even company level. Centered at Langres,[9] these schools taught a cornucopia of courses, from basic leadership, gas discipline, and tactics, to supply. For every task the soldier was called upon to perform, there was very likely a course or school program to teach it. During the training period, men were sent to the schools on a rotating basis, then sent back to their units. Once established the schools worked well for the most part, but after the spring of 1918, when the pace of the fighting picked up and the flood of untrained doughboys began arriving in France, many men received their training on the job.[10] Some learned well; others paid the ultimate price.

Pershing continued to mold the army in his own image, starting with his own staff and the higher-ranking officers. His standards and expectations were high, and he weeded out the unfit with ruthless disregard for rank or seniority. Those who did not measure up were sent to the picturesque town of Blois on the Loire River for reassignment or rotation home.[11] Orders for Blois became synonymous with banishment and disgrace, and the mere mention of the word sent shivers through even the most seasoned professional soldier. However, in this way the commander in chief surrounded himself with a group of talented officers, many of whom would later distinguish themselves in the Second World War. Among his protégés were George C. Marshall, Malin Craig, and George S. Patton, Jr.

On the other hand, there was a sense that the National Guard outfits and the officers who led them, as opposed to the regular army units and their officers, were somehow inferior, perhaps not trustworthy or up to the task. This attitude began at the top with Pershing himself and filtered down through headquarters.[12] It was to have serious consequences later in the war, in particular with the controversial relief and replacement of General Edwards of the 26th Division in October 1918, in the middle of the Meuse-Argonne fight. According to Capt. James Duane, an officer in K Company, 101st Infantry, Pershing did not make a favorable impression upon the men of the 26th Division when, in the course of a visit on November 11, 1917, he was overheard by many of them making numerous "sarcastic remarks."[13] The fact of the matter was that two of the first fully ready divisions were National Guard divisions, the 26th and 42nd, whose combat records were second to none.[14]

As the army played catch-up with men, American industry tried to make the transition from a peacetime to a wartime economy. The going was very slow. Initially, virtually all of the 75 mm artillery pieces were produced and supplied to our batteries by the French.[15] So too were artillery shells, both gas and high explosive. We had an arrangement whereby we manufactured the gas and shipped it to France where the shells were filled. Likewise, ammunition for rifles, and often the rifles themselves, were supplied by our allies.[16] Those doughboys who were lucky enough to have rifle practice before going overseas often found that the weapons with which they trained with were not the same make and model as those they were expected to fight with.[17] Some soldiers were required to carry gas masks of both British and French manufacture at the same time, in addition to a sixty-to-eighty-pound pack.[18] We had a tank on the drawing boards, but none rolled off the assembly line in time to be of service. The French Renault light tank had an American-designed International Harvester engine.[19]

Also at home, a wave of anti-German sentiment swept the nation, a country that prided itself on ethnic diversity, and where those of German ancestry made up the largest single block after those of English stock.[20]

As the new troops became acclimated to their surroundings, individual American battalions were sent into line to train with the British and French. Later the program would involve whole divisions.[21] The French generally let the Americans come and go with Gallic indifference, while the British were loath to part with any new blood and often had to be reminded of the temporary nature of the exercise. Among the first coalition partners, there was a natural reluctance to make divisions available, even in times of acute need. To some French commanders, reserves were just too important to squander, even where their use could easily stem a breakthrough.

On a more mundane note, the familiar campaign hat was discarded in favor of the soft "overseas" cap pursuant to an order dated January 9, 1918. The advantage of the latter was that it could be easily folded up when the soldier wore his steel helmet.[22]

The 26th Division: Winter in the Vosges Mountains

In October 1917, Neufchâteau was a market town of approximately 3,000 people, situated on the east bank of the Meuse River at its confluence with the Mouzon.[23] The town lay in the foothills of the Vosges Mountains in the heart of what was the old province of Lorraine. Saint Joan of Arc had been born and raised at Domremy, eight miles to the north, and a shrine had been built there in her honor. It is a farming region with hillsides dotted with cattle and sheep. The little towns are nestled in valleys or on hilltops and contain gray stone buildings with red roofs. From a distance, the effect is quite picturesque; however, up close the narrow, muddy streets of those days told a different story.[24] At that time, Neufchâteau itself boasted a distillery, a brewery, and two or three primitive hotels.[25] It was, more importantly, the locus of an excellent rail and road net, and it was here that the division set up headquarters.[26]

The Fourth Training Area was approximately 100 miles square and was in the heart of what was considered a "quiet," or rest, sector by both the French and the Germans.[27] Thus, it was an ideal location for training. AEF headquarters was at Chaumont, a scant thirty-four miles southwest of Neufchâteau. "Rest" was a relative term after the horrors of the Champaign and the Marne; still an unwritten understanding seemed to be in place to the effect that neither side would conduct *major* operations there. So far, nothing had happened to violate the relative calm. However, the area's proximity to the German front line meant that there was always activity of some kind, like a trench raid or sporadic artillery fire, and the presence of battle-hardened French troops meant that there were plenty of experienced trainers for the green Americans.[28]

The Germans were not the first problem that the doughboys had to contend with: housing was the number-one priority. At first, the soldiers were billeted in homes, barns, and lofts.[29] This was not a significant problem, since the area was virtually devoid of military-age men, the bulk of them dead or serving in the French army. However, this would not do for the long run. Camps with barracks needed to be constructed. Engineer companies, supplemented by work details from the various units, even German prisoners of war (POWs), worked hard to erect the flimsy structures. Typical barracks were approximately 100 feet long. They had dirt floors and small wood-burning stoves at either end.[30] The roofs leaked, and on November 25, 1917, a wind and hail storm blew the roofs off of several of these barracks.[31] The overall effect was not one of comfort.

A second problem was typical of the locality. This was an area of cattle and dairy farms.[32] The practice was to house the animals in barns and sheds attached to houses in town and to lead the animals to pasture outside of town. In addition, the universal observation of the soldiers who were stationed there was that a citizen's wealth appeared to be measured by the size of the manure pile in his front yard. When it rained, and it did often, the streets ran yellow with a combination of mud and manure.[33] Wells were shallow and polluted, and the latrines were unspeakable.[34] Add to this the flies and the smell, day after day, especially around mealtimes, and the reaction of the typical soldier is not hard to imagine. The situation was a nightmare for the medical officers charged with sanitation.[35] Much of the dough-boys' time was devoted to improving the sanitary conditions, as much for them-selves—such as with the building of showers and urinals—as for the locals, who at first, did not view this as a problem.

However, the greatest challenge remained the miserable weather, and there was not much that the engineers could do to ameliorate its effects. To make matters worse, that winter proved to be a particularly cold and wet one.[36] The troops were not dressed appropriately. They did not even have gloves.[37] Their biggest complaint was that because it often rained every day for weeks, boots and clothes never dried out.[38] When winter came, the frigid temperatures froze wet boots on beds.[39] Worse, the conditions meant that colds and influenza, along with other diseases and infections, such as trench foot and bronchitis, were rampant.[40] This was especially true since many of the soldiers were in large groups of men for the first time in their lives and were thus exposed to a plethora of new illnesses. The 101st Engineers suffered an outbreak of cerebro-spinal meningitis,[41] while the 103rd Infantry was plagued with a variety of childhood diseases.[42] A number of cases of scarlet fever broke out in a company of the 104th Infantry, and that unit was quarantined for a while.[43]

Training for the upcoming combat was the order of the day. Typical was the experience of the 104th Infantry, which was stationed in the small town of Rebeuville, about two miles south of Neufchâteau. The unit was assigned to the French 162nd Regiment for purposes of training. Its men were given individual instruction with the machine gun as well as unit practice in laying out trenches.[44] There were always training accidents. The first casualties in the 104th Infantry occurred on January 16, 1918, when several men were injured at grenade practice.[45]

Trench fever had dogged the Allied armies since 1914. In an act of exceptional bravery, sixty-four men from the 26th Division stepped forward when a call went out for volunteers to participate in trench fever research by the Red Cross. Every volunteer was from either an ambulance company or a field hospital. Those ultimately chosen to participate were picked from a group the size of four compa-nies—there was no shortage of brave men among the noncombatants. The men were isolated in a tent hospital behind the British lines for up to two months. They suffered recurrent bouts of the disease, and their average weight loss was twenty to twenty-five pounds, although some men lost forty to fifty pounds. To add insult to injury, German artillery found the town the hospital was located in a ripe target, pounding it day and night; the men had to be moved.[46]

Sanitary Trains: More Organizational Problems

Whatever the rest of the division suffered and experienced, the men from Sanitary Trains did also—inadequate clothing, poor housing and sanitation, and general discomfort. It rained on all troops alike, and the mud was everywhere. Many billets were without heat due to lack of fuel or to a very real danger from fire.[47] (On June 2, 1918, just such a fire destroyed all of the equipment of the 102nd Field Hospital.)[48] The men from Sanitary Trains, in particular the field hospitals, were responsible for the health of the entire division, and to the extent that their own rolls were short due to illness or injury, they had to take up the slack themselves.

Once in France, at least, the division never lacked for medical supplies.[49] Chaumont was close by as was the supply depot at Is-sur-Tille.[50] At that time, the latter was the site of what was considered to be the largest railroad terminal in the world.[51] The division also had the services of such specialists as an orthopedist, a psychiatrist, and a urologist. Consultants—experts in other fields, such as neurology—were also available, but coordination and supervision remained a problem. The urologist supervised the regular inspections for and the treatment of venereal disease. In addition, there were chief and assistant chief dental surgeons assigned to the division. It was at this time that a division dental lab was established, as well as a field lab and medical supply unit.[52]

Overall medical authority flowed down from the chief surgeon at Tours through his designee at AEF headquarters at Chaumont. Each division, in turn, had a surgeon, who had his own headquarters.[53] The bulk of the work was done by the individual ambulance and field hospital companies, four each to a division. Eight camp infirmaries were established and assigned to Sanitary Trains.[54] In addition, there were medical personnel attached to each regiment and battalion. On the most basic level, the individual soldier was responsible for some knowledge of first aid for himself and, more often, his buddy. The establishment of a unified command for sanitary personnel in the Yankee Division during this period was hampered because the various units, in particular the artillery, were scattered about with French units for purposes of training.

Another major problem was the continuing lack of motorized transportation. At first, the table of organization called for some units to have animal-drawn vehicles. This was found to be impractical, although horses and mules did have some advantages in mud—until late in the war one of the division's field hospitals and one ambulance company made use of such animals. However, in the interim, the division initially had to rely upon the already overtaxed French transport for the movement of supplies and personnel.[55] In an ironic twist, a detachment left Liffol-le-Grand on October 10, 1917, for a journey to St. Nazaire to pick up the long-awaited and much-needed ambulances, only to have the detachment *and* the vehicles turned over to the Quartermaster Corps to be used for the delivery of rations.[56] Later on the Provisional Truck Company was formed to handle transportation.[57]

By November 1, 1917, shortly after hospital and ambulance companies had settled into the Neufchâteau area, there occurred a final name change for the various units, pursuant to War Department orders. Henceforth, they would be called as follows:[58]

1st Ambulance Co.	became	101st Ambulance Co.
3rd Ambulance Co.	became	102nd Ambulance Co.
2nd Ambulance Co.	became	103rd Ambulance Co.
4th Ambulance Co.	became	104th Ambulance Co.
1st Field Hosp. Co.	became	101st Field Hosp. Co.
3rd Field Hosp. Co.	became	102nd Field Hosp. Co.
2nd Field Hosp. Co.	became	*103rd Field Hosp. Co.*
4th Field Hosp. Co.	became	104th Field Hosp. Co.

The basic model for the treatment and movement of sick and wounded from the battlefront was designed to provide prompt, appropriate care in stages.[59] In short, the area to be covered by the medical personnel was divided into three zones: the Zone of Activity, the Evacuation Zone, and the Distribution Zone (see appendix II). The second zone contained evacuation hospitals and the large base hospitals run by the Red Cross or the army. These facilities were generally well back from the front (although not immune from artillery and bombs).[60] They were fully staffed and equipped hospitals, where patients could receive more sophisticated care.[61] The evacuation hospitals were moveable, while the larger base hospitals were generally more permanent. In the immediate division area, base hospitals were established at Dijon (No. 17), Bazoilles-sur-Meuse (No. 18), and Chaumont (No. 15).[62] The Distribution Zone was in essence the network of hospitals at home, along with the ships and trains necessary to transport the wounded there. It was in the Zone of Activity, the forward zone, where the field hospitals and ambulance companies operated.

The ambulance companies were composed of litter bearers and drivers. Ambulance drivers braved shot and shell to take the wounded back to sorting stations, field hospitals, or evacuation hospitals in the rear areas in the shortest time possible. In spite of their efforts, speeding ambulances were not good for some patients, especially those suffering from shock or phosgene gas poisoning. To counter this problem, facilities for the preliminary treatment of gas and shock were provided closer to the front.[63] Many volunteer drivers of trucks and ambulances were to later to become high-profile people like John Dos Passos and Ernest Hemingway—but most were just ordinary men and women.

However, the real heroes were the litter bearers, the men who had to traverse the battlefield itself to bring their wounded comrades to safety. Traditionally, the regimental musicians had acted as litter bearers; later, litter squads were put together by drawing men from the various units in the battalion or regiment. This was found to be ineffective, since such bearers were a mixed lot and often not fully up to the task. Litter bearers had to be young, strong men, able to withstand the arduous duties carried out under combat conditions; likely candidates were not usually found among the members of the band. The division surgeon recommended that a permanent squad of twelve men from each of the rifle companies and two from each artillery battery be chosen, and further that all litter bearers "be selected from among the strongest, most intelligent and courageous Privates of the organization."[64]

This group of men had to retrieve the wounded where they lay and bring them to battalion aid stations.[65] After the wounds were dressed, those that could be moved were taken by a second group, the litter bearer section of the ambulance company, which was responsible for getting the wounded to the ambulance head farther back from the front line. In each case, the length or difficulty of the "carry" was a function of the terrain and the nature of the battle. George Patton was carried two miles on a litter to reach the ambulance head.[66] Near Samogneux, in the Neptune sector north of Verdun, the 104th Ambulance Company was ordered to move toward the rear due to intense shellfire. This only lengthened the distance of the carry to the ambulance head.

In theory, only two men were needed to carry a litter, but in places like Flanders, where the mud was like glue, sometimes eight or more were assigned to just one litter. It was hard, exhausting work.[67] Again, the situation in the Neptune sector was so difficult at times that often the litter bearers were only able to make just one round trip a day.[68] Where the men were required to make multiple carries, they often had to resort to improvisation. Litter bearers whose hands were tired and sore tied wire or rope around their wrists to loop over the litter handles.[69] Other innovations, such as the wheeled litter, were a help where available and where terrain permitted.[70] The hammock stretcher, another innovation, permitted movement through the twists and turns of the trenches.[71]

Ambulance companies also served as advanced dressing stations to which the wounded were brought from the field. The treatment was more sophisticated than the first aid administered at the battalion level, but the primary function was to stabilize the patient and remove him as quickly and safely as possible to the field hospital. Often, in times of extreme necessity, the litter bearers were under the supervision of a field hospital. The latter performed triage as well as surgery, often under very adverse conditions.[72] The ambulance companies were billeted together in Liffol-le-Grand, just across the street from the 101st Field Hospital. The small town, with a population of about 1,500, lay about six miles southwest of Neufchâteau.[73] Their camp, consisting of Adrian barracks, was described as "an island in a sea of mud."[74]

At first, during the training period, there was no attempt at specialization among the four field hospitals. That would come later, on something of a rotating basis.[75] Due to the lack of transport, the field hospitals actually performed the functions of base hospitals for much of this period.[76] The 101st Field Hospital (which also spent time at Bazoilles-sur-Meuse constructing barracks) established a hospital in a convent called Hospice St. Simon at Liffol-le-Grand, and the 104th occupied a hospital in barracks constructed for the French at Rebeval.[77] Both served as hospitals for contagious cases until the division moved up to the front.[78] The 102nd Field Hospital was temporarily broken up into detachments, which were sent to the various other hospitals and line organizations.[79]

The fall and winter weather was foul, and competition for available barrack and office space was keen, sometimes leading to conflict. A case in point was the hospital at Bazoilles-sur-Meuse. Originally, the plan called for a newly constructed Adrian barrack to be used as a ten-to-twelve-bed infirmary for the division sick. Companies B and C of the 101st Engineers had been hard at work building these structures and had appropriated one for their own use. Unfortunately for them, on November 25, following an inspection tour, Lt. Col. Bevans, the division surgeon, discovered their use as a barracks. In a memorandum to General Edwards he asked for, and obtained, an order that the hapless engineers vacate the premises immediately. A Captain Osborn, commanding officer of the engineer detachment, contended that the unit had been given permission to occupy the barracks by the division adjutant's office, but to no avail.[80] Bevans wasted no time in ordering the senior surgeon, Maj. John Towne, to take over the building and establish the infirmary.[81] On November 30, the division billeting officer, Capt. H. D. Cormerais, confirmed, in a short, handwritten memorandum to division headquarters, that the engineers had vacated the building.[82]

The incident at Bazoilles-sur-Meuse was not an isolated one. A short distance north and west, at Liffol-le-Grand, were stationed two battalions of the 103rd Infantry, a field hospital, three ambulance companies, as well as elements of the 103rd Machine Gun Battalion. Orders were issued to construct twenty Adrian huts, one of which was to be used as an infirmary by the regimental surgeon of the 103rd Infantry. Again, after an inspection of the area, the division surgeon discovered that the infirmary was not located in the barracks, which was occupied by men of the 103rd Infantry. In fact, the infirmary had been mistakenly placed in the nearby chateau by members of his own staff. This was a problem, since the latter building consisted of only fourteen rooms and was in the process of being converted to use as a 300-bed camp hospital. Lt. Col. Bevans ordered the infantry out, and they complied. However, when the regimental commander ordered the medical unit to set up the infirmary in the vacated barracks, a new problem arose—The French officer in charge of the area would not permit it. Instead, he assigned the infirmary to a building known as the "Hospice."[83] Once again, Bevans asked Edwards' assistance. In a memorandum dated December 7, he sought a solution to the "tangle," saying that he really did not care if the infirmary was located in either structure, only that it be set up somewhere, and soon, as it was "urgently required." His request was endorsed two days later, but the specific location was not indicated, only that "suitable space" was to be found.[84]

103rd Field Hospital Company: More Training

The men of the 103rd Field Hospital Company had hardly settled in at Bazoilles-sur-Meuse when orders dated November 1, 1917, were received to proceed to Dijon "at the earliest practicable date" to help establish Base Hospital No. 17. By this time, the field hospital must have occupied one of the newly constructed barracks, because the orders clearly specified that the barracks was to be turned over to the French engineers building the base hospital. The Quartermaster Corps was to furnish transportation, and two days' rations would be issued. The unit left Bazoilles-sur-Meuse on November 4, and arrived at its assigned duty station at 1 A.M. on November 5. At the time of this transfer, the effective strength of the unit was five officers and seventy-nine enlisted men.[85]

Base Hospital No.17 had been formed at Harper Hospital in Detroit, Michigan, in September of 1916.[86] The unit had sailed for France on July 13, 1917, and arrived at Dijon, by way of Southampton and LeHavre on July 29. Its personnel were directed to occupy the Hospital St. Ignace, which, at the time of their arrival was being operated as Auxiliary Hospital No. 77 by the French. The buildings and grounds were formally turned over to the Americans on September 2, although the hospital had started admitting American patients a little over a week before.[87] Nearby, on Rue Thurot, the army would later establish the Central Medical Department Laboratory in a building on loan from the University of Dijon.[88] The hospital was actually a group of buildings situated on a seven-and-one-half acre tract of land. The main building, erected about 1885, was an L-shaped, four-story structure, constructed of stone, plaster, and concrete, with a slate roof. Its main entrance, on the longer, north-south wing, faced west onto the Boulevard Voltaire, a wide, paved thoroughfare.[89] The shorter wing was connected to the north end of the main wing, and ran from west to east. Two rows of smaller outbuildings lay to the north and paralleled the shorter wing. The buildings in the farthest row were one story in height and contained storerooms and small shops. Those in the nearer row were two stories tall and contained, among other things, the kitchen for the entire hospital. All food was prepared there and carried across the alley and into the wards of the hospital. The whole complex was surrounded by an eight-foot-high brick wall. Several other buildings dotted the acreage and were used for various functions. One, in fact, had been leased by the hospital to a paper box factory. The main rail line from Dijon to Langres ran along the eastern boundary, and the freight depot stood a mere 700 yards away. For the most part the vacant land was covered with mature hardwood trees, including horse chestnut, as well as a vegetable garden.

When the base hospital personnel arrived, the building was still occupied by the patients and staff of the French hospital. On the first floor, the main entrance opened into a large hall, around which were offices. The two wings branched out from the main hall and were, in essence, long corridors with adjacent rooms containing, among other things, a pharmacy, a laboratory, a chapel, a mortuary, and an autopsy room. The second floor had a similar layout, but with operating rooms grouped around the main section and wards off the long corridors. The third and fourth floors were similar, but the rooms were smaller, since the corridors ran down the middle of each wing. The latrines were extremely primitive, consisting of eight inch pipes, flush with the floor, with no fixtures or water to carry the excreta away; gravity alone took the waste to cesspools just outside the foundation walls. These had loose-fitting covers and had to be cleaned out regularly. The stench permeated the rooms and halls of the hospital. The irony of the situation was that a main city sewer line ran along the boulevard just yards from the front of the main building. Fresh water was supplied by a single, small-diameter pipe with intermittent taps and drains throughout the building. The only source of hot water was a coal heater in the admitting room.

Heat, which was supplied by a combination of radiators and small stoves, was totally inadequate. Fire protection was nonexistent, and there were no fire escapes. There was no laundry on the premises, all work being done on a contract basis. Electricity was supplied by a local illuminating company and was sufficient neither to maintain the X-ray equipment nor to light the entire building at night. The wiring was very primitive and dangerous in the extreme, with exposed, unshielded wires and fuse boxes fused higher than capacity. Similarly, the gas supplied to the building flowed through leaking pipes and was found to be escaping in many places throughout the hospital. There was no elevator, and patients had to be carried up and down stairs in litters by hand. At the northeast corner of the hospital was an incinerator, which was used to burn soiled dressings deemed unfit for further use. Brick privies, similar to those in use in the hospital, were scattered throughout the garden.[90]

As a result of the report of his inspection, the commanding officer of Base Hospital No. 17, Maj. H. C. Coburn, proposed certain changes and improvements, the primary emphasis being upon a proper sewer connection as well as the installation of up-to-date plumbing fixtures. In addition, he asked for kitchen improvements, more barracks, steam heating, safer gas and electric connections, and fire safety measures, not to mention a fresh coat of paint and calcimine on the walls and ceilings. He also saw the need for an elevator. For the most part, his requests were granted, all except the steam heat and the elevator. A detail from the 16th Regiment of Engineers (Railroad) was assigned to the hospital to attend to the work; it was authorized to procure materials locally and to requisition added materials as needed.[91]

In addition to the physical problems with the building, there was not enough space to house the projected 1000 beds and at the same time, to house the necessary medical personnel. The French had calculated the hospital's capacity at about 600 patients. The housing problem was temporarily solved by the erection of a number of pyramidal tents in the graveled area just behind the main building, to be used by the enlisted personnel of Base Hospital No. 17. However, there was no room for officers and female nursing staff; they were allocated space in nearby rental properties. Arrangements were made for the leasing of 10 Boulevard Voltaire, a building fronting the main hospital, for the sum of 400 francs per month, as well as the nearby estate of Madame d'Aubraumont, for 22,000 francs per annum. The latter would be able to house up to forty-seven nurses.[92]

On November 5, 1917, the day that the 103rd Field Hospital Company arrived at Dijon to begin its tour, the commanding officer of Base Hospital No. 17 filed a progress report on the state of repairs and improvements. In it he stated that the digging of ditches and the laying of sewer pipe was "progressing satisfactorily." Most of the plumbing fixtures had been delivered. In addition, four barracks had been erected, three were in the process of construction, and the materials for five more had been delivered to the grounds. The one fly in the ointment was that the tenant in the paper box factory, whose building was needed by the hospital for storage, had refused to vacate on November 1 as originally agreed. The writer referred to the fact that in addition to his own troops pulled from their medical duties to join in the construction, there were sixteen members of the 16th Regiment of Engineers and a group of fifteen to thirty German prisoners (supplied and guarded by the French). He also referred to the men of the 103rd Field Hospital, newly arrived for "temporary station." If they had any illusions about advancing their medical training, these notions were soon laid to rest, since the commanding officer of the hospital made clear in a report his intentions that the men would be "utilized in construction work" while in Dijon. As an aside, he ended his report with the remark that "in view of the unskilled labor involved [the project] is progressing very satisfactorily."[93]

While the 103rd Field Hospital was stationed at Base Hospital No. 17, the men were broken down into various work details. Inside, Mess Sgt. Austin King was in charge of a permanent kitchen detail consisting of fifteen enlisted men whose duty it was to cook, clean up, and keep the fires going. This detail worked seven days a week, with the exception of the cooks and the butcher, who worked twenty-four hours on and twenty-four hours off. The next group was the mess hall detail. This seven-man detail was under the supervision of Sgt. Arthur T. Gormley. They served meals and cleaned tables, carried the nurses' food from the kitchen to their separate mess area, and kept the mess hall fires going. Each man received one day off in ten. The average day began at 6:30 A.M., with breaks between mealtimes, and ended at 7:30 P.M. There was small office detail consisting of four men under Sgt. 1/C Raymond Bliss, and one man assigned to keep the enlisted quarters in shape. Sgt. 1/C Burton P. Woodbury acted as quartermaster, and one man was assigned as a motorcycle driver for an officer.

The majority of the enlisted men were assigned to outside work, under the supervision of Sgt. 1/C John Harriss. This work was backbreaking and never ending. The men, separated into several groups, dug ditches in frozen ground, laid pipe, and carried sections of barracks for assembly. Others acted as plumbers' helpers, or worse yet, as helpers to the engineer detachment, for which, among other things, they poured concrete. They also hauled rails, coal, and wood. Gravel brought in by wagon to be spread between the new barracks was frozen and had to be broken up with picks. The weather was foul, and a fair number reported to sick call on a daily basis. Still, with the exception of Sundays and Christmas Day, the work went on. However, Friday, December 28, was an exception. That day dawned cold and stormy. Since the men had no gloves, Sergeant Harris requested that inside work be substituted for the outside duties. Even so, there was plenty of hard, manual labor to go around inside the hospital. The very next day they were back at work outside.[94]

Like the enlisted personnel of the base hospital, the men of the 103rd Field Hospital more than likely found billets in tents on the hospital grounds or in the newly constructed barracks. During the company's stay in Dijon its effective strength remained fairly constant, ranging between eighty-one and eighty-four men; however, during the week ending November 7, an additional person was carried on the rolls. Surviving patient reports indicate that the unit treated at least sixty-eight patients during its stay, for complaints ranging from measles to rhinitis. Virtually half of the patients had to be transferred to other hospitals, and two to their "home stations."[95] The others were treated and released to their quarters. The company's work as carpenters and ditch diggers must have been going well also, as was apparent from a progress report dated November 15, 1917. Major Coburn reported that five barracks had been erected, with seven more under construction. The sewer pipes supplying the main building had been laid, and ditches were being dug for the outside wards. The inside plumbing had been started during the past week. The only problem remaining was the continuing inability to evict the paper box factory. This was holding up, among other things, the set up of the YMCA hut in another building on the grounds, the contents of which had to be stored in the factory building. The matter had been turned over to the French authorities.[96]

On the basis of a telegram dated January 31, 1918, written orders were drawn up the next day transferring the 103rd Field Hospital back to Bazoilles-sur-Meuse. The unit was to prepare to join the division, which was itself being sent to train in the line with the French in the Chemin des Dames sector, near Soissons. The orders called for the transportation of five officers and eighty enlisted men.[97] The men drew rations for two days and boarded a train at Dijon on February 2, arriving at their destination later the same day.[98]

NOTES

1. Martin Gilbert, *The First World War* (New York: Henry Holt, 1994), 353–54, 361–65, 377.

2. Harvey Cushing, *From a Surgeon's Journal* (Boston: Little, Brown, 1936), 177.

3. Denis Winter, *Death's Men* (London: Penguin, 1979), 196–97.

4. Gilbert, *First World War*, 379–83.

5. Ibid., 385–87.

6. Philip J. Haythornthwaite, *The World War One Source Book* (London: Arms and Armor, 1996), 40.

7. Ibid., 122–23.

8. Edward M. Coffman, *The War to End All Wars: The American Military Experience in World War I* (Madison: Univ. of Wisconsin Press, 1986), 37–42.

9. Cushing, *From a Surgeon's Journal*, 346.

10. John Toland, *No Man's Land* (New York, 1980), 430.

11. Coffman, *War to End All Wars*, 330.

12. Ibid., 6; Cushing, *From a Surgeon's Journal*, 479; Emerson G. Taylor, *New England in France, 1917–1919: A History of the Twenty-sixth Division U.S.A.* (Boston: Houghton Mifflin, 1920), 53.

13. James T. Duane, *Dear Old "K"* (Boston: Thomas Todd, 1922), 20.

14. Paul Braim, *The Test of Battle: The American Expeditionary Forces in the Meuse-Argonne Campaign* (Newark: Univ. of Delaware Press., 1988), apps. 2–9.

15. Coffman, *War to End All Wars*, 42.

16. Braim, *Test of Battle*, 38.

17. Frank P. Sibley, *With the Yankee Division in France* (Boston: Little, Brown, 1919), 128.

18. Jonathan Gawne, *Over There! The American Soldier in World War I* (London: Greenhill, 1997), 10 and 43.

19. Coffman, *War to End All Wars*, 39.

20. David M. Kennedy, *Over Here: The First World War and American Society* (New York: Oxford Univ. Press, 1980), 67–68.

21. Braim, *Test of Battle*, 56–57.

22. General Order No. 7, G.H.Q., American Expeditionary Forces, January 9, 1918; Stars & Stripes, February 8, 1918. USMA; Gawne, Over There, 24.

23. James Lung Bevans, *Medical History of the 26th Division from Organization to June 24, 1918* (typescript, n.d.), 3. NA RG120; Sibley, *With the Yankee Division in France*, 37–38. Neufchâteau was located on the site of the ancient Roman town of Neomagus. *Encyclopaedia Britannica,* 1959, s.v. "Neufchâteau."

24. Woods Hutchinson, *The Doctor in War* (Boston: Houghton Mifflin, 1918), 200–24.

25. *Encyclopaedia Britannica,* 1959, s.v. "Neufchâteau."

26. Sibley, *With the Yankee Division in France,* 37–38.

27. Frederick E. Jones, *Historical Sketch of the Medical Department of the 26thDivision* (typescript, n.d..), with "Introductory Note" and other comments by R.S. Porter, 8 August 1919), 5. NA RG120.

28. Braim, *Test of Battle,* 46–47.

29. Bevans, *Medical History*, 3; Hutchinson, *Doctor in War*, 220–21.

30. Duane, *Dear Old "K,"* 13; Surgeon General, *Annual Report, 1919* (Washington, D.C., 1920), 3293.

31. Duane, *Dear Old "K,"* 22.

32. Hutchinson, *Doctor in War*, 209–11.

33. Jones, *Historical Sketch,* 6; War Department, *Report of the Surgeon General U.S. Army to the Secretary of War, 1919* (Washington, D.C.: GPO, 1920), 3294.

34. Hutchinson, *Doctor in War*, 218–19.

35. Laurence Stallings, *The Doughboys* (New York: Harper and Row, 1963), 35.

36. Bevans, *Medical History*, p. 3; Surgeon General, *Annual Report, 1919*, 3293; Porter, *History,* 346. Ambulance men suffered "many frozen hands" until Red Cross supplied gloves.

37. Duane, *Dear Old "K,"* 23.

38. Surgeon General, *Annual Report, 1919*, 3293.

39. Duane, *Dear Old "K,"* 23.

40. Surgeon General, *Annual Report, 1919*, 3294.

41. Ibid.

42. Ibid.

43. Duane, *Dear Old "K,"* 21–22.

44. Ibid., 16–17.

45. Ibid., 26.

46. Bevans, *Medical History*, 7; Sibley, *With the Yankee Division in France*, 35–37; *Stars & Stripes*, February 22, 1918, p. 1 (refers to sixty volunteers). USMA.

47. Bevans, *Medical History*, 3.

48. Surgeon General, *Annual Report, 1919*, 3297–98. See also Jones, *Historical Sketch*, 17.

49. Bevans, *Medical History*, 4.

50. Ibid., 4–5; Frederick A. Pottle, *Stretchers: The Story of a Hospital Unit on the Western Front* (New Haven, Conn.: Yale Univ. Press, 1929), 88.

51. Pottle, *Stretchers*, 88.

52. Bevans, *Medical History*, 6; Eben Putnam, *Report of the Commission on Massachusetts' Part in the World War*, vol. 1, *History* (Boston: Commonwealth of Massachusetts, 1931), 140; *Stars & Stripes*, February 8, 1918, p. 8. USMA.

53. Bevans, *Medical History*, 2 and 4.

54. Joseph H. Ford, ed., *The Medical Department of the United States Army in the World War*, vol. 2, *Administration American Expeditionary Forces* (Washington, D.C.: GPO, 1927), 284.

55. Bevans, *Medical History*, 4–5 and 9.

56. Jones, *Historical Sketch*, 6. Later forays to obtain vehicles proved more successful. The 103rd Ambulance returned with twelve Ford ambulances. The 101st Ambulance sent a second detail, which came back with thirty-six; the 102nd Ambulance was also successful. R. S. Porter, *101st Sanitary Train, 26th Division AEF, History, March 20th, 1919*, 346. MNGA.

57. Ibid., 9.

58. Putnam, *Report of the Commission*, 139. See also General Orders No. 7, Headquarters, American Expeditionary Forces.

59. W. W. Keen, *The Treatment of War Wounds* (Philadelphia: Saunders, 1917), diagram #35; Charles Lynch, ed., *The Medical Department of the United States Army in the World War*, vol. 8, *Field Operations*, "Schematic Diagram of Hospitalization & Evacuation System, AEF" (Washington, D.C.: GPO, 1925), 262.

60. Cushing, *From a Surgeon's Journal*, 201–2 and 399.

61. Jones, *Historical Sketch*, 6.

62. Bevans, *Medical History*, 3.

63. Lynch, ed., *Medical Department of the United States Army in the World War*, vol. 8, *Field Operations*, 456.

64. Jones, *Historical Sketch*, 28 (reference by Porter to Memorandum from R. S. Porter to commanding general, July 5, 1918 found in *Appendix* to Jones, *Historical Sketch*, 78–79.) NA RG120; Alistair Horne, *The Price of Glory: Verdun, 1916* (London: Penguin, 1993), 183.

65. Duane, *Dear Old "K,"* 105. "In addition to administering first aid, [bearers] often carried [litters] two to three kilometers to the dressing station."

66. Martin Blumenson, *Patton: The Man behind the Legend, 1885–1945* (New York: Quill, 1985), 114.

67. John Ellis, *Eye Deep in Hell* (Baltimore: Johns Hopkins Univ. Press) 106–7; Rod Paschall, *The Defeat of Imperial Germany, 1917–1918* (Chapel Hill, N.C.: Algonquin, 1989), 77.

68. Jones, *Historical Sketch*, 37.

69. Bert Ford, *The Fighting Yankees Overseas* (Boston: McPhail, 1919), 132 ("corns grew on his hands") and 144.

70. Cushing, *From a Surgeon's Journal*, 29.

71. Derby, *"Wade in, Sanitary!"* 14–15.

72. Surgeon General, *Annual Report, 1919*, 3294; John S. Haller, Jr., *Farmcarts to Fords: A History of the Military Ambulance, 1790–1925* (Carbondale: Southern Illinois Univ. Press, 1992), 94-95.

73. R. S. Porter, *101st Sanitary Train, 26th Division AEF, History* (manuscript, March 20, 1919), 344. MNGA.

74. Jones, *Historical Sketch*, 8.

75. Derby, *"Wade in, Sanitary!"* 38–41.

76. Bevans, *Medical History*, 4.

77. Jones, *Historical Sketch*, 8.

78. Putnam, *Report of the Commission*, 140.

79. Jones, *Historical Sketch*, 8.

80. Memorandum, Division Surgeon to Commanding General 26th Division, November 25, 1917. NA RG120.

81. Memorandum, Division Surgeon to C.O. Field Hospital Section, November 25, 1917. NA RG120.

82. H. D. Cormerais, Memorandum to HQ 26th Division, November 30, 1917. NA RG120. Captain Cormerais served as the top division billeting officer throughout the war despite a serious wound in the hand from a shell fragment suffered in the Toul sector. *Framingham News*, September 27, 1944, p. 7. FPL. General Edwards assigned him to escort the Chief of Staff, Gen. Peyton March around Camp Devens on April 19, 1919. *Boston Globe*, April 19, 1919, p. 2. BCL. (The printed name below his signature is given as "Cormorais," but the signature itself and the news articles spell it "Cormerais.")

83. No indication as to whether or not this was the same building occupied by the 101st Field Hospital, but in a small town, it most likely was.

84. Memorandum from Division Surgeon to Commanding General 26th Division, December 7, 1917 (together with endorsement of 9 December 1917). NA RG120. See reference to the size of the chateau in *The Medical Department of the United States Army in the World War*, vol. 2, *Administration*, 545.

85. Jones, *Historical Sketch*, 8; Special Order #26, paragraph 8, H.Q. A.E.F., November 1, 1917. See also Field Return Nov.1, 1917 to Nov. 10, 1917; Station List, Sheet #1, 103rd Field Hospital. NA RG120.

86. It was initially designated as United States Army Hospital No. 3, later redesignated as Base Hospital No. 17.

87. Ford, ed., *The Medical Department of the United States Army in the World War*, vol. 2, *Administration*, 643–44.

88. Ibid., 157.

89. The hospital complex is currently shown as the "Grand Seminaire" on *Dijon*, Plan Détaillé, Centre Ville, Scale:1/10,000, *Plan Guide Bleu & Or*, Editions Grafocarte (Bagneux, France).

90. Report on Hospital St. Ignace (Auxiliary Hospital No.77) Dijon, August 12, 1917, by Commanding Officer United States Army Hospital No. 3. NA RG120.

91. Memorandum, from Surgeon, Base Group and L.O.C. to Commanding Officer, U.S. Army Hospital No. 3, September 20, 1917. NA RG120.

92. Memorandum, from Commanding Officer, Headquarters, Base Hospital No. 17, to Commanding General, Lines of Communication, October 4, 1917. NA RG120.

93. Memorandum re Progress of Construction, from Commanding Officer Base Hospital No. 17, to Chief Surgeon, Lines Of Communication, A.E.F., November 5, 1917. NA RG120.

94. Miscellaneous Reports, November 5, 1917 to December 31, 1917, 103rd Field Hospital Company. NA RG120.

95. Daily Field Reports and Weekly Reports of Sick and Injured for months of November 1917 through January (including week ending Feb. 6) 1918, 103rd Field Hospital. The Nominal Checklists for November and December 1917 and January 1918 list only thirty-six patients by name. I have assumed that the higher number is more accurate. NA RG120.

96. Memorandum re Progress of Construction, from Commanding Officer Base Hospital No. 17, to Chief Surgeon, Lines of Communication, AEF, November 15, 1917. NA RG120. Shortly after the departure of the 103rd Field Hospital, an inspection was conducted at Base Hospital No.17. It was found that the bed capacity had reached one thousand as originally projected, while in the interim, plans had been revised to increase this by another 200. At that time, there were 402 patients in the hospital. The facility boasted twenty-six wooden buildings, in addition to the main structure. The YMCA had also established huts for the nurses and enlisted men. It had city water and sewer hookups and an internal telephone system. Fire extinguishers were in place, with plans to install fire plugs and hoses. The heating plant was deemed efficient for part of the main building, with stoves in use for the remainder. Even a new kitchen was finally in place, and a large icebox was scheduled to be installed. The old kitchen was turned over to the nurses for their mess. Only the main mess hall remained inadequate for the needs of the personnel. Report of Inspection, 18 April 1918, Base Hospital No. 17 (Harper Hospital of Detroit). NA RG120.

97. Order No. 32, Base Hospital No. 17, February 1, 1918. NA RG120.

98. Station List, Sheet #1, 103rd Field Hospital. NA RG120.

Chapter Three

First Taste—In and Out of Line (Chemin des Dames Sector)

Gentlemen, I have thought this program over very deliberately and will not be coerced.

—Gen. John J. Pershing

INCOMING TIDE: FEBRUARY 1918 THROUGH MARCH 1918

France

The Treaty of Brest-Litovsk was signed on March 3, 1918,[1] and the German high command began to transport divisions by rail from the eastern front to the west.[2] The much-anticipated German offensive could now begin. Ludendorff's objective was to drive a wedge between the French and British forces at their point of joinder and thus knock Great Britain out of the war. He very nearly succeeded. After a massive, twelve-day artillery preparation that began on March 9 and in which 500,000 mustard and phosgene gas shells were fired, dozens of German divisions smashed into Gen. Sir Hubert Gough's British Fifth Army on March 21. The surprise was nearly total; the British had anticipated an attack in another sector.[3]

Using the by-now-perfected "Hutier" tactics,[4] numerous small groups of German soldiers, armed with light machine guns and flamethrowers, drove quickly through the British lines, preparing the way for the larger assault forces. In desperation, General Gough appealed to Petain for French reinforcements, only to be summarily denied; the latter feared that a similar attack upon French forces was imminent, and he did not want to get caught short.[5] The Americans were not yet a factor. Although they had several divisions, or parts of divisions, in France, only about four were up to strength, and none had completed their training.[6] The British would just have to go it alone.

Gradually the attack spent itself, as British and French resistance stiffened. General Gough was relieved of his command. Meanwhile, on March 26, 1918, the Allies gave Ferdinand Foch overall command. He quickly ordered French troops currently in line in the St. Mihiel sector to move to the Somme to defend Amiens, if necessary.[7] It was not. Ludendorff called off this phase of the offensive on April 4, having gained at most about forty miles at the center of the attack, with only minimal gains at the margins. The lull was only temporary, however, and the question was, when and where would the next blow fall?

United States: Emphasis on Organization

The demand for more men, particularly riflemen and machine gunners, grew. In late March, the Supreme War Council itself emphasized that need.[8] However, in an effort to meet that demand, many U.S. processing centers did a poor job of screening. Men who for mental or physical reasons should have been weeded out in the United States, were inducted and sent overseas, passing along the problem to personnel in France, often overworked medical teams.[9] The convoy system was working, but still America did not have enough bottoms.[10] The sole emphasis upon infantrymen, without support personnel and munitions, would have negative effects later in the year when the actual fighting began.

Some divisions were sent over with the expectation that they would fight as a unit but were sorely disappointed. Many became replacement units and were constantly stripped of their men, particularly NCOs, who were always in short supply. For the most part, these were the National Service divisions, made up of draftees.[11]

Conditions at home that winter were bad. Coal was in short supply, and there were numerous railroad breakdowns.[12] Moreover, inductees training in the United States complained that they trained without weapons and that they were inadequately housed and clothed.[13] The War Department needed to get a handle on things, and quickly. In response to the continuing crisis, Secretary of War Newton Baker appointed Gen. Peyton March as chief of staff and directed him to improve the supply situation. March took steps to coordinate and centralize supply and to institute efficiencies. Things did get noticeably better, but even at war's end many problems still remained.[14] For his part, President Wilson appointed Bernard Baruch as chairman of the War Industries Board, with control over production of war material and the allocation of raw materials.[15]

In addition to the need for men, pressure was brought to bear upon Wilson to amalgamate American companies and battalions directly into British units.[16] The president and his secretary of war sent a mixed message to the Allies, to the effect that they did not object to such a course where dictated by military necessity, but that it was not their preferred option. Wherever possible, they wished Americans to fight in American units, led by their own officers. They considered this a military question, however, and deferred to Pershing.[17] The latter made only very limited concessions to the Allies.[18]

It was during this time that fully manned divisions like the 1st and the 26th began to train with the Allies at the division level, under the control of French or British armies or corps. The units actually took their places in the line and performed the work that they had come to do. Here, senior officers got the feel of commanding large bodies of men, a very valuable experience for some, for whom it which pay dividends later on.[19] It proved to be the breaking point for others, who came up short and had to be replaced.[20]

26TH DIVISION: IN LINE WITH THE FRENCH—SOISSONS FRONT

The Division on the Move

With Field Order No. 1 dated February 3, 1918, the division was placed under the tactical control of the 11th Corps of the French army, which was composed of three divisions. The 26th Division was ordered to move to the Soissons front in the Chemin des Dames sector.[21] Its area of responsibility lay between the Pinon Forest and Pargny-Filain. Division headquarters was in a chateau at Couvrelles.[22] The same day, in a ceremony at Neufchâteau, General Edwards presented its colors to the 101st Infantry.[23]

Within a week the division had entrained for its new station. The exercise was scheduled to last approximately thirty days, and it would give the various units a chance to work side by side with their French counterparts. The American units were gradually introduced to the fighting, first by company and then by regiment. When training was by company, two platoons went into line, while two remained in support. When regiments were introduced, one battalion went into line, one was in support, and the third remained in reserve. Experienced French officers and NCOs were assigned to each unit.[24]

North of the Marne and Aisne Rivers, the region was laced with chalk mines. For centuries the French had grown champagne grapes and stored the finished product in underground caves. During the last three years of war, both sides had taken advantage of the obvious attributes of these caves and had constructed very elaborate infrastructures within.[25] When the 104th Infantry came to the sector, it found that several large chalk mines had been converted into stables, fully equipped hospitals, headquarters, and sleeping areas.[26] The French had even given them names, such as "Pantheon," but generally referred to them euphemistically as "dugouts."[27] Lincoln Eyre, a correspondent with the *New York World*, on assignment in France, observed that:

Practically all units in Soissonais are quartered in places wrested from the Germans less than a year ago in the French offensive of April, 1917. Most of them actually live in trenches, dugouts, hutments and other shelters built and once inhabited by the Boches. Staffs are installed in neat little houses tucked under ledges of rock or camouflaged with painstaking Teutonic ingenuity.[28]

Soissons itself is an ancient city surrounded by wooded hills on the south side, or left bank, of the River Aisne. Though it had a population of less than 20,000 people, it was the locus of a regional road net linking it to Paris, Reims, Château-Thierry, and Meaux.[29] The city had been in German hands for most of the war, and its buildings, including churches and abbeys tracing their foundations back more than a thousand years, lay in ruins. Powerful artillery exchanges had seen to that. Frank Sibley, a correspondent for the *Boston Globe*, attached to the 26th Division, reported that upon entry into the city, the Yankees found that "The noble cathedral was a total wreck, and no street was without a ruined building. Two or three hotels were open, however, and there were plenty of shops doing business though they had very small stocks."[30]

Much of the division's time was spent in the trenches and patrolling at night to obtain information regarding the enemy.[31] Numerous aerial dogfights took place over the American positions, as each side's airmen tried to gather information and the other side attempted to drive them off. Once, American flyers dropped leaflets over the German lines with Wilson's Fourteen Points printed in German.[32] The Red Cross provided an occasional hot shower, a short march to the rear.[33] Secretary Baker toured the front in March 1918. Dressed in a trench coat, steel helmet, and borrowed boots, he visited the 1st, 42nd, and 26th Divisions. He narrowly escaped death when a shell burst only fifty yards from his automobile. His praise of the Yankees (both new and old) recalled New England's long history of rallying to the colors:

From the day of my arrival in France, I have been hearing praise of the New England Division, which has made good in its initial experience in the trenches. . . . Some of the men are probably descended from the Minute Men of the Revolution . . . [while] . . . [t]hose whose fathers came to America since the Civil War have had an opportunity to prove that their Americanism is of the same quality. . . . *Whether the soldier is from the factory towns or the farms or the Maine woods, the account I hear is equally good.*[34]

Wherever they went, the doughboys came upon village after village that, after years of war existed only as a map reference. Just ruins remained.[35] The weather proved just as bleak. In addition to rain, there was a heavy snowfall on February 28.[36]

On the night of March 16–17, 1918, the Germans conducted a large mustard gas bombardment that fell mainly on the Americans, in particular the 102nd Infantry, which suffered 175 casualties (168 in one company alone). The ill effects would manifest themselves a day or two later, due to a delayed reaction to the gas, which clung to clothing and was activated by sweat.[37] The shells fell both in front of and behind their unit's position, keeping relief as well as supplies from reaching them. The 51st Field Artillery retaliated with some punch of its own.

Sanitary Trains: Half a Loaf

During this period of unit training, tactical control of the division and its various units passed to the French, while administrative control was retained at division headquarters.[38] In addition, under the new staff system, administrative control rested with the personnel officer, or G-1, a non-medical officer often junior in rank to the division surgeon and some of his subordinates. However, the new system brought with it some practical efficiencies. Until the change, the chief surgeon had been under the aegis of Services of Supply at Tours. This presented some problems regarding the efficient disposition and administration of medical units in the field. Military operations had been coordinated from AEF headquarters in Chaumont. As a result of the change, which became effective March 21, 1918, the chief surgeon remained at Tours, but he designated a representative at Chaumont, referred to as G-4-B. In actuality, the chief surgeon's "designee" at Chaumont consisted of four medical officers of field rank and two officers of the Sanitary Service, together with a large clerical staff. The senior person of this group was the assistant chief of staff, G-4-B. As American troops entered the line at Cantigny and the Marne, an officer from the Chaumont was detailed to cover them. He was referred to as chief surgeon, Paris Group.[39] In addition, the supply system changed, so that requisitions for medical supplies could not be made directly to the medical supply officer at the Advance Section at Is-sur-Tille, which had gone into operation on November 18, 1917.[40] This new arrangement was not without friction until all parties got used to it. At division headquarters in the château at Couvrelles, a town just outside Braine, space was at a premium. Although the division surgeon and his staff were accommodated there, the attached consultants had to be billeted in a hotel in nearby Soissons.[41]

The division of tactical and administrative responsibilities created problems for the Yankee Division surgeon. The placement of field hospitals, ambulance sections, and the evacuation routes was considered tactical. On the other hand, the treatment of wounded was considered administrative. Consequently, though the training of individuals and companies was excellent, the coordination of the various units and the cohesiveness of the Sanitary Train suffered, because the units were parceled out among their French counterparts. In addition, the French had their own very definite ideas regarding the handling of the sick and wounded, and they were inflexible to an exasperating degree. As a case in point, many American division surgeons wanted to create more mobile hospitals and move the evacuation hospitals closer to the front. That way, the patients could be removed quickly from harm's way and receive better treatment sooner. However, earlier in the war the French had suffered severe losses of hospital beds and medical personnel and had opted to place their hospitals well to the rear. Thus, when the 26th Division liaison with the French 11th Corps went to the sector in advance of the division, he found that the "tentative plans" made for hospital placement were in fact set in stone. Try as he might, when the division surgeon later came on the scene, he found his logic and reason unavailing.[42]

While it may have taken longer than actually necessary to evacuate American sick and wounded, many of whom were treated in French hospitals, and been difficult to keep track of them, there was no question that they received good care. Indeed, despite administrative problems, our medical personnel learned a lot about the care and treatment of wounded soldiers, especially those suffering the ill effects of gas. The French method included bathing, treating, and reclothing such gas victims.[43]

Most American units were used as adjuncts to their French counterparts. The 101st Field Hospital, along with the laboratories and the Medical Supply Unit, were placed at Bois Roger, where they assisted in the construction of a French hospital. Another field hospital, the 104th, was assigned to assist the French at their evacuation hospital at Vasseny, while the 102nd was stationed at St. Paul Hospital in Soissons. The latter received all types of seriously wounded and gassed cases, primarily French.[44] Likewise, the ambulance companies were scattered among various French hospitals.[45] However, the 103rd Field Hospital was assigned (as we will see below) to the Château Muret-et-Crouttes. It alone operated autonomously, caring for the slightly sick and less seriously wounded.[46]

Whatever differences the medical staff of the Yankee Division may have had with the French medical authorities, they were minor, and no doughboy suffered because of them. However, major friction continued to exist between Chaumont and division headquarters. This was potentially more serious, since it undermined the division command structure and had a negative effect upon unit morale, in particular among the officer corps, most of whose members were National Guardsmen.

As a case in point, during the stay in the Chemin des Dames, Gen. Hunter Liggett, commander of 1st Corps, and his chief of staff, Col. Malin Craig, paid an inspection visit to division headquarters at Couvrelles. After making the rounds, Liggett returned to the headquarters of the French army commander for the night. However, Craig,[47] stopped off first in Soissons, where he was overheard by the division surgeon, James Bevans, to denigrate the division, in particular its sanitary practices. Although Lt. Col. Bevans was undoubtedly aware of the negative reports by French medical authorities regarding this very point,[48] he became incensed by Craig's remarks and went immediately to General Edwards. In spite of the late hour, Edwards sent for his car. He and Lt. Col. Cassius M. Dowell, his chief of staff, and Capt. Nathaniel Simpkins, his aide, raced to find Craig, by now back at French headquarters. Liggett was asleep at the time, but Craig was not, so he bore the brunt of Edwards' wrath. The general, never one to mince words, demanded an explanation then and there; he received a public apology the next day at Gen. Louis Maud'huy's headquarters. The victory may well have been Pyhrric, since Craig had a long memory, as Edwards would learn in the Argonne.[49]

103rd Field Hospital Company: "Gentle as a Woman"

On February 8, 1918, the men of the 103rd Field Hospital boarded a train pursuant to a telegram from division headquarters.[50] Their destination was Vasseny, a small village about seven miles east of Soissons; there they were to secure billets for the night of February 9. At 9 A.M. the following day, the men began a seven-mile march to the Château Muret-et-Crouttes through the towns of Couvrelles, Mont-de-Soissons, and Nampteuil-sous-Muret.[51] The unit was under orders to operate a hospital "for slightly wounded and slightly sick who will recover within fifteen days." In addition, the 102nd Ambulance Company, which was designated "in reserve," was ordered to provide a detachment of six ambulances.[52] The only French presence was an officer assigned to protect property and equipment.[53] In addition, during their stay in the sector, medical personnel in all field hospitals received instruction from the French in gas-proofing dugouts, neutralizing gas, and treating gas casualties.[54]

On February 10, 1918, the men of the 103rd Field Hospital Company arrived at the Château Muret-et-Crouttes, named for its proximity to the two neighboring villages of those names.[55] The beautiful dwelling, with its spacious grounds, was situated on a rise approximately seven miles southeast of Soissons by winding country roads, and, as the crow flies, about thirteen miles south of the front line, held at that point by elements of the 26th Division. It had already been used by the French as a hospital. In addition to the chateau itself, there were two Adrian barracks, several outbuildings, and two large, double-walled tents known as Bessonneau tents.

The chateau was used both as sleeping quarters for the officers and as wards for the more serious surgical and medical patients. At the time, there were beds for thirty-seven such patients, in two rooms. Inside was the main kitchen for the unit, but there was also an auxiliary kitchen in a "small wooden building" outside. Another small wooden building at the entrance to the chateau served as the company office. A cement outbuilding housed a four-bed isolation ward, a dispensary, an operating room for minor surgery, and twenty-three other beds. The latrines were both the box type, which required emptying, and the open-pit type. Hot water was provided by a French system, most likely the one in place when the unit took over the hospital.[56]

One of the Adrian barracks was divided by a curtain into two sections. One half was used as a receiving ward and the other as an observation ward. The other barracks was used as sleeping quarters for the enlisted men. In addition, the two Bessonneau tents were used as wards for ambulatory cases. They were capable of holding twenty-six patients each, and thirty in an emergency, although during the stay of the 103rd Field Hospital only one was utilized. Each of these tents was approximately twenty feet wide by sixty feet long. Often two tents were joined together to make one large ward. At each end, the flaps were extended to form storage areas. The tents were heated by a stove, which vented through a flap midway along one sidewall. Nine window flaps (eight on the stove side) admitted light. The spacing between the two layers of canvas provided an insulating pocket of air.[57] The bunks were wooden and contained straw mattresses, called "ticks."[58]

Two of the doctors assigned to the company at this time described the food as "of good quality" and "well cooked."[59] Not everyone agreed with this assessment, however. On March 3, 1918, after becoming ill, some members of Company K,

104th Infantry were evacuated to the 103rd Field Hospital. Several of these patients tried to leave the hospital early, their chief complaint being the poor quality of the food served there. They charged that they had been fed tomato soup cooked in the same containers that had held oil. They were quickly apprehended by the military police and returned to the hospital to complete their recuperation.[60]

First Lt. Clifford W. Renth was a dentist assigned to the 103rd Field Hospital Company during its stay in the Soissons sector. He also served as the officer in charge of patient clothing and equipment. Later, near Verdun, he would act as an anesthetist on one of the surgical teams formed by the hospital.[61] Dr. Renth carried a portable dental outfit. On February 12, 1918, he commenced inspections and treatment of the convalescent patients as well as of the field hospital and ambulance company personnel assigned to the unit. He was trying out a new system of examining convalescents, one that lent itself well to the mission of the hospital. What he found was "a prevalence of abscessed teeth," as well as a general "lack of care and use of [a] toothbrush." When word reached the neighboring townspeople, he was flooded with requests for treatment. However, for them he confined himself to "emergency extractions after hours." During this period, he also treated one man evacuated from the front line.[62]

Most if not all army hospitals, including field hospitals, had admission procedures.[63] These were determined by the type of patient the unit was designated to serve. Some hospitals treated seriously wounded and injured; others contagious, venereal, and skin-disease cases; while others might treat gas victims. Still others, like the 103rd Field Hospital, while stationed in the Soissons sector, were ordered to serve the ordinary sick and less seriously wounded. However, there were three basic functions common to all: screening for the illness or injury and for lice, cleaning of clothing and bathing of the patient, and treating patients or forwarding them to other treatment units.

When an ambulance bearing a patient arrived at the 103rd Field Hospital, it was greeted by the officer of the day. That doctor's responsibility was to screen for contagious or venereal diseases. Such cases were not admitted but were sent directly to other facilities. Those admitted, many of whom were covered with lice, were bathed and placed in appropriate wards. Their clothing was tagged and taken to the kitchen and placed on wooden racks in one of three large-mouthed galvanized-iron cans filled with water. The lids were then placed thereon and the contents boiled for one hour in order to kill the lice and their eggs. When a contagious disease did appear within the hospital, such as scarlet fever, the affected patients were immediately isolated and, if appropriate, transferred to a contagion hospital.[64] When a patient became ambulatory, he was transferred to one of the tent wards and, if warranted, assigned light duties.[65]

There were no female nurses with the 103rd Field Hospital at this time, so nursing duties devolved upon the inexperienced NCOs and enlisted attendants. Up to this point, while they had some classroom training, these men had been used largely as construction hands at Bazoilles-sur-Meuse and Dijon. The table of organization for a motorized field hospital, such as the 103rd, provided for three sergeants first class, six sergeants, three corporals, and fifty-five privates and privates first class. In addition, there were two cooks, one mechanic, and thirteen drivers, for a total of eighty-three enlisted men. Of the sergeants first class, one served as first sergeant known as "Top." Another was in charge of records, and the third was in charge of the wards. Of the six sergeants, two were wardmasters, and the others were assigned as the mess sergeant, an anesthetist, in charge of the supply room, and in charge of the operating rooms.[66]

The ward duties were divided into supervisory responsibilities, which were carried out by the wardmasters, and the daily nursing chores, which were carried out by the enlisted attendants (referred to in the navy and Marines as "hospital corpsmen"). The duty day was divided into shifts. The wardmaster, a noncommissioned officer, usually a sergeant, was in charge of each shift, reporting directly to the ward surgeon, a medical doctor. His basic responsibilities were both administrative and functional. For example, he was responsible for the order and cleanliness of the ward, security of the patient's valuables, and coordination with the mess sergeant to see that the proper meals were provided for the patients as ordered by the doctor. He filed patient records, which were to be kept confidential and released only to authorized persons, and he had to secure all drugs and alcohol (including liquor) to prevent their improper use. No patient was allowed into the ward without an admission card. It was the wardmaster's duty to attach a medical history to each patient's chart. In the event that a patient was also under arrest by military authorities, the wardmaster was held personally responsible if the terms of his admission and release were violated, or if he escaped.[67]

Enlisted attendants were responsible for basic nursing duties, whether ministering to the sick or cleaning up after them. They were urged to use "common sense sanitation." In wards for infectious diseases, attendants were issued white cotton coats and trousers to wear on duty; they were to be changed twice a week.[68] Also, when on duty in the hospital, enlisted personnel were exempted from wearing the hobnailed boots that were standard doughboy issue. Instead, they were permitted to wear the plain-soled garrison shoe.[69] Among other things, they bathed, clothed, and fed the sick, as well as changed bandages and soiled linens, and emptied bed pans. In addition, they administered medicines, took temperatures, and, where ambulatory convalescents were unavailable, kept wards clean. In contagious cases, they used paper napkins to wipe runny noses. The used wipes were then placed in paper bags attached to patient beds by adhesive tape. The bags and their contents had to be regularly disposed of by burning.[70] Many wards were "under canvas" and had dirt floors, or at best multiple layers of canvas tarp for floors. In those cases, cleanliness was a little harder. The attendants were constantly exposed to contagious diseases, and where they had not already developed immunities, had to be vaccinated or inoculated. Theirs was a thankless task, but they learned their jobs well and took great pride in what they did.[71]

The hospital at Château Muret-et-Crouttes had a total capacity of about 350 beds, although on any given day no more than 195 patients were treated.[72] All told according to available records the unit admitted 325 men. The average stay in the hospital was between five and eight days. More than two dozen types of medical problems were treated, from trench foot, scabies, and dysentery to broken bones and septic wounds.[73] There were no patient deaths during this period.

The effective strength of the unit remained roughly the same, between sixty-one and sixty-three officers and men.[74] This was well below the TOE for a field hospital. In fact, on March 31, 1918, the day before its transfer to the Toul sector, the effective strength of the hospital was fifty-six, eight officers and forty-eight enlisted.[75] The most likely explanation would be that some men were at special army schools, such as Langres, or were on temporary assignment. Also, from time to time more experienced personnel, especially commissioned and noncommissioned officers, were assigned to newer divisions. On February 14, 1918, Major King was relieved of his command and transferred to Blois. At various times, both Maj. Charles Walker and Capt. Leonard W. Hassett served as interim company commanders until the arrival of Maj. William Blanchard.[76]

The stay at Château Muret-et-Crouttes provided invaluable preparation for the dark days ahead, when the company would be called upon to treat the many hundreds of broken American bodies that would be delivered to them by ambulances fresh from the battlefield. For many enlisted men, the roles of orderly and nurse were new. In spite of their lack of previous experience, they performed well. Lt. Harold F. Parker made the following observation in his report of the company activities during this period:

The ward masters and attendants were from the personnel of the 103rd Field Hospital Co., and although new to this type of work from a practical standpoint they had all received lectures on ward management and care of patients etc. *and all took an interest in their work and performed it in a creditable manner.*[77]

Historian Ronald Schaffer quotes two doughboys, both former patients in other hospitals. The first commented upon the kindness of the medics and their willingness to help; it did him good "to see how tender the big tough American can be toward the patient." The other soldier described the man who bandaged his wounds as having been as "gentle as a woman."[78]

In a sad footnote to the unit's stay in the Soissons sector, the beautiful Château Muret-et-Crouttes was destroyed by the Germans during their retreat in July 1918.[79]

Movement: "A Fine Stretch of the Legs!"

On March 8, 1918, the various units of the Yankee Division were ordered to the Toul sector to relieve the 1st Division. Movement was to begin on March 18.[80] The new headquarters was to be located at Boucq.[81] The trip had originally called for train travel the whole way, but the orders were amended to one day by train and a march the rest of the way back to the Fourth Training area near Rimaucourt. To add insult to injury, the train depot at Braine was shelled and much of the division baggage, which was following behind, was destroyed.[82] The change to a road march was in part to help condition the men prior to a training exercise later in the month. During the movement, the division was temporarily headquartered at Bar-sur-Aube.[83] The march did not seem to faze the men. Along the route, new clothing was issued, and even though showers were not available, the men took advantage of the many streams and the spring weather to bathe and wash their clothing.[84] According to Maj. Emerson G. Taylor, later acting chief of staff for the 26th Division, they marched "easterly, along smooth roads, through a smiling farm country of rolling plains and little, clean rivers, with patches of ancient woodland with nowhere a sign of war and everywhere the signs of tender spring, past sleepy little towns of venerable age.[T]he warm sun sent down its blessing. It was a good war."[85]

The French had delayed the movement of the Sanitary Trains from Braine, and it was far behind the rest of the division, nearly full two days. Thus, when the men of the 102nd Infantry, while en route to their new station, experienced a delayed reaction to an earlier mustard gas attack,[86] it was fortunate that there were two small French hospitals nearby, since the Yankees had only one ambulance available.[87] On March 19, 1918, the 103rd Field Hospital finally departed from the rail station at Braine at 7 P.M. The unit traveled by train to Brienne-le-Château, where the medics boarded trucks for the remaining fifteen miles to their interim destination, Bar-sur-Aube. It was there that they found billets for the night of March 20.[88] The men of the 103rd Field Hospital were able to rest for a few days. On March 25, most of the Sanitary Trains began a twenty-five-mile journey by truck to the vicinity of Marault, a small town five miles north of Chaumont. The route took them through the towns of Colombey-les-deux-Eglises and Jonchery.[89] The 103rd Field Hospital did not have to travel quite that far, as it was transported sixteen miles to Blaisy, where the men spent the night. It then set off the next day on another twenty-five-mile ride to Lafauche, a short distance west of Liffol-le-Grand, in the original divisional training area, where the unit arrived sometime on March 26.[90]

After a few more days catching up, the exercise (along with anticipated and long-awaited leaves) was suddenly canceled on Easter Sunday, March 31, due to changes in the overall military situation. The 101st and 103rd Field Hospitals were ordered to proceed to Toul early the next day as part of an advance party to relieve their counterparts in the 1st Division.[91] The respective division surgeons were ordered to transfer their sick as well as the necessary medical supplies.[92] The third unit in the advance party was the 103rd Ambulance Company, which was ordered to Ménil-le-Tour, also to relieve its counterpart. Trucks were provided for transport. The route of the hospitals was by way of Neufchâteau and Colomby-les-Belles. The advance party was scheduled to leave the staging area just outside Camp Hospital No. 18 at 12:45 P.M., April 1, and to arrive at their respective duty stations later that day.[93] The balance of the Sanitary Trains, like the rest of the division, was trucked from Prez-sous-Lafauche to Toul to complete the relief, in vehicles supplied by the French.[94] In addition, the quartermaster was ordered to provide trucks to carry baggage and haul the rolling kitchens. Horse-drawn units were to set off at 7:30 A.M., April 2, and were allowed until April 5 to arrive at their assigned destinations.

The route was the same as that of the field hospitals, but billeting and cooking arrangements had to be made for the men.[95]

NOTES

1. Martin Gilbert, *The First World War* (New York: Henry Holt, 1994), 401.

2. Ibid., 386–87 and 411.

3. Ibid., 406 ff.

4. Rod Paschall, *The Defeat of Imperial Germany, 1917–1918* (Chapel Hill, N.C.: Algonquin,1989), 65 and 227–28; see also Paul Braim, *The Test of Battle: The American Expeditionary Forces in the Meuse-Argonne Campaign* (Newark: Univ. of Delaware Press, 1988), 28–29 (referred to as "by-pass tactics"); Edward M. Coffman, *The War to End All Wars: The American Military Experience in World War I* (Madison: Univ. of Wisconsin Press, 1986), 154.

5. Gilbert, *First World War*, 408.

6. Paschall, *Defeat of Imperial Germany*, 130–31 and 134.

7. Gilbert, *First World War*, 409–12.

8. Coffman, *War to End All Wars*, 171–72.

9. Harvey Cushing, *From a Surgeon's Journal* (Boston: Little, Brown, 1919), 375.

10. Coffman, *War to End All Wars*, 182.

11. Ibid., 67.

12. David M. Kennedy, *Over Here: The First World War and American Society* (New York: Oxford Univ. Press, 1980), 123–24.

13. Coffman, *War to End All Wars*, 64–68.

14. Ibid., 162.

15. Kennedy, *Over Here*, 129.

16. Coffman, *War to End All Wars*, 168–70.

17. Ibid., 169–70.

18. Ibid., 173; Kennedy, *Over Here*, 171.

19. Braim, *Test of Battle*, 52–53.

20. Ibid., 161.

21. Field Order #1, February 3, 1918, 26th Division (U.S.). MNGA; James Lung Bevans, *Medical History of the 26th Division from Organization to June 24, 1918* (typescript, n.d.), 8; *Chemin des Dames* means literally, the "Road of the Ladies," which refers to an ancient road along the ridge between Soissons and Reims traversed by the ladies of court. NA RG120.

22. Bevans, *Medical History*, 8.

23. James T. Duane, *Dear Old "K"* (Boston: Thomas Todd, 1922), 27.

24. Frederick E. Jones, *Historical Sketch of the Medical Department of the 26th Division* (typescript, n.d., with "Introductory Note" and other comments by Col. R.S. Porter, 8 August 1919), 9; Bevans, *Medical History*, 8. NA RG120.

25. Frank P. Sibley, *With the Yankee Division in France* (Boston: Little, Brown, 1919), 54.

26. Duane, *Dear Old "K,"* 29.

27. Ibid., 44.

28. *Stars & Stripes*, March 1, 1918, 1–2. USMA.

29. *Encyclopaedia Britannica*, 1959, s.v. "Soissons."

30. Sibley, *With the Yankee Division in France*, 53.

31. Duane, *Dear Old "K,"* 44; *Stars & Stripes*, March 8, 1918, 1. USMA.

32. Duane, *Dear Old "K,"* 43.

33. Ibid., 34.

34. *Stars & Stripes*, March 22, 1918, 2. USMA.

35. Duane, *Dear Old "K,"* 50–51.

36. Ibid., 46.

37. Bevans, *Medical History*, 11.

38. Sibley, *With the Yankee Division in France*, 51–52.

39. Charles Lynch, ed., *The Medical Department of the United States Army in the World War*, vol.8, *Field Operations*, (Washington, D.C.: GPO, 1925), 47–49 and 55–58.

40. Ibid., 27.

41. Bevans, *Medical History*, 9–10.

42. Ibid., 8.

43. Ibid., 9.

44. Jones, *Historical Sketch*, 11.

45. Bevans, *Medical History*, 9.

46. Jones, *Historical Sketch*, 11.

47. Malin Craig was born into an army family in St. Joseph, Missouri, on August 5, 1875. He graduated from West Point with the class of 1898 and took part in the Spanish-American War. Later, he served in the Boxer Rebellion in China and in the Philippine Insurrection. After the First World War he served as director of relief when the Mississippi flooded in 1927. The pinnacle of his career was reached in 1935, when President Franklin D. Roosevelt appointed him to the post of chief of staff of the army. He died on July 25, 1945. *Dictionary of American Biography, Supplement Three: 1941–1945,* (New York: Scribners, 1973), 193–94.

48. Circular Letter, February 27, 1918, Para. I.2., HQ 26th Division, Office of the Chief Surgeon. NA RG120. See also chapter 1 and Chapter 2.

49. Sibley, *With the Yankee Division in France*, 85–86.

50. Station List, Sheet #1, 103rd Field Hospital. NA RG120. But see Field Order #1, February 3, 1918, 26th Division (U.S.). The unit was ordered to station at Liffol-le-Grand no later than 11 P.M., February 9, 1918. I have assumed that the telegram changed these orders. MNGA.

51. Special Order #29, February 9, 1918, 11th Corps (Fr.) HQ, 3rd Division. NA RG120.

52. Note on Organization and Working of Sanitary Service in the 26th Division U.S.A., 11th French Corps, 1st Bureau, February 7, 1918. NA RG120.

53. Charles S. Walker, Report of Tour of Duty in Soissons Sector, April 13, 1918. NA RG120.

54. Jones, *Historical Sketch*, 12.

55. Station List, Sheet #1, 103rd Field Hospital. NA RG120.

56. Walker, Report; Harold F. Parker; Report of Tour of Duty in Soissons Sector, April 15, 1918. NA RG120.

57. Joseph H. Ford, ed., *The Medical Department of the United States Army in the World War*, vol. 2, *Administration American Expeditionary Forces*, ed. (Washington, D.C.: GPO, 1927), 260 and 275–76.

58. Walker, Report. In an early example of recycling, the Army reused the old mattress straw for horse feed. *Stars & Stripes*, April 12, 1918, 3. USMA.

59. Walker and Parker, Reports.

60. Duane, *Dear Old "K,"* 47–48.

61. See chapter 7; Richard Derby, *"Wade in, Sanitary!"* (New York: G.P. Putnam's Sons, 1919), 100. (It was common practice for dental surgeons to serve as anesthesiologists on surgical teams.)

62. Clifford W. Renth, *Report of Tour of Duty in Soissons Sector, Feb.10/18 to Mar.19/18.* NA RG120; Lettie Gavin, in *American Women in World War I,* describes the similar experiences of Dr. DeLan Kinney, who was on the staff of the American Women's Hospital No. 1 at Luzancy. Many residents of the Marne region had "lived a lifetime without a toothbrush." Dr. Kinney held "pulling clinics" and performed dental repairs for the area residents (p.162).

63. As an example of a more detailed procedure, see Frank A. Evans, *System of Admission, Base Hospital No. 18, A.E.F.,* 1–4. Base Hospital No.18, at Bazoilles-sur-Meuse, was a large facility. Although its procedures were similar, they were more detailed; personnel were assigned specific titles and tasks. Whether a clerk in the receiving office, a wardmaster or orderly, a stretcher bearer, or a vestiare clerk, all had assigned tasks. When the flow was too great for the regular staff to handle, others were temporarily assigned to receiving. Procedures in place in June of 1918, long after the 103rd Field Hospital had moved on, were typical. The first task of the inspecting medical officer was to determine the proper ward in which to place the patient and whether he was infested with vermin. A clerk took note on an index card of any valuables removed from him. If lice were found and his condition did not preclude his movement, the patient was sent to the bathing facility, where his clothes were removed for sterilization and he was bathed. He was then sent along to the proper ward. He was given a number by the vestiare clerk, and his clothing was inventoried. Clean clothing was placed in the locker with his number; upon discharge, all patients were assured of a complete uniform. At the same time, the patient's medical diagnosis and condition were noted on the medical card attached to his person. It followed him throughout his stay. NA RG120.

64. Walker, Report.

65. Parker, Report.

66. General Headquarters, American Expeditionary Forces, General Staff: First Section, Tables of Organization, Series A, January 14, 1918, Corrected to June 26, 1918, Sanitary Train, Maximum Strength, August 1, 1918, table 28.

67. Ward Rules and Regulations, Base Hospital No.17, Dijon, August 30, 1917 to October 16, 1917. NA RG120.

68. Circular Letter No. 56, February 27, 1918, A.E.F., Headquarters 26th Division, Office of the Chief Surgeon, citing para. 8, Circular No. 9, February 7, 1918, Chief Surgeon, G.H.Q. A.E.F. The circular letter was issued to "all medical, dental & veterinary officers," so there was apparently no distinction made between the personnel in field hospitals and those at base hospitals. In the treatment of meningitis, all medical personnel, including enlisted attendants, were directed to wear surgical gowns, caps, and gauze masks. NA RG120.

69. Frank W. Weed, ed., *The Medical Department of the United States Army in the World War,* vol. 6, *Sanitation: In the American Expeditionary Forces* (Washington, D.C.: GPO, 1926), 641.

70. Circular Letter No. 56, para. V. 11.

71. As an example of the enlisted man's devotion to duty, Pvt. 1/C Clarence Minkler of the 104th Field Hospital volunteered to work in the contagious ward. He died on December 11, 1917, of scarlet fever and nephritis contracted while on duty. R. S. Porter, *101st Sanitary Train, 26th Division A.E.F., History, March 20th, 1919,* 347. MNGA.

72. Weekly Report of Sick and Injured, Week Ending March 6, 1918, 103rd Field Hospital. NA RG120.

73. Walker and Parker, Reports. In comparing the Weekly Reports of Sick and Injured with the Nominal Check Lists (which list names and assigns distinct numbers to each man) for the same period, there is a wide variance. I have gone with the higher number, because of the method of identifying the patient. The Weekly Report for the period shows 223 admissions, while the Nominal Check Lists show a total of 325. Of these persons, twenty-nine were listed as injured, and the balance were sick.

74. Weekly Report of Sick and Injured, March 6, 20, 26, and 27, 103rd Field Hospital. NA RG120.

75. Strength Report, 31 March 1918, 103rd Field Hospital. NA RG120.

76. Roster Medical Department, 26th Division. MNGA; Weekly Report 26 March 1918, 103rd Field Hospital (signed "Maj. Leonard W. Hassett M.C. Commanding"). There is some question as to his rank at this time. In January 1919, when he took permanent command, his rank was still captain, but he was promoted to major on March 17, prior to taking the company back to the United States. NA RG120.

77. Parker, Report. Emphasis added.

78. Ronald Schaffer, *America in the Great War: The Rise of the War Welfare State* (New York: Oxford Univ. Press, 1991), 172.

79. Jones, *Historical Sketch*, 11.

80. Field Order #2, March 8, 1918, 26th Division (U.S.). MNGA.

81. Sibley, *With the Yankee Division in France*, 108.

82. Duane, *Dear Old "K,"* 54.

83. Jones, *Historical Sketch*, 12; Bevans, *Medical History*, 11.

84. Bevans, *Medical History*, 11.

85. Emerson G. Taylor, *New England in France, 1917–1919: A History of the Twenty-sixth Division U.S.A.* (Boston: Houghton Mifflin, 1920), 88–89.

86. During the night of March 16/17.

87. Bevans, *Medical History*, 11.

88. Field Order #2 (as amended by F.O.#4), March 8, 1918, 26th Division (U.S.). MNGA; Station List, Sheet #1, 103rd Field Hospital; Clifford W. Renth, Report of Duties to Division Dental Surgeon, 26th Division, A.E.F., 18 October 1918. NA RG120.

89. Station List, Sheet #1, 103rd Field Hospital. NA RG120.

90. Ibid., Sheet #2. Note that in the station list, the destination appears as "Draizy"; but see Michelin Map #61,"Paris, Troyes, Chaumont, 1cm:2km."

91. Station List, Sheet #1, 103rd Field Hospital. See also Jones, Historical Sketch, 12; Field Orders No.1 (Secret), 31 March 1918, Headquarters, 101st Sanitary Train, A.E.F., para.1.(b), 2., and 4. NA RG120.

92. Field Orders No.17 (Secret) and No.19 (Secret), 26th Division, March 31, 1918; Field Orders No.20 (Secret), 26th Division, 1 April 1918, para.3.(c). NA RG120.

93. Field Orders No. 17 (Secret), 26th Division, 31st March, 1918; Field Orders No. 1 (Secret), 31 March 1918, Headquarters, 101st Sanitary Train, A.E.F. NA RG120.

94. Jones, *Historical Sketch,* 11–12. Relates that trucks left from Liffol-le-Grand, but orders are very specific that they were to report to Prez-sous-Lafauche.

95. Field Orders No. 18, 26th Division, 31st March, 1918; Field Orders No. 2 (Secret), 1st April 1918, Headquarters, 101st Sanitary Train, A.E.F. NA RG120.

Chapter Four

A Front All Their Own
(Toul Sector)

Dim, through the misty panes and thick green light
As under a green sea, I saw him drowning.

—Wilfred Owen

HIGH TIDE (APRIL 1918 THROUGH JUNE 1918)

Western Front—Allied Woes

Like a boxer probing his opponent for a weak point, Ludendorff jabbed again. This time he chose the area beyond the Lys River. On April 9, 1918, following a four-and-one-half-hour artillery bombardment, fourteen divisions opened the attack on a ten-mile front. Another four divisions ploughed into a Portuguese division. The object of the attack was to cross the Lys, overrun the southern portion of the Ypres salient, and drive to the coast between Dunkirk and Calais. If successful, the attack would split the French and British forces. The initial results were the same as those of the earlier assault on Gough's Fifth Army. The British and their allies fell back, giving up in the process the hard-won ground at Paschendaele and Messines Ridge. The Germans created a gap three and one-half miles wide. Once again the Germans used an enormous quantity of gas. Two thousand tons of mustard, phosgene, and diphenylchlorarsine gasses incapacitated 8000 British troops, some of them blinded. On April 11, Douglas Haig gave his famous "Backs to the Wall" speech, but still they came on. More gas was used—9,000,000 artillery rounds containing yet another 2000 tons. The situation was considered so serious that conscription was extended to Ireland. Pershing finally relented and authorized the use of American troops. However, like the previous attacks, this too spent itself, since the Germans were simply too exhausted to achieve a breakthrough. The offensive was called off on April 29, 1918. The cost had been high—30,000 Germans died while killing 20,000 Allied soldiers, all in the space of just three weeks.[1]

One month later, Ludendorff landed a haymaker in the Chemin des Dames, the sector recently vacated by the American 26th Division after completing its training with the French 11th Corps. On May 27, he launched a massive attack across a twenty-four-mile front against the four French and four British divisions holding the ridge between Soissons and Reims. The results were spectacular—twelve miles gained in the first twenty-four hours. Within forty-eight hours the gap was forty miles wide and fifteen miles deep. Soissons fell on the 29th, and on the 30th the German army was on the north bank of the Marne at Château-Thierry, poised to cross over. In fact, on June 3, 1918, using specially built telescoping ladders, it did cross the Marne, six miles east of the town, and established a beachhead.

However, this was the Germans' high-water mark, and except for a brief, unsuccessful thrust in the area of Noyon-Montdidier between June 8 and 12, they never again had the opportunity to mount a serious offensive.[2] From now on, for the Germans, it would be mostly a defensive struggle.[3] The French and British could not possibly know this, and they were in near panic. The enemy was within fifty miles of Paris. It was shades of 1914 all over again.[4] The time of the Americans was at hand.

Western Front: The Time of the Americans

Ready or not, the Americans were definitely needed. Pershing relented and prepared to release his divisions. On June 15, 1918, in a pep talk to the officers of the 1st Division, he emphasized the fact that the American army was unfamiliar with defeat; they should meet the enemy "like Americans." That is, they should charge right at them.[5] The warm-up bout took place at a village called Cantigny, on the British front, near Montdidier. There, on May 28, 1918, a brigade of the 1st Division, with the assistance of French tanks and flamethrowers, wrested the town from the surprised German defenders. The fight was fierce, and against heavy odds the Americans held until relieved several days later.[6] It was an excellent beginning.

When the Allies called for assistance in the area of Château-Thierry, Pershing sent for the U.S. 2nd and 3rd Divisions. The former unit had an interesting history, in that it was not an all-army division. Early in the planning stages, the Marine Corps had discovered that it would not be part of the original American Expeditionary Force. Not to be denied its opportunity for glory, the Corps insisted upon and was granted inclusion.[7] Thus, the 2nd Division was cobbled together with two brigades, the 3rd Brigade, composed of the 9th and 23rd Infantry Regiments of the U.S. Army, and the 4th Brigade, composed of the 5th and 6th Marine Regiments. Brig. Gen. James Harbord, an army officer, took command of the Marine brigade.[8]

The 2nd Division was loaded onto French trucks, the drivers of which were Vietnamese, and raced overnight to the area slightly north and west of Château-

Thierry.[9] The French were in complete and demoralized retreat. Fleeing soldiers yelled to the new arrivals, "The war is over!" The Americans, who had waited and trained for this moment, were having none of this defeatism. "Retreat, hell! We just got here!" was the most common reply.[10] The 3rd Brigade entered the line near Vaux and the hotly contested Hill 204, an excellent site for the German artillery. The Marines were taken to Belleau Wood, near Bouresches and Lucy-le-Bocage.[11]

Much has been written about the Marines and their gallant defense and later capture of that wood which was renamed by the French in their honor. Not enough has been written about the rest of the 2nd Division, let alone the later exploits of other divisions, like the U.S. 3rd Division ("Rock of the Marne"), whose incredible containment of the German bridgehead just east of Château-Thierry, against heavy odds, was the stuff of legends.[12] That the army units went unrecognized was an accident of fate. At that time, censorship was tightly imposed by AEF headquarters at Chaumont. Unit names could not be used in press accounts to describe the fighting; however, the use of the word "Marines" was considered generic and thus was acceptable. Consequently, journalists stuck to the letter of the law, and most of the dispatches and the headlines centered around the exploits of that gallant band. It simply made good press.[13] Thus, a chapter was added to the tradition of the U.S. Marine Corps, and rightly so.

The Marines were inserted into the crumbling French line on June 2, 1918. After a desperate and often confused hand-to-hand defense, which lasted several days, they shifted to the offense. The fight was against a German defender who knew the value and the effective use of interlocking fields of fire from well-entrenched machine-gun nests. The Marines learned the hard way that these were not to be charged en masse, standing upright, but only after hundreds of them were killed or suffered grievous wounds.[14] Where leadership at the upper levels may have been inexperienced or ineffective due to lack of good communication, raw courage and enthusiasm were not lacking.[15] The latter prevailed after a bitter, three-week struggle. The line was held at the Marne.

26TH DIVISION: "BON SECTEUR, MONSIEUR"

It was time for the division to take over an entire sector, and the area around Toul was selected.[16] The only good thing to be said about it was that it was well established and was considered a quiet sector, or as the French said, a *"bon secteur."*[17] The division sector stretched for approximately fifteen miles on a line that ran generally from west to east, beginning near the town of Apremont and extending through Xivray-et-Marvoisin and Seicheprey to Beaumont, where it terminated.[18] Later, the division responsibility shifted somewhat, as the French took over the area around Apremont; the line of the 26th moved eastward to Flirey.[19] Unfortunately, by doing so the division gave up the highest and driest ground in the sector. The remaining land was wet and swampy, and the trenches were always full of water and mud; the dugouts required daily pumping. In fact, the trench system was described by some as the worst stretch of trenches on the western front.[20] To top it all off, the Germans had a well-established observation and artillery post on nearby Montsec, the highest ground in the vicinity.[21]

Lt. Col. James L. Bevans, the division surgeon, offers a very vivid picture of the conditions under which these men lived:

One typical camp of about a hundred men looked more like the hiding place of old time brigands than anything else. The men lived in little caves and dugouts. The whole camp was tramped into a mire, knee-deep with indescribable ruts and chuckholes where the horses passed. The cook-house was a half completed wooden building, the rain coming through in streams, and no attempt had been made at paving with duck-boards to prevent mud; the cooks waded about in rubber boots. The mess table, one board wide, without seats, was in the open and the men stood in the mud as they ate. *Inspection showed almost every one was suffering from scabies or lice.*[22]

His successor, Lt. Col. Frederick Jones, was just as graphic:

In many of the trenches the men were knee deep to waist deep in liquid mud most of the time. Men occupying them often had no shelter from the elements. Many slept in the mud on the firing steps. Sanitation was bad when we entered the area. Only two meals a day could be served to men in the trenches, the food-carry was long, the big marmite cans heavy and awkward to carry. *Lice were becoming a nuisance.*[23]

As in the Chemin des Dames, tactical control rested with the French—this time, General Passaga, commander of the French 32nd Corps.[24] Administrative control remained with division headquarters, now at Boucq, a town about thirteen miles northwest of Toul.[25]

This usually quiet area suddenly became the focus of an increase in activity; perhaps the Germans were determined to intimidate the newly arrived Yankees. The upshot was that the Germans launched a series of attacks. The first attack took place on April 10, 1918, at Bois Brûlé (near Apremont). After a day's pause, the attack resumed on April 12, continuing through the next day. The 103rd and 104th Infantry Regiments bore the brunt; as a result of its spirited defense, the latter had its colors decorated with the croix de guerre.[26]

However, the deadliest attack by far occurred on April 20, in the section of the trench line located at Seicheprey.[27] There, elements of the 102nd Infantry Regiment were surprised and very nearly overrun by a vastly superior force, following an artillery attack that included gas.[28] The fighting was fierce, and many casualties were incurred, even among the litter bearers and other medical personnel. Quite a number of prisoners were taken, some never to return.[29] Telephonic communications were severed, and reports filtered back to headquarters only as a result of intrepid runners. As it turned out, the German losses were also extremely heavy due to the ferocious defense put up by the Yankees, who fought to the death with anything and everything at hand, including their bare fists. Cooks and medics, as well as anyone else unfortunate enough to be within the village at that time, were involved in the fighting. Journalist Bert Ford, with the Yankee Division, describes the scene: "They fought the seasoned enemy troops with rifle, pistol, bayonet, and grenade. They fought them hand-to-hand in the streets and in the ruined houses, cellars and dugouts. They fought with their fists and they drove the enemy back."[30]

The Germans eventually withdrew to their own lines, leaving behind "souvenirs," including American bodies booby-trapped with grenades, for unsuspecting medics and litter bearers.[31] It was reported that when Pershing was informed about the attack, he became extremely upset about the losses and the lack of an immediate counterattack.[32] On May 3, a detachment from the 104th Infantry was sent to Seicheprey to repair the trenches and to act as a burial detail for some still unburied bodies.[33]

Headquarters felt it was time for a major counterpunch, and the 26th Division was chosen to stage what was to be the first large-scale, all-American effort.[34] The kickoff was scheduled for the night of May 30–31. The object was to seize prisoners in the area of Richecourt and Lahayville, approximately a mile and a half north, and slightly west, of the American line at Seicheprey. The leader of the raid was Maj. James F. Hickey of the 101st Infantry; the operation is sometimes referred to as "Hickey's Raid." Planning took place in secret for ten days; it covered all phases, including medical evacuation. A contingent of more than 300 volunteers was selected from the 101st Infantry.

At the appointed hour, the group selected to cut the wire and open a passage was sent out ahead. An artillery barrage followed. This was a "box barrage," designed to hem the defenders in but permit the attackers to advance in relative safety. Early in the raid, the Americans reported the unmistakable odor of gas. It was first thought to be from German counter-battery fire, but it was later determined to be deadly phosgene gas that had been included in the initial American barrage. The wind had shifted, and the gas was blowing back along a ravine near Lahayville up which the Americans were advancing. They continued, and the raid was initially called a success.[35] Some prisoners were taken, and our losses were only two killed, five wounded, and one man missing. A bag full of grenades carried by a soldier had exploded, killing him; when his buddy came to his rescue he too had been killed by a secondary explosion.[36]

The initial optimistic assessment had to be modified when hundreds of the soldiers were treated over the course of the next several days for delayed reactions to the gas.[37] Several of these men died agonizing deaths, including Sgt. Fred S. Murphy of Framingham, Massachusetts, a member of the 101st Infantry.[38]

Other German attacks occurred during the division's stay in the sector. One took place on May 27, at a place called Humbert Plantation, near Flirey, at the eastern end of the American sector. It was repulsed by elements of the 101st Infantry.[39] The last major German attack came on June 16, at Xivray-et-Marvoisin in the center of the sector. Again, the Germans were turned back, this time by the 103rd Infantry.[40]

All the while, artillery shelling from both sides was a constant fact of life. On June 7, one man from M company, 104th Infantry, was killed and several others crushed when German shells hit their billet. The medical officer, Maj. Stanhope Bayne-Jones, was cited for his good work with the victims.[41] Division headquarters ordered a projector gas attack at 2:00 A.M. on June 19. A thousand shells containing chloropicrin gas were fired. The Germans retaliated, hitting regimental headquarters and causing a number of shrapnel injuries.[42]

It was not all work for the Yankees during this time. Elsie Janis,[43] a popular and multi-talented entertainer spent most of a week with them in late May, midway through a six-month tour of France. She was well known both in England and the United States. She sang and danced, thrilled the boys with her famous cartwheels (on small, improvised stages no less!), and reduced them to gales of laughter with her imitations of other entertainers (like Dan Daly and Charlie Chaplin) and with her own renditions of popular songs of the day. Her trademark became "Over Here," a parody of "Over There" composed by her friend George M. Cohan. Mostly, she was Elsie, or as Stars & Stripes reported, she had a "pepful and pulchritudinous personality" and was "an oasis of color and vivacity in the midst of a dreary desert of frock-coated and white-tied legislators and lecturers who have been visited upon us for our sins and the sins of our fathers."[44] This could well have been a veiled reference to Secretary of War Newton Baker, who was currently on a tour of the AEF.

While in Toul, Elsie and her mother stayed in the Hotel de la Comedie. The rooms were not luxurious, but their top-floor location gave them a bird's-eye view of the goings-on, especially of the air war in the sector. The tour began on a Tuesday, when she and her mother were the guests of General Edwards and his staff at his headquarters in the Château at Boucq. For much of her tour she was escorted by the general's aide, Captain Simpkins. Edwards bent over backward to see to her comfort, extending every courtesy to her. He even issued her a "red motor pass" that entitled her to go anywhere in the sector, and that is just what she did. From the Bois de Rehanne to Royaumeix, in every type of venue from an airplane hangar and a brickyard to a prize-fight ring, she sang and danced her way into the men's hearts. She quelled a near riot at a YMCA hut by agreeing to a second performance to accommodate an overflow crowd. They loved their Elsie! In the rain and mud, in the noonday heat, at times hoarse, she performed for the infantry, artillery, and support troops alike. Somebody even painted a sign on her car that read, "Elsie Janis Division."

On Monday, May 27, after her last performance, General Edwards asked her if she would mind a visit to the hospital to cheer up a group of thirty division members wounded in a raid the night before. Many of them had likely seen her show. She gladly complied and walked through the wards, talking with and encouraging the men. This was not the first time she had shown such kindness, nor would it be the last. Although the visits were emotional for her, she felt that it was the least she could do for her boys. On Tuesday, May 28, she was en route back to Paris.[45]

All told, in her six months in France among her beloved doughboys, she gave more than 600 performances. She had hoped to remain for the duration, but the tour was at her own expense, and she had run out of money. Stars & Stripes called her the "Playgirl of the Western Front."[46] The doughboy's newspaper printed an open letter from Elsie to the troops in which she pleaded, "Please don't forget me."[47] She also encouraged the men to ask her to send them things. Not surprisingly, she received dozens of requests for all sorts of items, from "dice to evening gowns." She saw to it that the requests were filled. She sent a total of nine evening gowns (including one of her own) so that the "leading ladies" in the amateur shows would be properly clothed.[48]

Sanitary Trains: Trouble from the Start

The relief of the 1st Division on April 1, 1918, did not go smoothly at all. The movement took place at night so as to elude the notice of the German artillery; the effort was in vain. The Germans launched a heavy barrage that landed squarely upon the Sanitary Trains of both divisions, causing 200 casualties, most of them in the 1st Division. The 102nd Ambulance Company was on the scene, and it dressed and evacuated all of the wounded.[49] This would not be the first time that the Yankee medicos would suffer. In fact, the dressing station operated by the 102nd Ambulance Company at Mandres and the roads leading to it were under constant artillery fire for the following eight days, most of the shells containing gas. On April 8, the 104th Ambulance Company relieved the beleaguered men of the 102nd Ambulance.[50]

Many of the initial sites chosen for the field hospitals and other units were unsuitable. They had been inherited from either the French or the 1st Division, and they were used at first merely for convenience. Evacuation Hospital No. 1 was a prime example. This unit was located at Caserne Sebastopol, about five kilometers north of Toul, closer to the front lines than the field hospitals.[51] This was not the normal pattern, as evacuation hospitals were generally located toward the rear. Nevertheless, its men could not find another place to set it up, and there it remained.

The 101st Field Hospital was at Caserne Lamarche near Toul, and it treated the ordinary sick and gas cases that could be transported. During its stay in the sector, the hospital expanded to 900 beds, and its staff eventually included female nurses. Due to this expansion and to a shortage of enlisted personnel, the company commander of the 101st Field Hospital had requested twenty female nurses.[52] Concerned with the quality of care at these facilities, Lt. Col. Bevans endorsed the request, which was ultimately granted in part.[53] Mrs. Mabel Shaw and fourteen female nurses arrived at the hospital on May 23.[54] The 103rd Field Hospital, also located at Caserne Lamarche, had about 300 beds. Its function was to treat contagious sick, venereal diseases, and skin cases. Later, a separate camp was opened for the treatment of venereal diseases at Rangeval, just north of Boucq, and the 103rd no longer had that duty.[55] Both field hospitals were located between sixteen to twenty miles from the front line.

Due to the length of the line held by the division and the nature of the road net in the sector, two zones were established, each covered by a separate triage or sorting station. In the eastern half, the 102nd Field Hospital was assigned this mission, Initially, it was stationed in Ménil-le-Tour. However, due to poor traffic flow and other conditions, the unit was moved closer to the front line. It relocated to the town of Minorville, approximately six miles southeast of Flirey. The 104th

Field Hospital acted as the sorting station for the western zone. It was first located at Aulnois-sous-Vertuzey, moved to Vignot, and finally to Abbe-de-Rangeval, two miles northwest of division headquarters at Boucq.[56]

The ambulance companies were set up as advance posts along the roads leading to both sorting stations. Their mission was to take all gas and nontransportable cases to the sorting stations, all wounded to the evacuation hospital at Caserne Sebastopol, and the sick to the hospitals at Toul. The medical supply unit was headquartered at Toul. It had two substations, one at Aulnois and the other at Ménil-le-Tour.[57]

During the division's stay in the Toul sector, all of the medical units were engaged at one time or another. The ambulance companies saw their fair share of the action. During the period April 10 through April 13, at the Bois Brûlé, near Apremont, the 103rd Ambulance Company treated approximately 200 casualties. Eleven of their number were later decorated for bravery. The situation was more tragic at Seicheprey about a week later. At 3:30 A.M., Saturday, April 20, 1918, gas and high-explosive shells began to rain down upon the 104th Ambulance Company stationed at Mandres. At the same time, that unit, which was acting as an advance dressing station, experienced a sharp increase in casualties from Beaumont and Seicheprey. Working with gas masks on, the men began to treat and evacuate the wounded by ambulance to the 102nd Field Hospital, then at Ménil-le-Tour. It soon became apparent that the operation, whatever it was, was a large one. More ambulances and personnel were sent for, including two medical officers each from the 101st and 103rd Field Hospitals, who were dispatched to the 102nd Field Hospital.

All through the day and well into the early hours of the next, the work went on. It was dangerous and exhausting. Litter bearers went all the way into the front line, and ambulance drivers braved shot and shell racing over roads targeted by German artillery. Two ambulances were completely destroyed; the driver of one, a member of the 101st Ambulance Company, was killed and his orderly severely wounded. During the first day, 254 cases passed through the 102nd Field Hospital alone. In total, about 650 men were killed, wounded, gassed, or reported missing. At 8:30 P.M. that night, it became apparent that the position of the 104th Ambulance Company was untenable due to continuous shelling, and it was moved back to the Bois de Rehanne. When the fighting stopped during early Sunday morning, the Sanitary Train toted up its own losses. Fifty-four enlisted men and officers, most of them from the 104th Ambulance Company, had been either killed, wounded, gassed, or reported missing.[58]

Prior to Hickey's Raid on the night of 30/31 May 1918, careful preparation was made by the Sanitary Trains to ensure prompt evacuation and medical care of the expected casualties. To that end, Capt. (later Maj.) Stanhope Bayne-Jones was selected as surgeon of a sanitary detachment to accompany the raid. With him were thirty-eight combatant litter bearers, together with eight enlisted men from the medical department. Their equipment included thirty-two litters, some of which were the four-wheeled variety. Because of the advance notice, the detachment was able to rehearse with the other elements of the raid. The objective of the medical department was to provide a semi-autonomous service of evacuation from the point of attack to hospitals in the rear.[59]

At 2:30 A.M., just as the barrage commenced, the litter bearers, with a sergeant in charge, moved out from Seicheprey, "leap frog" fashion at intervals of a hundred yards, two each to the wheeled litters, which were stocked with medical supplies. Every fifty yards, one litter group stopped and maintained its position. Behind at Seicheprey were Captain Bayne-Jones, one sergeant, and four other enlisted men to serve as backups. The dressing station was located at Bois de Rehanne, and the wounded were transported there by Ford ambulance. From there, a GMC ambulance took the patients to the 102nd Field Hospital at Ménil-le-Tour, where records were made and necessary treatment given. The ambulances were provided by the 102nd Ambulance Company, together with a detachment from the 104th Ambulance Company. The vehicles were scattered around, two at Seicheprey, four at Beaumont, and three each at Ansauville and Bois de Rehanne. As one became full, another moved forward to take its place. Lines of evacuation to the right and left of this area were placed on alert. For further evacuation, the Evacuation Ambulance Company No.1 removed patients to Evacuation Hospital No.1 at Caserne Sebastopol, northeast of Toul.

The first wounded reached the 102nd Field Hospital at 4:30 A.M. and were evacuated within ten minutes. The last wounded arrived at 6:20 A.M. The wheeled-litter bearers had been ordered to follow the infantry back in so as to pick up all casualties. In his report to the division surgeon at 7:30 A.M. that same morning, Maj. Paul Waterman, commanding officer of the 101st Sanitary Train, reported that total casualties amounted to twenty-two, fifteen of whom were wounded (two seriously) and three were gassed. He ended his report with the observation, "*Other cases may be discovered or evacuated later.*" Little did he know, or could he know at that early hour, the devastating toll that would be exacted on his own troops by the gas shells that had been fired prior to the raid.[60]

On June 24, Lieutenant Colonel Bevans left the division, having been promoted promoted to chief surgeon of the 3rd Corps effective July 1. His place was taken by Lt. Col. Ralph S. Porter.[61]

103rd Field Hospital Company: Quiet No More

On March 31, 1918, the 103rd Field Hospital was directed to assume the duties of a contagious hospital then being carried out by the 2nd Field Hospital of the 1st Division. The exchange was to take place at 8:00 A.M., April 3. Along with the change in station, both division surgeons were ordered to make arrangements for the transfer of sick and necessary medical supplies.[62] The 103rd Field Hospital (along with the 101st) was to be located at Caserne Lamarche, on the outskirts of Toul.[63]

Toul is an ancient garrison town in northeastern France, in the upper Moselle River valley. The city lies on the west side of the river where the stream makes a large bend to the northeast. The city's relatively small size belies its importance in the defense of the country. Situated on the site of an old Gallic tribal center and later a Roman camp (Tullum), it is encircled by walls designed and rebuilt by the great Vauban about A.D. 1700. Entrance to the ancient center of the city is still gained through its four gates. The city was served by the Eastern Railway, and it largely escaped the ravages of the First World War, being located in a relatively quiet sector.[64] During the war, in the area surrounding the city was a railway yard, military camps, and barracks. A pass was needed to enter the town; the gates were guarded by military policemen, who also patrolled the streets to enforce the 9:30 P.M. curfew and to keep the doughboys out of the bars, which were "off limits."[65]

One such barracks was Caserne Lamarche, which was situated about a mile west of the city center on the Rue de Justice. It was part of the "Justice Group" of hospitals, which included Caserne Perrin, Caserne Tavier, and several others.[66] A *caserne* is a permanent military barracks designed to provide lodging for the infantry, artillery, and cavalry units scattered throughout the country; many such barracks in France, trace their origins back to the late sixteenth century. The earliest examples were often located within bastions or a citadels. Sometimes a caserne was composed of a single building, one or more stories in height, but often it was a small complex of buildings, including stables and administrative offices. The designs varied from simple to ornate, and the construction materials were eclectic as well.[67]

At Caserne Lamarche, which the unit shared with the 101st Field Hospital, three four-story buildings were grouped in an open square, with the entrance to the complex through the open side. Each building was constructed of stone and concrete and measured approximately 375 by 50 feet. The first floor was composed of administrative offices, operating rooms, and wards. The top three floors were fitted with eight wards, some connecting with each other at the long end, with several common hallways. The kitchen was in a separate building behind the hospital complex. There the staff and patients (except those with special dietary requirements which were provided by the Red Cross) took their meals. The mess also doubled as a recreation area for patients who were awaiting a return to duty, and for staff.[68] In fact, a series of small outbuildings, each with a specific function (bath, latrine, kitchen, storage, etc.) encircled the outer edge of the complex at the rear of the three buildings.[69] Each ward had a wardmaster and an orderly, and a sergeant was in charge of each floor. The enlisted personnel at the hospital were supervised by a sergeant first class. Surgeons were assigned to specific wards depending upon the type of case recuperating there.[70]

While the layout of the rooms made the complex generally well suited for use as a hospital, its amenities were few and far between. For starters, there were no lights. Worse yet, according to one source, "There were no bathrooms, no means of disposing of waste in the buildings, and running water was to be found in but one or two rooms in each building." The water itself came from one of two sources, either wells or the Moselle River, and it was strictly apportioned among the various hospital complexes. The latrines were the "box" type and were located outside; soiled dressings and excreta from the patients had to be carried outside and emptied into the cans, often a long way from the wards. Waste water, including that from the kitchen and bath, also had to be carried outside and dumped into sewer pipes and drains to be carried away.[71]

The weather during the division's stay in the sector was "cold and wet,"[72] and in late May the dreadful sanitary conditions in the trenches contributed to an epidemic of trench fever. In addition, there was an outbreak of scabies, due to the inability of the line companies to treat and contain it. Seventeen percent of all men on sick call had this problem. At first, only the most serious cases were treated at the 103rd Field Hospital. Later, all such cases were taken there. As a result of the vigorous efforts of this hospital, scabies was eliminated from the division. The 103rd Field Hospital also treated men with skin lesions caused by lice.[73] During this period, the division reopened the venereal camp at Rangeval (It had been discontinued by the 1st Division). This freed the men of the 103rd Field Hospital from what had to have been one of their less agreeable tasks.[74]

As of April 5, the 103rd Field Hospital had an effective strength of eight officers and forty-eight enlisted personnel. The list included two sergeants first class, six sergeants, four cooks, one mechanic, twenty-two privates first class, and thirteen privates. In addition, one sergeant and three enlisted men were listed as sick in the hospital, and one private first class was listed as on detached service with the division medical supply depot since February 7. Maj. William H. Blanchard was now the company commander. He was joined by Maj. Michael J. Thornton, Capt. Charles S. Walker, and Lts. Harold F. Parker, Clyde W. Pember, and Clifford W. Renth. Also temporarily attached to the unit were Lt. Roy F. Brown,[75] the acting supply officer for the field hospital companies, and Lt. Condict W. Cutler, Jr., the billeting officer for the 101st Sanitary Trains.[76] The mean strength of the outfit dropped slightly to fifty-four the following week, but as the unit became busier the rolls rose sharply to between eighty-three and ninety as the month progressed.[77]

April proved to be a very busy month for the hospital. The normal capacity of a field hospital was 216 beds.[78] In actuality, the hospital was acting more like a base hospital, since it had about 327. At the beginning of its tour in the Toul sector, the 103rd Field Hospital accepted the transfer of 249 patients from the 1st Division. Apparently there had been an outbreak of mumps, with 191cases reported in the "Big Red One" and left in the care of the New Englanders. In addition, in the month of April alone the unit admitted 595 new patients.[79] The majority of the sick were treated in the hospital, but some were treated and released to their respective organizations. On average, new admissions ran about 150 patients per week, or just under twenty per day. In the course of a typical day the hospital operated at fairly close to capacity, either caring for or treating an average of 292 patients. In addition to the mumps, the medicos had to treat pneumonia, scarlet fever, measles, and cerebro-spinal meningitis. On April 20, two medical officers from the 103rd Field Hospital, along with two more from the 101st, were sent to the 102nd Field Hospital at Ménil-le-Tour, no doubt to assist with the many casualties from Seicheprey.[80]

Sadly but inevitably, the unit now experienced its first patient deaths. The first occurred on April 10, when a soldier died of a pulmonary edema complicated by a kidney infection and erysipelas, an acute skin disease caused by the streptococcus bacteria. The second death occurred on April 29, when a patient died of cerebro-spinal meningitis. Reports indicate that only ten patients were absent without leave (AWOL) during the month.[81]

The next month proved even busier. In fact, on May 6, the hospital was divided into two sections. Weekly Reports for May are incomplete, however, the Nominal Check List for that month shows a total of 864 names. Based upon returns for the first two weeks alone, new admissions amounted to 372 patients. Looking at the month as a whole, the unit admitted on average nearly twenty-nine patients per day and almost 216 per week. This had to be a strain for a hospital with slightly more than 300 beds. In fact, for the first two weeks, the medicos cared for or treated an average of 439 patients on a daily basis.[82] Incidents of measles, scarlet fever, and cerebro-spinal meningitis seemed to taper off. Three more patients died, one each on May 1, 22, and 24. However, returns showed a marked increase in gas victims, twenty-eight in the first week alone. The greatest number came on May 30 and 31, when fifty-nine gas victims were admitted—some, no doubt, a result of Hickey's Raid.[83]

On Sunday, May 19, around 10:00 A.M., the personnel at the hospitals were treated to a gallant but foolhardy gesture in the sky directly overhead. The excitement began when a German two-seat observation plane was spotted flying toward the hospital complex, dodging French antiaircraft fire. The German aircraft descended toward the French cemetery behind the hospital. At a height of a hundred feet, the pilot dropped a floral wreath on the grave of a fellow German aviator who had been killed exactly two years before. The intruder tried to gain altitude in order to escape, but it was apparent that the aircraft had been damaged by the shellfire. The last the hospital personnel saw the observation plane, it was in full flight heading toward the German lines. Later, it was learned that the Boche were pursued by the American ace Raoul Lufbery, whom the German plane managed to bring down; the unfortunate Lufbery jumped to his death in order to escape the flames. The German aircraft was in turn brought down a short time later by French pilots—not by another American ace, Douglas Campbell, as was rumored.[84]

On the previous Thursday, May 16, a car belonging to one of the specialists at the 101st Field Hospital had caught fire while it was being fueled in a garage. The car next to it became involved. Both automobiles were pushed out into the open, but it was too late to extinguish them; the flames were allowed to burn themselves out. Exciting times!

By June, the impact of the war had begun to be felt at the 103rd Field Hospital. Until the end of the previous month, the unit had had to contend with disease alone, but now men suffering the effects of gas poisoning were being seen in larger numbers, most transferred from other hospitals. Two men from the 101st Infantry died on June 2 from the effects of phosgene. Scabies, measles, scarlet fever, syphilis, diphtheria, pediculosis, and impetigo all made their appearance. Consistent with orders, after treatment these men were discharged, most often to the Military Police for inspection and return to their commands. The medics also saw influenza and a number of cases referred to as "N.Y.D. (not yet diagnosed) Nervous," a euphemism for shell shock.[85]

However, at this time, the division was also hit with a large outbreak of what was referred to as "three-day fever," which was descriptive of the length of the high fever itself. In actuality, this was only the first, and milder, wave of the fatal influenza epidemic that was to occur in the fall. Even so, Lieutenant Colonel Jones reported that the epidemic was so large that "it turned our field hospitals into practically base hospitals."[86] As an example, on June 12, the 103rd Field Hospital treated 537 patients, including 189 new admissions. Of the latter, 148 were diagnosed with three-day fever. An additional fifteen were treated for influenza. The remainder were admitted for complaints ranging from pyoderma (a pus-causing skin disease) and scabies to pediculosis and hives. Most cases of three-day fever were released to their units.[87] In addition to the routine diseases, the hospital was responsible for the care of some seriously sick patients. For example, on June 22, four such cases were reported, one with no diagnosis, one with bronchopneumonia, and two with lobar pneumonia.[88] June had been an incredibly busy month, with a total of 2,237 new admissions.[89]

The hospital had adopted the French procedure of using the medical unit as the source of resupply for uniforms and equipment. For the most part this system worked well; however, there were some problems. Gas masks were a case in point. During the stay in the Toul sector, a total of seventeen patients were sent to the 103rd Field Hospital without gas masks. This required the supply officer to issue new masks from the unit's limited supply. On May 1, Major Blanchard addressed the problem in a memorandum to higher headquarters.[90]

Another Move: "Out of the Frying Pan and into the Fire"

Toward the end of June, rumors of an impending move must have been rife. As early as June 24, the Sanitary Train began making preparations for a move to another sector. The 325th and 327th Field Hospitals of the 82nd Division were ordered to relieve the 101st and 103rd Field Hospitals respectively, the procedure to be complete by 9:00 A.M. on June 28. Any patients who were sufficiently recovered at that time to return to duty were ordered to the division G-1 for processing. In the days following the changeover, the division surgeon of the 82nd Division would be responsible for issuing the necessary instructions.[91] During the last week before their transfer to the new sector there was a flurry of activity. Five hundred and forty new admissions were treated at the 103rd Field Hospital alone, along with 484 retained from the week before. When the week was done, 584 patients had been treated and returned to their commands, while an additional 438 still being cared for, were turned over to the 82nd Division to complete their recuperation.[92]

After each of the units of the 101st Sanitary Train was relieved, it proceeded to the town of Domgermain, a short distance south and west of Toul, where the company spent the better part of four days awaiting further orders. The 103rd Field Hospital arrived there on June 27.[93] The six-kilometer march took about an hour and a half. At Domgermain the men enjoyed a brief respite from all but essential duties; they were able to play ball or lounge about. They also took advantage of the town's location at the base of high hills whose summits afforded fine views of Toul and the surrounding countryside.[94]

Not all was rest and recreation. Many details regarding the move had yet to be worked out. Requests by the various units for truck transport had to be submitted to the motor transport officer. In addition, each unit was required to designate a noncommissioned officer to report to the billeting officer for the Sanitary Train at 10:00 A.M., June 27, to serve in an advance billeting party.[95] This detachment was scheduled to leave Toul at 2:00 P.M., July 1, and upon arrival at the destination to report to the senior town major. First Lt. Thomas A. Mann of the 102nd Field Hospital was detailed as the assistant billeting officer.[96]

On June 28, the division received its movement orders to leave the Toul sector and to join the fighting near Château-Thierry. The Yankees were to relieve the regulars of the U.S. 2nd Division.[97] The same day, the 103rd Field Hospital received detailed instructions to depart from Train Station No.1 at Toul at 10:00 P.M., Monday, July 1. The medics were issued two days' travel rations for what was scheduled as a twelve-hour journey.[98]

All of the medical units were directed to assign sufficient personnel to drive the Sanitary Train's motor vehicles to the new location. The motor transportation was to leave Domgermain for the outskirts of Paris in sufficient time to meet the bulk of the division, which was being transported by train. The motor column was to assemble on the Foug-Lay St. Rémy Road at 9:00 A.M., June 29. The enlisted men were issued four days' rations, along with two in reserve. Sufficient gasoline and oil were to be carried for a hundred miles travel, although the total distance to be covered was about 250 miles.[99] The division was also ordered to return the borrowed ambulance now at Boucq to its proper unit. At first, the 103rd Ambulance Company was to remain at the old location until the last unit had entrained; its personnel were to go by train, while its vehicles were designated to go over the road.[100] Later, in an apparent change of plans, all units proceeded by train (including the 103rd Ambulance Company); however, the 104th Ambulance Company was told to wait for a later train. Most of the Sanitary Train departed Toul during the evening of July 1 on Train No. 53, while the 104th Ambulance Company followed at 3:00 A.M. on July 2.[101]

The initial destination was Trilport, just to the east of Paris. After an all-night train trip, the various units of the Sanitary Train arrived at the outskirts of Paris, only to cool their heels for a day in the railroad yards in Trilport and La Ferté-sous-Jouarre. As the men got off the trains at the Trilport station, they met and spoke with a detachment of Marines fresh from the fighting at Belleau Wood and waiting to entrain for Paris. The Marines were detailed to march in the Fourth of July parade, and they had plenty of stories and advice for the Yankees. Trucks took the medics west to the small village of Villenoy, a short distance away; there they found billets during the night of July 3. The town had never quartered Americans, and the remaining inhabitants were naturally curious.[102]

NOTES

1. Martin Gilbert. *The First World War* (New York: Henry Holt, 1994), 412–14 and 418.

2. Ibid., 425–32.

3. Thomas E. Greiss, ed., *The Great War* (Wayne, N.J.: Avery, 1986), 144.

4. Gilbert, *First World War*, 431.

5. Ibid., 415.

6. Edward M. Coffman, *War to End All Wars: The American Military Experience in World War I* (Madison: Univ. of Wisconsin Press, 1986), 156–58; Gilbert, *First World War*, 426–27.

7. Robert Asprey, *At Belleau Wood* (Denton: North Texas Press, 1996), 8–9.

8. Ibid., 13 and 27.

9. Coffman, *War to End All Wars*, 215–16.

10. Ibid., 217.

11. Asprey, *At Belleau Wood*, 1–2.

12. Ibid., 58–60; Coffman, *War to End All Wars*, 224–27; Rod Paschall, *The Defeat of Imperial Germany, 1917–1918* (Chapel Hill, N.C.: Algonquin, 1989), 159–60.

13. Coffman, *War To End All Wars*, 214.

14. Asprey, *At Belleau Wood*, 345.

15. Ibid., 348. See generally, John Toland, *No Man's Land* (New York: Konecky, 1980), 277–88.

16. Emerson G. Taylor, *New England in France: A History of the Twenty-sixth Division U.S.A.* (Boston: Houghton Mifflin, 1920), 99; Meirion Harries and Susie Harries, *The Last Days of Innocence: America at War, 1917–1919* (New York: Random House, 1997), 239.

17. Laurence Stallings, *The Doughboys* (New York: Harper and Row, 1963), 49; Taylor, *New England in France*, 106 and 144–45; Tonie Holt and Valmai Holt, *Battlefields of the First World War* (London: Pavilion, 1993), 144.

18. James Lung Bevans, *Medical History of the 26th Division from Organization to June 24, 1918* (typescript, n.d.), 11. NA RG120; Frank P. Sibley, *With the Yankee Division in France* (Boston: Little Brown, 1919), 111–12; Taylor, *New England in France*, 101–2. See also R.S. Porter, *101st Sanitary Train, 26th Division A.E.F., History, March 20th, 1919* (typescript), 354. Up to that point, the longest continuous front held by the Americans was 18 kilometers. MNGA.

19. Bevans, *Medical History*, 11–12.

20. Ibid., 12 and 14–15; Daniel W. Strickland, *Connecticut Fights: The Story of the 102nd Regiment* (New Haven, Conn.: Quinnipiack Press, 1930), 121–23 (102nd Inf.); Duane, *Dear Old "K"* (Boston: Thomas Todd, 1932) 56–57 (104th Inf.); Harries and Harries, *Last Days of Innocence*, 212; Stallings, *Doughboys*, 46.

21. Frederick E. Jones, *Historical Sketch of the Medical Department of the 26th Division* (typescript, n.d., with "Introductory Note" and other comments by R.S. Porter, 8 August 1919), 13. NA RG120.

22. Bevans, *Medical History*, 14. Emphasis added.

23. Jones, *Historical Sketch*, 18. Emphasis added.

24. U.S. Army Center of Military History. *Order of Battle of the United States Land Forces in the World War: American Expeditionary Forces, Divisions.* (Washington, D.C.: GPO, 1988), 120–21.

25. Bevans, *Medical History*, 11; Sibley, *With the Yankee Division in France*, 112.

26. Sibley, *With the Yankee Division in France*, 116–20 and 160; Bevans, *Medical History*, 13.

27. Coffman, *War to End All Wars*, 148–49.

28. Strickland, *Connecticut Fights*, 133–48.

29. Eben Putnam, *Report of the Commission on Massachusetts' Part in the World War*, vol. 1, *History* (Boston: Commonwealth of Massachusetts, 1931), 140.

30. Bert Ford, *The Fighting Yankees Overseas* (Boston: McPhail, 1919), 141.

31. Ibid.

32. See note 30. See also Report of Action, 20th–21st April, 1918, dated April 27, 1918, by Brig. Gen. Peter Traub, as quoted in Strickland at pp. 148–50; also, comments by Gen. John J. Pershing in Memorandum 30 April, 1918, as well as Operations Report 23 April, 1918, by Maj. Gen. Clarence Edwards, both quoted in *United States Army in the World War 1917–1919*, vol. 3 (Washington, D.C.: GPO, 1968), 613–17 and 621.

33. James T. Duane. *Dear Old "K,"* 59.

34. It is an interesting twist of history, how the term "raid" reentered the American military lexicon. During the Civil War, large bodies of cavalry from both sides conducted what were referred to as raids, roaming the countryside to gather information and to disrupt communications and supply lines. After the war, European military officers, some of whom had observed fighting first-hand, added the concept of a raid to their own tactical repertoire. Basically, a raid, or *coup de main* as the French called it, differed from a "patrol" in the size of the force. Patrols were conducted almost nightly during World War I by each company in the front line. The purpose was to gain up-to-date information about the unit directly opposite, retrieve the dead and wounded, or to repair the barbed wire. Little advance planning was needed, and the patrols, usually by a very small group, generally followed the same basic routes. The raid was a more complicated affair. Planning was necessary, not only because more men were involved but also, because the purpose was generally a larger military objective, such as the seizing of prisoners or of a stretch of trench, or perhaps to keep the other side off balance. Lee Kennett, *Marching through Georgia* (New York: Harpers, 1995), 122; Duane, *Dear Old "K,"* 68; John Ellis, *Eye Deep in Hell* (Baltimore: Johns Hopkins Univ. Press, 1989), 72–79.

35. Sibley, *With the Yankee Division In France*, 169–76; Bevans, *Medical History*, 13; Duane, *Dear Old "K,"* 63.

36. Duane, *Dear Old "K,"* 75.

37. Statistics show that for the four-day period May 30, 1918 to June 2, 1918, that 211 members of the 101st Infantry were treated as a result of poison gas. Probably most, if not all, were very likely exposed to the gas on Hickey's Raid. Albert G. Love, ed., *The Medical Department of the United States Army in the World War,* vol. 15, *Statistics: Part Two* (Washington, D.C.: GPO, 1925), 1044–45 and 1050–51.

38. Sergeant Murphy was a typical Yankee doughboy. He was born in Framingham, Massachusetts, in April 1894. His father, an immigrant from Ireland, worked for the railroad, first as a switchman and later as a conductor. Fred was a shoemaker. He enlisted in the Massachusetts National Guard in 1914 and served with it on the Mexican border. George, his older brother, was also serving in France, in a different division. His promotion to sergeant came on March 12, 1918, shortly before his death. After being gassed due to a friendly fire incident on the night of May 30–31, he was taken first to the 102nd Field Hospital and later to the 103rd Field Hospital, where he died on June 2. He and the other dead were temporarily laid to rest in Ménil-le-Tour. At the request of his family, his remains were repatriated in July 1921, and he was reinterred at Saint Stephen's Cemetery, Saxonville, Massachusetts. War Records Section, Military Division, Adjutant General's Office, Commonwealth of Massachusetts. MNGA and author's personal files.

39. Sibley, *With the Yankee Division in France*, 164–66.

40. Ibid., 183–90.

41. Duane, *Dear Old "K,"* 77.

42. Ibid., 79.

43. Elsie was born Elsie Jane Bierbower, in Columbus, Ohio, on March 16, 1889. Her mother, Jane, the proverbial "stage mother," shortened it to Elsie Janis. She began her stage career as "Little Elsie" at the age of seven. Her mother was her constant companion. They sold the house in Columbus and bought and renovated the historic Phillipsburg Manor in Tarrytown, New York. Elsie starred on Broadway, vaudeville, and in silent films, and composed her own songs. She was known for her boundless energy. After the war, success followed her throughout the 1920s; however, thereafter her career faded. Later, she sold her beloved home in Tarrytown and moved to Hollywood, California. Several attempts at a comeback failed, and she died in Hollywood on February 26, 1956. *Dictionary of American Biography, Supplement Six, 1956–1960*, s.v. "Janis, Elsie;" *New York Times*, February 28, 1956, p. 1, col. 2 and March 11, 1956, p. 75, col. 1. USMA.

44. *Stars & Stripes*, March 15, 1918, 4. USMA.

45. Elsie Janis, *The Big Show* (New York: Cosmopolitan, 1919), 56–78. Due to the restrictions of censorship at the time, she kept in her diary, which was the source of this book, very few dates or names of units or their locations. She does state that her first performance with the division took place on a Wednesday. A photograph of her in the Bois de Rehanne, found in the Still Pictures Branch of the National Archives, has the date May 22, 1918, which was a Wednesday. Since she spent six days with the Yankees, I have assumed that her tour began on that date.

46. *Stars & Stripes*, March 29, 1918, 7. USMA.

47. *Stars & Stripes*, September 13, 1918, 6. USMA.

48. Janis, *Big Show*, 196–97.

49. Jones, *Historical Sketch*, 15.

50. Porter, *History*, 355.

51. Bevans, *Medical History*, 12.

52. John G. W. Knowlton, Memorandum to Division Surgeon, 26th Division, A.E.F., April 26, 1918. NA RG 120.

53. James Lung Bevans, Memorandum to G-1. April 28, 1918 (endorsement to Memorandum dated April 26, 1918, to the division surgeon requesting twenty female nurses for the 101st Field Hospital); Bevans, Memorandum to Chief Surgeon, American E.F., HQ. S.O.S, 29 April 1918, par. 6 (see also, paragraphs 3 and 4). As of date of his Memorandum to the chief surgeon, the 101st Field Hospital had 400 beds and 381 patients. It was expected to increase to at least 600 beds, in part due to an anticipated change in the number of patients, from 150 to 400, that needed to be on hand at Evacuation Hospital No. 1 before a request for a hospital train would be approved. At this time, the 103rd Field Hospital had 290 beds and 199 patients. NA RG 120.

54. *History Field Hospital Company 101–101 Sanitary Train, 26th Division, Part 4* (typescript, n.d.), 3. NA RG 120.

55. Ibid., 12; William H. Blanchard, Memorandum Re Change of Status, April 6, 1918. NA RG 120.

56. Bevans, *Medical History*, 12–13; Jones, *Historical Sketch*, 13–14.

57. Bevans, *Medical History*, 12.

58. Putnam, *Report of the Commission*, 140 (refers to three ambulances destroyed); Paul Waterman, Report of Action of 20 and 21 April, C.O. 101st Sanitary Train to Commanding General, 26th Division, 27 April, 1918. NA RG 120.

59. James Lung Bevans, Memorandum, 31 May, 1918, HQ 26th Division, Office of the Division Surgeon. NA RG120.

60. Paul Waterman, Memorandum to Division Surgeon, 31 May, 1918, HQ, 101st Sanitary Train. NA RG120. Emphasis added.

61. Bevans, *Medical History*, 20; Charles Lynch, ed., *Medical Department of the United States Army in the World War*, vol. 8, *Field Operations* (Washington, D.C.: GPO, 1925), 1020; Richard Derby, *"Wade in, Sanitary!"* (New York: G. P. Putnam's Sons, 1919), 182–83.

62. Field Order #18, March 31, 1918, 26th Division U.S. See also Field Order #19. MNGA; Blanchard, Memorandum Re Change of Status, April 6, 1918. NA RG120.

63. Paul Waterman, Memorandum Re Location of Units, April 8, 1918. NA RG120.

64. *Encyclopaedia Britannica*, 1959, s.v. "Toul."

65. Ernest H. Hinrichs, *Listening In* (Shippensburg, Penn.: White Mane, 1996), 48–50 and 72.

66. See "Map Showing Location of Hospitals, Justice Group, Scale 1″ = 1000′ Sanitary Squad 67, Date 1/17/19," *History of Justice Group*, Box 3218. NA RG120.

67. Françoise Dallemagne, *Les Casernes Francaises* (France: Picard, 1990), 195–210.

68. *History Field Hospital Company 101, 101 Sanitary Train, 26th Div., Part 4*, p.1. NA RG120.

69. Map, *"Water & Sewer–System, Justice Hospital Group, Toul, France, Scale 1 in. = 100 ft., Dec. 1918, Sanitary Squad 67,"* *History of Justice Group*, Box #3218. NA RG120.

70. *History Field Hospital Company 101, 101 Sanitary Train, 26th Div., Part 4*, p.1. NA RG120.

71. Joseph H. Ford, ed., *Medical Department of the United States Army in the World War*, vol. 2, *Administration American Expeditionary Forces* (Washington, D.C.: GPO, 1927), 614–15 and 671.

72. Jones, *Historical Sketch*, 18.

73. Ibid., 12.

74. Bevans, *Medical History*, 17.

75. Lieutenant Brown was one of the original six officers who mustered into the 103rd Field Hospital and sailed to France with the company.

76. William H. Blanchard, Report on Location of Officers and Enlisted Personnel, April 5, 1918. NA RG120.

77. See miscellaneous Weekly Reports of Sick and Injured, 103rd Field Hospital, 26th Division for April and May 1918. NA RG120.

78. Ford, ed., *Medical Department of the United States Army in the World War*, vol. 2, 284.

79. This figure is based upon admissions as shown on the Weekly Reports of Sick and Injured for the periods April 3, 10, 17, and 24, and a Five Day Report (French) for April 80. In fact, the Nominal Check List for the month of April 1918 varies slightly, listing the names of 622 patients.

80. Paul Waterman, Report from C.O. 101st Sanitary Train to C.G. 26th Division, 27 April 1918, p. 3. NA RG120.

81. Weekly Report of Sick and Injured, 103rd Field Hospital Co., 26th Div., Miscellaneous reports for April 1918. NA RG120.

82. Weekly Report of Sick and Injured, 103rd Field Hospital Co., 26th Div., "French Five Day Reports" for May 7 and 14 and Nominal Check List for Report of Sick and Wounded at 103rd Field Hospital, 26th Division, A.E.F., May 1918. NA RG120.

83. Daily Patient Returns, 103rd Field Hospital Co., 26th Div. NA RG120; Porter, *History*, 364. MNGA.

84. *History Field Hospital Company 101, 101 Sanitary Train, 26th Division, Part 4,* 2–3. (Text refers to "Sunday May 1st." That date was not a Sunday. I believe that there was most likely an error in the transcription of the author's notes or a typographical error. Two Sundays in May 1918 had the numeral "1" in them, May 12 and 19. Since other sources show Lufbery as being shot down on May 19, I have assumed that date to be correct. Moreover, the narrative of the typescript is written in chronological order, and the incident of the burning car on May 16 is set forth before the incident with the aircraft.). NA RG120. See also Norman Franks, *Who Downed the Aces in WWI?* (London: Grub Street, 1996), 131–32 and James J. Hudson, *Hostile Skies* (Syracuse, N.Y.: Syracuse Univ. Press, 1996), 75–76.

85. *Stars & Stripes*, September 20, 1918, 6. USMA.

86. Jones, *Historical Sketch*, 16–17.

87. *Adjutant General's Dept., Statistical Division, Daily Report of Casualties and Changes, Report No. 37 (four pages), June 12, 1918, 103rd Field Hospital, Podunk (Toul).* NA RG120.

88. Weekly Medical Report, Serious Cases, 103rd Field Hospital, Podunk, A.E.F. France, June 22, 1918. NA RG120.

89. Nominal Check List for Report of Sick and Wounded at 103rd Field Hospital, 26th Division A.E.F. for the periods June 1–15 and June 16–30. Through June 15, 1918, the hospital assigned a register number to each new admission. This practice stopped after that date. The final register number was 3334. NA RG120.

90. William H. Blanchard, Memo to C.O. 101st Sanitary Train, May 1, 1918. NA RG120.

91. Orders No. 19 (SECRET), HQ, 101st Sanitary Train, 25th June, 1918 (reference to Orders No. 94 and Orders No. 95, HQ, 26th Div. both dated June 24, 1918). NA RG120.

92. Weekly Report of Sick and Injured, 103rd Field Hospital, 26th Division, Week Ending June 25, 1918. NA RG120.

93. Field Order No. 3, June 27, 1918, H.Q. 101st Sanitary Train; Station List, Sheet #2, 103rd Field Hospital. NA RG120.

94. *History Field Hospital Company 101, Part 4,* p. 4, and *Part 5,* p. 1. NA RG120.

95. Orders No. 20 (SECRET), HQ, 101st Sanitary Train, 26th June, 1918. NA RG120.

96. Field Orders No. 4 (SECRET), HQ, 101st Sanitary Train, 28th June, 1918. NA RG120.

97. Field Order #46, 28 June, 1918, 26th Division (U.S.). MNGA; Bevans, *Medical History,* 20; Jones, *Historical Sketch*, 19.

98. Field Orders No. 4 (SECRET), HQ, 101st Sanitary Train, 28th June, 1918. NA RG120.

99. Ibid., para. 8 ("400 kilometers").

100. Albert A. Horner, Memorandum to the Commanding Officer, 101st Sanitary Train, 24 June, 1918. NA RG120.

101. Field Orders No. 4 (SECRET), HQ, 101st Sanitary Train, 28th June, 1918. NA RG120.

102. Field Order #46; 28 June 1918; Field Order #47, 30 June 1918; and Field Order #97, 28 June 1918, 26th Division, U.S. (the unit arrived at Trilport/Villenoy on July 3, 1918). MNGA. See also Field Order #4, 28 June, 1918, H.Q. 101st Sanitary Train; Station List, Sheet #2, 103rd Field Hospital; NA RG120; Porter, *History*, 366–67. MNGA.

Chapter Five

Killing Fields
(Aisne-Marne Offensive)

The bodies of the fallen heroes lay along the roadside, as well as in the thick
wheat fields. Machine guns also littered the fields along the roads.
—Stanley J. Herzog

It bears the same relation to other firearms that McCormick's Reaper does to
the sickle.
—Richard Jordan Gatling, on the machine gun

THE TIDE TURNS AGAIN (JULY 1918 THROUGH
AUGUST 1918)

Western Front—France

American troop strength in France had now reached 1,000,000 men. Munitions and
supplies were arriving at the rate of 20,000 tons per day.[1] The doomsayers in the
French and British governments had been proven wrong—Germany had not
achieved the significant dominance that they had once feared. However, it had come
close. While selected American troops were proudly parading in Paris to celebrate
the Fourth of July, Germany was preparing for yet another offensive. But so were
the Allies. The Germans sought to exploit their gains in the salient east of Château-
Thierry with a crossing of the Marne. They still hoped for that elusive breakthrough
that would split the Allies.[2] On the other hand, the French, in concert with the
relatively more experienced U.S. 1st and 2nd Divisions, along with the untried U.S.
4th Division, were preparing to pinch off the salient with attacks east and northeast
along a fairly broad front. The jump-off line ran in a roughly north to south direction,

beginning just south of Soissons and terminating at Château-Thierry on the Marne. Also preparing to participate was the U.S. 3rd Division, just east of Château-Thierry, as well as the 26th and 42nd Divisions, both of which had been transferred to the sector just days before.[3] In anticipation of the upcoming offensive, and as a precaution against possible German attacks, the French asked Haig for four British divisions to become part of the French reserve. As with similar previous requests by the British, the appeal fell upon deaf ears and was bluntly denied. So much for coalition warfare![4]

On July 15, in the wake of another enormous artillery barrage, including large quantities of gas, the Germans kicked off their push with great enthusiasm. However, they did not reckon with the U.S. 3rd Division. Though the unit was new and relatively unbloodied, the determination of its defense and the ferocity of its fight against long odds, earned it the sobriquet, "The Rock of the Marne." As French units beside them withdrew en masse, small groups of Americans held firm despite enormous casualties. On July 19 the Germans, their position untenable, retreated back across the Marne, abandoning their slight initial gains.[5]

Meanwhile, on July 18 the long-awaited Allied counteroffensive was launched. In the north and west, the French and Americans attacked across the Ourcq River; the ultimate objective was the recapture of Soissons and the reestablishment of an east-west line along the Aisne River. The movement would be like the swinging open of a large door, with the hinge near Soissons. The U.S. 4th Division was inserted in the line south of the U.S. 1st and 2nd Divisions, the latter having been pulled from the line elsewhere and reinserted alongside the men of the "Big Red One."[6] At the same time, the 26th Division replaced the U.S. 2nd Division near Vaux and Château-Thierry. Its mission was to move north and east from there through a sector called, aptly enough, the Pas Fini. Good gains were made in the north, while fierce fighting continued in the south. Eventually Vaux, by now in ruins, was taken by the Yankees, and Hill 204, which had been used by the Germans to rain down deadly artillery upon the attackers, was finally taken by the French. The hill had been heavily defended, because of its obvious attributes, both offensive and defensive. To that point, the French had, despite repeated attempts, been unable to dislodge its defenders. The Germans abandoned Château-Thierry on July 21, and the big push continued.[7]

In other sections of the western front more gains were achieved. On July 4, the Australians, along with attached American troops, launched a successful attack in the Somme sector, near the town of Hamel. That same day, the French achieved modest gains in an attack at Autrêches.[8] On August 8, the British launched further attacks along the Somme at Amiens, and later at Albert and Bapaume, both begun on August 21. These more or less simultaneous activities prevented the overextended Germans from shifting adequate forces to meet all the challenges. However, it was at Amiens that the crucial hammerblow was struck.[9] Orders had been cut to activate the U.S. First Army in early September.[10] The initiative was clearly with the Allies.

Home Front: Up to Speed

On July 4, 1918, the U.S. shipyards launched 95 ships, 17 in San Francisco alone.[11] Clearly, the production of war material was in high gear. Most major industries, including steel, had voluntarily complied with the regulations regarding prices—Why not? Orders were high, and so were profits.[12] Labor unions, while not always obtaining the recognition they sought, saw at least temporary implementation of some of their most important goals, including a shorter workday and better pay.[13] The strike fever of the previous year (4,450 in 1917 alone.)[14] had subsided. However, the spirit of cooperation between management and labor did not seem to apply to U.S. Steel; the adamant refusal of its chairman to deal with the union was to ultimately result in a strike in September.[15]

A shortage of workers started a mass exodus of blacks from the southern states to northern cities. In an ironic twist, southern politicians and businessmen raised a hue and cry, and they sought in vain to stem the labor drain with legislation. Industry was in the process of switching to more complicated machinery, in order to perform more cheaply and efficiently tasks formerly done by skilled craftsmen. This did not bode well for existing union workers, but for unskilled blacks it was a golden opportunity to break out of southern serfdom.[16]

Earlier estimates of military manpower requirements had to be revised drastically upward to nearly 3,000,000 men. The war in Europe was expected to continue well into 1919, and there would not be sufficient men to fill the ranks at the present rate of induction.[17] Accordingly, in August 1918 the Selective Service Act was amended to include men between the ages of eighteen and forty-five, with a new registration date of September 12.[18]

26TH DIVISION

In the Pas Fini: The End of the Road

Since early July, the division, now in the vicinity of Meaux, had been poised to take part in the ongoing offensive in the region. On July 7, the Yankees were ordered to relieve the U.S. 2nd Division, which was engaged in bitter fighting in the vicinity of Bouresches and Château-Thierry.[19] The division front would cover between three and four miles.[20] Two days earlier, the division had been trucked to the vicinity of the front line, and the next day elements went forward to reconnoiter.[21] Men from Battery F of the 103rd Field Artillery Regiment later described as enthusiastic the reception they received from the citizens of La Ferté-sous-Jouarre as their troop train arrived to support the advance.[22] The relief was completed on July 9.[23]

The division advanced slowly and methodically. Compared to its earlier experience in the trenches near Toul, this action was constant and intense—Attack and counterattack, and incessant shelling from both sides.[24] The fighting was particularly heavy in the area of the railroad station at Vaux and the nearby railroad bridge. The Yankees held the latter through sheer guts and determination; the capture of the station was a costly affair for both sides. The retreating Germans gave ground grudgingly. Four years of war had enabled them to perfect the art of the fighting withdrawal by small groups of dedicated soldiers. In addition, they continued to hold much of the high ground in the vicinity, which gave them a decided advantage in terms of effective artillery fire. A steady stream of casualties flowed through dressing stations all the way back to the field hospital at La Ferté-sous-Jouarre, some twenty miles to the rear.[25]

Early on the morning of July 15, the Germans launched a counterattack, preceded by a gas barrage. The Americans held.[26] On July 17, the Germans fired more gas, some said in retaliation for earlier setbacks.[27] That evening, in a barn near the front line, the men of the 104th Infantry were given general absolution by their chaplain.[28] July 18 brought a renewal of the Yankee attack. The division was at the apex of the Allied counterattack. For a week the men struggled in a narrow corridor, with little or no help from the French 167th Division on their left flank. The French themselves were having a difficult time with the retreating Boche. Later that day, heavy fighting took place at Taffourney Farm, and on July 20 at Genevrois Ferme. The Germans left deadly surprises behind as they retreated. In Company G, 104th Infantry, one man was killed and eight wounded by a booby trap. Such incidents resulted in few prisoners being taken.[29] Those that were lucky enough to be taken prisoner were fed and issued brand-new American uniforms, much to the annoyance of the doughboys, whose ill-fitting boots and tattered uniforms would have to do for a while longer.[30] As the Yankees pushed their way forward along clogged roads, the sight of those well-clothed Germans being taken rearward must have been dispiriting.

On July 21, 1918, the Germans gave up Château-Thierry for the last time, as the Yankees attacked at Lucy-le-Bocage and Grand Ru Farm.[31] The Allied advance pivoted slightly northeastward toward Epieds. There, on July 23, a fifteen-year-old Browning Automatic Rifle (BAR) man nicknamed "Scotty" died, but not before thirty-one Germans fell in the field before him.[32] Artillerymen following the advance testified to the intensity of the fighting. They told of dead bodies and dried blood on the road.[33] The steady stream of wounded clogged the roads; ambulances, ration carts, and trucks of all descriptions were used to take the casualties to the rear.[34] In the fight for Epieds and nearby Trugny, elements of the 101st Engineers had to be used as combat infantry.[35] Epieds fell on July 23, but what was left was in "shattered ruins."[36] On the July 24, the Yankee attack bogged down, as wave after wave of soldiers charged heroically through wheat fields near Courpoil to attack German machinegun nests, at great cost. One Yankee Division member who took part in the offensive referred to it as "our roughest fight."[37] The Yankees reached the edge of the Forêt de Fère, where they were relieved the next day.[38]

It was during this period that, once again, the unfortunate controversy between General Edwards and higher command began to exhibit itself.[39] Whether the roots of the problem ran deeper or farther back is open to speculation. Part of the problem was most certainly the decidedly negative feelings that many higher commanders, including Pershing himself, had for National Guard units and the officers who commanded them. Even a West Point graduate like Clarence Edwards was not immune.[40] The problem was worsened by an unfortunate mix of personalities and styles. Edwards was popular with his men but often a thorn in the side of his superiors. He was considered by some to be "volatile, argumentative, intractable [and] he trod a fine line between independent initiative and outright insubordination."[41]

Corps command was one contentious issue. In the course of creating the U.S. 1st Army, Pershing formed several corps. They were not large, unwieldy organizations, but rather made up of as few as two divisions. As an example, the 1st Corps was made up of the French 167th Division and the 26th Division.[42] Unfortunately for Clarence Edwards, the man chosen to lead the 1st Corps was none other than Maj. Gen. Hunter Liggett.[43] Except for his closeness to Pershing, it is highly unlikely that the overweight general would ever have been selected for high field command; Pershing, who himself was ramrod straight and fit, placed great stock in youth and military bearing. Hunter Liggett however, was an impatient perfectionist, and he insisted that the Yankees, who had not yet entered battle as a unified division, perform like experienced soldiers. (War, as the Americans were about to find out, did not always go according to the textbooks.) He also insisted that Edwards clean the deadwood out of his officer ranks. Edwards chose to ignore the latter order.[44] His troops performed with exceptional bravery under trying conditions as their casualty list attests. However, in Hunter Liggett's book (and, as it turned out, in the eyes of his chief of staff, Malin Craig), that was simply not good enough. He saw a failure of leadership; he simply filed his report and bided his time.[45]

On July 24 the German machinegunners had done their work efficiently and well. However, by the time the exhausted Yankees were relieved by the 42nd Division on July 25, they had stopped the German drive in its tracks and had also gained nearly eleven miles against fierce opposition, at a cost of more than 4,000 casualties.[46] The 51st Field Artillery remained in support of the 42nd Division until they were ultimately relieved on August 4.[47] While operating in that capacity on July 27, the men of Battery F had some unusually good luck; on that day they found a supply of shoes left behind by the fleeing Germans and simply helped themselves.[48] The men of the division had earned a rest.

On July 26, the infantry began to move to rest billets. It rained for several days, and the roads were a muddy mess. Still, this was their first rest in six months; rain or not, it must have felt good. They stopped first at Lauconnoise Ferme, before finally settling in at Caumont. Regimental headquarters for the 104th Infantry was at St. Aulde, and the Division headquarters was at Mery-sur-Marne.[49]

During the first week in August, Elsie Janis returned to the division for a short visit. This time she was a guest of the division commander at his headquarters in a chateau near Mery-sur-Marne. There was a touch of sadness, in that she could not help but notice that there were many faces missing from just two months before. She later confessed that she went back to her room after her performance and cried.

A short time later, she herself was the audience when the division put on a show for her benefit. The jokes were in her words for "gents only," although the boys tried to tone them down somewhat. She left after lunch the next day.[50]

Elsie was not the only performer to entertain the troops. In fact, in addition to operating the ever-popular "Y Huts," the YMCA sent more than 800 professionals (actors, dancers, musicians, etc.), both men and women, to France. There they joined the more than 500 entertainers already in France. Typical were the "The Hearons Sisters," a troupe that traveled a total of 25,000 miles by all means of transport and staged 2,000 performances.[51]

Sanitary Trains: Working Overtime

Orders issued on July 7, 1918, directed that the "101st Sanitary Train will relieve the 2nd Sanitary Train by special agreement between the respective Division Surgeons." Unlike previous reliefs, this one had to take place in the midst of an offensive. Patients and supplies had to be transferred without interruption of service or care. Instructions had to be given regarding the continued care of the non-transportable cases. Lives hung in the balance.[52] The 101st and the 104th Field Hospitals combined to form a hospital for the slightly gassed, sick, and other wounded at Luzancy, a small town on the Marne, approximately twelve miles west of Château-Thierry by road. The hospital was located in a large school.[53] The 103rd Field Hospital was located at La Ferté-sous-Jouarre.

The remaining field hospital, the 102nd, in addition to the 101st and 102nd Ambulance Companies, was located at Bézu-le-Guery, a small town a mere three miles behind the front line. It was designated as the division triage, or sorting station, and handled the casualties that poured in from all the ambulance companies. Personnel from the latter worked in dressing stations and as litter bearers.[54] The village was completely empty at this time, its inhabitants having fled with their possessions in anticipation of the fighting.[55] The hamlet lay just off the main road between Château-Thierry and La Ferté-sous-Jouarre. The town setting was described by Dr. Richard Derby, division surgeon for the 2nd Division as "a village of not more than fifty buildings, placed on the heights to the north of the Marne, built about one winding street. At the extreme northern end was a small church with a two-story schoolhouse adjoining." The church-school complex served as the field hospital.[56] The medics at Bézu-le-Guery developed a triage and treatment procedure for mustard gas poisoning using rubber blankets on inclined planes for draining water away from the patients.[57]

In addition, the 104th Ambulance Company in La Voie-du-Châtel served as the dressing station for the left half of the line, while the 103rd Ambulance Company at the chateau in Villiers-sur-Marne (now Villiers-St. Denis) handled the right side.[58] The regiments of the division that the medical units served were on a generally north-south line from Bussiares and Torcy to Vaux, in descending numerical order—from the 104th in the north to the 101st in the south.[59]

Unlike previous campaigns, the fighting was constant, so the medical work was constant. From July 7 through July 17 more than 2,000 casualties were treated by Sanitary Trains.[60] These were the result of the fighting around Vaux and Bouresches, the area the division had taken over from the 2nd Division. When the big push beyond Château-Thierry began on July 18, more casualties were treated. Along with the division, the Sanitary Trains were ordered forward. The 103rd Field Hospital remained at La Ferté-sous-Jouarre, but all other units advanced. On July 22, the 101st Ambulance Company was sent to Bouresches, and the 102nd, along with SSU No. 502, was detailed to La Sacerie. The 101st Field Hospital and the 103rd Ambulance Company were to proceed to Bézu-le-Guery to await further orders. Train headquarters also moved to Bézu-le-Guery. All in all, during the latter phase of the division's advance, the men of the Sanitary Trains had handled well over 4,000 additional patients.[61] The largest single-day number of patients evacuated by Sanitary Trains was 1,227 on July 23.[62] The following day, eleven fresh officers reported for duty at Train headquarters. They were immediately parceled out among the ambulance and field hospital companies, all except the 103rd Field Hospital.[63]

As if the enormous numbers of wounded and gassed were not enough, the good sanitary practices that the division had developed over their months of training lapsed in the heat of battle. In addition, the conditions that the men found in the area upon their takeover, including hundreds of unburied and partially buried bodies, both German and American, contributed to the unhealthy situation. This was coupled with abominable living conditions described in graphic detail by Lt. Col. Ralph Porter, the division surgeon:

Excreta was deposited whenever and wherever opportunity offered. . . . Such latrines as were found often contained a moving mass of maggots; and flies, which up to this time had rarely been seen, appeared in enormous numbers. Water was being used from every available source, often untreated. Food, when obtainable at all, was often sour and affected by long carries and its preparation under bad circumstances.[64]

As a result, at one time or another during the campaign virtually every man in the division suffered from diarrhea.[65] In order to combat this scourge, Maj. Paul Waterman, the commanding officer of the Sanitary Train, issued orders in early August to all his unit commanders that all existing orders and regulations on sanitation must be "scrupulously observed." In addition, each unit commander was directed to appoint a commissioned officer as a sanitary officer, who was "to assure observance." Finally, he named 1st Lt. Henry Christianson of the 101st Field Hospital as the sanitary officer, with overall supervisory authority over the entire Sanitary Train in that area.[66]

On July 29, 1918, as noted, the Sanitary Train was ordered to assemble at Lauconnois Ferme, just north of Château-Thierry. It had not been decided whether or not the division would continue the advance; if it did , the Sanitary Train would follow.[67] Instead, the Yankee Division was relieved by the 42nd Division. Orders were received at 8 P.M. on July 29 that the entire division would march to the La

Ferté-sous-Jouarre area on July 30 to stand down for a period of rest. Accordingly, Train headquarters closed at Lauconnois Ferme at 7 A.M., July 30, and set up in Luzancy two hours later. The advance billeting party had left the previous evening; its task was to locate suitable billets in the Luzancy area. According to division headquarters, Luzancy contained billets for only twenty officers and 600 enlisted men. This was not nearly sufficient to accommodate the entire Train as well as the 101st Machine Gun Battalion. It was anticipated that men not finding billets would bivouac. Likewise, at the same time, the 102nd Field Hospital was ordered to proceed to that town to set up a hospital in the building formerly occupied by the 101st and 104th Field Hospitals. The 104th was to bivouac at Bouresches and proceed to Luzancy. As soon as the 102nd Field Hospital was operational, the 101st Field Hospital was ordered to evacuate its patients to it and then close. All other elements of the Train were to assemble at Lauconnois Ferme at 6:30 A.M., July 30, and to leave for Luzancy half an hour later. Their route of march would take them south and west through Château-Thierry and along the Paris-Metz road.[68]

A Provisional Truck Company was organized on August 3, and 1st Lt. James F. Cobey was selected as the commanding officer. He was to assume all the duties that, up to then had been assigned to the motor transport officer. All trucks in the Sanitary Train were assigned to him. There was, however, subject to the needs of the Train, a permanent detail of two trucks each to every unit. Otherwise, the vehicles would be sent to the various units for specific duties and missions only upon proper request. The company consisted of twenty-eight cargo trucks, one motorcar, one motorcycle, three other trucks (one each for baggage and repair, and also a tanker), as well as a trail-mobile kitchen. As far as personnel was concerned, there were two commissioned officers (a captain and a first lieutenant), one sergeant first class, five or six sergeants, and between sixty-two and seventy other enlisted men. At this time, there were men from Train headquarters and the field hospitals and ambulance companies on temporary assignment with the Provisional Truck Company. They were ordered to remain with the new unit; however, they would be carried on the rolls of their respective units as "present, special duty." Given the limited number of trucks in the Train, the formation of this company would prove efficient and effective.[69]

103rd Field Hospital Company: "Chests, Heads, Abdomens, Compound Thighs"

On July 4, 1918, the men of the 103rd Field Hospital left their billets in Villenoy after a one-night stay and headed east along the Marne in the direction of Château-Thierry. While they were doing so, selected troops from the American divisions then serving in France were parading in Paris. The 103rd arrived later that day in Mery-sur-Marne, where they bivouacked for two days while awaiting further orders. The small town lay on the north bank, sandwiched between Luzancy and Saâcy, within one of the great loops of that stream.[70] Lt. Col. Porter, the division surgeon, described the village as "pathetic." It was virtually uninhabited, the villagers having deserted it in the face of the advancing Germans. Their wheat and oat fields lay untended. The Yankee medics were greeted with the following scene: "Babies cribs had been left just as they were when the child had been carried away. In some homes the beds hadn't been made nor the furniture dusted since the owners left. Clothing was left hanging in the closets for only small, light objects could be moved." The mayor turned the entire town over to the Americans, including all but two rooms of his own home.[71]

Meanwhile, in a memorandum to the division G-1 (Personnel), Lieutenant Colonel Porter requested authority to place his field hospitals and ambulance companies in their new duty stations. Specifically, he asked that the 104th Field Hospital be located at La Ferté-sous-Jouarre and that the 101st and 103rd Field Hospitals bivouac at Luzancy near the 15th and 16th Field Hospitals, their counterparts in the 2nd Division. He asked for a reply "as soon as possible." A similar request was sent to the French Mission the following day.[72] In the meantime, higher headquarters in Paris directed the 2nd Division surgeon, at the time of the relief, to transfer his excess blankets and litters to the 26th Division, and—so that there would be no mistake—he was to turn over five "serviceable" GMC ambulances. (He was not pleased to receive that order.) The order also included the transfer of the SSU No. 502 currently assigned to that division, as well as the operating teams and female nurses.[73]

Headquarters for the 101st Sanitary Train saw things a little differently and ordered the 103rd Field Hospital to La Ferté-sous-Jouarre. The orders specifically directed that the relief be completed by "7 o'clock, 9th July," and it referred to "3 surgical teams and 18 nurses."[74] According to a memorandum signed by Maj. William Blanchard, company commander of the 103rd Field Hospital, the relief was completed in two stages. In the first stage, two officers and twenty-two enlisted men made the hour-long journey from Saâcy to La Ferté-sous-Jouarre, arriving at 10 A.M. on July 5. The balance of the unit followed the next day and arrived at 3 P.M.[75] However, the official transfer was not completed until July 7, at 6 P.M.[76]

La Ferté-sous-Jouarre is a large market town approximately eleven miles east of Meaux. The marketplace and city center are north of the Marne, but the town as a whole straddles the river. La Ferté is at the junction of several important roads, in particular, the Paris-Metz road, as well as the main rail line from Paris. The 103rd Field Hospital was situated in a large convent, where it was designated to handle the seriously wounded.[77] The old building and grounds had been converted into a fully equipped surgical hospital with six operating rooms and a staff of thirty to thirty-five female nurses.[78] The previous occupants, the 23rd Field Hospital of the 2nd Division, had arranged the operating rooms, which were located within the building, while the wards were in tents set up in the courtyard. Ambulances unloaded at the gate, and the wounded were carried into the tents on litters to await treatment.

Richard Derby, division surgeon for the 2nd Division, gives a detailed account of the admission procedures at the hospital. The admission team was composed of one doctor, one nurse, and six enlisted men. A consulting surgeon divided his time between the admitting ward, sorting and prioritizing patients for later treatment, and the operating room. Newly arrived patients were placed on litter racks that lined both sides of the center aisle of the tent. Each was draped with a blanket to conserve body heat (sometimes small heaters were placed beneath the litters) and to ameliorate the effects of shock. If necessary, X-rays were taken. At the same time, the diagnosis and other relevant information was noted on the soldier's field medical card, which accompanied him throughout the course of his treatment.[79]

On June 15, 1918, the Medical Department of the AEF had implemented a change that was designed to cut down on paperwork and more important, provide better care for the sick and wounded. The field medical card—in essence, a medical chart—was to be folded twice over, fitted into an envelope, and fastened to the patient's uniform by a wire at the first point of treatment following the aid station, whether it was an ambulance, a field hospital, or evacuation hospital. The patient's treatment and diagnosis information, including laboratory reports, was noted on the card at each stage, so that medical personnel at successive facilities could see what treatment had been given at any point. It was based upon the British system then in effect, and it eliminated the necessity of preparing transfer cards each time the patient was moved. Thus, the complete record was prepared only once, when the patient was finally discharged to duty.[80]

Dr. Harvey Cushing, a celebrated Boston neurosurgeon then serving as a consultant in the AEF, visited the 103rd Field Hospital during its stay at La Ferté. He leaves us with the following account of the activities at the hospital during July 1918: "They've had heavy work the past few days, with four teams working in eight-hour shifts—very cramped quarters in the grounds of an old convent; *no field medical cards, merely slips of paper*; four Bessomeau [sic] tents for wards; only the very severe cases detained—chests, heads, abdomens, compound thighs, occasional multiples."[81] Cushing went on to say that in the course of three weeks the unit had handled nearly 500 "urgent cases" and that the mortality rate was high, due to the serious difficulty of transporting the wounded to more sophisticated facilities.[82]

During the ten days ending July 17, 1918, the heavy fighting around Vaux and Bouresches produced hundreds of seriously wounded casualties, many of whom were considered "non-transportable."[83] A glance at the Weekly Medical Report tells the story:

Beckwith, Lewis, Cpl.	Co. A, 102nd Inf.	10 July 1918	G.S.W. Vertibral reg. "S"
Berkial, Stefan, Pvt.	Co. C, 104th Inf.	7 July 1918	G.S.W. Serious
McGonigle, Jas. A., Pvt.	Co. H, 101st Inf.	9 July 1918	G.S.W. Lf. Chest & leg "S"
Porter, E. M., Sgt.	Co. B, 23rd Inf.	7 July 1918	G.S.W. Shoulder, back, rt. hip "S"
Vose, Frank L., Pvt.	Co. H, 104th Inf.	12 July 1918	G.S.W. Lf. & rt legs "S"[84]

Thirteen other patients that week had their conditions listed as "serious," indicating that they could not be evacuated to other facilities unless they improved. The 103rd Field Hospital admitted a total of 160 men during this time, 142 of whom were wounded. Of the latter, twenty-eight, or 19.7 percent, died. On a brighter note, seventy-four patients, almost all of them wounded, were treated and transported to other facilities. The mean strength of the unit at this time was eighty-nine officers and men.[85]

The Yankee Division took part in a big drive to close the salient and to push the Germans back across the Aisne River. In anticipation of the attack, the division made plans both for the evacuation of medical units as well as for their movement forward following the advance of the infantry.[86] In addition, the division surgeon requested and received augmentation by the three surgical teams then attached to the 23rd Field Hospital, 2nd Division. Company records indicate that the following surgical teams were attached to the 103rd Field Hospital:

Team I

Capt. Clarence A. McWilliams, MRC

1st Lt. William B. Hetzel, MRC

1st Lt. Thomas M. Coppedge, MRC

Team II

Capt. B. M. Bernheim, MRC

1st Lt. John C. Lyman, M.R.C

1st Lt. V. P. W. Sydenstricker, MRC

Team III

Capt. Joseph P. Brenen, MRC

1st Lt. Howard C. Fairbanks, MRC

1st Lt. Hugh C. McDowell, MRC

X-ray

1st Lt. Homer Grimm, MRC

1st Lt. J. P. Gillis, MRC

The response to his request for two additional teams was presumably favorable.[87]

The division attack commenced on July 18, and the next week and a half was especially busy for the medics. The field hospital was operating eighteen to twenty hours a day.[88] In the period ending July 24, one day before the division was relieved, the hospital admitted 343 patients, only twenty of whom were listed as sick. Two were admitted for gas. In keeping with the function of a field hospital, once a patient was stabilized and capable of being transported, he was evacuated by ambulance to an evacuation or base hospital in the rear for more sophisticated treatment. Most of the serious cases admitted the previous week had either died or been evacuated. However, seven patients had had to be retained and were still being treated during the week ended July 20.[89] Most of the wounds incurred in the new attacks were caused by machinegun bullets.[90] The Weekly Medical Reports (Serious Cases) for this period listed thirty-nine non-transportable patients, and they told the same story:

Benedetto, Joseph, Pvt.	Co. L, 103rd Inf.	18 July 1918	G.S.W. Head, neck, & rt. hand. Severe
Flanders, Arthur, Pvt.	Co. F, 104th Inf.	18 July 1918	G.S.W. Rt.arm, testinals [sic] "S"
Miller, Edgar, Pvt.	Co. M, 103rd Inf.	19 July 1918	G.S.W. Rt. Lung "S"
Shonle, William, Sgt.	Co. F, 103rd Inf.	18 July 1918	G.S.W. Chest & spine Serious
Stewart, Guy, Pvt.	Co. G, 104th Inf.	18 July 1918	G.S.W. Chest "S"[91]

Just one man returned to duty, and eighty men died as a result of their wounds, or a 24.7 percent mortality rate.

The versatile and energetic dental surgeon, Clifford Renth, gives an account of his activities during this period in the sector from July 17 through July 26. In addition to his dental practice, Dr. Renth was appointed as dental supply officer and the regular supply officer for the 103rd Field Hospital. He also censored mail for patients and personnel at the hospital. Perhaps of more importance, he served in both the operating room and in pre-op as an anesthetist, often at night after completing his day shift. When the unit moved up, he was part of the advance detail to set up in the new location.[92]

Earlier in the month, the division surgeon had visited the advanced dressing station operated by the 103rd Ambulance Company, located at Villiers-sur-Marne. The chateau and grounds, owned by a Madame Houard,[93] were used for this purpose. Lieutenant Colonel Porter found this an ideal location for use as an advance surgical hospital for the severely wounded. Specifically, he had the 103rd Field Hospital in mind. The problem, as he observed, was that it was also the site of a Marine battalion, the supply company for the 102nd Field Artillery, and an assortment of wagons, animals, and kitchens. In other words, it was a chaotic mess. Accordingly, he requested that the chateau and grounds be turned over to the exclusive use of the Medical Department. His request was approved on July 16.[94]

The 103rd Field Hospital was relieved at La Ferté-sous-Jouarre by the 162nd Field Hospital (42nd Division). It moved forward to the chateau at Villiers-sur-Marne on July 24, pursuant to verbal orders of the commanding officer of the Field Hospital Section.[95] The hospital continued to treat wounded even after the division's infantry was relieved the following day. It was finally relieved by the 168th Field Hospital on July 27.[96] A Weekly Report of Sick and Injured dated July 31, covering this period, showed that 136 men were admitted to the hospital, some from both the Yankee and "Rainbow" (42nd) Divisions. Only one of this number was sick. Twenty men died, so the mortality rate improved somewhat, to 14.8 percent. Thirty-two men, mostly from the 42nd Division, were listed on the Weekly Medical

Report (Serious) for July 27. All were gunshot wounds, the machinegun the likely culprit. Typical were:

Fatterfield, Kirk, Pvt.	Co. D, 167th Inf.	27 July 1918	G.S.W. Multiple "S"
Wingate, Rosier, Pvt.	Co. B, 167th Inf.	26 July 1918	G.S.W. Knee & Face "S"
Dickinson, Stanley, 1st Lt.	Co. G, 101st Inf.	24 July 1918	G.S.W. Rt. Arm, Chin
Upchurch, F., Pvt.	167th Inf.	26 July 1918	G.S.W. Head & Chest[97]

Overall, during the month of July, the hospital admitted 639 patients, nearly all (96 percent) of whom were injured and required surgical intervention. The mean strength of the unit during this period was eighty-eight officers and men.[98]

The distance from the front line did not make the American hospitals immune from German bombing and shelling.[99] The 103rd Field Hospital was the target of one such incident which took place during a German counterattack on July 15. The shelling began shortly after midnight and continued throughout the early morning hours. The nurses were evacuated to a shelter away from the hospital. However, when a shell struck the tent ward at 6 A.M. and killed a patient, the nurses, oblivious to the danger, went back to take care of their wards. One of the nurses was heard to say, "Our place is with our patients." Shortly thereafter, they helped move the patients to what was hoped to be a safer temporary location a few miles to the rear. They were wrong. The next night, German aviators dropped two bombs on the clearly marked tent hospital, followed by a second attack the following night, when one of the pilots also strafed the ward tents with machinegun fire.[100] Several nurses were specifically cited for their bravery, including Clara L. Zaung (night chief), Ruth Bridges, Elizabeth Harland, Elizabeth Roulstone, Sybella T. Haviland, Rosa I. Hall, Margaret Lowe, Ethel Randall, and Della A. McNamara.[101]

Female nurses had been attached to the 26th Division at least as early as the Toul sector, where they helped staff the 101st Field Hospital at Caserne Lamarche.[102] According to Col. Richard Derby, these women performed "*splendid and devoted work*," but were only "*temporary*" until such time as the "*hospital corps men became more skilled*."[103] There seems to be some confusion as to how many female nurses actually were attached to the 103rd Field Hospital, during its tour in the Pas Fini sector. One account places the number at thirty-five, but it is more likely that the actual figure was closer to thirty.

On July 5, eighteen nurses then thought to be on duty with the 2nd Division were ordered to report for duty with the 26th Division.[104] Further orders assigned these nurses to the 103rd Field Hospital to be carried as "attached."[105] One week later, Lieutenant Colonel Porter, the division surgeon, expressed his pique when he discovered that Major Blanchard had transferred two surgeons and four nurses to Evacuation Hospital No. 7 on the strength of a verbal order from a Col. P. C. Hutton.[106] In the exchange of memos that followed, it became apparent that the original transfer to the Yankee Division included fewer nurses from the 2nd

Division; only sixteen, and not the eighteen at first thought. That number, coupled with the fourteen already attached to the division, brought the actual total to thirty. Nurses Nellie Driscoll (originally with the 2nd Division), Mary E. Ray, Valerie Weil, and Mary C. Pancoast left the unit on July 15. Thus the number was further reduced to twenty-six, only eleven of whom had originally come into the sector with the division. While he accepted the fait accompli, Lieutenant Colonel Porter could not help but try to get in the last word; he recommended that "future orders regarding personnel of this division be transmitted *through the usual channels.*"[107] However, the actual last word came from Major General Liggett, through his chief of staff, Malin Craig. In a tersely worded "Special Order" dated July 31, the verbal order of the corps commander was confirmed as "being necessary in the military service."[108]

To make matters worse, while all this was going on, fifteen more nurses (all of whom had been previously attached to the 2nd Division) were released to Evacuation Hospital No. 8 on July 19, in a belated response to an order dated July 10.[109] Their numbers were dwindling. The message from 1st Army Corps (Paris Group) was clear; the original transfer to the 26th Division, and, in turn, to the 103rd Field Hospital, had been "without authority." The memorandum informing the division surgeon of the reasons for the transfer went on to chastise the unit for the delay in complying with the order and to state that the hospital had a complement of nurses greater than "at any similar divisional unit in this area." Moreover, two more nurses had accompanied a shock team that had arrived that day.[110] What was apparently lost upon many of the headquarters types was the fact that the 103rd Field Hospital was tending to hundreds of seriously wounded casualties from the offensive who would never make it to the hospitals in the rear without immediate, skilled intervention.

Lieutenant Colonel Porter's consternation is completely understandable when it is realized that the original order transferring the nurses to the division had emanated from the very office that now called it into question.[111] Belatedly, at the request of corps, the First Army found six female nurses for the division, and in a memo dated July 25, 1918 (the same date that the Yankee infantry was relieved in the sector), General Liggett informed General Edwards that the new nursing personnel would be released from Base Hospital No. 15, and that he would "be advised as to expected arrival."[112]

On July 28, the 103rd Field Hospital moved forward to Lauconnoise Ferme just north of Château-Thierry, in anticipation of a further advance by the division. It remained there two days.[113] Instead, the unit got the welcome news that it would march back to Luzancy, there to rest, recuperate, and await further orders. The motor transport officer for the Sanitary Train arranged for the movement. The troops were ordered to assemble at 6:30 A.M., with the march to begin thirty minutes later. The route took them along the Paris-Metz road through La Ferté-sous-Jouarre. The 103rd Field Hospital left Lauconnaise Ferme on July 30 and arrived at Luzancy the same day. It spent the following sixteen days bivouacked on the banks of the Marne.[114] The hospitals were situated in a private school building, which at one time must have been a chateau or large estate and had been used by the French and American medical personnel since the beginning of the war. The facility was located just a few hundred yards from a bridge over the Marne, which made it convenient for evacuation to the rear. The enlisted men were quartered in tents in a grove of pine trees behind the hospital. The building itself was ideally suited for a hospital, having "all modern improvements," including running water and hot and cold showers. Due to numerous shelling and air raids, there was a dugout behind the hospital. There was also a small American cemetery.[115] Frederick Pottle offers a description of the hospital in June 1918, which at the time was occupied by the 16th Field Hospital (2nd Division), just prior to its occupation by the Yankees; he writes of several "buildings of a large estate with a porter's lodge [that was] serving as the morgue."[116] A doctor who was stationed there in September 1918, after the Yankee Division had left, described the building as "a dear old place, with a frontage on the bank of the Marne."[117]

This was a time to obtain fresh clothing, swim in the Marne, and visit the recently stocked commissary in Nanteuil. Some forty-eight-hour leaves were granted. Fortunate officers (and a few enterprising enlisted men who were able to evade the vigilant MPs and French authorities) got to visit Paris. Most were content to visit La Ferté-sous-Jouarre or other neighboring villages.[118] However, so as not to let the men stay idle for long, on the morning of August 5 a mock exercise was conducted under the direction of Major Blanchard of the 103rd Field Hospital. Litter bearer detachments were ordered to report to "hypothetical" ambulance heads to remove simulated wounded patients, represented by field packs, from aid stations marked by guidons. After the drill, all units returned to Luzancy.[119]

Two Sectors in Two Weeks

This rest period lasted a little more than two weeks, when division orders were received to move out to a new sector. The infantry began the journey by rail on August 13, while the artillery set out on August 14. The troop trains left Château-Thierry and passed through Dormans, Epernay, and Châlons-sur-Marne (near the site of Attila the Hun's defeat in A.D. 451), where they turned south to their ultimate destination, Châtillon-sur-Seine, a small town located near the headwaters of the Seine, in the 12th Training Area.[120] The Sanitary Trains came last. Orders were issued to march to Château-Thierry on August 15, where the Field Hospital Section and the rest of the Sanitary Train would begin a journey by rail and truck.[121] The 103rd Field Hospital made its way to Château-Thierry and there, at 4:30 P.M. on August 15, boarded train No. 41.[122] As these units arrived at Chatilon-sur-Seine, they spread out into the surrounding area and established their camps. The 104th Infantry marched northeast approximately twelve miles to Riel-le-Eaux, where it encamped.[123] The ambulance sections were ordered to Laignes, ten miles west of Châtillon-sur-Seine.[124] While there, the 101st Ambulance Company became fully mechanized and transferred its horses to an artillery unit.[125]

Originally, the division surgeon had hoped to establish a hospital within Châtil-lon-sur-Seine, but when Lieutenant Colonel Porter arrived to make final arrangements, the officer in command of the area refused permission.[126] As a result, according to orders, the hospital units to bivouacked on the grounds of the chateau in the village of Villotte-sur-Ource, about five miles to the east of Châtillon.[127] At that time, Villotte was a small village of about 150 inhabitants, situated in a valley in rolling farm country. Upon arrival in the new area about 8:30 P.M., August 16, the hospital companies erected pup tents, ate dinner, and settled in for the night.

The mission of the 103rd Field Hospital was to set up and operate a tent hospital for the division sick across from the chateau at Villotte-sur-Ource.[128] The hospital was designated as the evacuation point for all the division sick. All seriously ill, as well as most surgical cases, were to be evacuated to Base Hospital No. 15, at Chaumont. Ordinary sick and minor surgical cases were to be sent to Camp Hospital No. 38. The 103rd Field Hospital arrived at this location on August 16, and by 8 P.M. the next day the hospital was fully operational. The 101st Field Hospital looked after skin and venereal patients, as well as the overflow from Chaumont and the camp hospital.[129]

This was not a period of inactivity, and the army insisted on regular training schedule for the field hospital companies. The training consisted of classes and drill Monday through Friday, inspections on Saturday; Sunday was a day of rest. Each day's training took four hours in the morning and an additional two hours in the afternoon. Typical classes included personal hygiene, camp sanitation, military courtesy, and minor surgery. Drill consisted of squad litter drills as well as platoon drill.[130]

During the first week of operation, the 103rd Field Hospital admitted 136 patients, eleven of whom were listed as injured, with the balance sick. Fifteen of the latter were venereal cases, their infections more than likely contracted during the two-week rest period. Sixteen were transferred to other hospitals, while eight were returned to duty. The remainder were retained.[131] The next week was more of the same. The unit admitted 130 patients—124 sick and six injured. Of the sick, there was one case of pneumonia and an additional sixteen venereal cases. One hundred nine were transferred to other facilities, and sixty-seven were returned to duty. Sixty-five remained when the tent hospital ceased operating at that location. Two of these patients were then transferred to other facilities, while the remainder were sent back to their units, presumably cured. While in this area, the mean strength of the organization was eighty-four officers and men.[132]

Mobile Surgical Unit No. 7 joined with the 103rd Field Hospital, transforming it into a Surgical Hospital. The company commander was then ordered to submit a requisition for a "nucleus of supplies" with which to complete the conversion.[133]

By the end of August, in anticipation of the upcoming St. Mihiel Offensive, the division was on the move again. This time the destination was a hundred miles north of Châtillon-sur-Seine, to the area surrounding Bar-le-Duc, with all the elements arriving between August 29 and 31. The Sanitary Trains moved out with the rest of the division during the last week of August. First Lt. Henry Christiansen was named billeting officer, and he led the advance billeting party to the new area. First Lt. Wentzle Ruml, Jr., was appointed as the entraining officer. On August 28, a detachment from the 101st Ambulance Company was detailed to proceed ahead of all other units to Bar-le-Duc. The balance of that unit, along with the 102nd Field Hospital, was ordered to leave at noon the same day, with an anticipated arrival in Bar-le-Duc at 1 A.M. on August 29. Detachments from the 102nd and 103rd Ambulance Companies were to provide evacuation service in the Châtillon-sur-Seine area until the departure of the last unit, after which they were to drive their vehicles to the new area. The headquarters of the Sanitary Train, located at Château Crépan, closed at 6 A.M. on August 29.

The 103rd Field Hospital was told to evacuate its patients unable to return to duty and to close its doors. At the same time, 101st Field Hospital was ordered to remain open until 9 A.M., August 30, and then close. Later that same day, the personnel of the field hospitals, less the 102nd, and their equipment were driven thirteen miles north by truck to Latrecey, where the men boarded train 52 at 8:13 P.M. They carried two days' rations for what was expected to be a seven-hour journey to Tronville-en-Barrois, in the area around Bar-le-Duc and Ligny-en-Barrois.[134]

NOTES

1. Martin Gilbert, *The First World War* (New York: Henry Holt, 1994), 437; Edward M. Coffman, *The War to End All Wars: The American Military Experience in World War I* (Madison: Univ. of Wisconsin Press, 1986), 222.

2. Rod Paschall, *The Defeat of Imperial Germany, 1917–1918* (Chapel Hill, N.C.: Algonquin, 1989) 159. (Germany hoped to gain something at bargaining table by capturing and holding an important piece of ground.)

3. Paul Braim, *The Test of Battle: The American Expeditionary Forces in the Meuse-Argonne Campaign* (Newark: Univ. of Delaware Press, 1988), 73.

4. Ibid., 64.

5. Coffman, *War to End All Wars*, 223–27; Paschall, *Defeat of Imperial Germany, 1917–1918*,159-60; Gilbert, *The First World War*, 442.

6. Coffman, *War to End All Wars*, 236–46.

7. Robert B. Asprey, *At Belleau Wood* (Denton, Tex., 1996), 343–44; Gilbert, *First World War*, 443–44.

8. Gilbert, *First World War*, 437.

9. Coffman, *War to End All Wars*, 248.

10. Braim, *Test of Battle*, 76. (The orders were dated August 10, 1918.)

11. Gilbert, *First World War*, 437 and 449–50.

12. Ronald Schaffer, *America in the Great War: The Rise of the War Welfare State* (New York: Oxford Univ. Press, 1991), 47.

13. Ibid., 67–69.

14. David M. Kennedy, *Over Here: The First World War and American Society* (New York: Oxford Univ. Press, 1980), 262.

15. Ibid., 272–74.

16. Ibid., 280–83; Schaffer, *America in the Great War*, 75.

17. Kennedy, *Over Here*, 169–71.

18. Ibid., 166–67 and 177.

19. Emerson G. Taylor, *New England in France, 1917-1918: A History of the Twenty-sixth Division U.S.A.* (Boston: Houghton Mifflin, 1920), 160–62.

20. Daniel W. Strickland, *Connecticut Fights: The Story of the 102nd Regiment* (New Haven: Quinnipiack Press, 1930), 176.

21. James T. Duane, *Dear Old "K"* (Boston: Thomas Todd, 1922), 81.

22. Stanley J. Herzog, *The Fightin' Yanks* (Stamford, Conn.: Cunningham, 1922), 61; Frank P. Sibley, *With the Yankee Division in France* (Boston: Little, Brown, 1919), 195.

23. Frederick E. Jones, *Historical Sketch of the Medical Department of the 26th Division,* (typescript, n.d.), with "Introductory Note" and other comments by R.S. Porter (8 August 1918), dated July 9, 1918, p. 20. NA RG120; Sibley, *With the Yankee Division in France,* 196; Taylor, *New England in France,* 160; U.S. Army Center of Military History. *Order of Battle of the United States Land Forces in the World War: American Expeditionary Forces, Divisions* (Washington, D.C.: GPO, 1988), 120–21. (Division HQ opened at Genevrois Ferme on July 10, so I assume that the relief had been completed the day before.)

24. Herzog, *Fightin' Yanks,* 74–75.

25. Sibley, *With the Yankee Division in France,* 222; Duane, *Dear Old "K,"* 98.

26. Gilbert, *First World War,* 440–41.

27. Duane, *Dear Old "K,"* 98.

28. Ibid.

29. Ibid., 101; Bert Ford, *The Fighting Yankees Overseas* (Boston: McPhail, 1919), 141.

30. Herzog, *Fightin' Yanks,* 81.

31. Gilbert, *First World War,* 444; Sibley, *With the Yankee Division in France,* 215.

32. Duane, *Dear Old "K,"* 102; *Stars & Stripes,* August 2, 1918, 1–2. USMA.

33. Herzog, *Fightin' Yanks,* 83 and 105.

34. Ibid., 80.

35. Taylor, *New England in France,* 196.

36. Herzog, *Fightin' Yanks,* 105.

37. Henry Berry, *Make the Kaiser Dance* (Garden City, N.Y.: Doubleday, 1978), 18.

38. Taylor, *New England in France,* 199–202. (An excellent summary of the division's activities during this operation can be found in *Stars & Stripes,* January 10, 1919 USMA.)

39. Taylor, *New England in France,* 77–78 (Chemin des Dames).

40. Harvey Cushing, *From a Surgeon's Journal* (Boston: Little, Brown, 1936), 479; Coffman, *War to End All Wars,* 13; Braim, *Test of Battle,* 161–62; Sibley, *With the Yankee Division in France,* 4–13.

41. Meirion Harries and Susie Harries, *The Last Days of Innocence: America at War, 1917–1918* (New York: Random House, 1997), 210 and 239; Cushing, *From a Surgeon's Journal,* 440 ("characteristically profane"); Coffman, *War to End All Wars,* 25 ("talkative").

42. Coffman, *War to End All Wars,* 250–51; Sibley, *With the Yankee Division in France,* 196.

43. Hunter Liggett (1857–1935). A member of the West Point class of 1879, Liggett was a staff officer for most of his long military career. Largely self-taught, he had a vast knowledge of military science and history, and he was universally admired for his brilliance in military matters. He attended the Army War College at the age of fifty-three, and within two years of his graduation he was appointed its president. Liggett retired from active service in 1921 and at the time of his death held the rank of lieutenant general. "Annual Report," *Assembly,* 11 June 1936, 125–27. USMA.

44. Sibley, *With the Yankee Division in France*, 133–34 and 227.

45. Coffman, *War to End All Wars*, 250–52.

46. Taylor, *New England in France*, 208–9; *The Immortal Yankee Division* (Boston: Young Men's Christian Association).

47. Herzog, *Fightin' Yanks*, 119.

48. Ibid., 108; Sibley, *With the Yankee Division in France*, 196 (August 5, 1918).

49. Duane, *Dear Old "K,"* 107; Field Orders No. 8 (SECRET), 29th July, 1918, HQ,101st Sanitary Train, par.VIII. NA RG120; Cushing, *From a Surgeon's Journal*, 417.

50. Elsie Janis, *The Big Show* (New York: Cosmopolitan, 1919), 182–83. The date was more than likely Thursday, August 1, 1918, when the divisional troupe of entertainers staged a minstrel and vaudeville show. The 102nd Artillery band formed the orchestra, and the 101st Infantry Band played French marches. *History Field Hospital Company 101–101st Sanitary Train, 26th Division, Part 5*, p.5. NA RG120.

51. Lettie Gavin, *American Women in World War I* (Niwot: Univ. Press of Colorado, 1997), 141–43.

52. Field Order #50, 7 July 1918, 26th Division U.S. MNGA.

53. Jones, *Historical Sketch*, 21.

54. Eben Putnam, *Report of the Commission on Massachusetts' Part in the World War*, vol.1, *History* (Boston: Commonwealth of Massachusetts, 1931), 140.

55. Ibid., 225.

56. Richard Derby, *"Wade in, Sanitary!"* (New York: G. P. Putnam's Sons, 1919), 57.

57. Jones, *Historical Sketch*, 24–25 and 80–81. See also R. S. Porter, Memorandum To Commanding Officer, Field Hospital 102 and Field Hospital 101–4, 18 July 1918. NA RG120.

58. Jones, *Historical Sketch*, 20–21.

59. Sibley, *With the Yankee Division in France*, 203.

60. Putnam, *Report of the Commission*, 140.

61. Ibid., 140. (For three week period July 7 through July 20, the division's four field hospitals handled 4,395 patients.)

62. Paul Waterman, Report of Operations from Period July 18 to July 25, 1918, Para. XI, 15 August 1918. NA RG120.

63. Field Orders No. 7, HQ, 101st Sanitary Train, 24th July, 1918. NA RG120.

64. Jones, *Historical Sketch*, 23–24.

65. Ibid., 24; Surgeon General, *Annual Report, 1919*, 3300.

66. Orders No. 25, HQ, 101st Sanitary Train, 4th August, 1918. NA RG120. The Order contained the following injunctions: (a) All practicable measures will be taken to prevent contamination of food by flies. (b) All latrines will be made flyproof. (c) Food will be kept under cover. (d) Drinking water will be chlorinated or boiled. (e) *Promiscuous defecation will be prevented.* [Emphasis added.] (f) Proper police will be maintained at all times.

67. Putnam, *Report of the Commission*, 140–41.

68. Ibid., 140–41; Field Orders No. 66 (together with accompanying Movement Table and Billeting Accomodations), Headquarters 26th Division, A.E.F., 29 July 1918; Field Orders No. 8 (SECRET), HQ, 101st Sanitary Train, 20 o'clock, 29th July, 1918. NA RG120.

69. *Orders No. 24, HQ, 101st Sanitary Train, 3rd August, 1918*; James Lung Bevans, *Medical History of the 26th Division from Organization to June 24, 1918* (typescript, n.d.), 18. Later, all of the division's trucks were consolidated under the division G-1 for maximum effectiveness throughout. NA RG120.

70. Verbal Order by Commanding Officer, 101st Sanitary Train, Station List, Sheet #3, 103rd Field Hospital. NA RG120.

71. R. S. Porter, *101st Sanitary Train, 26th Division A.E.F., History, March 20th, 1919,* 368. MNGA.

72. R. S. Porter, Memorandum for G-1, 1 July 1918. See also Walter Krueger, Memorandum for French Mission, 2 July 1918. NA RG120.

73. Letter Order, A.C. of Staff, G-4, Paris Group, to C.G. 2nd Division, July 3, 1918. NA RG120 (For the comments by division surgeon of the 2nd Division on the loss of his ambulances, see Derby, *"Wade in, Sanitary!"* 96.)

74. Memorandum to Section Commanders and M.S.O., 5 July 1918. NA RG120.

75. William H. Blanchard, Memorandum to C.O. 101st Sanitary Train, 7 July 1918. NA RG120.

76. Paul Waterman, Memo to Unit Commanders, 7 July 1918. NA RG120.

77. Paul Waterman, Memorandum to Division Surgeon, 26th Div., 8 July 1918. NA RG120.

78. War Department, *Report of the Surgeon General U.S. Army to the Secretary of War, 1919* (Washington, D.C.: GPO), 3299.

79. Derby, *"Wade in, Sanitary!"* 75–76.

80. *Stars & Stripes,* June 21, 1918, p. 1. USMA.

81. Cushing, *From a Surgeon's Journal,* 392–94 emphasis added. (The previous occupant, the 23rd Field Hospital, 2nd Division, shifted from twelve-hour shifts to three teams working eight hour shifts. Derby, *"Wade in, Sanitary!"* 78.)

82. Cushing, *From a Surgeon's Journal,* 393.

83. Jones, *Historical Sketch,* 75–77 (citing Memorandum, 2 October 1918, R. S. Porter to Commandant, Army Sanitary School.) Jones defines the term "non-transportable" wounded both in terms of the nature or seriousness of the wound, and of other factors, which could actually control, such as availability of transport, distance to a hospital of "definitive treatment," weather and road conditions, and the tactical situation. Nontransportability was to be determined by the commanding officer of the field hospital or of the sorting station.)

84. Abstract from Weekly Medical Report, Serious Cases, 103rd Field Hospital, La Ferté, 13 July 1918. NA RG120. ("G.S.W." stands for gunshot wound; "reg"stands for region. The date is that of admission.)

85. Weekly Telegraphic Report, 103rd Field Hospital, July 9, 1918 and July 17, 1918. NA RG120.

86. Memorandum #12, HQ First Army Corps, Office of the Chief Surgeon, 13 July 1918; Memorandum "Z" (SECRET), HQ 26th Division, Office of the Division Surgeon, 15 July 1918; Memorandum, For G-1, HQ 26th Division, Office of the Division Surgeon, 21 July 1918; Jones, *Historical Sketch,* 22 (reference to "leapfrog"). NA RG120.

87. Memorandum for G-1, Office of the Division Surgeon, 26th Division, 9 July 1918; Memorandum from Division Surgeon to Commanding Officer 101st Sanitary Train, 13 July 1918; Waterman, Report of Operations from Period July 18 to July 25, 1918, p. 1. NA RG120.

88. Porter, *101st Sanitary Train,* 372. MNGA.

89. Weekly Medical Reports, Serious Cases, 103rd Field Hospital. NA RG120. (For the weeks ended July 13 and July 20, 1918.)

90. Frederick L. Bogan, Report, Operations from July 18 to 26th, 1918, 102nd Field Hospital, 15 August 1918. NA RG120.

91. Abstract from Weekly Medical Report, Serious Cases, 103rd Field Hospital, 20 July 1918. NA RG120.

92. Clifford W. Renth, Report of Duties from 17th to 26th July 1918, 3 September 1918. NA RG120.

93. Derby, *"Wade in, Sanitary!"* 74.

94. R. S. Porter, Memorandum for G-1 (Re Advance Dressing Station, Villiers-sur-Marne), 11 July 1918 (Approval noted on Memorandum on 16 July 1918.). NA RG120.

95. Station List, Sheet #3, 103rd Field Hospital; Report on Action 18th–26th July, 1918, C.O. 101st San. Train to C. G., 26th Division, 2 August 1918. NA RG120.

96. William H. Blanchard, Memo to C.O. 101st Sanitary Train, 30 July 1918. NA RG120.

97. Weekly Medical Report, Serious Cases, 103rd Field Hospital Co., 27 July 1918. NA RG120.

98. Weekly Report of Sick and Injured, 103rd Field Hospital, 26th Division, A.E.F. (July 9, 17, 24, and 31, 1918). NA RG120.

99. Cushing, *From a Surgeon's Journal*, 201–2 (describes air raid upon American Base Hospital #5 at Camiers, 14 September 1917, in which two persons were killed. Reference to "daisy cutter" bombs); ibid., 399 (general reference); *Stars & Stripes, 19 July 1918*, 1 (attack upon Red Cross Hospital at Juilly on July 19, 1918, resulted in three enlisted men killed and one nurse and twelve patients wounded. The attack upon the hospital took place at 11 P.M., and the facility was clearly marked with a 30 meter white cross). See also *Stars & Stripes, August 30, 1918*, 6 (story about an attack on an American hospital by Gotha bombers and the bravery of the nurses). USMA; Harries and Harries, *The Last Days of Innocence*, 45–46; Lyn Macdonald, *The Roses of No Man's Land* (New York: Macmillan, 1989), 68; Derby, *"Wade in, Sanitary!"* 146–48 (two corpsmen died).

100. *Stars & Stripes*, August 23, 1918, 5. USMA.

101. William H. Blanchard, Citation for Meritorious Action; Sibley, *With the Yankee Division in France*, 222.

102. Bevans, *Medical History of the 26th Division*, 12; *History Field Hospital Company 101-101st Sanitary Train, Part 4*, 3 (fifteen nurses under Mrs. Mabel Shaw). NA RG120.

103. Derby, *"Wade in, Sanitary!"* 76. Emphasis added.

104. Memorandum to Section Commanders and M.S.O., A.E.F., HQ 101st Sanitary Train, July 5, 1918. NA RG120.

105. Memorandum from Division Surgeon to C.O. 101st San. Trains, 13 July 1918. NA RG120.

106. Cushing, *From a Surgeons's Journal*, 404. (Colonel Hutton was chief surgeon of the Paris Group, a fact apparently lost upon the company commander and Lieutenant Colonel Porter.)

107. R. S. Porter, Memorandum for G-1, July 20, 1918; William H. Blanchard, Memo to C.O. 101st Sanitary Train, July 20, 1918. NA RG120.

108. Special Orders No. 184, HQ First Army Corps, July 31, 1918. NA RG120.

109. Blanchard, Memo to C.O. 101st Sanitary Train, 20 July 1918. NA RG120.

110. Response to C. G. 1st Army Corps from G-4, Paris Group, 20 July 1918. NA RG120.

111. Letter Order, A.C. of S., G-4, Paris Group, July 3, 1918, par.3. NA RG120.

112. Memorandum from Liggett to Edwards, 25 July 1918. NA RG120. See also Lettie Gavin, *American Women in World War I*, 44 and 179–208. (All in all, as of June 30, 1918, nearly half of the 12,000 army nurses then on active duty were serving in France. By the war's end, more than 21,000 were in service. In addition, thousands more Red Cross nurses also served in hospitals overseas and at home during the influenza epidemic.)

113. Station List, Sheet #3, 103rd Field Hospital. NA RG120.

114. Ibid.; Field Orders No. 66, 26th Division U.S., July 29, 1918 (together with Movement Table); Field Orders No. 8 (SECRET), Headquarters, 101st Sanitary Train, July 29, 1918. NA RG120.

115. History Field Hospital Company 101-101st Sanitary Train, Part 5, p.2. NA RG120

116. Frederick A. Pottle, *Stretchers: The Story of a Hospital Unit on the Western Front* (New Haven, Conn.: Yale Univ. Press, 1929), 115.

117. Gavin, *American Women in World War I*, 160.

118. Sibley, *With the Yankee Division in France*, 241–45; Taylor, *New England in France*, 206–7.

119. Field Orders No. Y, HQ, 101st Sanitary Train, 4th August, 1918 and Memorandum to All Units, HQ, Ambulance Section, 101st San. Tr. American E. F., August 4,1918. NA RG120.

120. Its local museum is famous for its display of the "Vase of Vix," a gigantic Celtic ceremonial vessel (five feet tall) dating from the sixth century B.C., unearthed as part of a hoard of treasure at Vix, several miles to the north. A vauclusian spring called the "Douix" pours forth fresh water from the base of a bank of rock in the town center.

121. Order #147, 12 August 1918, 26th Division U.S. MNGA; Putnam, Report of the Commission, 141.

122. Order #147, 26th Division U.S., 12 August 1918. MNGA.

123. Duane, *Dear Old "K,"* 109; Herzog, *Fightin' Yanks*, 121.

124. Putnam, *Report of the Commission*, 141; Field Order #68, August 13, 1918, 26thDivision U.S. MNGA.

125. Jones, *Historical Sketch*, 27.

126. *History Field Hospital Company 101–101 Sanitary Train, 26th Division, Part 6*, p. 1; Memorandum from Division Surgeon, 26th Division to Assistant Chief of Staff G-1, 17 August 1918. NA RG120.

127. Field Order #68, 26th Division U.S., August 13, 1918. MNGA.

128. Orders No. 27, 101st Sanitary Train, 17th August, 1918, 18:30 o'clock; R. S. Porter, Memorandum for G-1, 17 August 1918. See also *History Field Hospital Company 101–101 Sanitary Train, Part 6*, p. 1. (The chateau is described as "quite modern in character," with a large woods behind, with paths for walking and a courtyard "artistically laid out by the landscape gardener." The 101st Field Hospital set up adjacent to the 103rd Field Hospital in a field along the Châtillon road, across from the chateau. The 102nd Field hospital set up tents behind the other two but did not operate as a hospital.). NA RG120. See also Field Order #68, 26th Division U.S., August 13, 1918. MNGA.

129. Memorandum for C.O., 101st Sanitary Train, 17.30 o'clock, 17 August [19]18; Station List, Sheet #4, 103rd Field Hospital. NA RG120.

130. Schedule of Training, Field Hospital Companies, Week Beginning 19 August 1918. NA RG120.

131. Weekly Report of Sick and Injured, 103rd Field Hospital, American E. F., for week ended August 21, 1918 (Form 211). NA RG120.

132. Weekly Report of Sick and Injured, 103rd Field Hospital, American E.F., (Form 211), for weeks ended August 28, 1918 and September 3, 1918. NA RG120.

133. Jones, *Historical Sketch*, 25; Memorandum to C.O. 101st Sanitary Train, 27 August 1918. NA RG120. See also Derby, *"Wade in, Sanitary!"* 10–11 (comments re concept of a mobile surgical hospital in war).

134. Orders No. 39 (reference to Orders No. 167, HQ, 26th Division), Headquarters 101st Sanitary Train, 27th August, 1918; Station List, Sheet #4, 103rd Field Hospital. NA RG120. See also *Stars & Stripes*, June 14, 1918, 7. USMA.

Chapter Six

Closing the Gap
(St. Mihiel)

"Don't worry, major; you never hear the one that gets you."
—Douglas MacArthur to George S. Patton, Jr., at St. Mihiel

FLOOD TIDE (SEPTEMBER 1918)

Western Front—Allies

Marshal Foch issued orders on September 3, 1918, for attacks along the whole length of the western front. He and Haig were confident that at long last the logjam was broken. All they had to do was push a little harder. They were convinced that Germany did not have the men and resources to meet challenges at every point, especially now that the U. S. First Army was in the picture, with more than a million and a half Americans in France. Pershing was still attempting to concentrate his forces, most of whom were in the St. Mihiel sector. Some, however, remained in reserve or with the British. The attacks continued. The last battle in the Arras campaign, begun on August 26, was a four-hour affair fought by the Canadians at Drocourt-Queant. The British attacked the Hindenberg Line at Havrincourt on September 12, and at Epehy from September 12 through September 18.[1]

Meanwhile, on the German side, the high command ordered a withdrawal from the Lys salient; it was completed by September 6. The Germans also ordered evacuation of the St. Mihiel salient, on September 8. The foe was shortening his lines to make them more defensible. At home, both Ludendorff and the kaiser spoke out against the defeatist attitude of many Germans. The kaiser went so far as to tell an audience of workers that such people should be hanged. His words were received in stony silence.[2]

Things were going well for the Allies—so well in fact, that Haig would soon suggest to Foch a change in strategy. This would bring on yet another confrontation between Foch and Pershing.[3]

Western Front, AEF: St. Mihiel

For four years the Germans had held what was known as the St. Mihiel salient, a 200-square-mile bulge in the western front just south of Verdun and centered on the town for which it was named. Roughly triangular in shape and stretching for forty-two miles, the west face began in the north near Haudiamont and followed a line southwest to the apex at St. Mihiel on the Meuse River, where it turned back southeast to a point just north of Pont-a-Mousson to form the south face. It contained a portion of the wooded Heights of the Meuse in the north and the swampy area of the Rupt-de-Mad in the south. The south also contained the dominating height of Mont Sec and some lesser hills. To the east, lay the Woëvre Plain, itself swampy from the recent rains.[4] The region was dotted with small towns. What roads existed were few and generally narrow and unpaved. The French answer to road maintenance was to place piles of crushed stone at intervals along these byways.[5]

The military value of the area lay in the fact that it effectively blocked the direct rail passage of raw materials and manufactured goods produced in the industrial part of France to Paris and other points west. It had been a thorn in the side of the French since the beginning of the war.[6] When presented with the challenge of reducing the salient, Pershing literally leaped at it; here was an opportunity to prove just what the newly formed U.S. First Army could do.

His plan was to execute a large pincer movement from the northwest and southwest, with his forces pinching in toward the east.[7] There were even those who, looking ahead, thought that continuation toward the fortress city of Metz and the Moselle River would make great sense and would help to shorten a war that it was thought, would continue well into 1919.[8] Pershing and his staff worked on their plans, but two factors unknown to them were about to come into play. First, as we have seen, in an effort to shorten his lines Ludendorff ordered his forces to begin a withdrawal from the salient on September 8,[9] literally on the eve of the big push, originally slated for September 10.[10] Secondly, Foch and Haig had sensed an opportunity to change their own plans. Each thought that, at long last, a big breakthrough was possible—but in the British sector near Cambrai, not at St. Mihiel.[11]

On August 30, 1918, Foch came to see Pershing at First Army headquarters, then at Ligny-en-Barrois. He had new orders, but "Black Jack" would have none of them. The Marshal wanted the Americans to scale back their plans at St. Mihiel and for Pershing to transfer troops to attack the Hindenburg Line in the Meuse-Argonne region, just west of Verdun. Pershing could see his newly formed army slipping away, once more under French control, in a joint attack toward Mezieres. Quite predictably, he refused. After some discussion, a compromise was reached. The

Americans would reduce the St. Mihiel salient but could not proceed any farther east; in other words, there would be no attack toward Metz. In addition, the Americans would assume an additional forty-eight miles of front to the north of the salient, north through Verdun and west through the Argonne. All told, Pershing's area of responsibility would stretch for nearly a hundred miles.[12]

After the fight at St. Mihiel, the U.S. forces would need to make a ninety-degree turn to the north. Pershing would have to move elements of his army, including supply and other services more than fifty miles, take over the Meuse-Argonne sector, and prepare to attack in conjunction with the Allies in a massive offensive all along the whole western front.[13] He had, in essence, to be ready to plan and fight two major battles in the space of one month, when his men had not yet fought one battle as a unified army. It would have been a daunting enough task for an experienced army.

Pershing's staff, which included Hugh Drum and George C. Marshall, set about the task with energy.[14] Five hundred thousand Americans and 110,000 French troops would take part in the assault.[15] Anticipating heavy casualties, planners arranged for more than 20,000 hospital beds.[16] Rails were laid and roads improved.[17] In addition to men, the French agreed to supply much of the artillery support and hundreds of light tanks. The British had agreed to supply heavy tanks (only to renege at the last moment and to keep them for their own use).[18] In total, nearly 3,000 artillery pieces would be used, as well as 200,000 tons of supplies and 50,000 tons of ammunition.[19] The Americans even resorted to deception as to the location of the attack, when false plans were planted in a hotel room wastebasket to be "found" by German spies.[20] A small detachment of tanks was unloaded in the vicinity of Belfort to support the deception, and false radio traffic was transmitted— So much work was involved that the date of the attack had to be postponed until September 12.[21]

On that date, following a massive artillery barrage that began after midnight, the U.S. forces, including the 26th and 42nd Divisions, jumped off in the rain and fog of early morning.[22] In the primary attack, which took place from the south face against relatively light opposition, the gains were nothing short of spectacular.[23] However, on the west face, in what was meant to be a secondary attack, the opposition turned out to be surprisingly heavy. Nevertheless, when the offensive was completed on September 16, all objectives had been taken.[24] The Germans had expected an attack somewhere along the front, but they had been taken by surprise at St. Mihiel; two of their divisions, as we have seen, were actually in the process of withdrawing to the rear.[25] The Allies captured 16,000 prisoners and large quantities of arms and material.[26] That is not to say that there was no cost involved; the retreating Germans exacted a high toll. The Americans suffered 7,000 dead, wounded, and missing, and another 3,000 casualties in the cleanup actions the following week.[27]

Scholars debate the significance of a victory over a greatly outnumbered enemy in the process of withdrawing, but that begs the real question. There were serious logistical problems, but these could be blamed in part upon the poor French road net, not simply upon the inexperience of Pershing and his staff in moving such large numbers of men and amounts of equipment.[28] In addition, it was to be expected that coordination between the participating units would improve the next time around. The important point is that the American army had come of age and proved that it could conduct a successful operation on a large scale. It was a confidence boost for both Pershing and his staff, as well as for the doughboy himself. This positive attitude would help in the weeks ahead, in the gloomy Argonne. As for the commander in chief, not content with the obvious success of his first major battle plan, he blamed the 5th Corps for not closing the gap quickly enough—a tough man, indeed.[29]

26TH DIVISION: STEPPING OUT AT ST. MIHIEL

The 26th Division was now part of Maj. Gen. George H. Cameron's 5th Corps.[30] It had been in France for nearly a year, and once again it was the rainy season. In fact, it rained nearly every day for two weeks.[31] From their interim encampment near Bar-le-Duc, the elements of the division began to move into position to take part in the great advance.[32] The division was scheduled to take over a new sector currently held by the French 2nd Division Cavalerie à Pied at 9 A.M. September 4. All troop movement was to take place at night between the hours of 10 P.M. and 4:30 A.M. During the day, all "persons and vehicles" were ordered to "remain concealed to the fullest practicable extent."[33] On September 5, Battery F, 103rd Field Artillery, moved from Tronville-en-Barrois to Rupt-en-Woëvre, a distance of about thirty-five miles north and east. The unit received orders on September 8 to move another two and one-half miles to Mouilly, and to take up support positions 700 meters behind the front line. No firing was allowed, for fear for fear of giving away its location, and shells were brought up in the dark, through the mud and rain. That night, a horse-drawn wagon carrying thirty 155 mm shells weighing 2,700 pounds turned over and rolled down an embankment. The driver was badly injured and had to be taken to a hospital.[34]

Meanwhile, the 104th Infantry was also ordered to hike to the Mouilly area; the unit set out in the pouring rain on September 6.[35] The rains persisted right up to the evening of the attack.[36] The positions assigned to the Yankees were just north of the line they had held in the Toul sector; the name Seicheprey was still fresh in their memories. Once again they faced the Prussian Guards.[37]

Those who found the time, diverted their attention to the World Series. Despite a loss to the Chicago Cubs in the second game on September 8, the Boston Red Sox went on to win the series. Their emerging star, lefthander Babe Ruth, won two games and went on to set a pitching record that stood for forty-five years.[38]

The 101st Infantry had been given the task of taking the towns of Hattonchâtel and Vigneulles, where it would link up with the U.S. 1st Division. The 102nd Infantry was held in reserve.[39] The objective was about nine miles from the jump-off position and was to be taken within the first twenty-four hours.[40] During the first phase of the attack, General Edwards moved his command post to a dugout at

Rupt-en-Woëvre, to be closer to the front line.[41] The area was near the northern hinge of the base of the salient and was more heavily defended, particularly in the area of les Eparges, opposite the division front.[42] The divisions on the western face would have fewer tanks in support than those on the southern, but that would be offset somewhat by a heavier artillery barrage than that preceding the attack from the south.[43] The weather also assisted the Yankees, since the drenching rain masked their signal flares.[44] But the ever-present mud was an impediment. Many horses and mules died in their traces struggling to pull their loads through the glue.[45]

By the afternoon of September 12, only one Yankee unit had reached its objective, and that only after the reserve had been used. Pershing was adamant that all objectives be reached. He ordered a night attack, and the job fell to the men from Connecticut, the 102nd Infantry.[46] They passed through the 101st Infantry lines and attacked down the Grande Tranchée de Calonne. The regiment reached Hatton-châtel about midnight and, finding it deserted, pushed on to Vigneulles. It arrived at 2:30 A.M. on September 13, well ahead of Pershing's favorites, the regulars of the U.S. 1st Division, who linked up with it several hours later as dawn broke.[47]

On September 14, the Yankee infantry was relieved by French troops. The Americans marched north about six miles to St. Remy Bois, in the vicinity of les Eparges, where they remained until September 17.[48] The artillery had moved the day before to the Forêt de la Montagne in order to support further action by the foot soldiers.[49] That was not long in coming. The 104th Infantry was ordered to the Waddonville sector and was billeted in Hannonville.[50] On September 21, First Army established its headquarters at Souilly, a town about twelve miles southwest of Verdun.[51] The long-awaited Meuse-Argonne campaign would begin on September 26.[52] The next two weeks were characterized by trench raids and movement around the Waddonville and Troyon sectors. Most notably, on September 26, the 102nd and 103rd Infantry took part in a diversionary raid at Marchévlle-Riaville, with the support of artillery.[53] As they captured German positions in the area, it soon became apparent that their enemy had made himself quite comfortable during his four years of occupation. Dugouts were well built and stocked with food, in particular cans of American ham and corned beef. Even the prisoners looked well fed.[54]

The division incurred many casualties during this period, including a junior officer who fell victim to a ruse perpetrated by German soldiers who pretended to have surrendered.[55] However, if the commanders were in the doghouse, the troops certainly were not. No less an authority than Gen. Hunter Liggett himself had nothing but praise for the soldiers of the division, from company to squad levels. Moreover, he found the artillery "first rate."[56] The 26th had gained fourteen kilometers and captured more than 2,500 prisoners, along with twelve artillery pieces, eight trench mortars, and 109 machine guns.[57]

Sanitary Trains: From the Valley to the Heights of the Meuse

The 101st Field Hospital and the 103rd Field Hospital set up hospitals at Chaumont-sur-Aire, a town about thirteen miles to the north of Tronville and

Ligny-en-Barrois, while the rest of the train established billets nearby and awaited further orders.[58] They were not long in coming. All unit commanders were to transfer all soldiers with uncomplicated venereal disease to the Division Disciplinary Detachment until "pronounced cured."[59] The Trains' stay at Chaumont-sur-Aire was short; after about five days, they moved about fifteen or twenty miles north and east along the Voie Sacrée so as to be closer to the front.[60] First Lieutenant Wentzle Ruml, Jr. was placed in charge of the move and was responsible for obtaining truck transportation and the maintenance of security.[61] The moves were made at night so as not to give the enemy any hint of the upcoming attack at St. Mihiel.[62] Sgt. Ernest Hinrichs, a member of the Radio Intelligence Section in the First Army, describes the night movements of the Army on September 6:

After dark and all night long there is a roar in the back areas like the traffic of a great city. During the day the roads are empty. At night they are crowded with ammunition and supply trains, artillery moving into close up camouflaged positions, men and wagons, and trucks, trucks, trucks. Miles of trucks end on end, without lights. No wonder the noise is awful tonight. *I wonder if the Germans can hear it?*"[63]

The initial placements of the field hospitals and ambulance companies in anticipation of the upcoming battle were on the plain along both sides the River Meuse. The Heights of the Meuse, an imposing range of hills, many of which were a thousand feet or more, rose abruptly from the narrow plain on the east bank of the river and blocked easy transit toward the Woëvre Plain beyond and farther east. What few roads that existed climbed through valleys up toward the Grande Tranchée de Calonne, an ancient road that traversed the top of the ridge forming the heights in a roughly north-to-south direction.[64] It was along that route that the division would be supplied and its wounded evacuated to the rear. However, the Germans had other ideas. They dug trenches and antitank excavations all around the jump-off point and thus prevented the movement of food and ambulances until the engineers arrived to make repairs and create roads. Heavy artillery fire had also done its work, leaving many shell craters in the roadways.[65]

The 101st Field Hospital set up a sorting station at Génicourt-sur-Meuse, on the east side of the river, and the 104th Field Hospital operated a hospital for gas casualties in the same building. The 102nd Field Hospital remained on the west side of the river and ran a hospital for ordinary sick and slightly wounded at the Château-le-Petite Monthairon. It was teamed with the 102nd Ambulance, which set up a dressing station there. The 103rd Field Hospital was also stationed at the chateau.[66] On September 10, the latter was ordered to Génicourt-sur-Meuse.[67]

Also on the 10th, Maj. Paul Waterman, commander of the Sanitary Train, revoked all orders having reference to "the United States Army as divided into separate and component forces of distinct origin," such as regular army, National Guard, Reserve Corps, etc. He quoted verbatim from Bulletin 59, issued by AEF headquarters on August 16, 1918: "This country has but one army." Henceforth the land forces in the service of the United States would be referred to as the "United

States Army." No more distinguishing insignia would be worn. This had to be good news for former National Guard divisions like the 26th, especially the officers, but seeing would definitely be believing. Old habits and ideas die hard, and the military certainly had enough of them.[68]

On September 11, as the big battle loomed, the ambulance companies were moved closer to the front. Headquarters for the section was set up at Rupt-en-Woëvre, along with the 103rd Ambulance Company. In order to preserve precious transport, an effort was made to direct walking wounded to this company. As a result, 112 wounded were treated there.[69] The 104th Ambulance Company was also stationed there, but in a reserve capacity. The 101st Ambulance Company set up a dressing station at Mouilly, a mere three and a half miles from the Grande Tranchée de Calonne. The unit established itself in the local church; its orders contemplated the removal of the pews, if necessary, with the injunction to keep any damage to a minimum. The 102nd set up a similar dressing station at Noyon. In addition, the commanding officer of the Ambulance Section and his subordinate company commanders were ordered to reconnoiter the routes of evacuation to and from the dressing stations.[70] The next day, the 103rd and 104th Ambulance Companies were detailed to follow the advancing regiments. Due to the condition of the roads, which had been heavily shelled, they were unable to comply fully. At one point, each of the ambulance companies formed ad hoc engineering detachments from its own personnel. These small groups went forward with minimal equipment and were able to "hasten considerably" the movement of ambulances and other vehicles.[71]

Evacuation of wounded was also facilitated by the drafting of twelve litter bearers from each infantry line company. Because of the poor condition of the roads during the initial stage of the attack, the wounded would never have reached the dressing stations but for the hand-carries of these brave men. The carry became longer and longer as the Yankees advanced toward their objective.[72] Communication was poor. Often messages got through only by runners or returning ambulances. Even this method was unsatisfactory as the distances increased. No saddle animals were available, nor were the motorcycles which were supposed to be assigned to each motor-driven ambulance company (six) and field hospital (four).[73] Gradually, the Medical Department was able to take hold and bring the situation under control. On September 15, the 104th Ambulance Company, with the 103rd in reserve, served the left of the line and set up at les Eparges. At the same time, the 102nd Ambulance Company concentrated at Dommartin-la-Montagne, with the 101st in reserve, and served the right.[74]

All this time, the men of the Provisional Truck Company were kept busy moving the medical units to their various locations, delivering daily supplies and gasoline for the ambulance companies, and in some instances evacuating wounded, as they did throughout September 13. As the battle progressed, the distribution point for gasoline and supplies was moved forward. On September 11, the advance supply depot had been located at Rupt-en-Woëvre. This was changed to Mouilly on September 13 and again on September 15, to Dommartin-la-Montagne, a small town just off the Grande Tranchée de Calonne, about seven miles from Vigneulles.[75]

After September 16, when all of the objectives of the division had been reached, its mission changed; as a result, so did that of the medical units. On September 21 there was more shifting of medical units, when the 102nd Field Hospital was moved across the river to Ambly, to be held in reserve until the mayor's office, together with adjacent buildings and nearby barracks, was made available, at which time it would be used to treat ordinary sick. The latter term was defined as those patients whose hospital stay was expected to be four days or less. Until that time, the 101st and 103rd Field Hospitals would act as the evacuating points for ordinary sick so as to ensure an uninterrupted flow of patients. After the 102nd Field Hospital commenced its new assignment, the other field hospitals were consolidated at Chappelle de Ferme de Notre Dame et Palameix (known simply as Notre Dame de Palameix), closer to the action. The 104th would serve as a gas hospital, while the 101st operated as a triage and evacuating point for the dressing stations. The 103rd would handle non-transportable wounded. All the hospitals would be "under canvas." The commanding officer of the Provisional Truck Company was ordered to provide transportation for the various moves.[76]

September 26 brought a renewal of the fighting, as the 26th Division was asked to create a diversion in support of the main attack in the Argonne. The result was a successful but costly raid at Marchévlle-Riaville. The 101st Ambulance Company followed right on the heels of the infantry and established a dressing station at Saulx-en-Woëvre, with ten squads from its litter bearer section well in advance. In addition, an advance dressing station was opened at Wadonville. The 102nd Ambulance Company was responsible for evacuation of the wounded to the field hospitals at Notre Dame de Palameix. The less seriously wounded, or "walking wounded," were directed to Combres.[77] At six o'clock that evening, the raid completed, the dressing station was moved back to Hannonville, and the field was cleared of wounded as the infantry pulled back under cover of darkness. For their gallant efforts the ambulance companies were shelled that night with gas and high explosive.[78]

On September 29, 1918, the Provisional Truck Company became an independent administrative unit of the Sanitary Train. All the enlisted personnel of the headquarters company and the various field hospitals who up to this time had been carried on the rolls of their respective units as on "special duty" were now permanently assigned to the new company.[79]

103rd Field Hospital Company: "Where the Ball Stops!"

The men of the 103rd Field Hospital Company arrived at Tronville-en-Barrois on August 31, after a truck ride from the railway station at Ligny-en-Barrois in the drizzling rain. They spent one night camped in tents beside the road about a mile outside of town.[80] During the night of September 1–2, the unit boarded trucks for a twenty-mile journey to Chaumont-sur-Aire where it arrived later, on September 2.[81] There the unit operated a hospital for the sick and injured. The hospital's final destination had not yet been determined. Originally, the hospital was to have been set up at Pont-de-la-Morlette, a kilometer west of Ancemont, on the Meuse.[82] As late as September 4, Lieutenant Colonel Porter was requesting its placement at Fontaine Brilliante, a kilometer or so north of Sommedieue. He was understandably anxious, because he knew that the St. Mihiel attack was imminent and that hospital units moved slowly, due to all the equipment that had to be loaded, unloaded, and set up. One thing was clear, however, and that was that wherever the hospital was assigned, one of its missions would continue to be the treatment of the seriously wounded.[83]

Finally, on September 6, orders were "cut," and once again, the hospital packed up and moved by truck about twelve miles farther north to the chateau at le Petit Monthairon, one kilometer north of les Monthairons, a town on the west side of the Meuse about fifteen miles south of Verdun. The move was made at night under an overcast sky that threatened yet more rain. The chateau had been used as a hospital by the French from the beginning of the war, and many casualties had been treated there during the battle for Verdun in 1916. Like the 101st Field Hospital, which had been initially stationed there before its transfer to Génicourt-sur-Meuse, and the 102nd Field Hospital, the men were billeted in either a building adjoining the chateau or as was more likely, in tents pitched in a wooded area on the grounds.[84] There at the chateau, the 103rd Field Hospital was to operate a sorting station and hospital for venereal patients, in conjunction with the 102nd Field Hospital.[85] The stay lasted all of four days, when further orders were received to transfer its remaining patients to the 102nd Field Hospital[86] and to proceed to the town of Génicourt-sur-Meuse, about three miles south, but on the east side of the Meuse. The men arrived on September 10, "to remain in a position of readiness," two days prior to the scheduled start of the St. Mihiel offensive.[87]

Earlier in the month, on September 2, the commanding officer of the 101st Sanitary Trains was ordered to form three surgical teams at the 103rd Field Hospital. He was further advised that the personnel had to come from within the division, since there was nobody to be spared elsewhere within First Army.[88] In compliance with the order, the following teams were proposed:

Team No. 1

1st Lt. Edward B. Sheehan (in charge)

1st Lt. Roy F. Brown (assistant)

1st Lt. Alfred A. Richman (anaesthetist)

Team No. 2

Capt. Karl S. Simpson (in charge)

Capt. Leonard W. Hassett (assistant)

1st Lt. John P. Murphy (anaesthetist)

Team No. 3

Capt. Edward W. Knowles (in charge—Mobile Surgical Unit No. 7)

1st Lt. William S. Schley (assistant)

1st Lt. Martin D. Westley (anaesthetist)

By and large, the team members were very experienced. Dr. Sheehan had interned at Boston City Hospital and had been most recently on the staff of the Free Hospital for Women in Brookline, Massachusetts. Captain Simpson had seven years' experience in general surgery and an additional four years in special surgery. John P. Murphy had spent nearly four years as an anaesthetist at Missouri Baptist Sanitorium in St. Louis, where he had administered anaesthesia to more than 5,000 patients. The head of the Mobile Surgical Unit, Dr. Knowles, had twelve years' experience in general surgery and, in addition had spent three months observing the French army surgeons work.[89]

The thousands of anticipated wounded from the St. Mihiel offensive did not materialize, but there were casualties enough to go around. In addition, the spate of bad weather had brought an increase in influenza.[90] After four days in Génicourt-sur-Meuse, on September 14 the hospital was shifted two and a half miles south to Troyon, there to operate a sorting station. Major Blanchard, the commanding officer, filed a handwritten memo indicating that his unit was open and ready to receive patients as of one minute after midnight on September 15.[91]

Its stay at Troyon lasted one week, when further orders were received to move to Notre Dame de Palameix, halfway up the Heights of the Meuse toward the Grande Tranchée de Calonne. The unit was designated as a hospital for the ordinary sick.[92] The hospital, with Mobile Surgical Unit No. 7 attached, would also treat non-transportable cases.[93] On Sunday, September 22, nine trucks from the Provisional Truck Company were detailed to transport the hospital to its new location. The 101st Field Hospital, as part of the group of three, was also sent to the same site at this time to serve as a sorting station, evacuation point, and a hospital for complicated venereal cases, scabies, pyodermia, and other skin diseases.[94] That unit's history offers the following description:

The only signs of any habitation in sight [being] a partially demolished factory situated about a half a kilometer in the rear of the hospital on the opposite side of which lay a small French Military Cemetery. Otherwise nothing in sight but a desolate waste of hill and valley, the latter being of a swampy nature and to say the least not inviting. Here and there the side of neighboring hills contained dug-outs which had been used by the French before our arrival. . . . While here we underwent both daily and nightly scenes of air activities and artillery fire.[95]

While at that station, the men lived in pup tents.[96] During the Marchéville-Riaville raid, this group of field hospitals was designated as the evacuation point for the dressing stations.[97]

Weekly reports of sick and injured for the month of September tell of moderate activity. However, it must be borne in mind that during the last week in August and the first week in September, the hospital was in transition to a new sector. On September 11, records showed 162 patient admissions, most likely all at Chaumont-sur-Aire and at le Petit Monthairon. Of these, only eleven were for injuries; of the sick, there were thirty-four more venereal cases. At the end of the period, all patients had been transferred to other hospitals. The following week, 226 patients were admitted. Two hundred four of these were sick, including six venereal cases. Once again, on September 18, the hospital evacuated all of its patients. By the last week in September, the pace had very definitely slowed. The returns for the period ending September 25 disclose only thirty-nine patients, all sick. Of that number one man died of acute cardiac dilatation (an abnormally enlarged heart). Mean strength for the unit for the month fluctuated between sixty-six and eighty-four officers and men.[98]

In addition to sick and injured, while at Notre Dame de Palameix the 103rd Field Hospital also treated seriously wounded. On September 28, Pvt. William Davis of D Company, 101st Infantry, was admitted for serious gunshot wounds to his chest and right shoulder. Again, on September 30, the surgeons treated Pvt. Arthur R. Kroeger, M Company, 101st Infantry, for multiple gunshot wounds ; his condition was listed as serious.[99]

The month of September also brought with it some changes in personnel. Dr. Renth returned to the unit on September 18 and a short time later was assigned to one of the surgical teams as an anesthetist. On August 31, he had been temporarily assigned to command the division dental laboratory while the regular commanding officer was away at the Army Sanitary Schools.[100] On September 23, Cpl. Joseph J. Carty was promoted to sergeant. Likewise, on September 29, Pvt. 1/C Edward J. Shay was promoted to corporal. Unfortunately, Joseph P. Dean was reduced in rank from sergeant to private, for unspecified reasons. Pvt. Wasyl Bakshta was transferred into the company. As of September 30, the unit had a total of seventy-seven enlisted men in its ranks.[101]

NOTES

1. Phillip Haythornthwaite, *The World War One Source Book* (London: Arms and Armor, 1996), 57; Thomas E. Greiss, ed., *The Great War* (Wayne, N.J.: Avery, 1986), 158.

2. Martin Gilbert, *The First World War* (New York: Henry Holt, 1994), 457.

3. Rod Paschall, *The Defeat of Imperial Germany, 1917–1918* (Chapel Hill, N.C.: Algonquin, 1989), 171–72; Edward Coffman, *The War to End All Wars: The American Military Experience in World War I* (Madison: Univ. of Wisconsin Press, 1986), 271.

4. Paul Braim, *The Test of Battle: American Expeditionary Forces in the Meuse-Argonne Campaign* (Newark: Univ. of Delaware Press, 1988), 77–78; Coffman, *War to End All Wars,* 273.

5. Harvey Cushing, *From a Surgeon's Journal* (Boston: Little, Brown, 1936), 303.

6. Paschall, *Defeat of Imperial Germany*, 1917–1918, 170.

7. Coffman, *War to End All Wars, 273–74.*

8. Greiss, ed., *Great War*, 160; Gilbert, *First World War*, 472.

9. John Toland, *No Man's Land* (New York: Konecky, 1980), 418.

10. Paschall, *Defeat of Imperial Germany, 1917–1918,* 170.

11. Coffman, *War to End All Wars,* 270.

12. Ibid., 272; Braim, *Test of Battle,* 82; Paschall, *Defeat of Imperial Germany,* 1917–1918, 172.

13. Paschall, *Defeat of Imperial Germany, 1917–1918*, 65.

14. Toland, *No Man's Land*, 429.

15. Tonie Holt and Valmai Holt, *Battlefields of the First World War* (London: Pavilion, 1993), 143; Paschall, *Defeat of Imperial Germany, 1917–1918*, 170.

16. Braim, *Test of Battle*, 83.

17. Paschall, *Defeat of Imperial Germany, 1917–1918*, 171.

18. Gilbert, *First World War*, 457.

19. Ibid.; Coffman, *War to End All Wars*, 268.

20. Gilbert, *First World War*, 457; Coffman, *War to End All Wars*, 269–70; Paschall, *Defeat of Imperial Germany, 1917–1918*, 173.

21. Paschall, *Defeat of Imperial Germany, 1917–1918*, 170 and 173.

22. Laurence Stallings, *The Doughboys* (New York: Harper and Row, 1963), 215; Cushing, *From a Surgeon's Journal*, 439 ("raw, cold, rainy").

23. Greiss, ed., *Great War*, 161.

24. Braim, *Test of Battle*, 85.

25. Ibid., 11–12.

26. Greiss, ed., *Great War*, 161.

27. Paschall, *Defeat of Imperial Germany, 1917–1918*, 178–79; Stallings, *Doughboys*, 213–14; Holt and Holt, *Battlefields of the First World War*, 143.

28. Greiss, ed., *Great War*, 161.

29. Braim, *Test of Battle*, 86.

30. Paschall, *Defeat of Imperial Germany, 1917–1918*, 170; Braim, *Test of Battle*, 84; Emerson G. Taylor, *New England in France, 1917–1919: A History of the Twenty-sixth Division U.S.A.* (Boston: Houghton Mifflin, 1920), 213.

31. Taylor, *New England in France*, 217; James T. Duane, *Dear Old "K"* (Boston: Thomas Todd, 1922), 111–12.

32. Taylor, *New England in France*, 213–15.

33. Orders No. 40, Headquarters, 101st Sanitary Train, 31 August 1918. NA RG120.

34. Stanley J. Herzog, *The Fightin' Yanks* (Stamford, Conn.: Cunningham, 1922), 123–24.

35. Duane, *Dear Old "K,"* 112.

36. Ibid.; Stallings, *Doughboys*, 215.

37. Herzog, *Fightin' Yanks*, 125–26.

38. Cushing, *From a Surgeon's Journal*, 435; Alex Chadwick, *Illustrated History of Baseball* (New York: Bison, 1988), 37–38 (twenty-nine and two-thirds consecutive scoreless innings in World Series play).

39. Paschall, *Defeat of Imperial Germany, 1917–1918*, 177; Duane, *Dear Old "K,"* 114–15; Holt and Holt, *Battlefields of the First World War*, 145.

40. Paschall, *Defeat of Imperial Germany, 1917–1918*, 177.

41. Cushing, *From a Surgeon's Journal*, 437; Taylor, *New England in France*, 217; Frank P. Sibley, *With the Yankee Division in France* (Boston: Little, Brown, 1919), 210.

42. Braim, *Test of Battle*, 77–78.

43. Stallings, *Doughboys*, 212–13.

44. Toland, *No Man's Land*, 418.

45. Coffman, *War to End All Wars*, 277; Herzog, *Fightin' Yanks*, 123.

46. Paschall, *Defeat of Imperial Germany, 1917–1918*, 177.

47. Ibid.; Daniel W. Strickland, *Connecticut Fights: The Story of the 102nd Regiment* (New Haven, Conn.: Quinnipiack Press, 1930), 221–23.

48. Duane, *Dear Old "K,"* 119.

49. Herzog, *Fightin' Yanks,* 124–25.

50. Duane, *Dear Old "K,"* 119–20.

51. Coffman, *War to End All Wars,* 304.

52. Greiss, ed., *Great War,* 162.

53. Sibley, *With the Yankee Division in France,* 287–89; Frederick E. Jones, *Historical Sketch of the Medical Department of the 26th Division* (typescript, n.d., with "Introductory Note" and other comments by R. S. Porter, 8 August 1919), 34; Taylor, *New England in France,* 234–40; Memorandum for Assistant Chief of Staff G-1 from Office of the Division Surgeon, 26th Division, 25 September 1918. NA RG120.

54. Coffman, *War to End All Wars,* 281; Herzog, *Fightin' Yanks,* 125–26.

55. Duane, *Dear Old "K,"* 120.

56. Stallings, *Doughboys,* 212.

57. Paschall, *Defeat of Imperial Germany, 1917–1918,* 178–80.

58. Eben Putnam, *Report of the Commission of Massachusetts' Part in the World War,* vol. 1, *History* (Boston: Commonwealth of Massachusetts, 1931), 141.

59. Orders No. 41, Headquarters, 101st Sanitary Train, 3rd Sept., 1918. NA RG120.

60. Putnam, *Report of the Commission,* 141.

61. Orders No. 40, Headquarters, 101st Sanitary Train, 31 August 1918, Para. I.4. and II.7.2. NA RG120.

62. Duane, *Dear Old "K,"* 125; Orders No. 40, Headquarters, 101st Sanitary Train, 31 August 1918. NA RG120.

63. Ernest H. Hinrichs, *Listening In* (Shippensburg, Penn.: White Mane, 1996), 59. Emphasis added.

64. John Laffin, *Panorama of the Western Front* (London: Grange Books, 1994), plate XI, 86–91.

65. Jones, *Historical Sketch,* 30–31.

66. Putnam, *Report of the Commission,* 141; Jones, *Historical Sketch,* 30.

67. R. S. Porter, Memorandum for A.C. of S., G-1, 10 Sept. 1918. NA RG120.

68. Orders No. 44, Headquarters, 101st Sanitary Train, 10th Sept., 1918. NA RG120.

69. Paul Waterman, *Report* (re: operation of 101st Sanitary Train, 11–15, September 1918), Sec. IX. NA RG120.

70. Ibid., Sec. I; Memorandum to Commanding Officer, 101st Sanitary Train from the Office of the Division Surgeon, 6 September 1918. NA RG120.

71. Charles Lynch, ed., *The Medical Department of the United States Army in the World War,* vol. 8, *Field Operations* (Washington, D.C.: GPO, 1925), 502.

72. Ibid., 501.

73. Table 36, Tables of Organization, U.S. Army, May 3, 1917 as shown in ibid., 1057.

74. Waterman, Report, Secs. III and V; Jones, Historical Sketch, 31.

75. Report, Commanding Officer, Provisional Truck Co. to Commanding Officer, 101st Sanitary Train, 18 Sept. 1918. NA RG120.

76. Orders No. 55, Headquarters, 101st Sanitary Train, 21st Sept., 1918; Memorandum for C.O. 101st Sanitary Train From Office of Division Surgeon, 21 Sept., 1918. But see Memorandum from Lieutenant Colonel Porter to Major Dolan (perhaps town major) dated September 20, 1918, where he requests, at the direction of G-1, that the mayor's office and attached buildings, as well as three barracks, be reserved for use by the 103rd Field Hospital upon vacation by the French. Obviously the plans changed overnight. NA RG120.

77. Memorandum for Assistant Chief of Staff G-1 from Office of the Division Surgeon, 26th Division, 25 September 1918. NA RG120.

78. Jones, *Historical Sketch,* 34–35; Taylor, *New England in France,* 234–35.

79. Orders No. 57, HQ, 101st Sanitary Train, 29th Sept., 1918. NA RG120.

80. Station List, Sheet #4, 103 Field Hospital; and History 101 Field Hospital Co., 101 San. Train, 26th Division, Part 6, 1. NA RG120.

81. Station List, Sheet #4, 103 Field Hospital. NA RG120.

82. Orders No. 40, Headquarters, 101st Sanitary Train, 31 August 1918. NA RG120.

83. Memorandum for Assistant Chief of Staff, G-1 from Office of the Chief Surgeon, 26th Division, 4th Sept., 1918. NA RG120.

84. Lyn Macdonald, *The Roses of No Man's Land* (New York: Macmillan, 1989), 133.

85. Memorandum from Division Surgeon to C.O. 101st Sanitary Train, 6 Sept. 1918. See also Report of Major William H. Blanchard (n.d.). NA RG120.

86. Orders No. 40, HQ, 101st Sanitary Train, 10th Sept., 1918 (16:30 o'clock), para. II. NA RG120.

87. Memorandum from Division Surgeon to C.O. 101 Sanitary Train, 10 September 1918; Station List, Sheet #4. NA RG120.

88. Memo from Office of Division Surgeon, 26th Division to C.O. 101st Sanitary Train, 2 September 1918. NA RG120.

89. Memo to Commanding Officer 101st Sanitary Train from H.Q. Field Hospital Section, 6 September 1918. NA RG120.

90. Taylor, *New England in France,* 232–33.

91. William H. Blanchard, Memo to C.O. 101 Sanitary Train, 15 Sept 1918 (handwritten); William H. Blanchard, Report (n.d.). (Apparently, orders were received to move on 13 September, but evidence indicates that the actual move took place during the evening of 14 September.) See also Paul Waterman, Report (n.d.). NA RG120.

92. Memorandum from Office of the Division Surgeon to C.O. 101st Sanitary Train, Sept. 21, 1918; Orders No. 7, HQ, Field Hospital Section, 101st Sanitary Train, 22nd September, 1918, para. 2. NA RG120.

93. Orders No. 55, Headquarters, 101st Sanitary Train, 21st Sept., 1918, Para.I.1. See also Orders No. 40, HQ, 101st Sanitary Train, August 1918, para. III. 3. NA RG120.

94. Orders No. 7, Headquarters, Field Hospital Section, 101st Sanitary Train, 22 September 1918; Station List, Sheet #5, 103rd Field Hospital. NA RG120.

95. History Field Hospital Company 101–101 Sanitary Train, 26th Division, Part 6, 3. NA RG120.

96. Ibid.

97. Memorandum for Assistant Chief of Staff G-1 from the Office of the Division Surgeon, 25 September, 1918. NA RG120.

98. Weekly Report of Sick and Injured 103rd Field Hospital (Form 211) for the weeks ending September 3, 11, 18, and 25, 1918. NA RG120.

99. Weekly Medical Reports, Serious Cases, 103rd Field Hospital, Notre Dame de Palameix [sic] 28 September and 5 October, 1918. NA RG120.

100. Clifford W. Renth, *Report of Duties, 18 October 1918, par. 8.* NA RG120.

101. Return of the Enlisted Force of the Medical Department, 103rd Field Hospital, 26th Division, American Expeditionary Forces, September 30, 1918. NA RG120.

Cpl. Edward J. Shay, *left*, and his brother Sgt. Frank H. Shay. On leave at Issodoun, February 26, 1919. Courtesy of Paul R. Shay.

Sgt. Fred Stephen Murphy. Framingham, Massachusetts, circa August 1917. Courtesy of Paul R. Shay.

Second Lt. John W. Gleason. Author's collection.

Pvt. Edward J. Shay, *far right*, with members of the 2nd Mass. Field Hospital, Camp McGuinness, Framingham, Massachusetts, Summer 1917. Courtesy of Paul R. Shay.

Pvt. Shay, *left*, with another member of the 2nd Mass. Field Hospital, Camp McGuinness, Summer 1917. Courtesy of Paul R. Shay.

Col. James Lung Bevans, original division surgeon. Courtesy of Still Pictures Branch, National Archives and Records Administration.

"Kitchen Canaries." Members of 2nd Mass. Field Hospital, Camp McGuinness, Summer 1917. Courtesy of Paul R. Shay.

Pvt. Shay, *right*, and buddy believed to be James J. Quinn ("Quinnie") on banks of the Marne at Luzancy, August 1918. Author's collection.

Front view of Base Hospital No. 17 at Dijon, September 1918. Courtesy of U.S. Army Military History Institute.

Flag Raising Stars and Stripes also Red Cross Flag
Base Hospital N° 17 — A. B P.
France (Nov 25 1917)

Flag raising at Base Hospital No. 17, November 25, 1917. The 103rd Field Hospital Company is in row closest to main building. Author's collection.

Inside a hospital ward at Base Hospital No. 17, built with the help of the 103rd Field Hospital Company, September 1918. Courtesy of U.S. Army Military History Institute.

Several hospital wards behind Base Hospital No. 17, September 1918. Courtesy of U.S. Army Military History Institute.

First Lt. Edward B. Sheehan, *left* (later with the 103rd Field Hospital), with patient on a wheeled litter in the Toul sector, May 31, 1918. Courtesy of Still Pictures Branch, National Archives and Records Administration.

Bessoneau tents, Evacuation Hospital No. 1 at Caserne Sebastopol in the Toul sector, May 7, 1918. Courtesy of Still Pictures Branch, National Archives and Records Administration.

Inside Bessoneau tent ward at Caserne Sebastopol, May 7, 1918. Courtesy of Still Pictures Branch, National Archives and Records Administration.

Motorized Medical Corps, 101st Ammunition Train at La Ferté-sous-Jouarre, July 9, 1918, with portable medical/dental equipment like Dr. Renth of 103rd Field Hospital would use. Courtesy of Still Pictures Branch, National Archives and Records Administration.

The "Cootie Machine." One of Yankee Division's Thresh-Foden disinfestors, August 10, 1918. Courtesy of Still Pictures Branch, National Archives and Records Administration.

Tent hospital of 79th Division at Notre Dame de Palameix, October 17, 1918. (The 103rd Field Hospital had occupied the same location until October 7.) Courtesy of U.S. Army Military History Institute.

Exhausted ambulance driver from 102nd Ambulance Company near Samogneux, in the Neptune sector, at rest following a fourteen-hour shift, October 27, 1918. Courtesy of Still Pictures Branch, National Archives and Records Administration.

Bow of RMS *Canada* following launch, May 14, 1896. Courtesy of Harland & Wolff Photographic Collection, © National Museums & Galleries of Northern Ireland, Ulster Folk & Transport Museum (#H43). Reprinted with permission.

SS *Winifredian* at outfitting jetty at delivery, July 1899. Courtesy of Harland & Wolff Photographic Collection, © National Museums & Galleries of Northern Ireland, Ulster Folk & Transport Museum (#H405). Reprinted with permission.

103rd FIELD HOSPITAL, 26th DIVISION
FOURTH TRAINING AREA
(NEUFCHÂTEAU)
OCTOBER 1917 and FEBRUARY 1918

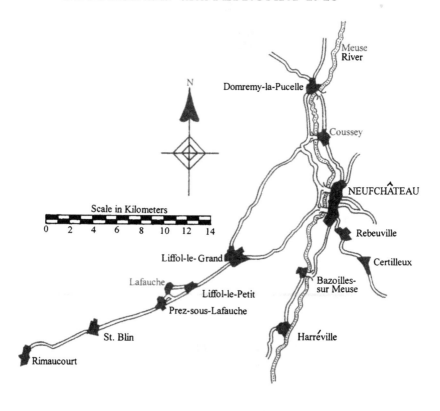

DIJON - BASE HOSPITAL #17
103rd FIELD HOSPITAL, 26th DIVISION
NOVEMBER 1917 - FEBRUARY 1918

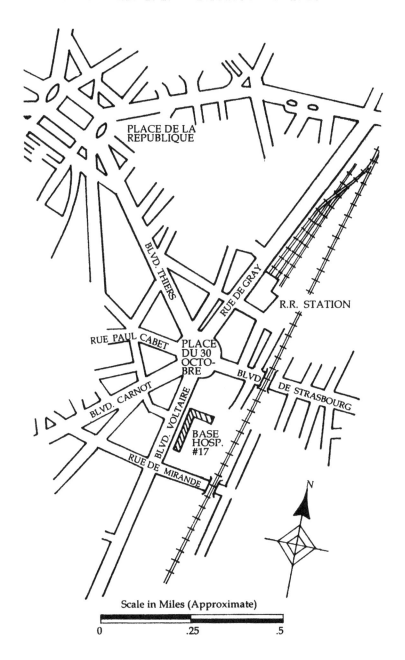

PLACE DE LA REPUBLIQUE

BLVD. THIERS

RUE DE GRAY

R.R. STATION

RUE PAUL CABET

PLACE DU 30 OCTO-BRE

BLVD

DE STRASBOURG

BLVD. CARNOT

BLVD. VOLTAIRE

BASE HOSP. #17

RUE DE MIRANDE

N

Scale in Miles (Approximate)

0   .25   .5

103rd FIELD HOSPITAL, 26th DIVISION
CHEMIN des DAMES SECTOR
FEBRUARY - MARCH 1918

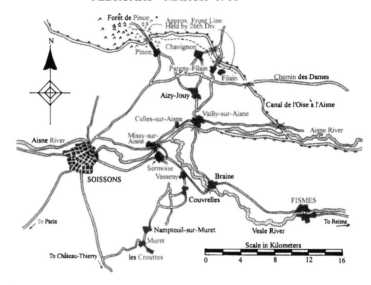

103rd FIELD HOSPITAL, 26th DIVISION
LA REINE and BOUCQ SECTOR (TOUL)   APRIL - JUNE 1918

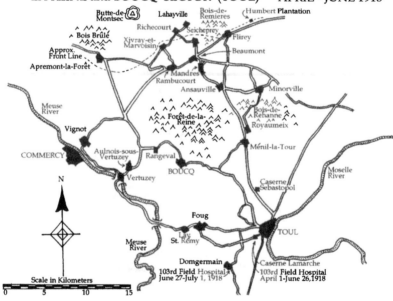

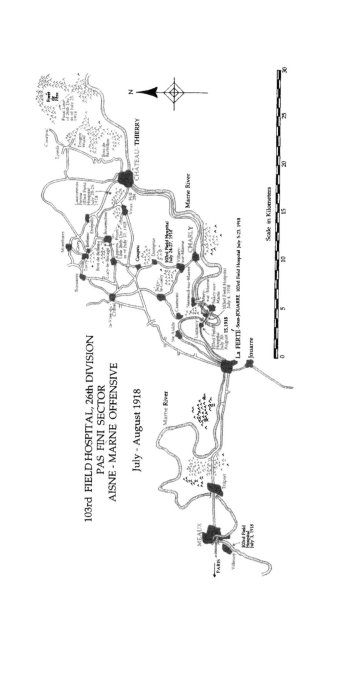

103rd FIELD HOSPITAL, 26th DIVISION
PAS FINI SECTOR
AISNE - MARNE OFFENSIVE

July - August 1918

Scale in Kilometers

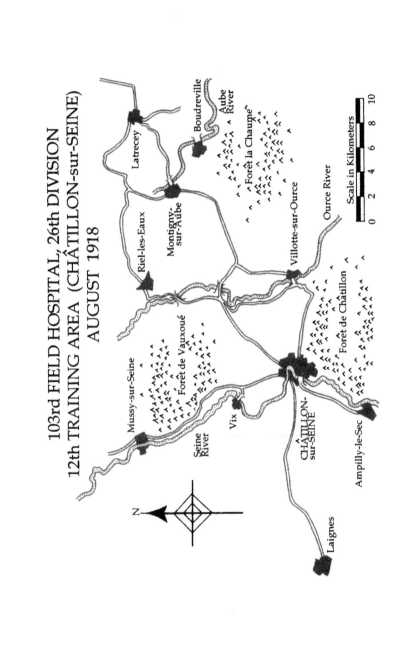

103rd FIELD HOSPITAL, 26th DIVISION
12th TRAINING AREA (CHÂTILLON-sur-SEINE)
AUGUST 1918

Scale in Kilometers

0   2   4   6   8   10

N

Latrecey

Boudreville

Aube River

Forêt la Chaume

Riel-les-Eaux

Montigny-sur-Aube

Villotte-sur-Ource

Ource River

Mussy-sur-Seine

Forêt de Vauxoué

Forêt de Châtillon

Vix

Seine River

CHÂTILLON-sur-SEINE

Ampilly-le-Sec

Laignes

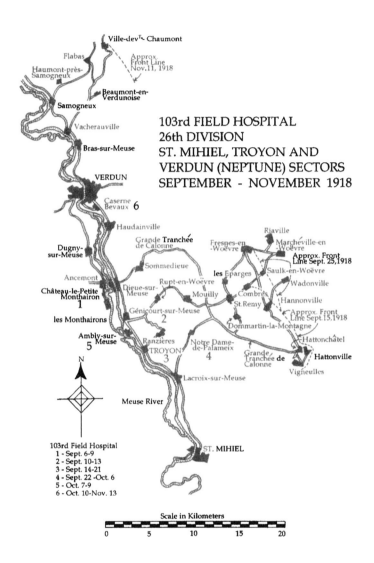

Ville-dev^{T←} Chaumont

Flabas

Haumont-près-
Samogneux

Approx.
Front Line
Nov.11, 1918

Beaumont-en-
Verdunoise

Samogneux

Vacherauville

Bras-sur-Meuse

VERDUN

Caserne
Bevaux **6**

Haudainville

Riaville

Dugny-
sur-Meuse

Grande **Tranchée**
de Calonne

Fresnes-en
-Woëvre

Marchéville-en
-Woëvre

Approx. Front
Line Sept. 25,1918

Ancemont

Sommedieue

les Éparges

Saulk-en-Woëvre

Château-le-Petite
Monthairon **1**

Dieue-sur-
Meuse

Rupt-en-Woëvre

Mouilly

Wadonville

Combres

St.Remy

Hannonville

Génicourt-sur-Meuse **2**

Approx. Front
Line Sept.15,1918

les Monthairons

Ambly-sur-
5 Meuse

Ranzières

TROYON
3

Notre Dame-
de-Palameix

Dommartin-la-Montagne

Hattonchâtel

4

Grande
Tranchée **de**
Calonne

Hattonville

N

Lacroix-sur-Meuse

Vigneulles

Meuse River

103rd FIELD HOSPITAL
26th DIVISION
ST. MIHIEL, TROYON AND
VERDUN (NEPTUNE) SECTORS
SEPTEMBER - NOVEMBER 1918

103rd Field Hospital
1 - Sept. 6-9
2 - Sept. 10-13
3 - Sept. 14-21
4 - Sept. 22 -Oct. 6
5 - Oct. 7-9
6 - Oct. 10-Nov. 13

ST. MIHIEL

Scale in Kilometers

0   5   10   15   20

103rd FIELD HOSPITAL, 26th DIVISION
8th TRAINING AREA (MONTIGNY-le-ROI)
NOVEMBER 1918 - JANUARY 1919

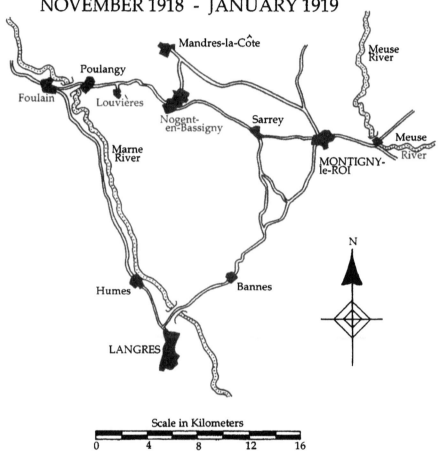

Mandres-la-Côte

Meuse River

Poulangy

Foulain

Louvières

Nogent-en-Bassigny

Sarrey

Meuse River

Marne River

MONTIGNY-le-ROI

N

Humes

Bannes

LANGRES

Scale in Kilometers

0   4   8   12   16

103rd FIELD HOSPITAL, 26th DIVISION
LE MANS EMBARKATION AREA
FEBRUARY - MARCH 1919

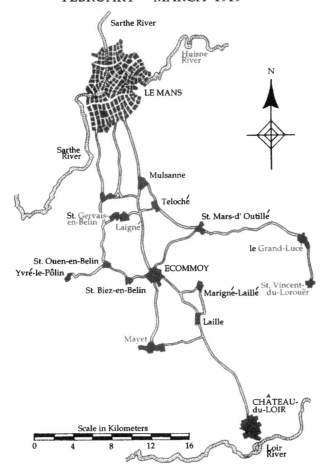

103rd FIELD HOSPITAL, 26TH DIVISION
BREST AND CAMP PONTANEZEN
MARCH - APRIL 1919

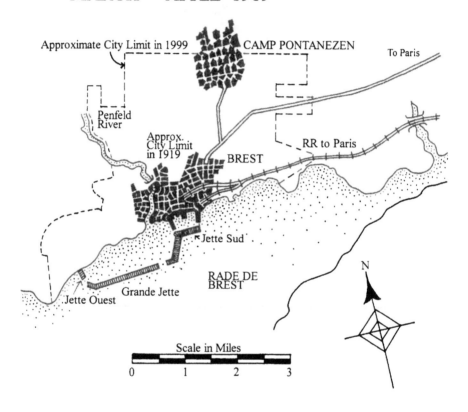

Approximate City Limit in 1999   CAMP PONTANEZEN   To Paris

Penfeld
River

Approx.
City Limit
in 1919   BREST

RR to Paris

Jette Sud

RADE DE
BREST

Grande Jette

Jette Ouest

N

Scale in Miles

0   1   2   3

Chapter Seven

The Tough Get Going
(Troyon Sector)

It seemed as though every truck and battery in France was trying to get to the same front by the same road that I was going.
—Capt. Harry S. Truman

The Americans have got to learn sometime. They are learning now, rapidly.
—Marshal Ferdinand Foch

THE SEAWALL (OCTOBER 1918)

Western Front—Allies

By October there were nearly 2,000,000 Americans in France.[1] On October 4, the Germans appealed to Wilson for an armistice, an appeal that, although rejected, was the beginning of a series of similar exchanges.[2] U.S. divisions were scattered up and down the line, some with the British and French, but most were with the American forces. The status of their equipment and the sufficiency of support troops were question marks; Allied emphasis upon infantrymen and machine gunners had left the newly arrived divisions with a lot of gaps.[3] Of more consequence was the state of their training. The divisions entering France no longer received the rigorous, staged training that the first four divisions had. Time and the military situation would not permit it. Consequently, many soldiers complained that they had never even fired a weapon in training—this on the eve of being thrust into combat.[4] In spite of these deficiencies, with few exceptions the American divisions performed well.[5]

A case in point was the attack on the Hindenburg Line at the St. Quentin Canal Tunnel. There, on September 29, 1918, the 27th and 30th Divisions, as part of the British Fourth Army, jumped off in a corps under the command of Australian general John Monash. Both U.S. units were National Guard divisions. The first was made up of New York soldiers under Gen. John F. O'Ryan. The latter consisted of men from the Carolinas and Tennessee and had the nickname "Old Hickory" Their division commander was Gen. Edward M. Lewis. The Americans were assigned the sector that included the tunnel complex. Their advance was swift—so swift, in fact, that having overrun the tunnel they found the still resisting Germans emerging from the ground at their rear. Their energy and inexperience had got them in over their heads; the attackers became the attacked. The Australians relieved them and completed the push on October 2. They went on to seize Beaurevoir between October 3 and 5, and in turn they were relieved by the "rested" Americans on October 6. Later on October 17, along with the rest of the British Fourth Army, the two divisions forced a crossing of the Selle River and began an offensive that lasted through October 25. That attack, and their earlier efforts at the St. Quentin Tunnel were not without a heavy price. By the time of their final relief on October 20, the divisions had between them more than 13,000 casualties. On September 29, the 107th Infantry Regiment alone suffered more than a thousand casualties, which amounted to 50% of its assault forces. According to historian Edward Coffman, this was the highest one-day loss of any American regiment in World War I. As a testament to such heroism, more medals of honor were awarded to the 30th Division than to any other division that saw service in France.[6]

All along the line during the month of October there was constant Allied activity. British cavalry saw action at the Second Battle of Le Cateau on October 6 through 12.[7] On a twenty-mile-wide front at the Somme, the British, with the assistance of some American units, fought and won the Second Battle of Cambrai on October 8 and 9.[8] In Flanders, another offensive at Ypres, this one more successful, was concluded on October 2.[9] Also, the Battle at Courtrai was fought between 14 and 19 October.[10] However, it was the American offensive in the Meuse-Argonne that was to garner the most attention. It was, as the title of Paul F. Braim's study suggests, the "test of battle" for the Americans.

Western Front, AEF: Meuse Argonne—Tough Slogging

Pershing's goals in the Argonne were ambitious—too ambitious by far, as it turned out. He envisioned a breakthrough of ten miles within twenty-four hours, all along the front.[11] Within ten days after his success at St. Mihiel, he had to turn his army north and be prepared to attack.[12] To some, it was a miracle that the troops ever got to the Meuse-Argonne in time. Supply was a very real problem; material and troops had to fight their way to the front lines along the inadequate French road net, all the while competing with the steady flow of wounded toward the rear.[13] Along the twenty-mile front, from west to east, lay the Argonne Forest, the valley of the River Aire, the looming height of Montfaucon, and the Heights of the

Meuse.[14] Thirty-seven divisions, some French but mostly American, were to take part in the offensive. They were to be supported by 700 tanks.[15]

The attack, which began in the early hours of September 26 after a massive bombardment by 2,700 guns, was still bogged down short of its goal when the month of October opened.[16] Elements of the 77th Division were surrounded and trapped in the Argonne Forest, having advanced with their flanks "in the air;" the French on their left had just not kept up. They became the celebrated "Lost Battalion" of legend, and they emerged from the woods much depleted in numbers.[17] (Their commander, Charles Whittlesey, a Wall Street lawyer turned soldier, would be awarded the Congressional Medal of Honor, but the memory would haunt him; he eventually took his own life, jumping overboard while on a cruise.)[18] Elsewhere, the 79th and 37th Divisions were having a rough go at Montfaucon. The mountain, with the adjoining village of the same name, stood astride the main attack route. For years, this height had been an important artillery and observation post for the Germans. In fact, from time to time the crown prince himself had visited to have a look at the front. (Today, a tall monument stands on the hilltop dominating and overshadowing the ruins of an ancient church also inhabiting the site.) The Americans finally captured the position, with heavy loss of life, after two days of bitter fighting.[19]

It was at this time that Sgt. Alvin York, conscientious objector turned soldier, earned everlasting fame and a Medal of Honor as a member of the 82nd Division, when he singlehanded killed twenty-eight Germans and captured 132 more near the town of Chatel-Chéhéry.[20] Capt. (later President) Harry S. Truman and his artillery battery, a part of the 35th Division, a National Guard unit, provided fire support for the offensive.[21] Also among those destined to be famous was Lt. Col. George S. Patton, Jr., who was severely wounded in action as he led a tank attack in support of the 35th Division near Cheppy.[22]

Patton, anxious to make a good showing in the first outing of his tank corps on the eve of St. Mihiel, exhorted his men with a hint of the hyperbole for which he would later be famed:

No tank is to be surrendered or abandoned to the enemy. If you are left alone in the midst of the enemy keep shooting. If your gun is disabled use your pistols and squash the enemy with your tracks. . . . AMERICAN TANKS DO NOT SURRENDER.[23]

Two weeks later, one of his young junior officers took those words to heart in the bitter fighting in the Argonne. For his "extraordinary heroism" under fire, twenty-five-year-old 2nd Lt. John William "Jack" Gleason was awarded the Distinguished Service Cross, the nation's second-highest decoration. On September 26, 1918, as a new second lieutenant, the intrepid Gleason led his tank platoon against machinegun and antitank positions at Cheppy; when his tanks ground to a halt, he continued to lead on foot through a minefield, under heavy fire. At Montrebeau Woods on September 28, he again led his platoon against heavy fire, and as if that were not enough, he took charge of a battalion of infantry and placed it in the positions he had just captured. Finally, on October 4, near Exermont, twice wounded, he refused to obey orders to go to the rear and continued to lead his men.[24] Patton received the same award for his actions at Cheppy.[25]

The advances toward the Kriemhilde Stellung (another name for the Hindenburg Line at this point) were uneven. Some units reached this interim goal on or about October 14, after much bitter fighting, while others took until the end of the month.[26] The line was relatively lightly manned at the start of the offensive, but the Germans were able to shift more men to this vital area over the next several weeks.[27] Four years of occupation had allowed them time to build a formidable series of defensive lines, named for the Valkyries of Wagnerian fame. The wooded, hilly terrain, cut by numerous valley streams and served by only a few, twisting roads, proved ideal for defense, a skill the Germans had honed to near perfection.[28] Allied casualties mounted to nearly ten times the number of dead and wounded at St. Mihiel. The Americans, many fighting in their very first engagement had developed neither the skills necessary to survive in battle nor the tactics that would have enabled them to take the numerous strong points and machinegun nests they encountered without undue loss of life.[29]

Pershing was frustrated, and many commanders, including high-ranking division commanders, lost their positions. The specter of Blois reared its ugly head.[30] Time was not the ally of the American soldier, and in the end it was only the sheer numbers of fresh men, unjaded by years of war, that carried the day.[31]

26TH DIVISION: IN ANOTHER PART OF THE FOREST

The Yankee Division did not take a direct part in the initial assault on the Argonne front. Headquarters felt that the division could be put to better use in diversionary attacks against the German troops just south of Verdun, perhaps sustaining the idea that Metz remained an important Allied objective.[32] As October dawned, plans were implemented for the division to be relieved by the 79th Division. Unit by unit, the division was moved out of line and set in motion northward toward Verdun. The line of march was on the west side of the Meuse, where the Yankees came under the command of the French 17th Corps, in the Neptune sector which included the infamous Morte-Homme.[33] While in Neptune sector the division participated in raids and attacks designed to secure the high ground on the east side of the Meuse. It was described by some as a meatgrinder, in which both French and American troops were constantly fed into line against well-entrenched positions without regard to casualties, simply to tie the Germans down.[34] These actions were, however, the key to the success of the main thrust on the west side of the river.[35]

On October 6, the 104th Infantry Regiment was treated to a bath and delousing, the men's first real bath in three months. This was just one day before they hit the road northward to Douai, on the Meuse. The next night they were settled in an old French artillery compound known as Faubourg Pava, on the outskirts of the ancient fortress city of Verdun.[36] On October 17, the 104th Infantry Regiment moved into the front lines. It had a rendezvous in a ravine called "Death Valley," near the town of Samogneux.[37]

Verdun stood on the site of a significant pre-Roman town, called Verodunum. Like Toul, the city is encircled by ancient walls, with bastions and fortified gates. Of the latter, only the Porte Chausse on the northeast side in 1918 had escaped significant damage from heavy, nearly incessant shelling. The Meuse River and the Canal de l'Est both flow through the middle of the city. At this point, the north-ward-flowing river coils serpentlike into a series of curves. The heights on both sides are set somewhat back, thus creating a small plain. The city was ringed by a number of forts, all occupying the high ground.[38] A medic, Frederick Pottle, on leave from Evacuation Hospital No. 8 just after the armistice, describes his experience walking through its streets:

Verdun is entirely enclosed by walls, the only entrances being through massive gate-ways. . . . We entered from the northern side. The destruction in this quarter was complete; the houses mere heaps of rubble, with occasionally chimneys or angles of walls standing up like ragged obelisks. . . . A shell had exploded in the street, laying open a huge vaulted passageway beneath it. . . . We passed along a street houses, the fronts of which looked comparatively uninjured. As we passed the open entrances, however, we saw that the roofs were entirely gone, and that the debris had run in rivers down the wide stairways.[39]

Pottle and his companions explored the bombed-out ruins of the Ecclesiastical Seminary with its library and museum, the wrecked railway station, and countless other buildings in a similar state.

The headquarters of the division was on the west side of the Meuse in the old citadel designed by Vauban and built over the site of a tenth-century abbey. Chambers deep within the walls of this fortress contained workshops, bakeries, barracks, and other amenities; they were the only areas of the city that were immune from the daily shelling.[40] On October 18 Edwards would move his headquarters forward to Bras. There, in a dugout in an embankment beneath the abutment of a ruined bridge, he would direct the fighting that was to come.[41]

While the men of the 104th Infantry were bathing on October 6, elements of the 102nd Infantry were being relieved by their counterparts in the 79th Division and some French units. On the night of the 7th, the regiment moved to Ranzières, northeast of Troyon, and by October 9 they were settled in and about Verdun. It was their turn for a brief rest, which included bathing, delousing, and refitting. They moved to the front line near Samogneux between October 16 and 18.[42]

During the night of October 10–11, the 51st Artillery Brigade was relieved by the 154th Artillery Brigade of the 79th Division. While the unit was waiting to move out, two men were killed and three wounded by German artillery fire. The brigade moved first to Rupt-en-Woëvre; the next day it marched north around Verdun to Baleycourt, where the men pitched tents in a wood to await further orders. On October 17 it too had moved to support the coming division offensive and took up positions in the Ravine de Vacherauville. All told, the artillerymen spent twenty-five days in the Neptune sector. The constant fighting was not without losses. During that time the brigade lost eight 75 mm guns and two 155s, either by direct hits or premature bursts.

Heavy rains during the night of October 18–19 resulted in many men in the 104th Infantry waking up in puddles of water. October 21 was used to reconnoiter the new front prior to a move the next day to Wavrille.[43] From October 23 through 29, when it was relieved, the 51st Infantry Brigade (101st and 102nd Infantry), along with the 104th Infantry and with support from the 51st Artillery Brigade, was engaged in a series of fights in an area of well-fortified hills and ravines. Place-names like Bois d'Haumont, Bois d'Ormont, and Bois des Caures became part of the lexicon of the Yankee Division during the waning weeks of the war.[44] Michael J. Perkins won the Medal of Honor posthumously; singlehanded, he captured a pillbox and silenced seven German machine guns, only to be killed when an ambulance transporting him to the rear for treatment of his wounds took a direct hit.[45] The next few days were characterized by attack and counterattack. The 104th Infantry suffered so many casualties that the second and third battalions had to be consolidated. At the start of the attack on the October 23, the two battalions were 600 men strong; by the time it was finished, they had been reduced to 258 men and three officers.[46] Although it was already theirs in all but name, official control over Neptune sector was transferred to the Yankee Division on October 30 by Field Order No. 97.[47]

As if the losses from the fighting were not enough, the 26th Division was now to suffer perhaps its greatest single blow. It had been clear for a long time that General Edwards was not in the good graces of Pershing and his staff, particularly Gen. Hunter Liggett, and his chief of staff, Malin Craig. The relief of Edwards was most likely the result of the cumulative effect of prior incidents and of attitudes that had not improved over time. There had been a certain inevitability once Liggett took over command of the First Army, of which the division was a part, and it was only a matter of time before he found an excuse to relieve Edwards. His opportunity came, ironically, with a communication from General Edwards himself, imparting certain information regarding German activities gleaned by a couple of his men while fraternizing with some German soldiers. Fraternization was definitely forbidden, but it had long been a custom on the western front, and the order was generally observed in the breach.

Liggett seized upon this breach, and by orders dated October 22 he sent Edwards packing as of October 24, with the sop that he was being sent home to train more soldiers.[48] This was a double blow to the general, who less than a week before had received news that his beloved daughter Bessie, his only child, had died of influenza at Camp Meade while in training to be an army nurse.[49] His troops did not buy the business about training and never forgave Liggett or Pershing. The latter, who he had lost his own wife and three daughters in that tragic fire in 1915, might easily have sympathized with Edwards' loss but chose instead to support his immediate subordinate.[50] Edwards, good soldier that he was, went home knowing that the division he had formed, nurtured, and had taken through battle would not be his to bring home, now that the war was nearly over.[51] Brig. Gen. Frank E. Bamford assumed command; however, his tenure was to be short-lived.[52]

Sanitary Trains: "Death Valley Days"

Upon receipt of verbal orders from the division surgeon October 7, 1918, the units of the 101st Sanitary Train began their movement to a new sector. The assembly point for the field hospitals and the ambulance sections was the town of Ambly-sur-Meuse. The 103rd and 104th Field Hospitals were ordered to close and to make the move during daylight. The 101st Field Hospital was to follow. Lastly, the 102nd Field Hospital was to make preparation to move but to remain open until relieved by its counterpart in the 79th Division. All of the ambulance companies were ordered to move to the staging area under the cover of darkness, during the night and early morning hours of October 7–8. Train headquarters would be at Troyon.[53]

The movement of the first elements of the Train to the vicinity of Verdun in the Neptune Sector was to take place on October 8; it would occur in stages between the hours of 6 P.M. that day and 6 A.M. the next. It rained hard all that day,[54] as units of the Sanitary Train of the 79th Division began the relief of their counterparts in the 26th Division. Soon elements of the Sanitary Train were on the road north toward Verdun.[55] Among the first group to set out were the various headquarters, the Advanced Supply Unit, the 104th Field Hospital, and 101st and 102nd Ambulance Companies. Nineteen trucks were allocated to carry this group; Lieutenant Ruml was in charge of the move and acted as guide. The destination was the cluster of buildings known as "Beaulieu" at Caserne Bevaux, a complex of French military barracks similar to those at Toul, one or two kilometers southeast of the outskirts of Verdun. The convoy's route would take it through Génicourt-sur-Meuse, Rattentout, Ancemont-sur-Meuse, and Dugny. Road guards were drawn from the Ambulance Section and posted at crossings to direct the horse-drawn ambulance company and field hospital, which, understandably, moved more slowly. This section was also required to furnish transportation for the billeting party. After unloading, the trucks were to return immediately to pick up the next group. Headquarters issued an injunction that was more easily said than done, when the convoy was to take "all precautions . . . against hostile shelling of the roads."[56]

The next group to move consisted of the 101st and 102nd Field Hospitals, along with the 101st Ambulance Company and Evacuation Ambulance No. 6. Once again the movement was to take place at night, this time between 6:30 P.M. October 9 and 6 A.M. the next day. Twenty-four trucks were allocated for the move, and the drivers were enjoined from using their lights upon arrival at Caserne Bevaux. The night was cold.[57] This time, the commanding officer of the Provisional Truck Company would be in charge of the movement. Upon arrival, the trucks were to promptly unload and return to Ambly-sur-Meuse to transport the remaining units of the Train to Bevaux, including, the 103rd Field Hospital, the field and dental labs, the Medical Supply Unit, and the Provisional Truck Company itself.[58] So there would be no mistake, specific orders were issued regarding, among other things, security and road discipline. All personnel were to remain under cover during daylight. No lights were to be visible at night, so windows had to be "camouflaged." Gas masks were to be worn "suspended from the right shoulder" with the mask "hanging at . . . [the] . . . left hip." Guards were to be detailed to watch and listen for airplanes. Upon the approach of any aircraft, friendly or hostile, all movement was to cease.[59]

The 104th Ambulance Company continued another eight miles north to Samogneux, where it established under canvas a dressing station to serve the left side of the Yankee line. The men, totally unprotected from artillery fire, were put to work digging individual shelters. The ambulance heads were placed forward from the dressing station, the first at Haumont, five kilometers away, and the second in "Death Valley," a part of Neptune sector. Aptly named, it was virtually devoid of all vegetation after years of uninterrupted fighting. Due to the shellfire, the 104th Ambulance was forced to close its station and into reserve. From that point on, the dressing station established by the 102nd Ambulance Company five kilometers to the rear, served that function. It had a greater capacity to handle the wounded, and it was better protected. At the same time, a detachment from the 104th Field Hospital established a station for walking wounded at Vacherauville.[60]

The remainder of the Train proceeded to Caserne Bevaux.[61] The 103rd Ambulance Company was held in reserve at Caserne Bevaux, but its ambulances were utilized in the evacuation of wounded. At that same location, the 101st Field Hospital operated a facility for the division sick, while the 102nd Field Hospital operated a sorting station. However, the 101st Field Hospital had only just arrived at Caserne Bevaux when it received orders to proceed to Vacherauville to open a triage station. Evacuation by the Ambulance Section was to be to that point. The division psychiatrist and orthopedist, in addition to the Mobile De-Gassing Unit and the divisional medical gas officer, were sent to the 101st Field Hospital. The Provisional Truck Company was to arrange for transportation. It was to leave four trucks at that location, returning the balance to the truck park at Caserne Bevaux. In addition, the commanding officer of the Field Hospital Section was ordered to station a sufficient number of ambulances from Evacuation Company No. 1 at Vacherauville to transport seriously wounded patients to Evacuation Hospital No. 4 at Fromereville. The route of evacuation was through Bras, Charny, and Villers-lès-Moines Farm. The balance of the 104th Field Hospital was used as the gas hospital, and the 103rd Field Hospital was held in reserve.[62] In the event, the active hospitals were kept quite busy, due to the continuous fighting and to an influenza outbreak of epidemic proportions. During July the flu outbreak had been relatively mild, but this strain was deadly. Soon the hospitals were full of both sick and wounded.[63]

The nature of the division's mission and the geography of its sector combined to create serious problems for evacuation and treatment of the wounded. The division was right at the hinge of the German line, which was virtually a right angle at this point. Well entrenched on the high ground, now virtually devoid of cover, the enemy had an incentive to hold; a withdrawal of either leg of the line could jeopardize the other and result in the severance of the primary rail line bringing supplies and replacements from Germany.[64] Moreover, the American ambulances had to move to and from the front on a route parallel to it, as opposed to the usual perpendicular axis, and were thus exposed to shellfire for the entire transit. As a result, the ambulance companies suffered many casualties.[65] In addition, the Yankee Division as a whole suffered more and more casualties, 8,000 in the month of October alone, and it became readily apparent that the line companies could not continue to provide their usual complements of litter bearers and still fulfill their missions. In fact, the problem was exacerbated by the decision to reduce infantry-company strength from 250 men to 175.[66] As a result, the field hospital companies at Caserne Bevaux were called upon to send detachments of litter bearers to the front lines.[67]

103rd Field Hospital Company: "No Rest for the Weary"

The first of October found the men of the 103rd Field Hospital still stationed at Notre Dame de Palameix, in that desolate valley among the Heights of the Meuse. As of October 4, 1918, they had a new commanding officer, Capt. Leonard W. Hassett, and the following day would mark the first anniversary of their arrival in France.[68] On October 7 the unit was ordered to close its doors and move to Ambly-sur-Meuse. It arrived there later that day to await further orders. Two weeks earlier, anticipating just such a move, the division surgeon had ordered that as soon as the French had vacated Ambly-sur-Meuse, the 103rd Field Hospital was to occupy the mayor's office and adjoining buildings, along with three nearby barracks, to be used later as a hospital.[69] The stay, however, was short, and no field hospital was set up. Within two days, the unit was on its way to Caserne Bevaux, just outside Verdun.[70]

During its final week in the Troyon sector, the hospital continued to treat the sick and seriously wounded of the division as well as German prisoners and the French troops stationed nearby. The Weekly Medical Report, Serious Cases for the week ending October 5 disclosed a veritable United Nations:

O'Brien, Robert	Pvt. Co. E 104 Inf.	2 Oct 1918	G.S.W. Abdomen "S"
Quimby, George	Cpl. Co. E 103 Inf.	2 Oct 1918	G.S.W. Chest "S"
Cinel, Bernard (Fr.)	Pvt. 8th Co. 12th Cuiss.	2 Oct 1918	Fr. Skull "S"
Moraud, Charles C. (Fr.)	Not known	2 Oct 1918	G.S.W. R. Thigh "S"
Leve, Frederick (Ger.)	15th Co. 13th Div.	1 Oct 1918	G.S.W. Head & Face "S"[71]

All told, for the week ending October 2 twenty patients were admitted to the tent hospital, of which sixteen were wounded. Of the latter, six died, all of gunshot wounds. The next week was more of the same; six new patients were treated, five of whom were wounded. Seven more men died that week. The unit strength for the period was between eighty-two and eighty-three officers and enlisted men.[72]

Earlier, when the division first moved to the Troyon sector, it had been attached to the 2nd French Colonial Corps. This coupled it with, among other units, the 12th Cuirassiers, an elite cavalry unit, now dismounted and fighting as infantry—*cuirassiers à pied.* The name derived from their vestigial armor, a breastplate or cuirass. The cuirassiers' traditional uniform included a maned helmet, red pants, yellow buttons, and either a dark blue or black tunic, depending upon whether the soldier was an enlisted man or an officer. At first, the helmet had been covered with fabric while in the field. However, as the war progressed, these troops adopted a long version of the standard horizon-blue coat, with a dark blue collar patch and trouser piping. They also wore the typical "Adrian" helmet of the *poilu,* and they no longer carried swords. Their only remaining concession to tradition was the crimson collar numeral designating the unit, and a double chevron and epaulettes of the same color.[73]

Seriously wounded French cavalrymen were taken to the 103rd Field Hospital for treatment. Muddy and bloody from their service in the line, they were hardly distinguishable from regular infantry. Again, the reports tell the sad tale of young flesh and blood coming into contact with bullets, shrapnel, and other deadly missiles. To Lieutenant Colonel Porter devolved the task of informing the commanding general of the 2nd Division of Cavalry on Foot (French) that three members of the 12th Cuirassiers had died of their wounds in the 103rd Field Hospital. Edèle Sale and Alfred Malapean, both privates, died on October 3; the former died of a fractured skull, while the latter died of multiple gunshot wounds. The next day their comrade, Pvt. Louis Tesson, also died as a result of multiple gunshot wounds. In addition, Pvt. Jean Tirel of the 15th Cuirassiers was treated for a severe gunshot wound to the face; on October 2, Charles C. Moraud, unit unknown, was evacuated to the hospital suffering a serious gunshot wound in the right thigh.[74] The same day, Pvt. Bernard Cinel of the 12th Cuirassiers was treated for a serious skull fracture.[75] The outcome of these men's treatment is not known.

According to a report filed by the company commander, the 103rd Field Hospital arrived at Caserne Bevaux on October 10. It did not function there as an active unit but was designated as a reserve hospital. However, it did furnish details of men to assist at the gas treatment unit set up at the 104th Field Hospital as well as the sorting station at the 102nd Field Hospital. In addition, the men were responsible for policing the grounds. These had to have seemed very mundane tasks following the previous nine months of intense work.

The designation "in reserve" did not mean that the unit was totally inactive or unprepared to fill a void should the need arise. Quite the contrary, the unit was ordered to designate two surgical teams. In compliance, Captain Hassett formed the following:

Team No. 1
Lt. Edward B. Sheehan, operator
Lt. Roy F. Brown, assistant

Lt. Clifford W. Renth (DC), anesthetist

Team No. 2

Capt. Edwin Knowles, operator

Lt. Wm. S. Schley, assistant

Lt. Martin Westley, anesthetist[76]

However, the 103rd Field Hospital was not destined to act as an autonomous hospital unit in the Meuse-Argonne fight, as it had done virtually continuously since February in the Chemin des Dames sector. At first, men not on duty had the opportunity to visit nearby Verdun on a regular basis. This practice was soon halted due to the increasing casualties from the nearly constant shellfire. However, even Caserne Bevaux was not safe from German air activity or from shells that fell close by.[77] On October 29, 1st Lt. William S. Schley, who had been with the 103rd Field Hospital from its very early days, was transferred to the 101st Ambulance Company. His place was taken by 1st Lt. John W. Williams, who had been with the latter outfit.[78] The very next day, Capt. Frank W. Stevens of the 104th Field Hospital was appointed survey officer to investigate the loss of a bicycle by the 103rd Field Hospital; the bike had disappeared on August 10, while the unit was resting at Luzancy, three months earlier.[79]

NOTES

1. Paul Braim, *The Test of Battle: The American Expeditionary Forces in the Meuse-Argonne Campaign* (Newark: Univ. of Delaware Press, 1988), 144. See also Philip J. Haythornthwaite, *The World War One Source Book* (London: Arms and Armour, 1996), 309.

2. Martin Gilbert, *The First World War* (New York: Henry Holt, 1994), 474.

3. Braim, *Test of Battle*, 71.

4. Ibid., 57 and 96.

5. Ibid., 146–50. (good overall assessment of performance of U.S. infantry).

6. Edward M. Coffman, *The War to End All Wars: The American Military Experience in World War I* (Madison: Univ. of Wisconsin Press, 1986), 291–98.

7. Haythornthwaite, *World War One Source Book*, 57.

8. Ibid.; Gilbert, *First World War*, 475–76; Coffman, *War to End All Wars*, 363.

9. Haythornthwaite, *World War One Source Book*, 57.

10. Ibid.

11. Rod Paschall, *The Defeat of Imperial Germany, 1917–1918* (Chapel Hill, N.C.: Algonquin, 1989), 186; Coffman, *War to End All Wars*, 313.

12. Laurence Stallings, *The Doughboys* (New York: Harper and Row, 1963), 223; Tonie Holt and Valmai Holt, *Battlefields of the First World War* (London: Pavilion, 1993), 153.

13. Braim, *Test of Battle*, 108 and 150–51; Paschall, *Defeat of Imperial Germany, 1917–1918*, 182; John Toland, *No Man's Land* (New York: Konecky, 1980), 429; Tonie Holt and Valmai Holt, *Battlefields of the First World War*, 153 (three usable roads).

14. Thomas E. Greiss, ed., *The Great War* (Wayne, N.J.: Avery, 1986), 162; Paschall, *Defeat of Imperial Germany, 1917–1918*, 182 (three roads).

15. Braim, *Test of Battle*, 91.

16. Paschall, *Defeat of Imperial Germany, 1917–1918*, 184; Holt and Holt, *Battlefields of the First World War*, 153–54; Coffman, *War to End All Wars*, 307.

17. Greiss, ed., *Great War*, 162; Paschall, *Defeat of Imperial Germany, 1917–1918*, 188.

18. Stallings, *Doughboys*, 278–79.

19. Ibid., 225; Coffman, *War to End All Wars*, 307–10.

20. Ibid., 324; Paschall, *Defeat of Imperial Germany, 1917–1918*, 189; Gilbert, *First World War*, 475.

21. David McCullough, *Truman* (New York: Simon and Schuster, 1992), 129–31.

22. Carlo D'Este, *Patton: A Genius for War* (New York: HarperCollins, 1995), 259–60; Martin Blumenson, *Patton: The Man behind the Legend, 1885–1945* (New York: Quill, 1985), 112–14.

23. D'Este, *Patton*, 233.

24. Harry R. Stringer, *Heroes All!* (Washington, D.C.: Fassett, 1919), 164. John W. Gleason was born in Rutland, Massachusetts, of Irish stock. His paternal grandfather, Dennis, a famine immigrant from County Leix (then Queens), owned a large farm near Demond Pond. Jack's father, Michael, was a teamster. Likewise, his maternal grandfather, Daniel O'Leary, emigrated from County Waterford in the 1840s. He too earned his living as a farmer in Rutland, with a homestead on Pleasantdale Road. Prior to joining the army, Jack obtained a degree from Worcester Polytechnic Institute. Information from author's family history files.

25. D'Este, *Patton*, 277.

26. Greiss, ed., *Great War*, 162.

27. Braim, *Test of Battle*, 122.

28. Frank P. Sibley, *With the Yankee Divsion in France* (Boston: Little, Brown, 1919), 302–303; Toland, *No Man's Land*, 429.

29. Coffman, *War to End All Wars*, 299.

30. Ibid., 330; Emerson G. Taylor, *New England in France, 1917–1919: A History of the Twenty-sixth Division U.S.A.* (Boston: Houghton Mifflin, 1920), 270. See also Stars & Stripes, 23 August 1918, p. 2. USMA.

31. Paschall, *Defeat of Imperial Germany, 1917–1918*, 223 and 231; Braim, *Test of Battle*, 116.

32. See chapter 6.

33. Sibley, *With the Yankee Division in France*, 302 and 304–5.

34. Frederick E. Jones, *Historical Sketch of the Medical Department of the 26th Division* (typescript, n.d., with "Introductory Note" and other comments by R. S. Porter, 8 August 1919), 36. NA RG120.

35. Braim, *Test of Battle*, 123.

36. James T. Duane, *Dear Old "K"* (Boston: Thomas Todd, 1922), 122–24.

37. Ibid., 125; Harvey Cushing, *From a Surgeon's Journal* (Boston: Little, Brown, 1936), 304–307.

38. John Laffin, *Panorama of the Western Front* (London: Grange, 1996), 76–85; *Encyclopaedia Britannica*, 1959, s.v. "Verdun."

39. Frederick A. Pottle, *Stretchers: The Story of a Hospital Unit on the Western Front* (New Haven, Conn.: Yale Univ. Press, 1929), 272–75.

40. Cushing, *From a Surgeon's Journal*, 475; *Encyclopaedia Britannica,* 1959, s.v. "Verdun."

41. Sibley, *With the Yankee Division in France*, 306 and 311–312; Cushing, *From a Surgeon's Journal*, 475 ("Clarence Edwards and his staff living majestically in the Citadel").

42. Daniel W. Strickland, *Connecticut Fights: The Story of the 102nd Regiment* (New Haven, Conn.: Quinnipiack Press, 1930), 257 and 262–63.

43. Duane, *Dear Old "K,"* 126.

44. Strickland, *Connecticut Fights*, 267 et. seq.

45. Duane, *Dear Old "K,"* 128.

46. Ibid., 131 (Second and Third Battalions combined).

47. Field Order #97, 26th Division, 30 October 1918. MNGA; Sibley, *With the Yankee Division in France*, 316.

48. Bert Ford, *The Fighting Yankees Overseas* (Boston: McPhail, 1919), 151 ("In wrong with the powers that be"); Sibley, *With the Yankee Division in France*, 308; Stallings, *Doughboys*, 305; Coffman, *War to End All Wars,* 330–31; Braim, *Test of Battle*, 131–33 ("personal animosity") and 250–51 (Malin Craig's assessment of the 26th Division.); Connell Albertine, *The Yankee Doughboy* (Boston: Brandon Press, 1968), 303–304. (In yet another possible explanation, Albertine believes that Edwards and Pershing had an "incident" before World War I and that his chief of staff, Duncan Major, was somehow responsible for the relief itself. Major was seen by many as rigid and dictatorial and full of self-importance; it is easy to see why he might be assigned some blame.)

49. Sibley, *With the Yankee Division in France*, 307.

50. Roger J. Spiller, ed., *Dictionary of American Military Biography,* Vol. II, H–P (Westport, Conn.: Greenwood, 1984), 847.

51. Coffman, *War to End All Wars*, 331; Stallings, *Doughboys*, 305.

52. Stallings, *Doughboys*, 305.

53. Orders No. [59] (SECRET), Headquarters, 101st Sanitary Train, 7th October 1918. NA RG120.

54. History Field Hospital Co. 101–101 Sanitary Train, 26th Division, Part 6 (typescript, n.d.), 3. NA RG120.

55. Jones, *Historical Sketch,* 35.

56. Field Orders No. 10 (SECRET), Headquarters, 101st Sanitary Train, 8th October, 1918. NA RG120.

57. *History Field Hospital Co. 101–101 Sanitary Train, 26th Division, Part 6,* 3.

58. Field Orders No. 12 (SECRET), Headquarters, 101st Sanitary Train, 9th October, 1918. NA RG120.

59. Orders No. 60, Headquarters, 101st Sanitary Train, 9th Oct., 1918. NA RG120.

60. Jones, *Historical Sketch,* 35; Charles Lynch, ed., *The Medical Department of the United States Army in the World War,* vol. 8, *Field Operations* (Washington, D.C.: GPO, 1925), 727.

61. Eben Putnam, *Report of the Commission on Massachusetts' Part in the World War,* vol. I, *History* (Boston: Commonwealth of Massachusetts, 1931), 141; *History Field Hospital Co. 101–101 Sanitary Train, 26th Division, Part 6,* 6. NA RG120.

62. Putnam, *Report of the Commission,* 141; Jones, *Historical Sketch,* 35–36.

63. Paschall, *Defeat of Imperial Germany, 1917–1918,* 188; Toland, *No Man's Land,* 527–28.

64. Sibley, *With the Yankee Division in France,* 302–5; *The Medical Department of the United States Army in the World War,* vol. 8, 525–26.

65. R. S. Porter, Note in Jones, *Historical Sketch,* 37. NA RG120; Ford, *Fighting Yankees Overseas,* 30–31; Albert M. Ettinger and A. Churchill Ettinger, *A Doughboy with the Fighting 69th* (Shippensburg, Penn.: White Mane), 151–52.

66. Paschall, *Defeat of Imperial Germany, 1917–1918,* 191.

67. Porter, *Note* in Jones, *Historical Sketch,* 37–38 (also included members of Provisional Truck Company and the Medical Supply Depot). NA RG120.

68. Major Blanchard was relieved as commanding officer of the 103rd Field Hospital and assigned to the 103rd Field Artillery on October 3, 1918. He left the company the next day. Daily Report of Casualties and Changes, 103rd Field Hospital, 5 October 1918. NA RG120; Captain Hassett took command on October 4. Roster Medical Department, 26th Division. MNGA.

69. R. S. Porter, Memorandum to Major Dolan, 20 September, 1918. NA RG120.

70. Station List, Page #5, 103 Field Hospital. NA RG120.

71. Weekly Medical Report, Serious Cases, 103 Field Hospital, Notre Dame de Palameix, 5 October 1918. NA RG120.

72. Weekly Report of Sick and Injured, Form 211, 103 Field Hospital, for weeks ending October 2 and October 8, 1918. NA RG12073. Haythornthwaite, *World War One Source Book,* 180–81.

74. R. S. Porter, Memorandum to A.C. Of Staff, G-1, 5 October 1918. NA RG120.

75. Weekly Medical Report, Serious Cases, 103 Field Hospital, Notre Dame de Palameix, 5 October 1918. NA RG120.

76. Leonard W. Hassett, Memo to C.O. 101 Sanitary Train, 24 October 1918. NA RG120.

77. *History Field Hospital Co. 101–101 Sanitary Train, 26th Division, Part 7,* 1. NA RG120.

78. Special Orders No. 101, Headquarters, 101st Sanitary Train, 29th October, 1918. NA RG120.

79. Special Orders No. 102 (EXTRACT), Headquarters, 101st Sanitary Train, 30th October, 1918. NA RG120.

Chapter Eight

The Final Push
(Meuse-Argonne)

Silence laid a pall on everything that first night after the Armistice. The guns
of four long years were still at last.
—Pvt. Elton E. Mackin U.S.M.C.

My work is finished. Your work begins.
—Marshal Foch to Premier Clemenceau

THE BREACH: NOVEMBER THROUGH DECEMBER 1918

Western Front—Allies

One by one, the kaiser's allies each sued for a separate peace. Austria, one of the
prime movers at the outbreak of the war, asked for an armistice on October 28,
1918, to become effective on November 4.[1] In the meantime, Germany and Austria
were retreating on all fronts. The German navy, once the proudest in Europe save
only the Royal Navy, was in the midst of a mass mutiny.[2] Fear of a Bolshevik revolt
on the order of the recent upheaval in Russia gripped the leaders of Germany.
Ludendorff had finally resigned on October 26, and there were many who thought
that it was time for the kaiser himself to go.[3] However, as in any crisis, there were
also hard-liners—those who said, "Fight on." Some felt that if the country could
hold on through the winter, another offensive could be launched. The more realistic
saw the fresh levies of Americans arriving at the rate of 10,000 per day, and they
knew that the end was a foregone conclusion.

By the end of October, British forces had reached the River Scheldt and were
poised to cross. In an attack on November 1, the French broke the German line

north of the Aisne River. On November 4, the British resumed their drive, capturing 10,000 prisoners and 1,200 guns.[4] (The world lost a brilliant young poet that day; Wilfred Owen was killed near the village of Ors, leading his men across the Sambre Canal.)[5] The Canadians retook Mons on November 10.[6]

The channels of communication remained open between the Allies and Germany, but the former insisted that there would be no temporary cessation of hostilities, with the armies holding in place. They were determined to carry on the fight until their adversaries surrendered. Negotiations could then begin on a peace treaty. The German leaders rightly foresaw that the terms of such an armistice would be nothing short of unconditional surrender. Germany and the kaiser thought that too humiliating; nevertheless, on November 7 they sent word that they would accede. Almost immediately word spread around the world, and celebrations took place—prematurely, as it turned out. On November 9, the German delegation reached the appointed location in the Forêt de Compiègne. In the meantime, the kaiser left Germany for exile in neutral Holland on November 10.[7] At 5:10 A.M. on the morning of November 11, following lengthy negotiations, the surrender document was signed in a railway car. The peace was to become effective at 11 A.M. No American officers were present.[8]

On December 1, the first British troops crossed into Germany. On December 4 they reached Cologne; they crossed the Rhine nine days later.[9] Germany was retreating by agreement, but her soldiers were doing so in an orderly fashion, still in possession of their arms. They did not exhibit the attitude of a beaten foe. Quite the contrary, they were angry at their leaders for quitting. They had carried the war to France and Belgium, and until then, no foreign troops had set foot upon their sacred soil. There had been a number of bombing raids, but compared to the Allied naval blockade, the effects of these had been negligible.[10] France now insisted that the blockade continue as an incentive to the Germans to make concessions at the peace table. The Germans thought that France was acting vindictively toward an honorable foe. She felt that there was blame attached to all of the participants—that it was unfair for Germany to be singled out for punishment in the form of territorial losses and large reparations.[11]

Western Front, AEF: Meuse Argonne—Second Wind

Originally, the attacks in the American sector were scheduled to resume on October 28, but they were delayed until November 1, following talks with General Gouraud, commander of the French Fourth Army.[12] For two days prior to the attacks, American artillery had fired 36,000 rounds containing mustard gas on the four German divisions defending the sector. In addition, naval guns were brought up to the front to pound the positions even harder.[13] Pershing was now in overall command of two American armies, the First under Maj. Gen. Hunter Liggett, and the Second under Maj. Gen. Robert L. Bullard.[14] To date, the First Army had borne the brunt of the American effort, and it continued to occupy an east-west line encompassing the Argonne Forest and the Heights of the Meuse north of Verdun.[15]

The Second Army occupied a generally north-south line east of the Meuse and south of Verdun.[16] The soldiers of the Second Army were awaiting their chance to prove themselves.

Gen. Max von Gallwitz had the unenviable task of defending the sector against the American forces. He was a good choice, because of his experience and his hard-line attitude. He had been ordered to withdraw his forces slowly and to re-form on a new line behind the Meuse River, much closer to Germany.[17] The First Army began the attack with six divisions abreast. The 2nd Division, with eighteen tanks in support, was in the center, along with the 89th Division. The former division experienced unexpected initial success from November 1 through November 3, then resistance stiffened. Beaufort fell to the men of the 89th Division on November 4, but only after a bitter fight. On November 5, Pershing issued controversial, even confusing, orders; though the city of Sedan had been designated as a French army objective, he ordered the 1st Division to take it. The order very nearly led to tragic consequences, as division boundaries became mixed. The American drive regained momentum, however; gains were registered all along the front. Unit after unit reached the Meuse River. The 42nd Division, which had relieved the 78th Division, took the heights just above Sedan on November 8. The division shelled the city heavily and forced the Germans to begin evacuation, leaving behind many supplies. Ultimately Pershing relented and gave the French the honor of entering the city first, thus avenging the bitter memories of 1870.[18] The Second Army kicked off its offensive on November 10, but by then the war was all but over.[19] Looking back, General Ludendorff would offer high praise for the doughboy: "The American infantry in the Argonne won the war."[20]

Once the armistice became effective, a haunting quiet reigned, punctuated only by flares fired up and down the lines like fireworks. Fires were lit and their flames flickered throughout the cold night.[21] Thoughts drifted homeward; for some, the trip home would be relatively soon, but for others, those who would comprise the occupation forces, the wait would be much longer. The author of a history of the 101st Field Hospital describes that moment:

The 11th of November, now famous in history broke cold and gray, the artillery being still heavily engaged on both sides right up to the eventful hour of eleven, when as if on signal all sounds of hostilities ceased, the quietness of peace filling the air where only a moment before death dealing shells held sway. This lasted a few minutes when everyone realizing that one of the many rumors we had been hearing was an actual fact, the air resounded to the cheering of everyone present.[22]

Lest their troops get caught up in the euphoria of the moment, commanding officers reminded their officers and enlisted men that under no circumstances were they to cross the front lines for the purpose of fraternization with the enemy. Gas discipline, censorship, and security measures would continue to be enforced until further notice.[23] Evidently, the message did not reach a few enlisted men, for it was repeated two days later with the terse injunction, "THIS MUST STOP!!"[24]

President Wilson arrived in France on Friday, December 13, 1918, the same day as the men of the U.S. 2nd Division crossed the Rhine River at Remagen, Germany, to begin a period of occupation duty.[25] Replacements now filled the ranks—fresh troops, unburdened by the memories of the past six months.[26] All along the route of march, through a cold drizzle and slippery mud, the men could not help but notice the stark contrast between the peoples and countrysides of France and Germany. The former had suffered greatly from four years of war. Her people were hungry, and her towns and fields that had been within artillery range lay devastated. Germany, on the other hand, was virtually untouched. There were no shell holes, trenches, or strands of barbed wire. Her people, those that cared to stand by and watch the Americans, appeared well fed, their fields plowed. The dreary German villages were still intact.[27] Little wonder that returning German soldiers felt somehow let down by their leaders.[28]

The arrival of Wilson, for the first ever visit by a sitting president, was a joyous celebration. He was feted and honored throughout France.[29] The warmth of the people was genuine, but beneath the surface, the old hands like Clemenceau simply bided their time. What did it matter what Wilson said? Each European leader had his own agenda, which was immutable. Ultimately the foreign leaders prevailed, and the president's plans, let alone his hopes and dreams for a better world, were of little consequence. If any of the 2,000,000 Americans in France hoped that the president would pay a visit to any of the battlefields so recently the scenes of their exploits, they were sorely disappointed. Given the contribution of the doughboy and the great pride felt by those back home who had lost sons in the effort, Wilson displayed a remarkable lack of sensitivity and enormous hubris when, as commander in chief, he pointedly declined to visit the battlefields or the graves of the honored dead. Unlike Lincoln, the president missed opportunities to sanctify and recognize their great sacrifice—such as at Château-Thierry, the site of the first large-scale European battle in which U.S. forces played a major role, and most certainly a household word back home.[30] Likewise, he declined to review troops at Montfaucon, one of the more difficult fights during the Meuse-Argonne campaign.[31]

For most American soldiers, the journey home would be made in stages over the next several months. Some who had survived shot and shell would not be going home, felled by a silent killer ravaging the ranks—influenza.[32]

26TH DIVISION: HINGE OF FATE

Before he was relieved as noted, General Edwards had moved his operational headquarters to a dugout near Bras-sur-Meuse so as to be closer to the fighting. Some command functions remained at the citadel at Verdun, four miles to the south.[33] The division, along with the 79th Division, continued to hold the far right of the First Army position at the juncture with the nascent U.S. Second Army. After a brief lull, the division was ordered to resume its attacks; however it was to shift its axis somewhat toward the east, so as to drive the Germans out of the hills and ravines and onto the flat Woëvre Plain, where they would be fair game for the Second Army.[34] The German defenders were having none of it. Nearby were the battlefields of 1916, where so many French and Germans had lost their lives in the fight for Verdun. The conditions in the sector continued to be miserable.[35] The rain was constant, and the exhausted troops pushed forward against stiff opposition. Flabas was taken on November 8,[36] and the division received some much-needed replacements. General Bamford measured the worth of his division by the number of its casualties. Despite the enormous toll that the fighting had taken to date, he was not satisfied; he found the division to be only adequate when compared with the 1st Division which, had suffered considerably more. Bamford obviously could not fully appreciate the worth of his command, nor would he be given ample opportunity to learn.

The 104th Infantry was ordered to mount an attack at 9:30 A.M. on November 11. The orders were rescinded, but then reissued. The attack went forward, and men died.[37] The armistice could not have been signed too soon. Joyous celebrations took place up and down the line. The band of the 101st Infantry led a parade of French and American soldiers through the streets of Verdun.[38] After the fighting had ceased, the division calculated that it had advanced about three and one-half miles during its month-long stay in the Argonne.[39] A fearful price had been paid for those few miles—nine times the casualties incurred at St. Mihiel.[40]

Orders were received to proceed south to Montigny-le-Roi to rest and refit.[41] On November 23, division headquarters was set up there, just twenty miles southeast of AEF headquarters at Chaumont. The area was about thirty miles below Neuf-château, where the division had commenced its training more than a year before. The march was conducted in stages over a period of eight or ten days.[42] The artillery was ordered to Tronville, south and east of Bar-le-Duc, there to await further orders. It would not join the rest of the division until Christmas. While there, it turned in its guns and disposed of most of its horses, retaining only those animals necessary to haul the supply wagons. The artillerymen were loath to part with these faithful friends that had carried them and their guns to battle.[43] As the men of the division began to march south, some of the weight of the war was lifted from them as they received regular meals, showers, and clean clothing. The salutary effects were visible.[44]

On November 12, 1918, the division insignia was approved by Chaumont, and orders were issued that each officer and enlisted man had to have the patch on the left shoulder of his uniform by no later than November 20. "Strict compliance" was expected, no exceptions. The design was a diamond of khaki cloth, four inches by three and a half, with a blue "YD" superimposed. In typical military fashion, commanders were advised that orders had been placed for the patch, but that it was doubtful that the official patches would arrive in time for compliance. So each unit was given the option to purchase khaki and blue cloth, which was in sufficient supply, for forty-two to forty-five francs per yard, to make the obligatory patches. However, orders for the fabric had to be placed, prepaid, no later than noon the next day. Unit commanders were further cautioned that higher authorities desired to "secure uniformity" even if the homemade method was adopted.[45]

On November 19, 1918, General Bamford was replaced by Maj. Gen. Harry Clay Hale a friend and classmate of Clarence Edwards (U.S. Military Academy, class of 1883). He had been born in Knoxville, Illinois, on July 10, 1861. Hale was an excellent selection, since he recognized and respected the bond that had developed between the men of the division and General Edwards.[46]

As had been the experience of his friend Edwards, Hale's first assignment as a newly minted second lieutenant had been the guard detail for the temporary tomb of the assassinated President Garfield. However, it was during his second assignment, which took him and his bride to Fort Bennett, on the west bank of the Missouri River in South Dakota, that he earned the respect of his superiors and the native peoples alike. There, following the death of Sitting Bull in 1890, during a frigid winter on the northern plains, he singlehandedly located and returned a band of 150 Sioux to the Standing Rock Reservation.

Later, he had served with distinction in the Philippines, where he was wounded in action. His other service had included a tour of duty in China as well as various staff positions. When the United States entered the First World War, he had been promoted to the rank of brigadier general and shortly thereafter to major general. He trained the 84th Division ("Lincoln Division") and brought it to France in August 1918. There he received the unhappy news that his division would be broken up, with separate detachments parceled out to various other divisions for the upcoming Meuse-Argonne fight. It was Hale who took the 26th home.[47]

At this time, AEF headquarters finally relented and issued orders permitting long-overdue furloughs for the men. The plan was to grant ten-day leaves (*permissions*) to all enlisted personnel, in blocks of 600 men at a time. While Paris was still generally "off limits," although as we have seen an occasional doughboy slipped through the ring of vigilant military police, the south of France was a popular destination. Enlisted men went, by and large, to an area near Aix-les-Bains, while officers sojourned on the Riviera.[48] By order of the president, November 28, 1918, was declared a day of thanksgiving, and General Hale excused all men of the division from duty, with the exception of those carrying out essential tasks.[49]

Sanitary Trains: More of the Same

By the beginning of November, all of the division field hospitals were at Caserne Bevaux, on the southern edge of Verdun.[50] There was no letup in the fighting, so the casualties continued to flow through these units in large numbers. In addition, the cold, wet weather and the abominable living conditions of the men certainly contributed to the epidemic of influenza that raged across both sides of the western front during the fall and would continue that winter. Even Capt. Nat Simpkins, General Edwards' favorite aide, had not been immune.[51] Lt. Col. Emerson Taylor, who served as the division adjutant, described the conditions in the Neptune sector:

The disease was aided by very bad weather conditions—continual rain, cold autumn river mists, and also by the appalling state of the ground where the troops were forced to live and seek shelter. Flooded dugouts, hillsides which were merely quagmires, broken roads, great difficulty in providing or procuring sufficient hot food, continually wet clothes and blankets, all tended to sap the strength of the battalions posted in the gas-drenched hollows or on the slopes which were whipped at all hours by snipers and artillery.[52]

As part of the last-minute push, the 101st Field Hospital was ordered north to Vacherauville to operate a sorting station. The unit opened its doors at 6 P.M., Sunday, November 10. The placement of the hospital across the road from a large railroad gun drew fire from the German artillery upon the men as they went about their duties.[53]

On Thursday, November 14, the Yankee Division was relieved by the 6th Division. Relief and march tables, as well as subsequent field orders, set the route of march.[54] The ultimate destination of the Sanitary Train was Camp Hospital No. 8, just outside Montigny-le-Roi, a small town in the Eighth Training Area, near the valley of the upper Meuse and about thirty miles south of Neufchâteau. The field hospitals and ambulance companies, except the horse-drawn 104th Field Hospital and 104th Ambulance Company, were scheduled to reach Montigny-le-Roi on November 23. There the men were to secure billets.[55] The weather was cool, but definitely not as bad as the previous year. However, some confusion regarding temporary billets along the way resulted in great discomfort for some unlucky soldiers.[56]

As in any large troop movement, the Sanitary Train had not only to move itself, but also to continue to perform its primary mission, to provide for the treating and evacuating sick and injured division personnel. Since the move to the new sector was to be largely by foot, a sufficient number of ambulances had to be available for each marching unit should the need for them arise en route. Of more importance, there could be no break in the availability of medical services. As a result, the field hospitals "leapfrogged" each other as the division moved to the new area. At least one hospital would remain open in the former area, generally performing as a triage, until another was open and in place at the next day's destination. Billeting details from both the field hospital and ambulance sections were sent ahead to the next village to secure housing.

On November 14, the 101st Field Hospital was ordered to close and move to its new station at Courcelles-sur-Aire, a town twenty-three miles west then south of Verdun, as soon as truck transportation could be obtained. The 102nd Field Hospital was to remain behind as the triage and evacuation point. The 103rd Field Hospital, along with Mobile Surgical Unit No. 7, received orders to proceed to the same station and open a "receiving and forwarding station."[57] The 101st and 103rd Ambulance Companies also selected details to remain behind at Caserne Bevaux and keep that station open until relieved by their counterparts in the 6th Division. Trucks would be used to move the equipment only, not to evacuate patients. Furthermore, in an effort to keep them from "straying," vehicles were ordered to drive in a convoy each way, then "promptly unload" and return to Caserne Bevaux. Along the way, the Train had to pass through the towns of Nixéville, Vadelaincourt, St. André-en-Barrois, and Amblaincourt. Billets were found in Courcelles-sur-Aire.[58]

On Friday, November 15, all units of the Sanitary Train were ordered to Longchamps-sur-Aire, a distance of about three and one-half miles, where the headquarters would also be located. The personnel of the 101st and 103rd Field Hospitals and the 101st, 102nd, and 103rd Ambulance Companies had been specifically directed to "proceed by marching." The movement began at 9 A.M., and commanding officers were enjoined to maintain strict march discipline; in other words, there were to be no stragglers. The equipment and baggage went ahead by truck. The Sanitary Train remained there two days.[59]

The next stopover was at Saulx-en-Barrois, seventeen miles down the road. The 103rd Field Hospital closed its doors at 4 P.M., November 17. On the way, it passed through Villotte-sur-Aire, Lignières-sur-Aire, and Domremy-aux-Bois. On November 18, the Train was off to Marson-sur-Barboure, between five and six miles farther south. Again the men marched, and the trucks carried the equipment. The trucks were not to leave until after noon; except for the 103rd Field Hospital, which set off at noon, the other units began their march at 3 P.M. The billeting party, which consisted one NCO from each section, was detailed to report to the commanding officer of the Ambulance Section. The latter was to provide transportation for them. The 103rd Field Hospital reopened as a forwarding and receiving station at 2 P.M.[60]

At 9 A.M. on Tuesday, November 19, the horse-drawn elements of the Sanitary Train, the 104th Field Hospital and the 104th Ambulance Companies, preceded only by the billeting party, left Marson-sur-Barboure, destination Houdelaincourt. At 9:30 A.M., the 101st, 102nd, and 103rd Ambulance Companies followed suit in marching columns. Fifteen minutes later, they were followed by the 101st and 102nd Field Hospitals, likewise on foot. The 101st Field Hospital was expected to reach Houdalaincourt in time to set up a triage facility by 2 P.M. the same day. The motor vehicles and baggage would leave at noon. Dead last was the 103rd Field Hospital, which was ordered to close and follow the others at 2 P.M. The route of the march took the men through the towns of Reffroy, Demange-aux-Eaux, and Baudignécourt; it covered between seven and eight miles. Headquarters for the Train would be with the other elements at Houdelaincourt, while the division headquarters would be at Neufchâteau.[61]

Wednesday, November 20, was a repeat of the day before, only the orders called for an earlier start all around. The destination for that day was Domremy-la-Pucelle, about thirteen miles down the road. The Provisional Truck Company was scheduled to clear Houdelaincourt at 7:30 A.M., followed by the 104th Field Hospital and the 104th Ambulance Company fifteen minutes later. By 8 A.M., the remaining ambulance companies, along with the 102nd and 103rd Field Hospital Companies, were to begin their long march. The following day (November 21) had been declared a day of rest, and there would be no marching. This must have helped lift spirits. As customary, the billeting party had gone ahead of the column to obtain quarters for the night. This time the 101st Field Hospital would bring up the rear; it was ordered to close at 1 P.M. and proceed to Domremy-la-Pucelle. When it closed, the 103rd Field Hospital was already in place at the new location and had opened as a forwarding and receiving station. The route of march was through the towns of Gondrecourt-le-Château and Vouthon-Haut.[62]

Hopes for a one-day respite were quickly dashed when the previous day's order regarding the day of rest was rescinded; the move would instead continue on November 21, with a march to the twin villages of Pompierre and Sartes, twenty-two miles away. The commanding officer of the Provisional Truck Company led the motor section out of town at 7:30 A.M. The hospital trucks would proceed to Pompierre and the ambulance trucks to Sartes. The 101st, 102nd, and 103rd Ambulance Companies would march out of Domremy-la-Pucelle at 7:55 A.M., destination Sartes. Likewise, the 101st and 102nd Field Hospitals would follow en route to Pompierre. This time, the marching troops would be followed at 8:00 A.M. by the horse-drawn 104th Field Hospital and the 104th Ambulance Companies. There must have been a complaint about straggling, as two officers from each marching company were ordered to march behind their respective companies to prevent it. A break was allowed every ten minutes before the hour every hour of the long march. Again, the billeting party went on ahead to arrange for accommodations for the night. Maj. Robert DeCue was detailed as billeting officer for Sartes, and his counterpart for Pompierre was 1st Lt John A. Rogers. The route took the men through Neufchâteau, Rebeuville, and Circourt-sur-Mouzon. Train headquarters was at Pompierre that night. The 101st Field Hospital was ordered to set up a forwarding and receiving station at Pompierre at 1 P.M., at which time the 103rd Field Hospital was to close and to proceed by truck to the new station.[63] There, all the men of the Sanitary Train received welcome news; they could put their tired feet up for while, for there would be no more marching. The rest of the journey would be by truck.

In keeping with the well-established pattern, the next day the billeting party set off for Montigny-le-Roi in advance of the column. Their task was to find billets there for all but the 104th Field Hospital and the 104th Ambulance Companies. These two horse-drawn units had their own billeting party, which was responsible for finding accommodations at their intermediate destination and at their ultimate one in the town of Sarrey. Major DeCue was to find billets for the ambulance companies (less the 104th) in the town of Sarrey. As in the move to Caserne Bevaux, the trucks would ferry men and supplies in a convoy, quickly unloading at Montigny-le-Roi and returning to Pompierre and Sartes. The Provisional Truck Company oversaw the move, and the various units assigned loading details so that there would be six men to each truck. The move began at 8 A.M., Friday, November 22, and overall, took two days to complete. The 101st Field Hospital remained open until 1 P.M. that day so as to give the 103rd Field Hospital time to open in the new station. Finally, on November 22, the first of the weary wanderers set out for their final destination at Montigny-le-Roi, another twenty-two and one-half miles away;

the lead elements arrived later that same day. The route carried the medicos through the towns of Soulaucourt, Damblain, and Sarrey.[64]

About this time, Lt. Col. Ralph S. Porter requested his own relief. He had seen the division through the end of its training and had been with it throughout the bitter fighting that followed. Porter recommended Maj. Thomas Jenkins to succeed him as division surgeon, and Maj. Frederick E. Jones as commander of the Sanitary Train.[65]

It was soon learned that on a date as yet unspecified, during the month of December 1918, the president of the United States would review the division. At first, the pass-by was to occur on the Montigny–Neufchâteau road, one-half kilometer north of Camp Hospital No. 8. The troops were placed on one hour's notice; they would form up on both sides of the road. The uniform of the day would be overcoats, brassards (arm bands), and overseas caps, but no packs.[66] These orders were rescinded the very same day; the division was now ordered to form up in single file on the south side of the Mandres–Montigny-le-Roi–Dammartin road, facing north. The president would be journeying from west to east, from Mandres to Dammartin, in an automobile. Company officers were to stand in front of their units. Each ambulance company was to provide "thirty-two fours" (128 men), and each field hospital company had to provide "twelve fours" (forty-eight men). The men were to wear helmets and overcoats with brassards on the outside, and to carry a short pack, gas mask, canteen, arms, a lunch, and as many litters "as can be made available."[67] The day ultimately selected for the review was Christmas.

In addition, the president had indicated that he would like to have Christmas dinner with some enlisted members of the 26th Division in conjunction with the review.[68] The Yankee Division had been selected for the honor because it had been in France longer than any other complete division. Pursuant to an order from division headquarters, a collection was taken up among the units to pay for the president's dinner, which was to consist of beef stew, bread, and coffee.[69] Christmas Day was a Wednesday. The presidential visit took place at 10:30 A.M. in a wet and muddy field at Humes, a small town just northwest of Langres on the road to Chaumont. However, Wilson ate his Christmas dinner—not with the enlisted men as planned, but rather with a group of officers of the division at Montigny-le-Roi. He then inspected a barracks and some billets in Mandres, and called it a day.[70]

103rd Field Hospital: "On the Road Again"

The month of November opened with the same appalling conditions as had the previous month. The men of the Yankee Division were feeling the adverse effects of combat, climate, and disease. As the fighting continued right up to what everyone sensed was the end for the German army, a new call went out for litter bearers. On November 9, a detail from the 103rd Field Hospital, led by Capt. Edward B. Sheehan and composed of two NCOs and forty enlisted men, was sent to the front to act as litter bearers.[71] A similar detail from the 104th Field Hospital was also sent. The duty must have been arduous, since the medics filtered back in small groups over a twenty-four-hour period starting at 7 P.M., November 11.[72] Their war had lasted just a little while longer.

On November 14, the Sanitary Train, including the 103rd Field Hospital, set out south from Caserne Bevaux toward Montigny-le-Roi. The men would hike much of the way and be taken by truck for the remainder.[73] The route assigned to them was not the more direct road along the Meuse River but rather a more roundabout way over country roads and through small villages. For much of the way along the route, the unit continued to carry out triage for the division sick.[74] During the week ending November 19, the 103rd Field Hospital treated a total of fifty-one patients, forty-eight of whom were sick and three injured. Of the sick, two were venereal patients, who were transferred to another hospital.[75] There were no patient deaths during this period. The mean strength of the unit was seventy-six officers and men.[76]

In the meantime, since the emergency surgical treatment of the wounded was no longer a priority, Mobile Surgical Unit No. 7 was disbanded and its personnel returned to duty with other units. Accordingly, orders issued by the division surgeon on November 17 required Capt. Edward Knowles and 1st Lt. Paul B. Roen to report immediately to the 103rd Field Hospital. Likewise, eight of the ten enlisted men released were sent to the company, including:

Sgt. Thomas J. Prendergast

Cpl. Percy A. Sharpe

Pvt. Clarence Bryant

Pvt. William A. Johnson

Sgt. Henry J. VonKameke

Pfc. Patrick H. Fitzgerald

Pvt. Albrie L. Jette

Pvt. Christian O. Larsen[77]

Camp Hospital No. 8 was established in June of 1918 and served the Eighth Training Area. It was organized as a "Type B" unit. In many respects, Camp Hospital No. 8 was a typical unit of its type. It had a normal bed capacity of 300, but in an emergency, the basic hospital could accommodate 520, provided tents could be found for the staff. At no time during its history did it reach this level. In a crisis, such as the flu epidemic, a camp hospital had a maximum capacity of a thousand beds, through the addition of tents in the expansion area on both sides. Accordingly, during the influenza epidemic of the fall and winter of 1918–19, the hospital was expanded by the addition of the 101st and 103rd Field Hospitals, which set up tents adjacent to it as soon as they arrived. Both units were detailed to treat the milder cases, while the main hospital handled the serious ones. A camp hospital like No. 8 was designed to provide only the barest necessities for medical care, but it was supposed to have operating rooms and an X-ray laboratory; however there was no X-ray machine at Camp Hospital No. 8. The standard "footprint" of the typical complex was 600 feet square. It had a central block of service buildings constructed of wood, including administration, officers' quarters, and a clinic/operating room. Two side blocks contained rows of six buildings each, two of which housed and fed hospital personnel, with the remaining ten buildings used as wards. Each ward was a hundred feet by twenty and held thirty patients. Type B camp hospitals were scattered throughout France; when the war ended, there were sixty-six in place.[78]

At the beginning, Camp Hospital No. 8 handled surgical cases referred by Base Hospital No. 15 at Chaumont. However, eventually its admissions were generally from units stationed in the Eighth Training Area, such as the 83rd, 91st, and 26th Divisions. Its greatest period of activity was from November 1918 through January 1919, when the influenza epidemic was raging within the Yankee Division. At that time, it admitted a total of 1,540 patients, nearly one-half of the 3,351 it served during its existence. Evacuations were normally to Langres, Chaumont, and Baziolles-sur-Meuse.

The records of this camp hospital were poor at best, but what emerges is the story of a medical stepchild. The problem likely stemmed as much from inattention to detail as from neglect by higher authorities. In addition to its lack of an X-ray machine, its laboratory was not up to standard. Its streets, left unmaintained and unrepaired, were described as "impassable." Trucks, even only "moderately loaded," became mired on a daily basis. There was no recreation or entertainment provided for either staff or patients. Food supplies were drawn from the army commissary at Montigny-le-Roi only with great difficulty and in insufficient quantity; the mess officer and mess sergeant had to search the area personally for food. Fresh milk for patients was obtained from local farms (it was pasteurized). Medical supplies, like the food, were drawn only after considerable red tape and delay. The officer in charge at the depot at Is-sur-Tille refused to release supplies to trucks from the unit but insisted on sending them by rail to the railhead at Meuse, about three kilometers east of Montigny-le-Roi. In many instances, the shipments were misdirected and never received. Laundry was not done at the hospital. At first it was done by local civilians, and only later, and very poorly, was it done by the army laundry at Rimaucourt.[79]

Although the flu epidemic in the Yankee Division was largely confined to two infantry battalions, the number of sick exceeded the capacity of the small camp hospital. The men of the 103rd Field Hospital had just arrived when they were ordered to set up a hospital for the mildly sick, the overflow from Camp Hospital No. 8. The unit opened a tent hospital annex at 1 P.M., November 22. Tents were pitched in the muddy ground adjacent to it. For the remainder of the troops, the epidemic was kept under control by proactive measures, including the requirement that the men sleep head to foot.[80]

For the week ending November 26, a transition period that included the journey to Camp Hospital No. 8, the 103rd Field Hospital treated a total of 131 patients. One hundred twenty-three were sick, most likely from flu, and eight had suffered injuries of one kind or another. All patients were evacuated to other facilities. There were no patient deaths, and the mean strength of the unit for this period increased to eighty-eight officers and men.[81] For the week ending December 3, hospital admissions jumped to 282. Of these, 270 were ill, three with pneumonia, together with a like number of venereal cases. The injured numbered twelve. One patient was returned to duty, and all of those remaining were treated and evacuated. The mean strength of the company again increased, to ninety officers and men. No patient deaths were reported.[82]

A report dated December 6 indicates that as of midnight there were seventeen patients in the hospital. However, an additional forty-six patients had been seen and evacuated to Camp Hospital No. 8 next door. As an indication of how quickly things change, on the next day, Saturday, the hospital admitted a total of sixty-six patients, the great majority for influenza. In addition, three men were returned to duty and one sent to the divisional disciplinary camp on the basis of a gonorrheal infection. Thirteen more men were evacuated to Camp Hospital No. 8, eight of them diagnosed as having influenza.[83] Admissions peaked during the period ending December 10, when 379 men were treated. There were four injuries, but the great bulk of those admitted were sick. Among them were three venereal cases, and one each of pneumonia, measles, and cerebro-spinal meningitis. Seventeen men were returned to duty. Two hundred twenty-one were treated and evacuated, and 141were held over for further treatment. Again, there were no patient deaths, but the mean strength of the organization dropped to eighty-five officers and men.[84]

Over the next three weeks, there were eighty-three new admissions,[85] all for sickness, with one exception. These, coupled with the holdovers, kept the tent hospital very busy. In fact, the unit treated an average of ninety-two patients per week. Eighty were treated and transferred to other facilities, and 103were returned to duty. One soldier went AWOL from the hospital. The irrepressible dentist Clifford Renth was permanently transferred to the 102nd Field Artillery on December 20. While at Montigny-le-Roi, he had operated his portable dental outfit in conjunction with the Division Dental Laboratory. In addition, he was appointed mess officer and had been temporarily assigned (eleven days) to the Third Battalion of the 103rd Infantry, stationed at nearby Sarrey. The hospital company's loss was certainly the artillery's gain.[86]

At 9 A.M. on Sunday, December 22, the Sanitary Train established a triage hospital at Bannes, a village seven or eight miles south of Montigny-le-Roi on the road to Langres. The triage site and billets would be located at 49 Main Street, at the home of Gustav Giradot, and at an old French infirmary on the same street, 160 yards from the crossroads, in a building that could be identified by the large red cross on it. All contagious cases were sent to Camp Hospital No. 8, and all other cases were sent to Langres. Inexplicably, the order stated that pneumonia and influenza were not to be treated as contagious. The order applied to evacuations from the 51st Artillery Brigade, 101st Ammunition Train, the Mobile Ordnance Repair Shop, the Motor Repair Shop, the 104th Infantry, and portions of the 103rd stationed at Chauffourt.[87] Capt. Edward Sheehan, along with a detail which included men from the 103rd Field Hospital, was ordered to help man the station at Bannes.[88]

A week later, on December 29, there were thirty-four patients in the hospital. Four patients had been admitted that day, two of them evacuated from the 104th Field Hospital, the others from the 101st. In addition, eight men were released, seven of them to their duties. One of these was Pvt. William Johnson of the 103rd Field Hospital, who was suffering from coryza, a severe head cold, marked by an acute inflammation of the nasal mucous membrane. Pvt. Johnson had transferred to the company from Mobile Surgical Unit No. 7 just six weeks before. Another member of the company was Pvt. Claude L. Cater, who was suffering from nephritis. A third man, Albert E. Richardson, a cook in the 103rd Field Hospital, was not so fortunate. He was transferred to the Division Disciplinary Battalion, because he was being treated for a venereal disease. Two men had been admitted for dental treatment, but by that time Dr. Renth was gone.[89] As the new year dawned, forty-four remained to recuperate. Unit strength remained fairly constant at between eighty-eight and eighty-nine officers and men.[90]

NOTES

1. John Toland, *No Man's Land* (New York: Konecky, 1980), 518; Martin Gilbert, *The First World War* (New York: Henry Holt, 1994), 491.

2. Rod Paschall, *The Defeat of Imperial Germany, 1917–1918* (Chapel Hill, N.C.: Algonquin, 1989), 215–16; Gilbert, *First World War,* 491 and 493.

3. Thomas E. Greiss, ed., *The Great War* (Wayne, N.J.: Avery, 1986), 163 (10/26/1918); Paschall, *Defeat of Imperial Germany, 1917–1918,* 217 (10/26/1918); Gilbert, *First World War,* 483 (10/25/1918).

4. Gilbert, *First World War,* 489–90 and 492–93.

5. Ibid., 492; Wilfred Owen, *The Collected Poems of Wilfred Owen,* ed. C. Day Lewis (New York: New Directions, 1965), Introduction, 23.

6. Gilbert, *First World War,* 499.

7. Ibid., 494–500.

8. Edward M. Coffman, *The War to End All Wars The American Military Experience in World War I* (Madison: Univ. of Wisconsin Press, 1986), 355.

9. Gilbert, *First World War,* 506.

10. Greiss, ed., *Great War,* 163; Paschall, *Defeat of Imperial Germany, 1917–1918,* 231.

11. Stanley Weintraub, *A Stillness Heard Round the World* (New York: Oxford Univ. Press, 1985), 58–59.

12. Paschall, *Defeat of Imperial Germany, 1917–1918,* 212–13.

13. Gilbert, *First World War,* 490.

14. Coffman, *War to End All Wars,* 329.

15. Paschall, *Defeat of Imperial Germany, 1917–1918,* 182; Paul Braim, *The Test of Battle: The American Expeditionary Forces in the Meuse-Argonne Campaign* (Newark: Univ. of Delaware Press, 1988), 87.

16. Braim, *Test of Battle,* 129.

17. Paschall, *Defeat of Imperial Germany, 1917–1918,* 222.

18. Coffman, *War to End All Wars,* 345–46 and 349–54.

19. Paschall, *Defeat of Imperial Germany, 1917–1918,* 219.

20. Braim, *Test of Battle,* 167.

21. Coffman, *War to End All Wars*, 355–56; Frank P. Sibley, *With the Yankee Division in France* (Boston: Little, Brown, 1919), 340–41; Richard Derby, *"Wade in, Sanitary!"* (New York: G. P. Putnam's Sons, 1919), 176–77; Robert Graves, *Good Bye to All That* (New York: Doubleday, 1985), 202 ("when the guns stop").

22. *History Field Hospital Co. 101–101 Sanitary Train, 26th Division, Part 7* (typescript, n.d.), 1. NA RG120.

23. Orders No. 71, Headquarters, 101st Sanitary Train, 11th November, 1918. NA RG120.

24. Memo to All Unit Commanders, Headquarters, 101st Sanitary Train, 13th November, 1918 (citing Instructions No. 118, HQ, 26th Division, 13th November, 1918). NA RG120.

25. Derby, *"Wade in, Sanitary!"* 195.

26. John W. Thomason, *Fix Bayonets!* (New York: Scribner's, 1970), 160.

27. Gilbert, *First World War*, 506; Thomason, *Fix Bayonets!* 164.

28. Toland, *No Man's Land*, 591.

29. Meirion Harries and Susie Harries, *The Last Days of Innocence: America at War, 1917–1918* (New York: Random House, 1997) 423–24.

30. David Fromkin, *In the Time of the Americans* (New York: Knopf, 1995), 244.

31. Gilbert, *First World War*, 507.

32. Emerson G. Taylor, *New England in France, 1917–1919: A History of the Twenty-sixth Division U.S.A.* (Boston: Houghton Mifflin, 1920), 240.

33. Sibley, *With the Yankee Division in France*, 306 and 311–12.

34. Taylor, *New England in France*, 264; Braim, *Test of Battle*, 141 (The Second Army moved into the Woëvre Plain on November 9, 1918); Stanley J. Herzog, *The Fightin' Yanks* (Stamford, Conn.: Cunningham, 1922), 129.

35. Daniel W. Strickland, *Connecticut Fights: The Story of the 102nd Regiment* (New Haven, Conn.: Quinnipiack Press, 1930) 289.

36. Sibley, *With the Yankee Division in France*, 321; Taylor, *New England in France*, 267.

37. James T. Duane, *Dear Old "K"* (Boston: Thomas Todd, 1922), 153–55; Albert G. Love, ed., *The Medical Department of the United States Army in the World War*, vol. 15, Part 2, *Statistics* (Washington, D.C.: GPO, 1925), 1092 (101st Inf. [1], 102nd Inf. [3], 103rd Inf. [3], and 104th Inf. [2] killed in action November 11, 1918.).

38. Duane, *Dear Old "K,"* 156; Sibley, *With the Yankee Division in France*, 343.

39. Sibley, *With the Yankee Division in France*, 342.

40. Love, ed., *Medical Department of the United States Army in the World War*, vol.15, Part 2, *Statistics*, 1072–73, 1082–83, and 1092. During the period September 12 through September 16, 1918 (St. Mihiel offensive), the four infantry regiments of the 26th Division (101st–104th) incurred a total of 360 men gassed and wounded by bullets: a total of sixty-one died from those causes. During the period October 16 through November 11, 1918 (last half of Meuse-Argonne offensive), the same regiments incurred a total of 3,207 men gassed and wounded by bullets, and a total of 490 men died from those causes.

41. Field Order #108, 26th Division, U.S., 13 November 1918. MNGA.

42. Taylor, *New England in France, 1917–1919*, 280 (11/23/18).

43. Herzog, *Fightin' Yanks*, 133–34.

44. Carlo D'Este, *Patton: A Genius for War* (New York: HarperCollins,1995), 278–79; Alonzo L. Hamby, *Man of the People: A Life of Harry S. Truman* (New York: Oxford Univ. Press, 1996), 79; Coffman, *War to End All Wars*, 358.

45. Orders No. 72, Headquarters, 101st Sanitary Train, 12th November, 1918. citing Orders 219, HQ, 26th Division, 12th November, 1918. NA RG120. The color scheme must

have changed soon thereafter to the now-familiar dark blue letters on an olive drab diamond. See Taylor, *New England in France*, 281–82. Lieutenant Colonel Taylor states that the design was submitted for approval on October 23 but that the dates of the order and for compliance were November 9 and 29 respectively. He refers to an "olive drab" diamond and "dark blue" letters. See also Charles Lynch, ed., *The Medical Department of the United States Army in the World War*, vol. 8, *Field Operations* (Washington, D.C.: GPO, 1925), 986. ("dark-blue monogram YD on diamond-shaped field of olive drab").

46. Taylor, *New England in France*, 281–82.

47. "Annual Report," *Assembly*, July 1946, 3–4 (Major General Hale died on March 21, 1946. He was buried in Arlington National Cemetery beside his wife, who had died forty years earlier.) USMA.

48. Taylor, *New England in France*, 283–84 and 292.

49. Bulletin No. 203, HQ 26th Division, Para. II, reprinted in Strickland, *Connecticut Fights*, 301.

50. Eben Putnam, *Report of the Commission on Massachusetts' Part in the World War*, vol. I, *History* (Boston: Commonwealth of Massachusetts, 1931), 141.

51. Sibley, *With the Yankee Division in France*, 306 and 309 (Captain Simpkins died).

52. Taylor, *New England in France*, 249.

53. History Field Hospital Co. 101–101 Sanitary Train, 26th Division, Part 7, 1. NA RG120.

54. Field Order #108, HQ 26th Division, U.S., 13 November 1918. MNGA.

55. Field Orders #116 and 117, HQ 26th Div., U.S., 21 November, 1918. MNGA.

56. Sibley, *With the Yankee Division in France*, 345.

57. The term appears to be used interchangeably with triage facility.

58. Field Orders No. 29 (SECRET) (together with accompanying Relief Table), Headquarters, 101st Sanitary Train, 14th November, 1918. NA RG120.

59. Field Orders No. 31 (SECRET), Headquarters, 101st Sanitary Train, 15th November, 1918, Para. 4. NA RG120.

60. Field Orders No. 33 (SECRET), Headquarters, 101st Sanitary Train, 17th November, 1918, Para. 7; Station List, Sheets 5 and 6, 103rd Field Hospital. NA RG120.

61. Field Orders No. 34 (SECRET), Headquarters, 101st Sanitary Train, 18 November, 1918. NA RG120.

62. Field Orders No. 35 (SECRET), Headquarters, 101st Sanitary Train, 20 November,1918. NA RG120.

63. Field Order No. 36 (SECRET), Headquarters, 101st Sanitary Train, 21 November, 1918. NA RG120.

64. Field Orders No. 37 (SECRET), Headquarters, 101st Sanitary Train, 21 November, 1918. NA RG120.

65. Sibley, *With the Yankee Division in France*, 345–46; Major Jones (later lieutenant colonel) took over as commanding officer of the 101st Sanitary Train on December 10, 1918, per General Orders No. 113, para. III, Headquarters 26th Division, A.E.F. He replaced Maj. William Denton. See also Taylor, *New England in France*, 290.

66. Orders No. 83, Headquarters, 101st Sanitary Train, 15th December, 1918. NA RG120.

67. Field Orders No. 38 (SECRET), Headquarters, 101st Sanitary Train, 16th December, 1918. NA RG120.

68. Strickland, *Connecticut Fights*, 302 (the president also inspected barracks at Mandres); Sibley, *With the Yankee Division in France*, 348.

69. Duane, *Dear Old "K,"* 159–60 (15ff per company).

70. Taylor, *New England in France*, 285–86; Bert Ford, *The Fighting Yankees Overseas* (Boston: McPhail, 1919), 164–65; Memorandum, Chief of Staff, 1st Army A.E.F., 20 December 1918, reprinted in Duane, *Dear Old "K,"* 196; Strickland, *Connecticut Fights*, 302–3.

71. Leonard W. Hassett, Memorandum to Commanding General, 26th Division, 17 November 1918, Report of Activities in Verdun Sector. NA RG120.

72. Frank W. Stevens, Report of Activities of 104th Field Hospital in the Verdun Sector. NA RG120.

73. Clifford Renth, History of Duties and Stations for October, November, and December, 1918, 9 January, 1919. NA RG120.

74. Return of 101st Sanitary Train, 26th Division, November 1918. NA RG120.

75. Weekly Report of Sick and Injured, 103rd Field Hospital, Week Ended November 19, 1918. NA RG120.

76. Form 211, Weekly Report of Sick and Injured, 103 Field Hospital, Week Ended 19 November 1918. NA RG120.

77. Special Orders No. 117, Headquarters, 101st Sanitary Train, 17th November, 1918. NA RG120.

78. Joseph H. Ford, ed., *The Medical Department of the United States Army in the World War,* vol. 2, *Administration American Expeditionary Forces* (Washington, D.C.: GPO, 1927), 257–58 and 752–53.

79. *History of Camp Hospital No. 8* (n.d.). Medical Section, Case 28, Drawer 4. NA RG120.

80. Jones, *Historical Sketch,* 38–39; the Return of 101st Sanitary Train, 26th *Division* for the month of December 1918, indicates that the 103rd Field Hospital performed division triage from December 1 through 10 and as a hospital for the divisional sick for the rest of the month. This would explain the large bulges in admissions and transfers during the first ten days. However, the transition, if any, was more than likely gradual, and the hospital probably functioned in both capacities to some degree for the entire period. As evidence of this, by December 10, it had retained 141 patients while transferring 221.

81. Form 211, Weekly Report of Sick and Injured, 103 Field Hospital, Week Ended 26 November 1918. NA RG120.

82. Form 211, Weekly Report of Sick and Injured, 103 Field Hospital, Week Ended 3 December 1918. NA RG120.

83. Daily Reports of Casualties and Changes, 103rd Field Hospital Company, 26th Division, 6 and 7 December 1918. NA RG120.

84. Form 211, Weekly Report of Sick and Injured, 103 Field Hospital, Week Ended 10 December 1918. NA RG120.

85. There appears to be an error in the count on the Weekly Report for December 24, 1918. Assuming that the counts of patients in hospital at the beginning and the end of the period covered are accurate, the error most likely occurred in a double-count of two patients transferred or returned to duty. Either of these categories would then be too high. The total of the two should read "11" not "13."

86. Renth, History of Duties and Stations.

87. Order No. 85, Headquarters, 101st Sanitary Train, 21st December, 1918. NA RG120.

88. Miscellaneous notes from National Archives. NA RG120.

89. Daily Report of Casualties and Changes, 103rd Field Hospital Company, 26th Division, December 29, 1918. (Richardson undoubtedly got his venereal disease under

control, because he sailed home with the 103rd Field Hospital on the *Winifredian.*) NA RG120.

90. Form 211, Weekly Reports of Sick and Injured, 103 Field Hospital, Weeks Ended 17, 24, and 31 December, 1918. NA RG120.

Chapter Nine

A Little Piece of
Me—Going Home

I tell you, these Boche are dangerous! They have too many children.
—Capt. John W. Thomason, USMC

CALM WATERS (JANUARY 1919 THROUGH APRIL 1919)

Western Front: Allies

The Paris Peace Conference opened on January 18, 1919. Early on, the German colonial territories were divided up among the principal parties under "mandates" of the League of Nations. On January 25, the conference set up a committee to determine reparations. Lloyd George of Britain began to have second thoughts as he contemplated the long-range implications of an oppressive settlement. He proposed that reparations be determined in two years, after the world economy settled down and prices came down from their inflated wartime highs. March brought a series of stormy sessions. Finally, on May 7, a draft treaty was presented to the German delegation. It balked, especially at the proposed admission of "war guilt." On June 22, it agreed to sign the treaty if the offending article was deleted. The Allies held firm, and the Germans relented on June 28, but not before the German navy had scuttled seventy-four of its warships at Scapa Flow. The Allies were angered at what they saw as a gesture of incredible bad faith. The Germans saw the scuttling as a defiant gesture to preserve some degree of honor, which had otherwise been denied them.[1]

A multinational victory parade was held in Paris on July 14. Marshals Foch and Joffre led the march on horseback. General Pershing rode at the head of the American contingent. This was some months before Austria and Bulgaria signed treaties with the Allied powers. The treaty was to be effective June 10, 1920. The U.S. Senate, in the exercise of its constitutional power, rejected it. This was a direct slap in the face to Wilson, and since the United States was to be a key partner in the treaty's enforcement, this act gutted its overall effectiveness. Europe and the world became doomed to repeat the tragedy of the past four years.[2]

Western Front: United States

American soldiers were sent home during the spring of 1919 at the rate of about 300,000 per month. The last combat division set sail from Brest on September 1.[3] At home the men were given discharge papers in addition to their uniform and overcoat, a pair of shoes, and a sixty-dollar bonus.[4] Many would never go home. When all was said and done, more than 50,000 American soldiers had been killed in battle or died of their wounds.[5] Another 50–60,000 had succumbed to disease or accident.[6] All in all, there were approximately 70,000 graves at war's end, mostly in France.[7]

The United States furnished the Third Army,16,000 men, as the nucleus of the American occupation forces, which were to be stationed at Coblenz, Germany.[8] This occupation force would not leave Germany until 1923.[9] At the close of the fighting, another 18,000 men remained in France recuperating from wounds and illness, most of them in Brest awaiting transport home. There were not sufficient hospital beds at home to accommodate them all; in Brest itself, there were 10,000 patients for 8,000 beds.[10] New medical units would continue to arrive in France for some time in order to alleviate the shortages of medical personnel.[11] The AEF was still building hospitals, one half-finished at Kerhoun, on the heights above Brest.[12]

Beneath all the cheering flowed a dark undercurrent. The two-year honeymoon between industry and organized labor was unraveling. Government appeals to patriotism and support for the troops had cobbled together an uneasy peace; now all bets were off. Production was curtailed, and labor was looking to make up for deferred wages and benefits. Industry was looking to roll back concessions it had made to boost production and profits during the war. New England telephone workers went on strike in April, and a dockworker strike was threatened.[13]

Still, within twenty-four hours after the arrival of the Sanitary Trains, one of the last units of the 26th Division to come home, it was business as usual for the people of Boston. The next day, April 19, was Patriots' Day in Massachusetts, and in the traditional Boston Marathon, Carl W. A. Linder from Finland was the winner, with a time of two hours, twenty-nine minutes and 32.5 seconds.[14] That same day, however, did not end happily for the Boston Braves, who dropped both ends of a doubleheader to the Dodgers. It was their home opener for the new season.[15]

26TH DIVISION: "THE SACRIFICE DIVISION"

At first, The Yankee Division had been considered for occupation duty; however, given the poor physical condition of the men in its depleted ranks, the decision was made to send it home.[16] By the end of January 1919, the division was in motion for the embarkation area near Le Mans. The latter had been designated as the embarkation center for the ports of Brest and St. Nazaire; it was capable of accommodating 250,000 men.[17] The trip was made by rail.[18] However, it was marred by a train wreck near Montiéramey, eleven miles southeast of Troyes, on January 31. Six members of the 103rd Machine Gun Battalion were killed instantly, and two died later at a hospital. Sixteen others were injured.[19] The division established its headquarters at Ecommoy, a town twelve miles southeast from Le Mans.[20] The various units of the division were billeted in the surrounding area. The 104th Infantry was located at Fillé,[21] while the 103rd Field Artillery settled in at Pontvallain.[22] On January 25, the division passed from the First Army, in which it had served throughout the tough fighting the previous fall, and came under the authority of the Services of Supply.[23]

Of universal concern with commanders was the morale of the men following the armistice. The enforced idleness and the natural boredom after months of tense combat needed to be addressed.[24] As a consequence, by order of General Hale, the division conducted military-athletic games on the southern outskirts of Ecommoy along the Tours road, on March 10 through 12.[25] Officers from the various units, including the Sanitary Train, were detailed to act as judges. For Monday, March 10, Capt. James F. Cobey of the 102nd Field Hospital was selected to judge "platoon inspection," while on the same day, Capt. Howard L. Cecil, also of the 102nd Field Hospital, judged "football passing, mental alertness, and the gas mask race." On the next day, Capt. Harry W. Steckel, a psychiatrist attached to the 102nd Field Hospital, was assigned the "company march." Finally, Capt. Elmer R. Edson of the 101st Field Hospital was to judge the "relay race, equipment race, and tent pitching." All judges were ordered to meet on the tournament grounds at 2 P.M. in the afternoon of March 7 in order to discuss their responsibilities.[26] That day, Captain Cobey was relieved of his duties as a judge, and Capt. Roy E. Fallas of the 103rd Field Hospital was detailed in his place.[27] In connection with the tournament, on March 10 the Field Hospital Section set up a first aid station on the grounds, and operated it throughout the games. Consistent with these orders, the booth was well marked and stocked with chlorinated water for the participants.[28] At the tournament's end, the men of the 104th Infantry walked away with the silver cup.[29]

In addition, General Pershing gave orders to set up an "A.E.F. University," so that the men could use their time to take advantage of the splendid facilities for higher learning in France. (Given the short time period, one has to wonder how much of a benefit this actually was. However, if it improved morale any and at the same time absorbed idle hours, then it was certainly a help.)[30] As a possible indicator of the overall response, Capt. (later Major) Leonard Hassett, commanding officer of the 103rd Field Hospital, reported to higher headquarters that no one under his command, officer or enlisted, was interested in attending classes at a French or British university.[31] Also during its stay in the area, the 101st Engineers constructed a YMCA hut in Le Mans, with funds contributed by the citizens of York, Maine. The building, located in the heart of the city across from the cathedral in the Place des Jacobins, boasted a canteen, movie theater, and a social room, all for the use of the men of the 26th Division and others passing through on their way home.[32] Within twenty-four hours after General Hale had announced the gift to the people of Le Mans, a seventy-five-man detail from Company B, 101st Engineers, began work— the same unit that began work on the barracks at Bazoilles-sur-Meuse in the fall of 1917. The hut was massive , with 15,000 square feet of floor space; the six trusses supporting the roof of the theater were decorated with the shields of each of the New England states. Inside was a massive fireplace, and the walls bore the regimental insignia of the Yankee Division.[33]

On March 15, 1919, orders were received to proceed to Billeting Section No. 6 at Camp Pontanezen, near Brest, which was to be the embarkation point for home.[34] The journey there was to take place by train from Ecommoy. A flurry of orders emanated from headquarters. The division would leave behind animals and animal transport, field ranges and heating stoves, quartermaster property, tentage, athletic equipment, and salvage property. Baggage was to be loaded one hour before departure of the train, and each man was to carry two days' reserve rations.[35] The 104th Infantry left the Le Mans area on March 21 and was the first to reach Camp Pontanezen. It was followed in order by the 103rd, 101st, and finally the 102nd. Artillery and Sanitary Trains brought up the rear on March 28.[36]

Brest is an ancient port city at the westernmost point in Brittany, in the department aptly named Finistèrre. The town had grown up on both sides of the River Penfeld, whose steep banks obliged its citizens to build steps up from its wharves. The streets were narrow and lined with two-story stucco houses with chimneys at both gable ends. Its natural harbor had been recognized by the French very early on, and it has been a busy port since the seventeenth century.[37] A doughboy seeing it for the first time in May 1918 as his troopship made its way up the estuary wrote in his diary, "Of all the lands and cities, is any lovelier than Brittany, or more picturesque than Brest?"[38]

At this time, Billeting Section No. 6 was located about two miles outside the city, at Pontanezen Barracks. The facilities at and around Brest came under the jurisdiction of the Services of Supply, which was located in Base Section No. 5 and covered Brittany and portions of adjacent French departments.[39] In the spring of 1919, Camp Pontanezen, as it was called, was well-equipped and sanitary.[40] However, that had not always been the case. In fact, conditions had been so bad there the previous autumn that an investigation had been conducted and improvements made.[41] The camp was built around an old Napoleonic-era caserne. The original site covered about fifteen acres and was composed of six large, stuccoed stone barracks, several smaller buildings, and a chalk parade ground, all surrounded by a high stone wall. The site was on a hillside facing south, and its final dimensions were about one mile wide and one and one-half miles long. The camp had grown in size, to accommodate the arriving troops and later the departing ones—it was well over a thousand acres.[42]

The landscape all around it was one of beautiful farms and fields. Frederick Pottle describes the area:

The country is beautiful as a dream, a Corot landscape everywhere. The vegetation is all very dark green and wonderfully luxuriant. The trees beside the fields have been cut off to prevent their shading the crops, but are allowed to cover themselves with green shoots so as to make quaint dwarf trees. The fields are small, and divided off by hedges of raspberry and other low bushes. There are many trees I never saw before, smothered with ivy and dense with foliage . . . sunken roads . . . [and] . . . walled chateaux with long avenues of horse chestnuts and immense iron gates.[43]

In spite of the scenery, the camp had been a disaster from the beginning; troops entered France faster than it could accommodate. There were insufficient kitchens, mess halls, bathing, and laundry services to name just a few deficiencies. The farm soil was quickly churned into a sea of "deep and tenacious" mud. In addition, there were not enough trained personnel on hand to staff the facility.

However, after a thorough investigation, significant improvements were made, and by April 1919, the camp was in good shape. At this time, there were 450 wood-framed, corrugated-iron barracks, each with a capacity of 110 men, and another 5,000 six-man tents with floors. The camp was divided into fifteen separate sections, not only for efficient sanitary control of the large facility but also to accommodate fifteen entire military units like the 26th Division. Each section had an up-to-date troop kitchen 375 feet long; in actuality six separate, fully equipped kitchens, complete with appliances, food storage, concrete floors, sewer, and water. The mess halls were 300 feet long and could feed 5,000 men in forty minutes. Latrines were both the cement-lined pit type, complete with urinals, and the all-too-familiar box type. The contents of both had to be emptied, hauled away, buried, and ultimately, soaked with gasoline and burned.[44] All told, the camp could accommodate 80,000 men, along with a permanent party of 13,500. On average, there were 60,000 men in camp at any one time, with a normal stay of between one and five days. Fully one-third of the American Expeditionary Force embarked for home through Brest.[45]

Since the function of the camp was to prepare each organization for embarkation, it was important to separate out individuals unfit to travel. At the northern end of the facility was the "segregation camp," built to accommodate 1,500 soldiers diagnosed with scabies, venereal disease, or communicable diseases. Floored tents were provided for these unlucky souls. (In a sadly, punning irony, black and white venereal patients were kept separate within this area.) Camp Pontanezen also had a hospital, a canteen, and a YMCA hut with a capacity of 2,000 men.

Within twenty-four hours of an organization's arrival, the men were directed to report to the central bathing facility at specified times, 240 men at a time at ten-minute intervals. The men stripped to their undershirts and placed their clothing on numbered benches, stood up on the benches and faced the next row while a doctor inspected them for vermin and venereal disease. They then stepped down and had throats checked. Those with lice or nits were sent for a thorough delousing, while those with venereal disease or other contagious condition were sent to the segregation camp for further treatment. The remaining men were given a four-minute hot shower and issued clean socks and underwear. They then dressed in their old uniform and went back to their organization areas. The goal of each division was to obtain a clearance certificate. The paperwork from the inspection was forwarded to the Troop Movement Office for review. If it was satisfactory, the coveted certificate was issued; however, the organization had to sail within six days of issuance or risk having to repeat the entire process. Those left behind came with later shipments. One last screening was necessary within twenty-four hours prior to departure; it involved taking the soldiers' temperatures and checking their throats. Those unlucky souls whose throats were suspect or whose temperatures were more than one degree above normal were segregated from the rest. They had all of one day to recover or remain behind.[46]

Sanitary Trains: Home at Last

At Montigny-le-Roi, Sanitary Trains continued to provide medical care for the division. Eventually, the field hospitals were permitted to evacuate their patients to nearby base hospitals at Chaumont, Langres, and Bourmont.[47]

As a first step in the process of winding down and going home, the 26th Division, including the 101st Sanitary Train, received two days' notice that the various units would be inspected on January 4, 1919. The 102nd and 104th Field Hospitals were ordered to assemble on the south side of the Montigny-Langres road, near the barracks occupied by the former. The 101st and 103rd Field Hospitals were to be lined up outside of Camp Hospital No. 8. The ambulance companies were to be inspected separately, and the times of the inspections would be announced later. Billets were to be "thoroly [*sic*] cleaned and scrupulously inspected" beforehand by an officer of each unit. The men were to wear clean uniforms and carry or wear the following items: helmet, gas mask, complete hospital corps belt, pack carrier (containing one blanket, shelter half, pole, pins, and mess gear), an overcoat, and, with the exception of officers, a brassard. All unit records, including sick and morning reports, hospital fund statements, and service records, were subject to inspection and had to be arranged so that they would be "instantly accessible" to the inspector.[48]

While the men awaited further orders regarding their return, another effort to recycle materials, commenced on Thursday, January 9. The various units were ordered to collect and flatten all empty tin cans, which would be turned in each morning at 9 A.M.[49] Shortly thereafter, the commanding officer of the Field Hospital Section was ordered to supervise the turn-in of all surplus and unnecessary equipment. All medical property "not necessary for the care of the ordinary sick of the division, or for venereal prophylaxis," or personal property, had to be immediately turned in to Capt. Marshall A. Welbourne, the medical salvage officer, at the railhead at Meuse. Field hospitals could keep, if available, up to twenty litters per company and a liberal number of dressings. Prior to departure from Montigny-le-Roi, all quartermaster property, from wheeled transportation to horses and mules, in addition to all rolling kitchens, water wagons, and trail-mobiles, as well as any material pertaining thereto, had to be turned in to the division quartermaster at Meuse. Basically, if an item was not necessary to the treatment of the ordinary sick, it was to be turned in. Stoves were to be left in the nearest barracks. Finally, on January 16 all unnecessary firearms and ammunition had to be turned in to the division ordnance officer. A similar directive applied to the Ambulance Section.[50]

Field Order No. 3, dated January 15, 1919, ordered the Sanitary Trains to proceed by rail to Ecommoy, near Le Mans.[51] In anticipation of the movement, the headquarters of the Train made arrangements to provide trucks and transport for the field hospitals and other units under its command to the entraining point. Forty-three trucks would be needed for the equipment and another twenty-four "if the men ride."[52] The extra trucks were not needed, since the men marched. The whole Sanitary Train would require forty flatcars and forty-eight boxcars to transport it to Ecommoy.[53] The troop trains were equipped with two lanterns in each boxcar for "the comfort of the men" during their journey. Unit commanders were issued strict instructions to make sure the lanterns were returned to the convoy officer so that succeeding trains with homebound men could use them.[54]

As for the animals, they were turned in to the division remount officer over the course of three successive days. Orders specified that the horses from both the Ambulance Section and the Field Hospital Section were to be brought to the junction of the Avrecourt–Bourbonnes-les-Bains road in Montigny-le-Roi, at 9 A.M., Sunday, January 26. The following day all mules, together with harness and escort wagons, of the Ambulance Section, were to be turned over to the supply officer of the 104th Infantry. The Field Hospital Section's mules, harness, and escort wagons were taken by the division remount officer at 9 A.M. on January 28.[55]

All was in readiness at 3 P.M., Sunday, January 27, when the Ambulance Section set off on its march from Bannes to Foulain, the entraining point. The men would spend the night there in billets before boarding their train the next day. However, the orders were amended, and their departure was delayed for twenty-four hours, until 8:30 A.M. on January 29. The route of march took the section through the villages of Lannes, Rolampont, Vesaignes-sur-Marne, and Marnay-sur-Marne. Truck transportation was to be provided for the remaining equipment, and the commanding officers of the various units were to provide loading details.[56] Unit commanders were told to provide all men with a third blanket, and when the men marched at a "route step" they were to be permitted to smoke.[57] Sanitary Train headquarters would be at Marigné-Laillé, not at Ecommoy as originally planned.[58]

While in the embarkation area, the Sanitary Train was asked to provide details to work at nearby Camp Hospitals No. 52 and No. 72.[59] The Sanitary Train operated a hospital for the slightly sick at Ecommoy; it evacuated patients with more serious illnesses to those two camp hospitals. Also, the process of delousing the men was continued.[60] The 102nd Field Hospital set up the division triage station at Ecommoy.[61] The business of "general police" for the town fell to the Ambulance Section. Its commanding officer was directed to select a noncommissioned officer and four enlisted men to work under the direction of the Train sanitary inspector to keep the town clean.[62]

However, the minds of most of the men must have been on home, and their idle hours were filled with lighthearted games—so much so that Maj. Frederick Jones[63] issued an order that "the practice of playing games in the streets will be stopped at once."[64] In order to alleviate the boredom and to fill some of the enlisted men's hours, division headquarters ordered that post schools be established to teach a variety of subjects, to include: "Reading and Writing, Arithmetic, Civics and Citizenship, U.S. History, Geography and French." A wide variety of topics within the general areas were to be offered, and the list was to be read to each company at the afternoon assembly on February 5. Anyone interested could sign up with the section school officer prior to 5 P.M. that date. Attendance was voluntary, but anyone who signed up for a course was required to attend.[65] Textbooks were sent to each school officer in advance of classes, which were to begin on Monday, February 24. Each class was held in the evening and lasted half an hour, five nights per week. The exact time of each class was left to the discretion of the school officers. Instructors were to meet on Saturday, February 22, to receive their textbooks and to inform themselves as to the content of the first lesson. Each was also encouraged to maintain a copy of the textbook to show prospective students. Enrollment must have remained open in spite of the earlier deadline, because school officers were later advised to canvass the four companies of their sections on a regular basis, so as to advertise the courses thoroughly.[66]

Preparations for a divisional review by the commander in chief began on February 8. The day and time had not yet been announced. All officers and enlisted men were ordered to participate, the only exceptions being one NCO in each office, personnel that "may not be spared" from the care and transport of the sick (this number was to be "reduced to the absolute minimum"), as well as one cook and one man on "kitchen police" for each kitchen.[67] Each field hospital company, except the 102nd Field Hospital (which was functioning as the division hospital) and the ambulance companies, would participate. There would be no field music, and participants were ordered to wear brassards (armbands) on their overcoats.[68] The 102nd Ambulance Company was shorthanded; its ranks were filled by a twenty-five-man detail from the field hospital section. The strength of each field hospital company participating was forty-eight, and each ambulance company was to provide twelve squads. All were to assemble in front of the church in Ecommoy and have left that point for the review site at 7:30 A.M. The men were weighed down by full packs, each including a shelter half, blanket, haversack and carrier, medical belt, canteen, first aid pouch, and mess kit. They wore overcoats and slickers. Officers were specifically directed not to wear white collars and cuffs, but to carry a stripped pack and medical belt. All were given cooked lunches to carry in their haversacks, along with the injunction that "Care will be taken that remains of this lunch do not appear on the Review Field."[69] General Pershing reviewed the division at the rifle range near St. Biez-en-Belin on Wednesday morning, February 19.

It was at this time that General Hale approved a new logo for the Sanitary Train, to be painted on the helmets of all officers and enlisted men "*at once.*" The design was "a red cross composed of five equal squares. Red cross to be two inches in diameter with half-inch figures, in white, superimposed upon center of red cross composed of numerals '101.' Beneath the right and left arms of the cross the letters 'S' and 'T' will be stenciled in white." The insignia was to be painted on the crown of the helmet, in front of the center, three-quarters of an inch above the junction of the crown with the brim.[70]

Long overdue and certainly well-deserved leaves played a large part in maintaining good morale. Up to this point, many men had not been much farther away from their units than the nearest town, or army schools, during their entire stay in France. On February 13, the Sanitary Train was allocated fifteen seven-day leaves to the town of St. Malo in Brittany. Travel time was not included. Seven men each were selected from the field hospital and ambulance sections. The final slot was to be chosen from among the personnel of the Medical Supply Unit, Dental Laboratory, and the Field Laboratory. 1st Lt. Joseph B. Edwards had the duty to escort the men to the station at Ecommoy on Monday, February 17, and to turn them over to the three officers of the 52nd Brigade who would accompany them on the journey. Officially, the leave began the following day in St. Malo. Prior to leaving their units, the men were deloused. Unit commanders were also to check to make sure the men had sufficient funds for the trip. The men deposited their gas masks and helmets in the places designated and took along three blankets and extra pairs of field shoes. At the entraining point, the army quartermaster provided them with travel rations and straw for their comfort on the ride—obviously, they did not travel first class.[71] Leaves continued to be allocated among the personnel of the division. On February 17, twenty more men from the Sanitary Train were awarded leave. Two had three-day leaves (travel not included), while the remainder received fourteen-day passes (travel included).[72]

Lice remained a plague, even in the Sanitary Train, and their eradication became nearly an obsession with higher authority. Beginning Friday, February 28, the Bathing and Delousing Station was assigned to the various field hospital and ambulance companies on a rotating daily basis. The facility was to remain open from 8 A.M. until dark. Even those who requested baths on a day other than assigned were to be accommodated. Headquarters personnel and officers could use it at any time. Prior to bathing, the soldier was told to tie his underwear and socks loosely together with his ID tags. These were then boiled by the attendants and returned to him afterward. Likewise, his uniform was to be first moistened with a cloth damp with 3 percent cresol oil and then ironed by the attendant. If a soldier was found to be "infested with vermin," he was directed to wash his "hairy parts" with 3 percent cresol oil following his bath. The names of all bathers and their organization were furnished the next morning to headquarters by the NCO in charge of the facility.[73]

In addition, unit commanders were directed to conduct "vermin inspections" every Saturday morning. Any man found to be infested was to be reported to headquarters by noon that day. Men returning from leave were to be subjected to immediate inspections for vermin and for venereal and contagious diseases. Corrective measures were to be employed at that time.[74] As of March 9, the problem persisted, and another memo was sent to all unit commanders, to be posted on all company bulletin boards. Effective the next day, any man found to be infected with vermin was to be dropped at once from his company's rolls and transferred (with his records) to the Casual Detachment at the Belgian camp near Le Mans.[75] Orders issued the same day praised those units found to be vermin free, and ordered them to continue to adhere to the bathing and delousing schedule in order to maintain their good standing. Those organizations found to have been infested were chided for their "lack of personal initiative and slackness." They were to submit to two delousings during the week of March 10, under supervision; anyone still infested would be segregated and kept segregated until a subsequent inspection found them clean.[76]

Unfortunately, the problem still persisted, and the 103rd Ambulance Company and its commanding officer were singled out for criticism. With a sense of exasperation, and all else failing, Lieutenant Colonel Jones appealed his men's sense of honor regarding that unit and its duty to the overall organization. Daily vermin inspections of the unit were ordered in hopes of eradicating the lice and of wiping the "blot from the fair repute of the Train." He even appealed to the commanding officer of the ambulance company to "rub out the blot upon its escutcheon."[77] Perhaps the final appeal worked, because two days later General Hale singled out the 101st Sanitary Train for "exceptional excellence in equipment, appearance, and discipline."[78] This was confirmed when Jones revoked the order regarding the 103rd Ambulance Company, and congratulated the Train for its "persistent and successful efforts" in eradicating the pest. As a result, all inspecting officers, except the Train bathing and delousing officer, were relieved of that irksome duty. However, weekly vermin inspections were to be maintained, with the company commander present.[79]

During the last two weeks of March, the Sanitary Train, along with the remainder of the division, began unit by unit the move to Brest, and ultimately home.[80] However, prior to departure from the embarkation area, certain tasks had to be performed. In addition to the preparation of lists of the men embarking with the division, each commanding officer was required to inspect the billets occupied by his men and to obtain a clearance certificate from the town major. He also had to file with the Sanitary Train headquarters a certificate that he had inspected his command and that it contained no men with vermin or venereal disease. All excess medical equipment—that is, items not necessary for the care of the division en route to Camp Devens, Massachusetts, was to be turned in to the division medical supply officer. However, each unit was allowed to retain one Lister bag and a supply of chlorinating tubes to ensure clean drinking water. Lieutenants Sheldon and Cohen were ordered to settle all claims arising out of the stay in Montigny-le-Roi before leaving the Ecommoy area. Enlisted personnel were to have a complete set of equipment, and any shortages were to be reported. All officers were required to carry helmets and gas masks and to wear their "OD" (olive drab) overcoats. Bed sacks were to be cleaned, stacked, and turned in by 9 A.M. on March 27.[81]

The Sanitary Train, less the 102nd Field Hospital and the Medical Supply Unit, was ordered to assemble on the Laille-Ecommoy road, about one mile south of Ecommoy, at 1:45 P.M. on Friday, March 28. The men were to march a short distance to the entraining point at Ecommoy. The remaining field hospital was to close its doors and follow at the end of the column. Full field equipment was to be carried, and overcoats and OD caps were to be worn. The night before, five trucks reported to the Field Hospital Section, prepared to load and carry its baggage to the entraining point at 7 A.M. the next day. After delivering that baggage, the trucks returned to the Ambulance Company Section and took its baggage in turn. As a final task, they returned once again and cleared the baggage of the 102nd Field Hospital and the Medical Supply Unit. The Train headquarters had already closed at 5 P.M. the previous evening.[82] The train trip to Brest was scheduled to take about sixteen hours.[83]

While the organization was at Brest, plans went forward for its return. The Sanitary Train was assigned to Billeting Area No. 6. One of the rules to be strictly adhered to was that there would have to be guards at the latrines at all times. Likewise, two barracks guards were to be assigned to keep the building policed and orderly. Washing was to be done in the ditches outside the company billets only, and water was to be obtained from spigots near the Brest road or at Troop Kitchen No. 6. As a precautionary measure, all men had to sleep head to foot. Those eligible could apply for wound chevrons. Finally, all officers and enlisted men were strictly forbidden to purchase any food items from the French canteen located within the camp, with the exception of fruit, nuts, and canned goods.[84] Capt. John W. Buchanan of the 104th Field Hospital was put in charge of the exchange of money. All French francs were to be turned in to him, in bundles of ten bills of the same denomination pinned together. The rate of exchange was 5.45 francs to the dollar. A special effort was to be made to accomplish this task by 9 A.M. March 31.[85] Between 2:10 and 2:40 P.M., March 30, the various units of the Train were ordered to report to the main delousing plant, located at 3rd Street and the Brest road, for a medical inspection. Each company was to be accompanied by one commissioned officer.[86]

On March 19, Capt. Harold S. Parker of the 103rd Field Hospital had been appointed entraining officer, Capt. James H. Malonson of the 101st Field Hospital the "hold baggage" officer, and Capt. Joseph B. Edwards of the 101st Ambulance Company the "stateroom baggage" officer. In addition, details from all the various units in the Sanitary Train were chosen to assist these officers.[87] Strict weight limits based on rank were assigned for all baggage, from 400 pounds for a field officer down to seventy-five pounds for corporals and privates. All baggage was to be inspected by each unit's commanding officer. Government pistols were to be turned in, as well as unauthorized government property and "excess personal property." The personnel records of the individual officers and men, however, were not to be packed away in boxes or trunks, or worse yet, stowed in the holds of ships. They were to be well guarded but remain accessible throughout the movement to the United States. Items that had to be tagged were tagged at both ends.[88]

Train headquarters issued what was most likely one of its last orders on French soil on Tuesday, April 1. At this time, Capt. Frank A. Willis replaced Captain Edwards as the stateroom baggage officer. The enlisted men of the Medical Supply Unit were ordered to report to him for this detail. Each unit commander was ordered to report to him with the number of bedding rolls as well as a list of office equipment. Baggage was to be pooled and checked in front of Troop Kitchen No. 5[89] (opposite Train headquarters). Spitting and throwing water on the barracks floor was specifically forbidden. Finally, when orders were received to clear Brest, all unit commanders were ordered to "assure themselves that all barracks and the vicinity thereof are scrupulously clean, this to include officer's barrack."[90] The men had their minds on going home, but the army did not let up.

103rd Field Hospital: Winding Down

The 103rd Field Hospital began the new year with forty-four patients in its tent wards. The weekly report for January 7 showed that an additional twenty-five patients were admitted, all ill. By week's end, one patient had been transferred to a different facility, and eighteen had been returned to duty. This left fifty patients on hand.[91] During the next week ending, January 14, eleven new patients were admitted. Of the patients treated that week, twenty-six were transferred out, and thirty-five returned to duty. No patient deaths were reported during the last two weeks of operation.[92] Both reports show the strength of the unit as ninety-five officers and men.[93] Capt. Leonard W. Hassett was promoted to the rank of major on February 17, 1919.[94]

At this point, orders having been received to move to the embarkation area near Le Mans, the unit closed its doors for the final time and ceased to function as a hospital. In February of 1918, when it opened in the Chemin des Dames sector, the 103rd Field Hospital had been the first of the division hospitals to operate as a virtually autonomous medical unit. In nearly a year of continuous operation the hospital had handled almost 6,500 patients, with complaints ranging from illness to serious wounds. Most recovered completely, or at least sufficiently to be transferred to other medical facilities—which was, in essence, the function of a field hospital in time of war. Given the serious nature of the surgical cases, especially in July 1918, it is not surprising that more than 140 died at their unit.[95]

At 10 A.M., on Thursday, January 24, the 103rd Field Hospital, along with the 101st and 104th Field Hospitals, was to parade in a column of fours, with full field equipment and packs (including two blankets), in Montigny-le-Roi, along the same street on which the 104th was billeted. Major Jones, the commander of the Sanitary Train, would review the men as they passed by. Later that same day, at 11 A.M., General Hale would review the marching columns in the square at Montigny-le-Roi.[96]

On Tuesday, January 29, at 8 A.M., the 103rd Field Hospital marched out of Montigny-le-Roi with the rest of the Field Hospital Section, accompanied by the Division Field and Dental Laboratories. The intermediate destination was sixteen miles away, in the town of Foulain, the entraining point; there the unit would board trains the next day for the long journey to the Le Mans embarkation area. It had originally been scheduled to move out earlier, but the movement had been postponed for twenty-four hours.[97] The men drew one day's rations and filled their canteens just prior to setting out with full packs on a route that took them through the towns of Sarrey, Odival, Nogent-en-Bassigny, Louvières, and Poulangy. Strict march discipline was to be observed.[98] The advance billeting party had already gone ahead to locate sleeping quarters. The hospital company was to be stationed at Laille, a small village about three and one-half miles southeast of Ecommoy. The train carrying the 103rd Field Hospital departed Foulain at 8:30 A.M. on January 30.

While at Laille, in compliance with orders from headquarters of the Sanitary Train, the company provided a small detail of men to Camp Hospital No. 72 at Château-du-Loir, a town twelve miles south of Ecommoy. The assignment was to make records of any officer or enlisted man of the Yankee Division who had entered the hospital there without first passing through the triage set up by the 102nd Field Hospital at Ecommoy. In charge of the detachment was Pvt.1/C Alfred Woollacott; his detail consisted of Privates Clarence S. Cullum, Fred Fuller, and James Hoover. The detail was expected to bring its own typewriter and a sufficient supply of blank Form 22s. In addition, it was required to fill out a large and a small card for each patient whose name appeared on Form 22. However, in typical army fashion, the men were advised that since the cards were "in the process of preparation" they could not be furnished at that time.[99] Camp Hospital No. 72 had been established on September 26, 1918. At first, the hospital was located in four rooms in the Hotel de la Gar, but it later moved to the École Primarie Supérieure des Garçons, a modern boy's school, a short distance from the center of town. The building was three stories high and consisted of twenty-six large, well-lighted rooms. The hospital had a capacity of 300 beds. It ceased to function as a hospital on May 14, 1919, and some of its personnel and supplies were transferred to Camp Hospital No. 114 at Ecommoy. The staff was not large—fifteen officers, eleven nurses, and eighty-eight enlisted men.[100]

Tuesday, February 25, and every Tuesday thereafter, was assigned to the 103rd Field Hospital as its bathing day.[101] Also at this time, the 101st Sanitary Train issued orders for fourteen-day leaves for certain personnel. Among those company members given leave were Sgt. Roy Jackson, who was bound for Dijon, and Cpl. Edward J. Shay, who went to Issoudun. Each was to be paid sixty cents per day to cover food and other expenses.[102]

During February and March, while the unit was stationed at Laille, its effective strength fluctuated between a high of 107 to a low of eighty-seven. Undoubtedly, the company was getting ready to go home, and many may have merely passed through it looking for rides home. On March 12, orders were issued authorizing certain officers and enlisted men to purchase and wear a third service chevron. Each chevron represented six months' service. Only two officers were mentioned, Capt. Edward B. Sheehan and Capt. Harold F. Parker. Among the forty-three enlisted men was Corporal Shay, who was authorized to wear the third chevron as of March 15. In addition, three men were authorized to wear two stripes, and another twenty-six received approval to wear one.[103]

The 103rd Field Hospital joined the other units at Billeting Section No. 6 at Camp Pontanezen. There was nothing to do there but follow the procedures for processing prior to boarding the transport home. Like the other units, the men gathered their baggage, exchanged their French francs for dollars, and were subjected to barracks inspections. Sunday, March 30, brought the long-awaited order to report to the main delousing plant at 2:30 P.M. that day, for a final medical inspection.[104] On or about April 1, as the men were making ready to sail, a final list of enlisted personnel leaving for home was prepared. The roster (see Appendix IV) showed eighty-nine present and accounted for, as well as an additional four men who had already sailed with the division headquarters detachment.[105] Comparison of this list with the passenger list of September 16, 1917 (see Appendix III), makes clear that there had been many changes. Of the original group of eighty-two enlisted men, only thirty-three were returning with the company.

GOING HOME

The division's stay at Brest was relatively short, and most units set sail by the beginning of April on an assortment of ships from the *Mount Vernon, Agamemnon,* and *Mongolia,* to the *America* (a confiscated German vessel formerly called the *Amerika*).[106] The voyage lasted about a week, and the ships landed at Commonwealth Pier within days of one another.[107] Disembarking at Boston, the first of the returning division troops received a tumultuous hero's welcome.[108] On Sunday, April 6, fifteen troop trains left Boston, one every twenty minutes. All along the train route to Camp Devens people stood to wave and cheer. Factory and train whistles blared constantly. Church bells pealed. As they passed through South Framingham, the men remembered that September day in 1917 when they had marched to the trains that would take them to Hoboken, New Jersey, and Montreal, Canada.[109]

At 8 A.M. on Sunday, April 6, 1919, the day that the first Yankee Division troops set foot in Boston, the men of the Sanitary Train assembled on Jetee de L'Est; later that day they boarded the passenger liner SS *Winifredian* for the voyage home. It was their turn. Col. Warren E. Sweetser was the commanding officer. Other units included the 101st Supply Train, the 101st Ammunition Train, as well as assorted "casuals."[110] The latter included several women, like reconstruction aide Lillian M. Reilly of Worcester,[111] and a telephone operator, Isabelle Villiers of Reading.[112] The ship, the last remaining vessel in the fleet of the Frederick Leyland Company, Ltd., had been pressed into wartime service as a troopship. She was familiar with the North Atlantic route, since she had been plying the waters between Liverpool and Boston for fifteen years prior to the war.[113] On board, the Sanitary Train continued to function, albeit in a different manner. On April 7, Cook Fred Brown was ordered to report to the ship's steward to serve as a cook in the officers' mess, while Pvt 1/C Arthur Lambeau of the 102nd Ambulance Company was detailed there as a waiter. Each was to be reimbursed by the steward for his services.[114] On April 12, while still aboard, Capt. James F. Cobey relieved Capt. Frank A. Willis as officer in charge of baggage for the Sanitary Train.[115] The *Winifredian* was due to arrive in Boston sometime during April 15; however, for unexplained reasons she was delayed, and the USS *Patricia* preceded her.[116]

Friday, April 18, 1919, was a beautiful, sunny day in Boston, although a chill breeze blew in off the water. The crowd of family and well-wishers filling Commonwealth Pier tried to stay in the sunshine, but they forgot everything when the *Winifredian* steamed into the harbor, hours late, the American flag on her foremast and the Yankee Division pennant on her mainmast. Bands played, and the crowd cheered. On deck, Maj. Leonard W. Hassett, commanding officer of the 103rd Field Hospital, and several officers were taking in the sights, including the approach of the Coast Guard cutter *Ossipee*. The major noticed a small boy hanging over the railing and remarked that the youngster would surely fall into the harbor. He asked for and received a pair of field glasses, and when he trained them on the ship, found to his horror that the boy was his own son. Luckily, an alert crewman pulled the child in and averted a tragedy.[117]

As the *Winifredian* docked at 10:45 A.M., family members shouted to the anxiously awaiting doughboys. The men returned the shouts and broke out in the popular song, "Till We Meet Again." To those fortunate enough to have relatives waiting on the dock a one-hour pass was given to visit them in a roped-off area. As those lucky few came down the gangway, they were offered coffee and doughnuts— many declined them or just brushed by, so anxious were they to see their loved ones. General Edwards had taken a subchaser out into the harbor and boarded the troopship in order to be with the returning men. So he was on hand when they debarked, and when he saw an anxious crush of people without passes, he simply wrote them out in longhand for every parent or sweetheart who wanted one. He later commented, "I couldn't refuse these mothers and fathers." The visit was short, and the men were loaded on waiting trains and taken to Camp Devens. When asked by reporters about their journey home, some men complained about the food, while others said that because they had not been allowed on the promenade deck, they had felt like steerage passengers. A ship's officer said that was according to "British custom." Originally, it was expected that the men would all be on their way by noon; however, it was late afternoon before the last train pulled away from Commonwealth Pier.

As had been the case with the trip over in 1917, much baggage was lost. Worse, it had been picked over in Brest by those responsible for loading the ships, looking for the souvenirs and trophies the men had acquired.[118] This sad occurrence was to be repeated in Boston; as three longshoremen were arrested by federal agents on April 16. The charge was theft from the baggage of members of the 26th Division.[119]

Once at Camp Devens, near Ayer, the men received baths, and most were placed in comfortable quarters, although some did spend a few days in tents.[120] Passes were issued, but most men who had families and friends nearby simply took "French leave."[121] A consolidated review of the division was conducted on April 22, with the New England governors in attendance.[122] The final review was a march down Commonwealth Avenue past the Statehouse in Boston. Originally scheduled for Saturday, April 26, the parade commenced at 1 P.M. on Friday, April 25. Nearly a million people turned out along the five-mile parade route.[123] The day was raw and overcast, and a northwest wind brought the temperature close to the freezing point.[124] However, both the crowd and the doughboys were oblivious to it. The previous Saturday, state police had arrested forty would-be profiteers at Camp Devens; they concocted a scheme to obtain, and sell at a premium, grandstand tickets for the parade. These precious ducats were supposed to be only available through the soldiers themselves and were primarily for their families.[125] As was only fitting, the two friends Clarence Edwards and Harry Hale led the march and reviewed the troops.[126] Once again, the six New England governors were present to pay tribute to the 18,000 to 21,000 marching men. When the final set of orders was cut detailing the march down Commonwealth Avenue, Boston, the Sanitary Train was almost dead last.[127]

The men were taken back to Camp Devens, where they made bonfires from the straw they had emptied from their mattresses and "whooped and danced" around them.[128] They were mustered out over the next several days.[129] The men of the 103rd Field Hospital Company were discharged along with the rest of the Sanitary Train at Camp Devens at 10 A.M. on Tuesday, April 29, 1919.[130]

EPILOGUE

If the 26th Division was unappreciated by higher headquarters at Chaumont, that certainly was not the case with its French allies. Almost universal praise and commendation were heaped upon the officers and men. They were referred to as "the Saviors of Paris," "shock troops," and the division itself was called the "Sacrifice Division" as a result of the demonstrated bravery and tenacity of its soldiers.[131] Even the enemy recognized the division's fighting qualities. The elite Prussian Guards could not believe their ill luck to have met the Yankees on almost every battlefield. On January 14, the First Battalion of the 102nd Infantry Regiment had its colors decorated by Marshal Petain with the croix de guerre for its fight at Marcheville on September 26, 1918.[132] This was the second time that a Yankee unit was accorded this honor, the colors of the 104th Infantry Regiment having been decorated the preceding April.[133] In fact, nearly a thousand Yankee doughboys were awarded the croix de guerre.[134] According to Frank P. Sibley, General Passaga recommended General Edwards for the croix de guerre, but Chaumont would not permit it. Five times he was recommended for the Legion of Honor; each time, higher headquarters blocked it. General Degoutte was incredulous. Edwards was the only commander of a fighting division who went home undecorated by either the French or the Americans.[135]

Clarence Edwards had returned home to Boston to assume command of the Northeastern Department, but his tenure was to be brief. He retired from the army after more than forty years service on December 1, 1922.[136] He returned to his estate "Doneroving," in Westwood,[137] Massachusetts, and entered the family business, the William Edwards Company. He received several honorary degrees, including awards from Trinity College, Syracuse University, and Boston College. His wife,

Bessie, died in 1929.[138] On January 15, 1931, he was operated on for an intestinal blockage. A second operation became necessary on February 13, but it too failed to solve the problem. He had already been transfused twice; when the call went out for blood for yet another transfusion following the second operation, the response from old Yankee Division men was overwhelming.[139] His longtime aide and friend, Col. John Hyatt, went so far as to say that the general "had a fighting chance to recover."[140] It was all to no avail, for he died Saturday morning, April 14.[141]

His body lay in state in the Hall of Flags at the Statehouse. More than 21,000 mourners paid their respects, and an additional 5,000 had to be turned away due to the lateness of the hour. An estimated 50,000 people lined the streets that clear, cold night as the procession took his body from the Statehouse to the South Street Station for transport to Washington, D.C., for burial at Arlington National Cemetery beside his wife and daughter.[142] The funeral ceremony on Monday the 16th was full of military pomp and was crowded with dignitaries, including a group of Yankee Division veterans who acted as an honor guard. However, one man was missing— John J. Pershing had a cold and declined to attend.[143]

The Yankee Division was the first complete division to reach France, and it spent a total of 193 days in the line, most of it continuous.[144] Only the favored 1st Division exceeded this total, and not by much.[145] The New Englanders advanced twenty-three miles against fire—eighth out of twenty-nine U.S. divisions. They incurred 15,619 casualties (sixth out of twenty-nine),[146] including 2,281 battle deaths and 11,383 wounded.[147] When the division went over to France, it was virtually an all-volunteer force. According to one source, it returned with only about 15 percent of its original members.[148] The Yankee Division had paid its dues.

The Sanitary Train had certainly seen its share of war. The concept of a mobile, efficient system to deliver medical care as close to the front as possible was shown to be workable. In spite of bad roads and other impediments, the American system of hospitals and evacuation procedures proved quite good. Time and time again, the men in the ambulance companies put aside fear and placed themselves in harm's way to render assistance to their fallen comrades in the infantry. Many paid the price. The field hospitals themselves were not immune from enemy shelling and bombing, despite large white crosses placed on their tents.[149] The role of the medicos drew just praise from correspondent John Nelson: "Of the ambulance companies and field hospital companies of the Division no praise could be too great. Noncombatants, in action they were always compelled to receive punishment and never permitted to retaliate. They had much to do, and they did it well."[150]

This relatively small group of men, fifty officers and 1,008 enlisted,[151] cared for more than 60,000 men during their tour of duty which encompassed 208 days in the line.[152] In the process they suffered 155 casualties, including nineteen dead, seven of whom were killed in action. Seven of their number were captured and made prisoners of war when they refused to abandon their wounded at Seicheprey. Individual soldiers received numerous decorations, including eight croix de guerre (one with palm), seven Distinguished Service Crosses, and 147 citations in orders. The Sanitary Train or its various units received a total of twenty-two citations from either the French or American armies.[153] Colonel Jones describes their spirit of self-sacrifice:

Forced at all times to work in the midst of dangers and discomforts, surrounded by the brutalities and disillusionizing influences of war, there seemed deep bedded within them the consciousness that their service was one of kindliness, thoughtfulness, and the self-sacrifice of the true humanitarian. War only intensified their idealism.[154]

NOTES

1. Martin Gilbert, *The First World War* (New York: Henry Holt, 1994), 508 and 513–18.

2. Ibid., 519–22.

3. Edward Coffman, *The War to End All Wars* (Madison: Univ. of Wisconsin Press, 1986), 359.

4. Gilbert, *First World War,* 519; Frederick Pottle, *Stretchers: The Story of a Hospital Unit on the Western Front* (New Haven, Conn.: Yale Univ. Press, 1929), 359; *Stars & Stripes*, April 18, 1919, 1 (uniform and basic equipment, including helmet and gas mask). USMA.

5. Paul Braim, *The Test of Battle: The American Expeditionary Forces in the Meuse-Argonne Campaign* (Newark: Univ. of Delaware Press,1988), 144 (50,280). But see Coffman, *War to End All Wars*, 363 (50,475).

6. Meirion Harries and Susie Harries, *The Last Days of Innocence: America at War, 1917–1918* (New York: Random House, 1997), 451; Gilbert, *First World War,* 540 (62,000 influenza deaths in the U.S. Army).

7. Stars & Stripes, February 28, 1919. 1. USMA.

8. Coffman, *War to End All Wars,* 359–60.

9. Jonathan Gawne, *Over There! The American Soldier in World War I* (London: Greenhill, 1997), 72.

10. Harvey Cushing, *From a Surgeon's Journal* (Boston: Little, Brown, 1936), 504–505. See also *Stars & Stripes*, April 18, 1919, 3. (As of April 1919, there were 50,000 AEF sick and wounded in hospitals.) USMA.

11. Stars & Stripes, November 22, 1918, 1. USMA.

12. Laurence Stallings, *The Doughboys* (New York: Harper and Row, 1963), 369.

13. Worcester Evening Post, April 18, 1919, 1. WPL.

14. Boston Sunday Globe, April 20, 1919, 1. BCL.

15. Worcester Telegram, April 19, 1919, 16. WPL; Boston Herald, Saturday Morning, April 19, 1919, 1; Boston Globe, April 19, 1919. BCL.

16. James Duane, *Dear Old "K"* (Boston: Thomas Todd, 1922), 157.

17. James G. Harbord, *The American Army in France, 1917–1919* (Boston: Little, Brown, 1936), 552.

18. Field Orders No. 3, 26th Division, U.S., 15 January 1919. MNGA.

19. *Roster Medical Department, 26th Division*. MNGA; Bert Ford, *The Fighting Yankees Overseas* (Boston: McPhail, 1919), 119 (refers to fifteen injured).

20. Frank P. Sibley, *With the Yankee Division in France* (Boston: Little, Brown, 1919), 350.

21. Duane, *Dear Old "K,"* 161.

22. Stanley J. Herzog, *The Fightin' Yanks* (Stamford, Conn.: Cunningham, 1922), 135.

23. U.S. Army Center of Military History. *Order of Battle of the United States Land Forces in the World War: American Expeditionary Forces, Divisions* (Washington, D.C.: GPO, 1988), 128; Emerson G. Taylor, *New England in France: A History of the Twenty-sixth Division U.S.A.* (Boston: Houghton Mifflin, 1920), 288.

24. Carlo D'Este, *Patton: A Genius for War* (New York: HarperCollins, 1995), 278–79; Alonzo L. Hamby, *Man of the People: A Life of Harry S. Truman* (New York: Oxford Univ. Press, 1996), 79; Coffman, *War to End All Wars*, 358–59.

25. Sibley, *With the Yankee Division in France,* 350–51; Taylor, *New England in France, 1917–1910,* 299–300.

26. Orders No. 19, Headquarters, 101st Sanitary Train, 5th March, 1919 (citing Memorandum, HQ, 26th Division). NA RG120.

27. Orders No. 22, Headquarters, 101st Sanitary Train, 7th March, 1919. NA RG120.

28. Orders No. 20, Headquarters, 101st Sanitary Train, 6th March, 1919. NA RG120.

29. Sibley, *With the Yankee Division in France,* 350–51; Taylor, *New England in France, 1917-1919,* 299–300.

30. Coffman, *War to End All Wars,* 358.

31. Memo to C.O. 101 Sanitary Train, 11 February, 1919. NA RG120.

32. Sibley, *With the Yankee Division in France,* 351; Taylor, *New England in France, 1917–1919,* 300.

33. *Stars & Stripes,* March 28, 1919, 8. USMA.

34. Field Order No. 6, 26th Division U.S., 15 March 1919. MNGA; Frederick E. Jones, *Historical Sketch of the Medical Department of the 26th Division,* typescript, n.d., with "Introductory Note" and other comments by R. S. Porter, 8 August 1919, 39; Orders No .29, Headquarters, 101st Sanitary Train, March 25th, 1919 (reference to Troop Movement Order No. 21, Headquarters, A.E.C., March 16th, 1919. NA RG120.

35. Orders No. 29, Headquarters, 101st Sanitary Train, March 25th, 1919. NA RG120.

36. Ford, *Fighting Yankees Overseas,* 229; Orders No. 29, Headquarters, 101st Sanitary Train, March 25th, 1919. NA RG120.

37. *Encyclopaedia Britannica,* 1959, s.v. "Brest."

38. Pottle, *Stretchers,* 77. See also W. G. Hudson, *The War Diary of W.G. Hudson 1917–1918,* entry for April 28, 1918. CHS.

39. U.S. Army Center Of Military History, *Order of Battle of the United States Land Forces in the World War. American Expeditionary Forces: General Headquarters Armies, Army Corps, Army Services of Supply Separate Forces,* vol.1 (Washington, D.C.: GPO, 1988), 67–69.

40. Ford, *Fighting Yankees Overseas,* 228.

41. Pottle, *Stretchers,* 81–82.

42. Joseph H. Ford, ed., *The Medical Department of the United States Army in the World War,* vol. 2, *Administration of American Expeditionary Forces* (Washington, D.C.: GPO, 1927), 465; *Historical Report of the Chief Engineer: Including All Operations of the Engineer Department, American Expeditionary Forces 1917–1919* (Washington, D.C.: GPO, 1919), 338 (report says "5,000 acres," but given the dimensions of one mile by one and one-half miles this is not realistic.). See also Harbord, *American Army in France, 1917–1919* ("one thousand seven hundred acres").

43. Pottle, *Stretchers,* 81.

44. Ford, ed., *Medical Department of the United States Army in the World War,* vol. 2, *Administration,* 465–69.

45. William E. Haseltine, *The Services of Supply of the American Expeditionary Forces: A Statistical Summary* (Washington, D.C.: GPO, 1919), 33 and 36. (Refers to 700 corrugated iron barracks, which must have included barracks for permanent party.). See also *Historical Report of the Chief Engineer*, 338 ("about 850 buildings for officers and men.")

46. Ford, ed., *Medical Department of the United States Army in the World War*, vol. 2, *Administration*, 469–71.

47. Jones, *Historical Sketch*, 39.

48. Orders No. 1, Headquarters, 101st Sanitary Train, 2nd January, 1919. NA RG120.

49. Orders No. 2, Headquarters, 101st Sanitary Train, 9th January, 1919. NA RG120; For yet another attempt by the army to recycle, see the plan to use kitchen wastes for the manufacture of soap and munitions. *Stars & Stripes*, November 1, 1918, 1. USMA.

50. Orders No. 3, Headquarters, 101st Sanitary Train, 15th January, 1919. NA RG120.

51. Field Orders No. 3, 26th Division, U.S., 15 January 1919. See also Field Orders No. 4, 21 January, 1919. MNGA.

52. Memorandum, Entraining Officer, 101 Sanitary Train, 9 January 1919, para. 2. NA RG120.

53. Ibid., para.2.

54. Memorandum to Unit Commanders, Headquarters, 101st Sanitary Train, 2nd February, 1919 (quoting from Memorandum No. 10, "Instructions to Commanders of Troop Trains," Headquarters, American Embarkation Center, A.P.O. 762, January 28th, 1919). NA RG120.

55. Orders No. 7, Headquarters, 101st Sanitary Train, 25th January, 1919. NA RG120.

56. Field Orders No. 5, Headquarters, 101st Sanitary Train, 21st January, 1919, as amended by Field Orders No. 7 (25th January) and Field Orders No. 8 (27th January). NA RG120.

57. Orders No. 5, Headquarters, 101st Sanitary Train, 21st January, 1919. NA RG120.

58. Field Orders No. 7, para. 4, Headquarters, 101st Sanitary Train, 25th January, 1919. NA RG120.

59. Orders No. 10, Headquarters, 101st Sanitary Train, 6th February, 1919. NA RG120.

60. Jones, *Historical Sketch*, 39.

61. Orders No. 10, Headquarters, 101st Sanitary Train, 6th February, 1919. NA RG120.

62. Orders No. 14, Headquarters, 101st Sanitary Train, 13th February, 1919. NA RG120.

63. Prior to his promotion to lieutenant colonel.

64. Orders No. 8, Headquarters, 101st Sanitary Train, 4th February, 1919. NA RG120.

65. Memorandum to Unit Commanders, Headquarters, 101st Sanitary Train, 4th February 1919. NA RG120.

66. Memorandum to Battalion School Officers, Hqtrs., 101st Sanitary Train, 21st February, 1919. NA RG120.

67. Orders No. 11, Headquarters, 101st Sanitary Train, 8th February, 1919. NA RG120.

68. Supplemental Instructions to Orders No. 12, Headquarters, 101st Sanitary Train, 8th February, 1919. NA RG120.

69. Field Orders No. 5, 26th Division, U.S., February 17, 1919. MNGA; Supplemental Instructions No. 2, Orders No. 12, Headquarters, 101st Sanitary Train, 16th February, 1919. NA RG120.

70. Orders No. 21, Headquarters, 101st Sanitary Train, 7th March, 1919. NA RG120. See also Connell Albertine, *The Yankee Doughboy* (Boston: Brandon Press, 1968), appendix (sketch of the logo).

71. Orders No. 15, Headquarters, 101st Sanitary Train, 13th February, 1919. NA RG120.

72. Special Orders No. 30 (Extract), Headquarters, 101st Sanitary Train, 17 February, 1919. NA RG120.

73. Instructions for use of Bathing and Delousing Plant, Headquarters, 101st Sanitary Train (n.d.). NA RG120.

74. Memorandum to Unit Commanders, Headquarters, 101st Sanitary Train, February 25 [1919]. NA RG120.

75. Memorandum to Unit Commanders, Headquarters, 101st Sanitary Train, 9th March, 1919. NA RG120.

76. Orders No. 23, Headquarters, 101st Sanitary Train, March 9th, 1919. NA RG120.

77. Orders No. 25, Headquarters, 101st Sanitary Train, 17th March, 1919. NA RG120.

78. Bulletin No. 1, Headquarters, 101st Sanitary Train, 21st March, 1919 (citing Letter from Harry C. Hale, Major General, 19th March, 1919). NA RG120.

79. Orders No. 27 (as amended by Orders No. 28, 24th March, 1919), Headquarters, 101st Sanitary Train, 22nd March, 1919. NA RG120.

80. Field Orders No. 6, Headquarters 26th Division, A.E.F., 15 March 1919. MNGA. See also Jones, *Historical Sketch,* 39.

81. Orders No. 29, Headquarters, 101st Sanitary Train, March 25th, 1919. NA RG120.

82. Field Orders No. 9, Headquarters, 101st Sanitary Train, 26th March, 1919. NA RG120.

83. Field Orders No. 6, Headquarters 26th Division, A.E.F., 15 March 1919. NA RG120. But see Ford, *Fighting Yankees Overseas,* 88 (eight hours).

84. Orders No. 31, Headquarters, 101st Sanitary Train, 30th March, 1919. NA RG120.

85. Orders No. 32 (as amended by Orders No. 33, 30th March, 1919), Headquarters, 101st Sanitary Train, 30th March, 1919. NA RG120.

86. Orders No. 30, Headquarters, 101st Sanitary Train, *30th March, 1919.* NA RG120.

87. Extract, Special Orders No. 57, Headquarters, 101st Sanitary Train, March 19, 1919. NA RG120.

88. Orders No. 29,Paras. 11, 13, 14, and 16, Headquarters, 101st Sanitary Train, March 25th, 1919. NA RG120. Captain Sheehan was reassigned to the 101st Infantry on March 20, 1919 per Roster Medical Department, 26th Division. MNGA.

89. This is somewhat confusing, since the Sanitary Train was definitely assigned to Billeting Section No. 6. Perhaps the troop kitchens for both Sections No. 5 and No. 6 were adjacent to each other.

90. Orders No. 34, Headquarters, 101st Sanitary Train, 1st April, 1919. NA RG120.

91. Weekly Report of Sick and Injured, Form 211, 103 Field Hospital, Montigny, France (week ending January 7, 1919). NA RG120.

92. Ibid. (week ending January 14, 1919).

93. There seems to be some inconsistency in the preparation of these reports regarding the unit strength. The form clearly refers to both "officers and men" to be shown on one line as a consolidated figure. I am certain that many of these reports simply list the number of enlisted only.

94. Roster Medical Department, 26th Division. MNGA.

95. After a review of the materials contained in boxes 3613 through 3615 in Record Group 120 at the National Archives regarding the 103rd Field Hospital Company, including daily, weekly, and monthly reports, my best estimate is that the unit admitted a total of 6,420 patients. There were 151 patient deaths recorded, most as a result of serious injuries and wounds treated during July 1918. The records are often incomplete and at variance (some greatly) with each other. I have relied on the monthly Nominal Check List for the period

August 1917 through and including June 15, 1918. These lists contain a numerical listing of all patients, beginning with Register No. 1 and ending with number 3,334. Presumably, the hospital maintained a register, but none was contained within these boxes. Inexplicably, after that date, the Nominal Check List merely records the patient's service number and not the register number. Not surprisingly, in my view, from that point on the list is less accurate, grossly undercounting admissions. For the period June 16, 1918, through April 1919, I have relied on the Weekly Report of Sick and Injured (Form 211), which seemed to be the most complete record. Even so, these valuable reports are missing for May 15, 1918, through and including June 18, 1918, and for that period I have used the Daily Reports and the Nominal Check List. This fact impacts upon the accuracy of the number of patient deaths, which are more than likely somewhat undercounted.

96. Orders No. 6, Headquarters, 101st Sanitary Train, 23rd January, 1919. NA RG120.

97. Orders No. 8, Headquarters, 101st Sanitary Train, 27th January, 1919. NA RG120.

98. Orders No. 5, Headquarters, 101st Sanitary Train, 21st January, 1919. NA RG120.

99. Company Order #4, 103rd Field Hospital Company, 6 February 1919 and Orders No. 10 (corrected copy), Headquarters, 101st Sanitary Train, 6th February, 1919. NA RG120.

100. Ford, ed., *The Medical Department of the United States Army in the World War*, vol. 2, *Administration*, 779–80; *History of Camp Hospital No. 72 at Château du Loir (Sarthe)* (typescript, n.d.). NA RG120.

101. Instructions for use of Bathing and Delousing Plant, Headquarters, 101st Sanitary Train (n.d.). NA RG120.

102. Extract, Special Orders No. 30, Headquarters 101st Sanitary Train, 17 February 1919. NA RG120.

103. Company Order #7, 103rd Field Hospital Company, 12 March 1919. NA RG120.

104. Orders No. 30, Para. 1, Headquarters, 101st Sanitary Train, 30th March, 1919. NA RG120.

105. Return of the Enlisted Force of the Medical Department, 103 Field Hospital, 101 Sanitary Train, 26th Division, American E.F. (No date). NA RG120.

106. Sibley, *With the Yankee Division in France*, 351 (first ship *Mount Vernon*); Duane, *Dear Old "K,"* 164 (SS *America*, formerly German ship *Amerika* took the 104th Infantry home.); Taylor, *New England in France*, 301 (Reference to *Mount Vernon, Agamemnon,* and *America*.); Ford, *Fighting Yankees Overseas*, 229–30 (reference to *Mount Vernon, America, Agamemnon,* and *Mongolia*).

107. Taylor, *New England in France*, 301.

108. Ford, *Fighting Yankees Overseas,* 250.

109. Duane, *Dear Old "K,"* 166; Ford, *Fighting Yankees Overseas,* 248–51.

110. Embarkation Order #154 (Revised), Troop Movement Embarkation Section, Base Section #5, April 5th, 1919 (The order included 2,288 officers and enlisted men from 101st Train HQ, 101st Supply Train, 101st Sanitary Train, a portion of 101st Ammunition Train [HQ, Motor Bn. HQ, Co. A and Co. B], Field Hospital #338. In addition, there was a group of "casuals," composed of forty-five officers and forty enlisted.). NA RG120. See also *Stars & Stripes*, April 18, 1919, "Recent Sailings," 2, column 1. USMA.

111. *Worcester Evening Post*, April 19, 1919. WPL.

112. *Worcester Evening Post*, April 18, 1919, 2. WPL. The six other reconstruction aides were: Miss Margaret Cobb, East Orange, N.J.; Miss Grace Courter, Newark; N.J.; Miss Mildred Hadley, Evanston, Ill.; Miss Ruth B. Pickett, Des Moines, Iowa; Miss Elizabeth Melzer, New London, Conn.; and Miss Virginia Fox, Riverside, Conn. According to the

Boston Herald, Isabel Villiers was from Reading, not Boston. *Boston Herald*, April 19, 1919, 14, col. 2. BCL.

113. *Lloyd's Register of Shipping* describes the vessel as of British registry, with a home port of Liverpool. She was built in Belfast, Ireland, in 1899, by the firm of Harland & Wolff. Her overall length was 552.5 feet, her width 59.3 feet, and her draft 28.9 feet. However, Kludas lists her overall length as 570 feet. Her gross registered tonnage was 10,422 tons. She was a single-screw, steel-hulled, four-masted, schooner-rigged vessel and was capable of fourteen knots. The ship was sold to the Red Star Line in 1927 and made several runs between Antwerp and New York prior to being sold for scrap in 1929. See Arnold Kludas, *Great Passenger Ships of the World*, vol.1, *1858–1912* (Cambridge: Patrick Stephens, 1975), 67 and Frederick Emmons, *The Atlantic Liners* (New York: Bonanza, 1972), 38–39.

114. Extract, Special Orders No. 65, Headquarters, 101st Sanitary Train, April 7, 1919. NA RG120.

115. Special Orders No. 66, Headquarters, 101st Sanitary Train, April 12, 1919. NA RG120.

116. *Worcester Telegram*, April 10, 1919, 1 and April 17, 1919, 1. WPL.

117. *Worcester Evening Post*, April 18, 1919, 2. WPL.

118. Duane, *Dear Old "K,"* 161.

119. *Worcester Telegram*, April 17, 1919. WPL.

120. Duane, *Dear Old "K,"* 167.

121. Herzog, *Fightin' Yanks*, 136.

122. Taylor, *New England in France*, 302 (April 22, 1919). But see Ford, *Fighting Yankees Overseas*, 251. Ford states that the review took place on April 23, 1919. Taylor is correct, and Ford is in error.) *Boston Daily Globe*, Wednesday Morning, April 23, 1919, 1. BCL.

123. Taylor, *New England in France*, 302 (April 25, 1919). But see, Duane, *Dear Old "K,"* 169, which sets the 26th as the day of the parade, but he is in error. Ford, *Fighting Yankees Overseas*, 258. MNGA. See also *Boston Sunday Globe*, April 20, 1919, and *Boston Evening Globe*, April 25, 1919, 1. BCL.

124. *Boston Evening Globe*, April 25, 1919, 1. The temperature at 1 P.M. at the start of the parade was 37 degrees and the warmest it would get all day. BCL.

125. *Boston Sunday Globe*, April 20, 1919, 1. BCL.

126. *Worcester Telegram*, April 26, 1919, 1–2. WPL.

127. *Boston Sunday Globe*, April 20, 1919; *Boston Evening Globe*, April 25, 1919. BCL.

128. Ford, *Fighting Yankees Overseas*, 258.

129. Duane, *Dear Old "K,"* 169.

130. Final Regimental Return, 101st Sanitary Train, Camp Devens, Mass., 29th April, 1919. NA RG407.

131. Bert Ford, *Fighting Yankees Overseas*, 85 ("Phalanx of Aces"); *"Immortal Yankee Division"* (pamphlet), 5–6 ("Sacrifice Division" and "Shock troops par excellence."); Harry A. Benwell, *History of the Yankee Division* (Boston: Cornhill, 1919), 4 (quoting Ferdinand Foch, "Saviors of Paris"); John Nelson, *A Brief History of the Fighting Yankee Division A.E.F., on the Battlefront February 5, 1918–November 11, 1918* (Worcester, Mass.: Worcester Evening Gazette, 1919), 3 and 10 (quoting General Degoutte, "shock troops par excellence").

132. Daniel W. Strickland, *Connecticut Fights: The Story of the 102nd Regiment* (New Haven, Conn.: Quinnipiack Press), 307 (text of Orders No. 19, H.Q. 26th Division, A.E.F., 13 January 1919).

133. Sibley, *With the Yankee Division in France*, 160.

134. *Immortal Yankee Division 1917–1919*, 19.

135. Sibley, *With the Yankee Division in France*, 353–54. But see "Annual Report," *Assembly*, June 10, 1931, 200. Edwards ultimately received, the Legion d'Honneur (Commandant) and the croix de guerre from the French, the Order of Leopold (Grand Cross) from the Belgians, and Haller Swords from the Polish government.

136. "Annual Report," *Assembly*, June 10, 1931, 199. USMA.

137. *Worcester Evening Post*, February 14, 1931, 2. WPL.

138. "Annual Report, *"Assembly*, June 10, 1931, 198–201; Connell Albertine, *The Yankee Doughboy* (Boston: Brandon Press, 1968), 304. (Buried with wife and daughter. The gravesite is located in Section 3, Grave 4073. ANC.)

139. *Worcester Evening Post*, February 14, 1931, 1–2. WPL.

140. *Worcester Telegram*, February 14, 1931. WPL.

141. *Worcester Evening Post*, February 14, 1931, 1. WPL.

142. *Worcester Telegram*, February 16, 1931, 1 and 7. WPL.

143. *Worcester Evening Post*, February 16, 1931, 1–2. WPL.

144. Braim, *Test of Battle*, appendix 4, 178; *Immortal Yankee Division*, 5 ("First full division to arrive in France. . . . No other division has seen so long and continuous service on the front"). See also Ford, *Fighting Yankees Overseas*, 29 and 164–65; Taylor, *New England in France*, 29–30.

145. Braim, *Test of Battle*, appendix 4, 178 (1st Division 220 days versus 193 days for the 26th Division).

146. Ibid., appendix 5, 179 and appendix 7 (calculation of casualties includes "dead, wounded, and evacuated for illness").

147. Stallings, *Doughboys*, appendix, 375. But see Ford, *Fighting Yankees Overseas*, 258 (1,730 dead); Sibley, *With the Yankee Division in France*, 342 (11,955 casualties); Taylor, *New England in France*, 302 (footnote: 2,168 killed in action and 13,000 wounded).

148. *Immortal Yankee Division 1917–1919*, 3. But see Taylor, *New England in France,*302. (footnote refers to 14,441 replacements for the division). See also *Stars & Stripes*, February 28, 1919, 2. USMA. Confirms number of replacements received for the period May 1, 1918 to November 13, 1918. The article indicates that many replacements were actually existing division members returning from treatment for sickness or wounds. Division strength stood at 20,709 at the time of the armistice. If the division went home at full strength of 28,000 and we assume that all replacements were not original division men, total replacements would be 21,732, leaving 6,268 original members of the division, or 22.4 percent and not 15 percent. That clearly would not be the case. If we subtract the 4,236 deaths and assume that two-thirds of the remaining replacements were not original members, a total of 11,664, the grand total of new replacements would be 15,900 (4,236 plus 11,664), or 56.7 percent. Thus, the remaining percentage of original men would be 43.3 percent. This compares favorably with the percentage of original returnees from the 103rd Field Hospital (40 percent). Without comparing passenger lists, and assuming higher turnover rates for the combat sections, I would estimate that, overall, a more accurate percentage of original members returning to the United States with the division would be between 30 percent and 35 percent.

149. See generally, chapter 5.

150. Nelson, *Brief History of the Fighting Yankee Division*, 7.

151. *Immortal Yankee Division 1917–1919*, 14.

152. Worcester Evening Post, April 18, 1919, 2 (quoting Lt. Col. Frederick Jones). WPL. For a sketch of the activities of the Medical Department during the war, see *Stars & Stripes*,

April 18, 1919, 1. USMA. Compare days in line with endnote 141 (193 versus 208). The lower figure may be tied to the establishment of the division headquarters in the various sectors. Some individual units served for longer periods in line. For example, the 51st Field Artillery Brigade was attached to the 42nd Division for ten days following the relief of the rest of the Yankee Division in the Pas Fini sector.

153. Porter, *History*, 381–82. See also Eben Putnam, *Report of the Commission on Massachusetts' Part in the World War*, vol. 1, *History* (Boston: Commonwealth of Massachusetts, 1931), 141 (Putnam refers to twelve Massachusetts men killed, but Sanitary Trains contained men from all over New England.). Roster Medical Department, 26th Division refers to Lt. Joseph P. Burke and six others captured at Seicheprey and returned at the armistice. MNGA.

154. Jones, *Historical Sketch*, 39.

Appendix I: Division Medical Organization Table

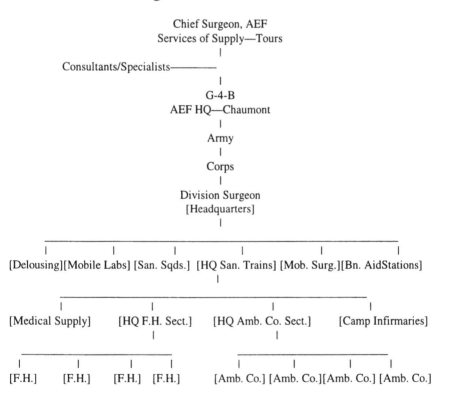

Chief Surgeon, AEF
Services of Supply—Tours
|
Consultants/Specialists————
|
G-4-B
AEF HQ—Chaumont
|
Army
|
Corps
|
Division Surgeon
[Headquarters]
|

[Delousing]	[Mobile Labs]	[San. Sqds.]	[HQ San. Trains]	[Mob. Surg.]	[Bn. AidStations]

[Medical Supply]   [HQ F.H. Sect.]   [HQ Amb. Co. Sect.]   [Camp Infirmaries]

[F.H.]	[F.H.]	[F.H.]	[F.H.]	[Amb. Co.]	[Amb. Co.]	[Amb. Co.]	[Amb. Co.]

Source: Based on Table 4, Final Organization, Medical Department, AEF, Charles Lynch, ed., *The Medical Department of the United States Army in the World War*, vol. 8, *Field Operations* (Washington, D.C.: GPO, 1925), 49.

Appendix II: Collection and Evacuation of Wounded

Zone	Station	Function	Means of Transport
Collecting	Battalion Aid Station	First Aid	Company Litter Bearers

↓

Zone	Station	Function	Means of Transport
Collecting	Dressing Station	Dress Wounds and Forward Patients	Litter Bearer Section Amb. Co

↓

Zone	Station	Function	Means of Transport
Collecting	Field Hospital	Surgery and Treatment; Sort and Forward	Motor Section Ambulance Company

↓

Zone	Station	Function	Means of Transport
Evacuation	Evacuation Hospital	Sophisticated Surgery and Treatment	Evacuation Ambulance Company

↓

Zone	Station	Function	Means of Transport
Evacuation	Base Hospital (Red Cross or Army)	Full Service	Ambulance, Train, or Ship

↓

Zone	Station	Function	Means of Transport
Distribution	Special or General Hospitals in Home Territory	Treatment or Convalescence	Hospital Ships or Trains

Source: Based on Figure 35, diagram of the U.S. Army evacuation organization, W. W. Keen, *The Treatment of War Wounds* (Philadelphia, 1917), 18, and Chart II, Charles Lynch, ed., *The Medical Department of the United States Army in the World War*, vol. 8, *Field Operations* (Washington, D.C.: GPO, 1925), 262.

Appendix III: Passenger List RMS *Canada*, September 16, 1917

Name	Rank	Next of Kin
Commissioned Officers:		
Frederick A. King	Major	Mrs. Elizabeth King, Mother 1 Cumberland St. Boston, Mass.
Harold F. Parker	First Lieutenant	Mrs. F. R. Parker, Mother 192 Dartmouth St. Boston, Mass.
Joseph R. Helff	First Lieutenant	Mrs. J. G. Helff, Mother 37 Prospect St. Keene, N. H.
James Y. Rodger	First Lieutenant	Mrs. Irene W. Rodger, Wife 366 Worthen St. Lowell, Mass.
William S. Schley	First Lieutenant	Mrs. Frances E. Schley, Wife 19 Dixwell St. Jamaica Plain, Mass.
Roy F. Brown	First Lieutenant	Mrs. Lillian Brown, Wife Provincetown, Mass.

Noncommissioned Officers:

Burton P. Woodbury	Sergeant First Class	Mrs. Helen M. Dickey, Mother 80 Lynn Street Everett, Mass.
John Harriss	Sergeant First Class	Mr. H. J. Harriss, Father 608 Hancock St. Abington, Mass.
Raymond Bliss	Sergeant First Class	Mr. F. P. Batchelor, Step Father 411 Massachusetts Ave. Boston, Mass.
Charles E. Burrill	Sergeant	Mr. Edward H. Burrill, Brother Central Street Saugus, Mass.
Joseph P. Dean	Sergeant	Mrs. Gilligan, Sister 127 Eustis Street Boston, Mass.
Authur F. Gormley	Sergeant	Mrs. G. Gormley, Mother 18 Creighton St. Jamaica Plain, Mass,
Roy Jackson	Sergeant	Mr. Purcell Jackson, Brother Bay State Railroad Lynn, Mass.
Austin J. King	Sergeant	Mr. C. H. King, Father 27 Brantwood Rd. Arlington, Mass.
George W. Quilty	Sergeant	Mr. Robert Quilty, Father 35 Topliff St. Dorchester, Mass.

Enlisted Men:

John P. King	Cook	Mr. F. King, Father 55 Benefit Street Worcester, Mass.
George L. Sullivan	Cook	Mrs. M. J. Sullivan, Mother Murray Street Lynn, Mass.
James P. Cronin	Mechanic	Mrs. Mary Cronin, Mother 133 Hudson Street Somerville, Mass.
Stewart J. Aldous	Private First Class	Mr. Frederick A. Aldous, Father Pine Street Dedham, Mass.
Andrew Allen	Private First Class	Mr. Andrew Allen, Father 48 Cranston Street Boston, Mass.
Thomas L. Aylward	Private First Class	Mrs. Catherine Aylward, Mother 14 Belmont Street Charlestown, Mass.

Richard G. Brine	Private First Class	Miss E. Griffin, Friend 51 White Street Waverly, Mass.
Gerard A. Carty	Private First Class	Mr. Thomas M. Carty, Father 126 Eustis Street Boston, Mass.
Joseph J. Carty	Private First Class	Mr. Thomas M. Carty, Father 126 Eustis Street Boston, Mass.
John J. Casey	Private First Class	Mrs. M. Casey, Mother 32 Mozart Street Jamaica Plain, Mass.
John J. Campbell	Private First Class	Mrs. A. Campbell, Mother 6 Wise Street Jamaica Plain, Mass.
Charles W. Chisholm	Private First Class	Mrs. M. Chisholm, Mother Halifax, Nova Scotia
Leslie W. Connor	Private First Class	Mrs. Anna Connor, Mother 18 Middlebury Street Lawrence, Mass.
Lester F. Comley	Private First Class	Mr. Henry R. Comley, Father 6 Sherman Street Lexington, Mass.
William F. Cody	Private First Class	Mrs. Patrick Cody, Mother 13 Linden Street Somerville, Mass.
Patrick H. Fitzgerald	Private First Class	Mr. M. H. Fitzgerald, Father 52 Meridan Street East Boston, Mass.
William A. Flynn	Private First Class	Miss Margaret Flynn, Sister Rhode Island State Hospital Providence, R. I.
Olin A. Goodale	Private First Class	Mrs. A. E. Goodale, Mother 53 South Street Jamaica Plain, Mass.
John Goss	Private First Class	Mr. D. J. O'Brien, Friend 22 Cowperwaithe Street Cambridge, Mass.
George N. Geer	Private First Class	Mrs. Alfred Geer, Mother 325 School Street Bennington, Vt.
Hyman Herold	Private First Class	Mr. L. Segall, Friend 51 North Washington Street Boston, Mass.
Myer H. Hillson	Private First Class	Mr. Joseph Hillson, Father 44 Powder House Boulevard Somerville, Mass.
Leroy R. Hogan	Private First Class	Mrs. A. Hogan, Mother 12 Cliff Street Roxbury, Mass.

Oliver W. Hood	Private First Class	Mr. Hood, Father 60 Aster Street Lynn, Mass.
Clayton G. Locke	Private First Class	Mr. O. A. Locke, Father 14 Oakland Street Lexington, Mass.
Daniel La Chappelle	Private First Class	Mr. Joseph E. La Chappelle, Father 17 Cross Street So. Bridge, Mass.
Fred H. Mealey	Private First Class	Mrs. C. Mealey, Mother 137 H. Street South Boston, Mass.
John J. Milan	Private First Class	Mrs. M. Milan, Mother 925 East Broadway South Boston, Mass.
Joseph P. McLaughlin	Private First Class	Mrs. Mary McLaughlin, Mother 11 Lake Avenue Woburn, Mass.
Walter D. Neville	Private First Class	Mrs. D. J. Neville, Mother 16 Dearborn Place Roxbury, Mass.
William M. Neville	Private First Class	Mrs. D. J. Neville, Mother 16 Dearborn Place Roxbury, Mass.
Oscar Norlin	Private First Class	Mrs. A. Norlin, Mother 359 Trapelo Road Waverly, Mass.
David T. Percy, Jr.	Private First Class	Mr. David T. Percy, Father 11 Water Street Arlington, Mass.
James J. Quinn	Private First Class	Mrs. James J. Quinn, Mother 11 Rutland Street Malden, Mass.
Albert E. Richardson	Private First Class	Mrs. A. Richardson, Mother 54 Myrtle Street Medford, Mass.
Percy Sharpe	Private First Class	Mrs. F. W. Sharpe, Mother 26 Rowell Street Dorchester, Mass.
Lewis Sheffield	Private First Class	Mr. William Sheffield, Father 72 Summer Street Revere, Mass.
George K. Slater	Private First Class	Mrs. __. B. Slater, Mother 20 Ballard Street Jamaica Plain, Boston, Mass.
Robert Sullivan	Private First Class	Mrs. J. Sullivan, Mother 5 Hayes Street Cambridge, Mass.
Harry Swanson	Private First Class	Mrs. N. K. Swanson, Mother 164 Beach Street Waverly. Mass.

David Swartz	Private First Class	Mrs. M. Swartz, Mother 67 Clifford Street Roxbury, Mass.
Clarence Tichell	Private First Class	Mr. John M. Tichell, Father 22 Washington Avenue Chelsea, Mass.
Herbert P. Thompson	Private First Class	Mr. H. S. Thompson, Father 5 Jacob Street Windsor, Vt.
Henry Von Kamecke	Private First Class	Mrs.M. E. Blake, Friend 4 Adams Street Waltham, Mass.
Harold D. Wetzler	Private First Class	Mr. D. Wetzler, Father 45 Lunt Street Norfolk Downs, Mass.
Cornelius Wharton	Private First Class	Mrs. M. H. Wharton, Mother 6 Elm Street Brookline, Mass.
Lawrence H. Woodbury	Private First Class	Mr. George I. Woodbury, Father 713 Broadway Everett, Mass.
Edward L. Zimmerman	Private First Class	Mrs. S. Zimmerman, Mother 301 Columbia Street Cambridge, Mass.
James Buchan	Private	Mr. Robert Buchan, Brother 96 Pleasant Street Concord, N.H.
Percy M. Chapman	Private	Mrs. Julia M. Chapman, Mother 56 Summer Street Norwich, Conn.
Joseph E. Carroll	Private	Mrs. John Carroll, Mother 6 Holborn Park Roxbury, Mass.
Henry J. Garrant	Private	Mrs. Emily Garrant, Mother 26 Alynn Street Hartford, Conn.
Fred Geer	Private	Mrs. Alfred Geer, Mother 325 School Street Bennington, Vt.
Norman B. Grimshaw	Private	Mrs. William Grimshaw, Mother 15 Peter Parley Road Jamaica Plain, Mass.
Everett A. Hanley	Private	Mrs. Nellie E. Hanley, Mother 99 Canterbury Street Worcester, Mass.
George W. Heffernan	Private	Mr. Charles T. Heffernan, Father 66 Chestnut Avenue Jamaica Plain, Mass.
William Keenan	Private	Mr. W. H. Keenan, Father 35 Woodman Street Jamaica Plain, Mass.

Edward McLaughlin	Private	Mrs. John E. McLaughlin, Mother 10 Forest Hills Street Jamaica Plain, Mass.
Charles E. Magill	Private	Mrs. Margaret Madden, Grandmother 23 Gayhead Street Jamaica Plain, Mass.
Stephen X. Mahoney	Private	Mrs. D. J. Neville, Friend 16 Dearborn Place Roxbury, Mass.
Joseph Malouin	Private	Mrs. J. Malouin, Mother 91 Buffum Street Lynn, Mass.
Thomas H. Marshall	Private	Mrs. G. N. Marshall, Mother 5 Elliot Place Jamaica Plain, Mass.
Michael McCullock	Private	Mrs. C. McCullock, Mother 156 Water Street Eastport, Maine
Peter L. McGorty	Private	Miss Frances A. McGorty, Sister 610 Cambridge Street Allston, Mass.
Thomas Milne	Private	Mrs. J. Milne, Mother 4 Hagar Street Jamaica Plain, Mass.
John Morriss	Private	Rev. D. Thompson, Friend Glace Bay, Nova Scotia, Canada
Charles D. Rooney	Private	Miss E. Rooney, Sister 42 Mystic Street Charlestown, Mass.
Edward J. Shay	Private	Mrs. James P. Shay, Mother 7 Curve Street Framingham, Mass.
Charles R. Tyner	Private	Mrs. L. Tyner, Mother 160 O Street So. Boston, Mass.
Harry Waite	Private	Mrs. M. Waite, Mother Pasadena, Calif.
Joseph P. Quinlan	Private	Mrs. Patrick Quinlan, Mother 100 Endicott Street Worcester, Mass.
Charles W. Zimmerman	Private	Mrs. Anna Zimmerman, Mother Bridge Street Dedham, Mass.
Alfred Woollacott	Private	Mr. John Woollacott, Father 94 Phillips Street Fitchburg, Mass.

Appendix IV: Enlisted Men Ready to Sail, April 1, 1919

Sergeant First Class:

Charles E. Burrill*	Arthur T. Gormley*	Percy A. Sharpe*

Sergeant:

Joseph J. Carty*	Roy Jackson*	Austin J. King*
Michael A. McCullock*	George W. Quilty*	Henry Von Komecke*

Corporal:

Charles W. Chisholm*	Joseph P. Dean*	Edward J. Shay*

Cook:

John P. King*	Albert E. Richardson*	

Mechanic:

Olin A. Goodale*		

Wagoner:

Stewart J. Aldous*	William F. Cody*	Lester F. Comley*
Myer H. Hillson*	Daniel J. LaChapelle*	Thomas Milne*

Private First Class:

Thomas L. Aylward*	Alan C. Barnard	Harold O. Batcheller
Lee R. Buffington	James T. Cronin*	Ollie L. Davis
Theodore J. Fendel	Patrick H. Fitzgerald*	Wesley M. Jones
Willie B. Kerr	Charles H. Mahn	Stephen X. Mahoney*
Joseph Malouin*	Fred H. Mealey*	Walter D. Neville*
William M. Neville*	Drew Pruitt, Jr.	Daniel M. Rogers
John T. Scanlon	Harry E. Whitman	Alfred Woollacott*

Private:

Alvin J. Abrahams	Albert B. Goods	Wilfred O. McCulloch
Gottfried Andersson	William J. Hearst	Fred McDonald
Ralph O. Bemis	Claudio G. Hollowell	Thomas W. Munroe
George Bengel	James A. Hoover	Leonard J. Parish
Paul O. Bennett	Jesse H. Hutchinson	John W. Rainbolt
George L. Benson	Vincent Jaskola	Franklin Reisinger
John A. Brittian	Alberic P. Jette	Guy G. Summers
James F. Buchan*	William A. Johnson	Benjamin F. Taylor
Gerard A. Carty*	Frank S. Koslowski	William K. Thompson
Clarence S. Cullum	William Laforgee	Clarence Tichell*
George A. Delaplane, Jr.	Thomas H. Lewis	Gustave A. Tufteland
Albert F. Dicterle	Milton Logston	Percy H. Waite
Harry J. Fagan	George C. Long	Lee Wonderly
Eastman A. Fountain	Herbert B. Lord	
Fred Fuller	Joseph A. McCourt	

*Indicates also on passenger list of RMS *Canada* as of September 16, 1917.

Note: Sgt. Eugene E. Harden, Pfc., Temple F. Catron, Pfc., Emil C. Haugue, and Pvt. Ron A. Fifield sailed earlier with Headquarters Detachment, 26th Division.

Source: National Archives, Record Group 120.

Appendix V: Sick Call
(Treatment of Disease)

The high incidence of all contagious diseases was cause for concern on the part of the chief surgeon, AEF. In a circular letter directed to all medical officers, dated May 4, 1918, he observed that these diseases, primarily scarlet fever and diphtheria, were particularly prevalent among the newly arrived troops. He attributed the outbreaks to overcrowding, personal uncleanliness, and *"promiscuous spitting."* He urged doctors to take a more proactive role and actually seek out men with sore throats rather than waiting for the daily reports to filter back to them. However, what really concerned him was the fact that the death rate among doughboys from these infectious diseases was twice that of men in the same age group in the civilian population. Statistics for the months of January, February, and March of 1918 showed that out of a total of 784 deaths among the officers and men of the AEF from all causes other than combat, 523 were due to infectious disease. Of the latter, pneumonia and meningitis led the list with a combined total of 461 deaths.[1] Later on, just prior to the fatal influenza epidemic, the *Stars & Stripes* reported that during the first year in France the AEF had experienced 131,075 cases of sickness, with mumps the leading malady, followed by bronchitis and venereal disease. Of that number, there were only 923 deaths reported.[2] Some of these diseases, such as the common cold, were not immediately life threatening, but as long as large groups of soldiers suffered from any of them, not only were the men less effective in performing their duties but the problems were likely to spread.

Medical personnel had two weapons in the fight against infectious diseases, quarantine and sterilization. The rules concerning quarantine were taken very seriously, as is evidenced by a circular letter issued on December 26, 1917, which declared, "UNAUTHORIZED BREAKING OF QUARANTINE SHOULD BE SEVERELY PUNISHED." Depending upon the disease, quarantine often included those who had been in contact with persons known to have contracted the disease—seven days in the case of scarlet fever, twenty-one days for measles or small pox. Medical personnel were urged to isolate patients immediately until they could be sent to a contagious hospital, and to wash well after contact. The straw in patients' beds was to be burned, and their clothing and blankets sent along with them. Their mess kits, clothing, and blankets were not to be washed with those of other personnel. When a patient left the hospital, his sheets and pillow cases, as well as other bedding and hospital clothing had to be sterilized prior to washing.[3] Recognizing that there was not enough equipment for large-scale steam sterilization of blankets, clothing, and mattresses, the top brass authorized the less effective alternative of formaldehyde. Lieutenant Colonel Bevans described this method as "slightly more than a surface disinfection." It was emphasized that formaldehyde was not an insecticide; that it would not kill lice, roaches, or bed bugs. Also, even though this method was effective in killing bacteria, it was ineffective in penetrating fabric to remove stains made by sputum or other bodily discharges.[4]

"NITS MAKE LICE": TRENCH FEVER, TYPHUS, AND SCABIES

Lice were a universal plague. The men had many euphemisms for them, from "cooties," to "arithmetic bugs," to "trench dandruff."[5] The British Tommie called them "gray backs."[6] Every diarist at one time or another referred to regular "shirt readings"[7] to remove the pests. Many a soldier idled away time squishing these creatures between thumb and forefinger like grains of rice. The British referred to this as "crumbing up" or "chatting" after yet another name for lice ("chatts").[8] These creatures infested soldiers on both sides equally. In *All Quiet on the Western Front*, Erich Maria Remarque's hero Paul Baümer describes the process: "Killing each louse is a tedious business when a man has hundreds. The little beasts are hard and the everlasting cracking with one's fingernails very soon becomes wearisome. . . . We set around with our shirts on our knees, our bodies naked to the warm air and our hands at work."[9] Some men dripped hot candle wax on the creatures and collected the hard wax when it cooled. Both methods were ineffective.[10] The most common problem was itching; soldiers afflicted with numerous lice were constantly scratching the bites.[11] Historian Denis Winter describes the soldier's plight:

The physical side was unpleasant, for the lice could be felt moving about and men could become so sensitive that, after a fortnight of infestation, each bite could be felt. Scratching, in the filthy conditions of trench life, risked boils, impetigo or ulcers particularly around shoulders and waist where clothing was closest to skin and activity most vigorous.[12]

The human louse is known to be the carrier of several diseases, including typhus fever and louse-borne relapsing fever. These ailments are associated with the generally unsanitary conditions attendant upon war and natural disasters. The louse is a small, wingless, parasitic insect that has been around mankind since the dawn of civilization. Unless they are passed from one person to another, lice live their whole lives—from eggs, which cling to hair and clothing, to adulthood—on a single host.[13] Typhus is transmitted by a louse that itself has been fatally infected with a microorganism called rickettsia (*Rickettsia prowazekii*). The fecal matter of the louse, which contains the disease, is deposited in the lesions and abrasions in the skin produced by scratching. Chills and fevers follow, along with nausea, headache, loss of appetite, and general malaise. Recovery can take more than two weeks. It does not usually prove fatal in younger persons, but when it does, the patient usually becomes delirious and then comatose; heart failure then ensues.

It was also learned that lice cause trench fever which manifests itself with sharp pains in the shins and results in a high fever. Weeks of recovery were needed.[14] During the early days of American participation on the front in France, the cause of the malady was unknown. The louse was considered the chief suspect, but this was confirmed only when volunteers from the 26th Division agreed to participate in an experiment conducted by the Red Cross (as discussed earlier). Some of the volunteers were injected with infected blood, while others had bags taken from the clothing of men who had trench fever tied to their forearms. Those who were inoculated came down with the disease within four to six days. The others held on for eighteen to twenty-one days. The symptoms of the disease included severe frontal headaches and high fever, along with "mystagmus" affecting the eyes, muscular weakness, and listlessness. This was followed by conjunctivitis ("pink eye"), spots on the abdomen, a stiff neck, and pain in the lumbar region, as well as the shins, elbows, and wrists. Finally, the doctors noted an enlarged spleen and some effect upon the heart. The patients were confined to bed. Reading was out of the question because of the eye problems, as was exercise, due to the general feeling of weakness and lethargy. Atropine was tried, but that dried up the skin, and the men found that food tasted like "wood shavings."[15]

In addition to trench fever and typhus, scabies, a mite-borne infestation, made its appearance among the troops. The mite is a popular name for another parasitic insect found the world over. Scabies is often referred to as the "Itch." The disease is characterized by intense itching (especially at night), a rash, and follicular papules or vesicles.[16] The condition was often further complicated by the soldier himself. The lesions were sources of intense itching, and men who scratched repeatedly soon became infected, due to the deplorable conditions under which the soldier had to exist.[17]

More showers and an effective laundry service helped with lice and mites. However, hot water alone was not enough, since it did not kill all the louse eggs, most of which were secreted in the seams of the garment and hatched within hours of washing.[18] The recommended treatment was a hot shower with "green" soap and the application of a sulphur ointment. This was repeated the second day. On the third day, a hot shower only was taken. The problem was kept in abeyance by the regular application of a 3 percent sulphur ointment.[19]

In the Yankee Division, the situation improved somewhat when the 101st Sanitary Train placed in service a mobile bathing and delousing station. At first the efficiency of this unit was limited, since the vehicle was drawn by two horses.[20] However, the division later obtained two large, steam-powered Thresh-Foden Disinfestors. The boiler that drove the engine also made steam for two large cylinders mounted on the truck chassis. Inside each cylinder was a basket to hold the clothing being disinfested. These monsters lumbered along at a speed of four miles an hour, visiting each unit in turn. Each truck had a crew of two, and a sergeant was in charge of the operation. So heavy were these vehicles that the crews often had to repair roads and shore up bridges before proceeding.[21] In addition, clothing had to be washed and returned to the soldiers who had been deloused.[22] In typical doughboy humor, the delousing process was referred to as a visit to "Scratchville-by-the-Sea."[23]

TRENCH FOOT

In a circular letter dated November 18, 1917,[24] Lt. Col. James L. Bevans, the Yankee Division surgeon, described the causes for the all too common malady known as "trench foot," as well as the cure for it. The report was based upon his firsthand observation of more than a thousand student officers and enlisted men in the 1st Corps schools. Of that number, more than 300 had suffered from trench foot. He blamed the abominable weather and the conditions under which the men had to live and study, from poorly heated tents and dirt-floored barracks to constantly wet shoes and socks. Trench foot, he concluded, came in four stages. During the first stage, the patient's feet were "*hyperemic* and *edematous*" (swollen with blood and body fluids), and he usually complained of a severe burning sensation. The second stage saw the formation of small blisters the size of split peas, containing a gelatinous substance; the patient complained of a numbness in an area away from the blisters. During the third stage, bluish or violet spots appeared near the base of the big toe, at the joints of the smaller toes, or in some cases the outer edge of the sole of the foot or on the heel. The areas beyond those points would become cold and lifeless. By the fourth stage, the skin over the discolored areas cracked, and ulcers formed.

Most of the cases Lieutenant Colonel Bevans observed were in the first stage, and these men remained on duty. They were, however, required to keep their feet dry, change their socks and shoes two or three times daily, and refrain from wearing tightly wrapped puttees. In addition, all afflicted men were required to submit to a three-step prophylactic treatment. First, their feet were washed with a lather composed of green soap, pulverized camphor, and a powdered borate of sodium. Next the feet were thoroughly dried, and a dusting powder was applied, a combination of talcum powder and powdered camphor. Finally, on the following morning, the feet were rubbed with whale oil just prior to putting on clean, dry socks. The results of this treatment/prophylaxis were excellent, and all but two first-stage patients were cured. Better yet, it showed that a soldier could be treated for this disability at an infirmary within his own battalion, and that, if caught in time, it caused a negligible loss of his services.

For those cases in the second, or "blister," stage, the patient was confined to bed, and he was given much the same treatment as those with a first-stage problem. In addition, large blisters were excised and compresses applied. These were changed daily, and soaked in a solution composed of camphor and ether. Usually the patient returned to duty within five to seven days. Serious cases were transferred to a field hospital for treatment. So successful was the treatment for the first-stage cases that all students at the school were required to follow the prophylaxis.

Shortly after Lieutenant Colonel Bevans issued his circular letter, the AEF published a bulletin confirming his findings. Since trench foot was now known to be preventable, the condition of a soldier's feet was considered a matter of good discipline. As a result, unit commanders were to be held personally responsible for regular foot inspections and prophylaxis. Commanders were required to maintain an ample supply of dry woolen socks and serviceable shoes and boots.[25] Ten months later, at the beginning of the fighting in the Argonne, the new division surgeon, Maj. Frederick E. Jones, issued a circular letter that anticipated the fall and winter seasons. In it he emphasized the preventable nature of the problem and the need for all medical and line officers to conduct regular foot inspections. In addition, he reminded them that the 26th Division Disciplinary Battalion was currently operating a laundry to clean and return socks, and that each man was to be issued a box with either oil or powder for his feet and a can of "dubbin" (a mixture of tallow and oil) to apply to his boots in order to waterproof and preserve the leather.[26]

VENEREAL DISEASE

Pershing made venereal disease a special target.[27] His approach was contrary to those of the French and British commands, which were more pragmatic and less puritanical.[28] In fact, it was in sharp contrast to Pershing's own policy during the Mexican incursion, when the army had licensed and sponsored brothels,[29] and during the fighting in the Philippine Islands, when the U.S. Army had run the largest licensed brothel in the world.[30] Now, however, he quickly rebuffed Premier Clemenceau's offer to help set up licensed brothels for the American troops.[31] Stern punishments, including court-martial and forfeiture of pay, were threatened, and chaplains could be counted on to back him up with fire and brimstone. A poster went so far as to declaim that, *"A soldier who gets a dose is a Traitor!"*[32]

However, the moral aspect of the issue was not the most important factor. Pershing was under extreme pressure from the Allies to increase American troop strength, and he needed the maximum number of "effectives" in the field. The British policy was to remove any man infected with a venereal disease from the line and send him for treatment at a base hospital, often up to a hundred miles away. The result of this policy was that the British were treating from 18,000 to 23,000 venereal cases, the equivalent of two full divisions. Although the French policy was to leave infected men closer to the front, by late 1917 they had treated nearly 1,000,000 venereal cases![33] Pershing chose Dr. Hugh H. Young, a noted urologist from Baltimore, Maryland, as the chief consultant in urology to the AEF. As a part of his duties, he helped design the policy for and the treatment of venereal cases. The procedures from a military standpoint resulted in General Orders No. 6, 34, and 77. The latter involved all unit commanders in the problem, directly tying their efficiency ratings to how effective they were in dealing with the disease. In addition, Pershing requested (and received) a daily report on the incidence of venereal disease within the ranks.

In 1910, Dr. Paul Erlich, a German scientist, introduced an arsenical compound called Salvarsan ("606") as a cure for syphilis.[34] At first the British and American armies adopted a time-consuming and painful procedure using this compound; a solution of Salvarsan was injected intravenously, and on alternate days the patient received an injection of mercurial oil in the buttocks. The French used a newer and more efficient procedure called the Levy-Bing method. After observing the French, Dr. Young recommended that their procedure be adopted by the AEF. It consisted of a hypodermic injection of the compound Novarsenobenzol every other day, and an intravenous injection of oxycyanide of mercury. The method was not only less painful but gave the medical corps the ability to treat more patients within a short period of time, as well as the flexibility to treat the problem at the regimental level.[35] Gonorrhea was also treated by chemotherapy, with a compound called Acriflavine.[36]

Division surgeons and their subordinates were trained in the procedures for treating venereal disease, and each regiment was issued a urological set.[37] In the Yankee Division, recovering patients were assigned to a special "venereal detachment," as a part of the Disciplinary Battalion, where they were put to work on roads and other projects behind the lines, thus freeing up infantrymen who might otherwise have been detailed to such tasks. The medical officers found virtually no ill effects in the patients stemming from the work details.[38] As a result of these policies and procedures, the AEF achieved an extremely low rate of venereal disease.[39] The policy continued even after the armistice. While medical records of venereal cases were confidential and were not to be used against a soldier, there was no doubt as to how these men would be dealt with. In a terse statement to all Yankee Division officers, the division surgeon, Maj. (later Lt. Col.) Fred E. Jones warned, *"Venereals will not go home with this Division."*[40]

Shortly after the Yankee Division arrived in France, the division surgeon issued a circular letter outlining the reasons for, and the methodology of treatment of venereal disease, in particular syphilis.[41] The proposed plan called for the treatment of venereal patients at the infirmary level, close to their units; it was the firm conclusion of Lieutenant Colonel Bevans that the disease was curable if treated as early as possible following its discovery. The added bonus was the underlying message to a soldier that a venereal disease did not automatically result in a trip to the rear. However, some cases were serious enough to warrant more specialized attention, and those men were sent on to camp hospitals or a special venereal hospitals. The watchwords were early diagnosis and treatment. Soldiers were encouraged to seek prophylaxis immediately after sexual encounters. The Yankee Division took the issue very seriously, but Major Jones might well be accused of stating the obvious when, in a circular letter directed to all medical officers, dated November 26, 1918, he stated, "Many realize the value of the prophylaxis but do not realize the importance of taking it immediately after exposure. *To take the prophylaxis the morning after spending the night with a woman is a doubtful procedure.* ... It is necessary to take the prophylaxis within three hours after intercourse.)[42]

DYSENTERY

Dysentery, bacillary and amoebic, along with diarrhea, were also scourges. The term "dysentery" covers a multitude of diseases exhibiting the same symptoms, principally blood and mucus in the stool, together with abdominal pain and tenderness. The colon is described as "contracted, painful and spastic." The onset is usually abrupt and accompanied by a high fever. The causative agents range from a bacteria (e.g., *Shigella shigae)* to an amoeba (e.g., *Endamoeba histolytica).*[43] With the bacillary type, death results from dehydration and intoxication. It is spread by water or food contaminated by the common housefly. The course of the disease can be mild or acute, with death taking place in two to three days. Doctors treated the disease with a polyvalent antidysenteric serum, and at the same time cleared the bowel with a saline solution. Salt volume was also restored through the administration of a hypertonic salt solution. Ipecac and opiates were not used, since they stopped bowel movements and thus kept the bacteria inside the intestine. With the later use of sulphur drugs, the treatment was much improved—too late, however, for the doughboys.

On the other hand, amoebic dysentery is generally characterized by high fever and diarrhea, together with occasional vomiting. The disease can become chronic and is often accompanied by complications including peritonitis, conjunctivitis, neuritis, and dysenteric arthritis. The protozoan agent feeds off the cells of the intestinal wall and causes the formation of cysts. The latter are the means by which the disease is transmitted, by water contaminated by fecal matter. Some persons appear to be merely carriers of the disease, which has an incubation period of up to sixty days. Death results from either the perforation of the large intestine and the peritonitis that follows, from hepatitis, or from gangrene of the bowel. It is quite common to experience no symptoms for long periods between bouts, often a year or more. The treatment used for amoebic dysentery was the subcutaneous administration of one grain of a medication called Ementine, an alkaloid of ipecacuanha. In acute cases, this relieved the symptoms but did not kill the amoeba. There were also potential side effects of the medication that could damage the heart. Doctors accompanied the treatment with ten to twelve drops of tincture of opium.[44]

Medical officers worked hard to eradicate the problems of dysentery and diarrhea. During the Yankee Division's stay in the Chemin des Dames sector, the French sanitary inspectors found substandard sanitary conditions. Among the problems noted were kitchens "almost universally in bad condition," failure to follow orders with regard to the "chlorination and boiling of water," and "indiscriminate defecation."[45] On an inspection tour of field kitchens in the same sector, Capt. William H. Blanchard, commanding officer of the 103rd Field Hospital, found the French kitchens to be "very good" but their American counterparts "quite poor." It was his observation that the kitchen personnel had "let down in the care of cooking material and handling of food" and that the ration, while satisfactory in terms of "quantity and quality," was "invariably spoiled," since insufficient time was taken to prepare it. He recommended that field hospitals receive garrison rations, augmented with milk and eggs, as well as "such other foods as necessary in diets for the sick."[46] These lessons were not fully learned, as evidenced by the breakdown of sanitary practices four months later in the fight above Château-Thierry in July 1918, where a full 70 percent of the division troops engaged suffered from dysentery or diarrhea. The incidence overall seemed to be higher among officers than among enlisted men, and higher during the summer months.

The Medical Department made three simple suggestions to prevent the occurrence of the problem: chlorinate drinking water, care for the latrines and properly dispose of all fecal matter, and bury the dead properly.[47] The department also made an effort to diagnose and isolate the disease at an early stage, not only those suffering with it but the carriers of the disease as well. In addition, Sanitary Train personnel urged unit commanders to destroy flies and to prevent their breeding. Since proper food handling was essential, special care was taken in the selection of men as cooks. To that end, medical personnel checked the stools of all cooks and food handlers, as well as water handlers and the drivers of water wagons. Any man found to be a carrier was not employed as a cook, and the findings were noted in his service record.[48]

Although there was a school for cooks at Langres,[49] the position of cook, like so many others, was most often filled by men without previous experience. Whether or not the experience of the men of a company was satisfactory was likely to depend upon the enthusiasm of the individual cook and the materials he had to work with. A typical field hospital company had two men assigned as cooks. An ambulance company had three cooks, and the headquarters of each section had one man assigned to the officers' mess.[50] Most cooking was done on portable cookers on wheels, or rolling kitchens, which were towed behind trucks. In the artillery, the contraption was connected to a limber, on which one of the cooks rode, and which was pulled by horses. Artilleryman Horatio Rogers of the 102nd Field Artillery describes one as follows: "The main part of it was a two-wheeled cart containing a firebox and a grate in the center, surrounded by metal containers for hot food and covered with a flat iron top on which broiling or frying could be done. A three-foot stovepipe gave it a far-fetched resemblance to a gun."[51]

In fact, the men referred to it as a "Slum Gun" or the "Soup Gun."[52] However, a "75 mm" it was not. Because the cooker was not as sturdily built as an artillery piece, on long trips it would often shake apart, or its bearings would freeze up; it would have to be abandoned or left behind for repair.[53] When that occurred, the company missed a hot meal. Each field hospital was assigned one rolling kitchen, sometimes referred to as a "Liberty" rolling kitchen.[54] However, just because the meal was served in a hospital did not guarantee its good quality. Alfred Ettinger spent some time recuperating at the U.S. base hospital at Allerey, where he described the food as "awful."[55] The unsung heroes of the war were the enlisted attendants who had to treat the unlucky souls suffering with dysentery. One such sufferer was Sgt. Arthur H. Lynch, who, after being confined to a ward with twenty-six other dysentery patients, wrote a letter to the editor of the *Stars & Stripes*. In it he observed:

There's only one ward in any hospital which is a meaner place to work in than the place filled with patients suffering from dysentery. And here these big, healthy men are diligently, carefully and patiently making it easier for the men who have become so weak that they cannot control the action of their organs. . . .

From early morning till late at night the same faces may be seen moving about the ward washing men, changing foul bedding, emptying refuse cans, taking temperatures and pulses. . . . Nothing seems too much trouble for them, and I've never heard one of them growl at the rankest, rottenest job a man can picture. . . . [They] are men to their backbones, but are seldom lauded.[56]

However, in spite of all efforts, throughout the war in France dysentery and other diarrheal ailments remained a problem for the doughboys.

CEREBROSPINAL MENINGITIS AND SCARLET FEVER

There was a relatively low incidence of cerebrospinal meningitis in the American armed forces, either at home or abroad. However, its high mortality rate (34 percent in the United States and 43 percent in the AEF) made it a force to reckon with. Overall, it ranked sixth as a leading cause of death. It was known as a "barracks disease" and had a tendency to be more prevalent during mobilization. There were many outbreaks in the United States at the various training facilities.[57] It favored enlisted men over officers. The culprit is the meningococcus bacteria, which is normally found in the posterior nasopharynx. The infection results in an inflammation of the meninges, the membranous covering of the brain and spinal chord. Man appears to be the only creature in which the infection is "spontaneous." There is a greater prevalence of the disease in the winter and early spring. Some persons are known "carriers." The infection is spread by "droplet infection" under conditions of close contact between carriers and those susceptible to the disease. Factors that contribute to the incidence of cerebrospinal meningitis are fatigue and hardship as well as other infections that tend to lower a person's resistance. The incubation period is four to five days. The disease progresses in three stages. The first stage begins in the nasopharynx and moves to the second stage, when the bacteria enter the bloodstream. The symptoms are rarely evident at this time. It is the third, and critical stage, in which the normal symptoms appear, such as vomiting, severe headache, and a stiff neck.

In order to diagnose the disease accurately, doctors had to examine the spinal fluid of the patient. The method was to puncture the spine and withdraw a sufficient quantity of fluid to test for the bacteria. Nasopharyngeal cultures could help, but there was no substitute for the spinal tap. The primary treatment was the injection of a Polyvalent Antimeningococcic Serum ("horse serum"), which was supplied by the Rockefeller Institute in the United States and the Pasteur Institute in France. The best results were achieved when the serum was administered within the first three days. Still, the results varied depending upon the numbers and types of antibodies in the serum and the strain of meningococcus that was infecting the patient. Normally between thirty and eighty strains of meningococci were used in the preparation of the serum. A hypodermic needle with 30 cc to 60 cc of the serum was injected in the spine immediately following the diagnostic lumbar puncture. If the examination of the fluid showed the presence of meningococci, the dose was repeated within twelve hours, then daily. A serious case could require six to ten injections.

In addition to the injections, the patient was placed in an isolation ward, since it was found that the meningococcus bacteria died quickly outside of the body. His bed was further isolated from others in the ward by sheets drawn around it to form a cubicle. Attendants (and sometimes the patient) wore caps, gowns, and even gauze masks. Antiseptic solutions, like Dichloramine T,[58] silver nitrate, and tincture of iodine, were used to wash hands, and sometimes as gargles or nasal sprays. Persons ministering to these patients, including doctors, nurses, and enlisted ward attendants, were required to have cultures taken every four days; unless the results were negative, they could not be assigned to other duties.[59] Efforts were made to make the patient comfortable and relieve his pain. His surroundings were kept quiet; he was given plenty of fluids, but medics took steps to make sure that he did not retain urine. Where contact carriers were found, they too were treated. Sometimes there were complications like hydrocephalus, arthritis, nephritis, bronchitis, or pneumonia. Often, the disease was accompanied by the measles, mumps, scarlet fever, diphtheria, or influenza.[60]

From time to time, there were outbreaks of scarlet fever in the units. This acute infectious disease is also caused by a streptococcus bacteria (*Streptococcus scarlatinae*). It is also spread by droplet infection, from contaminated food and drink, and from infected wounds. The incubation period is normally two to seven days after exposure. Patients exhibit a sore throat, headache, and a fever that lasts a week or more. In addition, the disease is recognized by the appearance of small red spots, redder and more diffuse than in measles. Treatment consisted of bed rest and plenty of fluids. The side effects could range from mastoiditis, arthritis, and nephritis, to rheumatic fever.[61]

IN THE GRIP OF THE GRIPPE: INFLUENZA

During the spring of 1918, an epidemic of influenza spread throughout the army on both sides of the Atlantic.[62] There is evidence that it began at Fort Riley, Kansas, in March.[63] Many soldiers contracted the disease and the pneumonia that often followed. In fact, between then and September, nearly one-quarter of the American army contracted some form of respiratory disease. Twenty-four camps in the United States alone were affected.[64] This initial outbreak was referred to by many army doctors as "three-day fever," because it usually lasted three to four days.[65] However, this was just a prelude to a far more deadly version that was to arise later that year.[66] Beginning with an outbreak on a ship in Boston Harbor during the last week in August 1918, the scourge spread quickly over a wide area. Particularly hard hit were military installations with large concentrations of men.[67] Up to that point, the good sanitary practices implemented by the armed services had resulted in a very low level of sickness among the military population.[68] All that was about to change.

Called the Spanish influenza, or simply "Spanish flu," once contracted the disease took a week or two to run its course. At first, in order to minimize concern, the doctors continued to refer to it as the "three day fever," but that was a misnomer.[69] Its symptoms included a high fever, aches and pains, headaches, and significant perspiration.[70] The worst complication was the pneumonia that often developed. In fact, virtually all of the fatalities from flu had contracted pneumonia. Those unlucky souls continued to have a high fever and were restless and delirious. Their complexion was described as blue or a "muddy, claylike pallor." Death usually resulted, if it did, within a week.[71] Aspirin and bed rest was the normal treatment, but any fluid built up in the lungs had to be pumped out.[72] Medical personnel wore gauze masks when ministering to patients.[73]

In spite of the awful weather and appalling battle conditions, for some reason the epidemic hit the stateside troops harder. The earlier flu outbreak may have left some with immunity, or perhaps the troops that had been fighting in France were more hardened and used to living among large bodies of men.[74] However, that is not to say that the effects were not serious in Europe. On the contrary, from September through November 1918, new cases were appearing at the rate of 11,000 per week—16,000 during the week ending October 5 alone.[75] At this time, the U.S. 2nd Division was evacuating 400–500 men a day, only 20 percent of whom were battle casualties.[76] During the Meuse-Argonne campaign, transportation of wounded and sick became a serious problem, due to poor and crowded roads.[77] Because of the overflowing hospital wards in France, Pershing asked in October that 1,500 nurses be sent immediately in place of the same number of combat troops.[78] General Pershing himself became ill with flu.[79] The disease peaked during mid-October,[80] but before it was through there were nearly 50,000 army deaths from flu. This figure, when added to the more than 5,000 sailors who succumbed, exceeded American battle deaths for the entire war.[81]

NOTES

1. Circular Letter No. 73, 4 May 1918, Office of the Division Surgeon (quoting from *Letter* from chief surgeon, A.E.F., 22 April 1918). NA RG120. In addition to pneumonia and

meningitis, the diseases were tuberculosis, typhoid fever, measles, syphilis, anthrax, scarlet fever, diphtheria, and mumps.

2. *Stars & Stripes,* August 9, 1918, 1. USMA.

3. Circular Letter No. 20, American Expeditionary Forces, Office of the Chief Surgeon, Headquarters 26th Division, December 26, 1917. NA RG120.

4. Circular Letter No. 60, March 12, 1918, Office of the Chief Surgeon, Headquarters 26th Division. NA RG120.

5. James T. Duane, *Dear Old "K"* (Boston: Thomas Todd, 1920), 45 and 119; Denis Winter, *Death's Men* (London: Penguin, 1978), 96–97; Ronald Schaffer, *America in the Great War: The Rise of the War Welfare State* (New York: Oxford Univ. Press, 1991), 164 ("pants rabbits" and "seam squirrels").

6. Lyn Macdonald, *The Roses of No Man's Land* (New York: Macmillan, 1989), 108.

7. David M. Kennedy, *Over Here: The First World War and American Society* (New York: Oxford Univ. Press), 209; Duane, *Dear Old "K,"* 21.

8. Winter, *Death's Men,* 97.

9. Erich Maria Remarque, *All Quiet on the Western Front,* (New York: Fawcett, 1967), 48–49.

10. Winter, *Death's Men,* 96–97.

11. *Encyclopaedia Britannica,*1959, s.v. "louse." There are two orders of lice, biting lice and sucking lice. The latter order *Anoplura,* or *Siphunculata* have claws well adapted to clinging to hair and clothing, and extrusable mouths capable of piercing the skin and sucking the host's blood or tissue fluids. Each type of louse is different, and there is distinct "host specificity." That is, one species of the louse is restricted to a distinct host species. The most common louse afflicting man belongs to the family *Pediculidae,* which comes in two varieties—the head louse (*Pediculus humanus capitas*) and the body louse (*Pediculus humanus corporis*). One other louse infests mankind, although it is not thought to be a serious carrier of disease. That is the pubic, or crab, louse. This creature commonly inhabits the pubic region, but can also be found in the eyebrows and beard.

12. Winter, *Death's Men,* 97.

13. *Encyclopaedia Britannica,*1959, s.v. "typhoid and paratyphoid fevers."

14. John Ellis, *Eye Deep in Hell* (Baltimore: Johns Hopkins Press, 1989), 57.

15. James Lung Bevans, *Medical History of the Twenty-sixth Division from Organization to June 24, 1918* (typescript n.d.), 7; Frank P. Sibley, *With the Yankee Division in France* (Boston: Little, Brown), 35–37; *Stars & Stripes,* February 22, 1918, 1 (refers to sixty volunteers). USMA.

16. *Encyclopaedia Britannica,*1959, s.v. "mite," and s.v. "scabies." The mite belongs to the order *Aracnida* as do spiders and ticks. Those that are human parasites, the cutaneous mites, belong to either of two families, one called *Sarcoptidae,* the other called *Demodicidae.* The culprit is the species known as *sarcoptes scabiei,* the fertilized female of which burrows into the host's skin and lays her eggs, and, as a consequence, is very difficult to eradicate. Larvae and nymphs are found in hair follicles, although mating occurs on the skin surface. Mites are prolific breeders. Fertilized females are passed from body to body by human contact. Follicular mange is caused by members of the species known as *Demodex folliculorum.* These are also difficult to eradicate, since they infest the hair follicles and sebaceous glands.

17. Harvey Cushing, *From a Surgeon's Journal* (Boston: Little, Brown, 1936), 276; Ellis, *Eye Deep in Hell,* 58.

18. Ellis, *Eye Deep in Hell,* 57.

19. Joseph F. Siler, ed., *The Medical Department of the United States Army in the World War*, vol. 9, *Communicable and Other Diseases* (Washington, D.C.: GPO, 1928), 556.

20. Bevans, *Medical History*, 7.

21. Richard Derby, *"Wade in, Sanitary!"* (New York: G. P. Putnam's Sons, 1919), 42–44; Jonathan Gawne, *Over There! The American Soldier in World War I* (London: Greenhill, 1997), 56–57.

22. Bevans, *Medical History*, 7.

23. *Stars & Stripes*, May 31, 1918, 2. USMA.

24. Circular Letter No. 6, Nov. 18, 1917, Office of the Division Surgeon. NA RG120. See also Frederick E. Jones, *Historical Sketch of the Medical Department of the 26th Division* (typescript, n.d.), 6. It was rare that a soldier died of trench foot, and that was only after gangrene had set in. In those instances, it was normal to remove the afflicted toes, and occasionally the foot. NA RG120.

25. *Stars & Stripes*, February 22, 1918, 8. USMA. See also Robert Graves, *Good Bye to All That* (New York: Doubleday, 1985), 173.

26. Circular Letter No. 97, 30 Sept. 1918, Office of the Division Surgeon. NA RG120; *The American Heritage Dictionary of the English Language*,1969, s.v. "hyperemia" and "edema."

27. Edward M. Coffman, *The War to End All Wars: The American Military Experience in World War I* (Madison: Univ. of Wisconsin Press, 1986), 132–33.

28. Winter, *Death's Men*, 150–52; Graves, *Good-Bye to All That,* 180 (the British marked the houses of prostitution with blue lamps for officers and red lamps for enlisted men).

29. Hugh Young, *A Surgeon's Autobiography* (New York: Harcourt, Brace, 1940), 301.

30. Schaffer, *America in the Great War*, 99. Pershing's detractors would contend that his puritanical attitude was somewhat hypocritical, since the general had been twice afflicted with gonorrhea, who preached continence and declared the delights of Paris off limits for most soldiers, and traveled regularly to the "City of Light" to visit his own mistress! Meirion Harries and Susie Harries, *The Last Days of Innocence: America at War, 1917–1918* (New York: Random House, 1997), 121–22; Schaffer, *America in the Great War*, 104; Gene Smith, *Until the Last Trumpet Sounds* (New York: John Wiley and Sons, 1998), 219.

31. Coffman, *War to End All Wars*, 133–34.

32. Kennedy, *Over Here*, 186–87. Emphasis added.

33. Young, *A Surgeon's Autobiography*, 276–77 and 284.

34. *Encyclopaedia Britannica*,1959, s.v. "Erlich, Paul."

35. Young, *A Surgeon's Autobiography*, 283–84.

36. Ibid., 253. See also W. W. Keen, *The Treatment of War Wounds* (Philadelphia: Saunders, 1917), 34–35.

37. Young, *A Surgeon's Autobiography*, 292.

38. Jones, *Historical Sketch*, 29 (Note by R. S. Porter); Young, *A Surgeon's Autobiography*, 358–59.

39. Young, *A Surgeon's Autobiography*, 312 and 320.

40. Circular Letter No. 101, 26 November 1918, Headquarters 26th Division, Office of Division Surgeon. NA RG120. Emphasis added.

41. Circular Letter No. 7, HQ 26th Division, Office of the Division Surgeon, November 19, 1917. NA RG120.

42. Circular Letter No. 101, 26 November, 1918, Headquarters 26th Division, Office of Division Surgeon. NA RG120. The prophylaxis involved washing the genitals with bichloride of mercury, followed by the injection of Argyrol into the urethra by means of a penis

syringe, after which the penis was smeared with calomel ointment. Byron Farwell, *Over There: The United States in the Great War, 1917–1918* (New York: W. W. Norton, 1999), 142. Emphasis added.

43. *Encyclopaedia Britannica,* 1959, s.v. "dysentery."

44. Siler, ed., *The Medical Department of the United States Army in the World War,* vol. 9, *Communicable and Other Diseases,* 324–49.

45. Circular Letter No. 56, Para. I. 2., February 27,1918, Headquarters 26th Division, Office of the Chief Surgeon. NA RG120.

46. Blanchard, Memorandum to Division Surgeon, 14 April 1918. NA RG120.

47. Siler, ed., *The Medical Department of the United States Army in the World War,* vol. 9, *Communicable and Other Diseases,* 324–34.

48. Ibid., 350–51; Circular Letter No. 20, 26 December 1917, Office of the Chief Surgeon, Headquarters 26th Division. NA RG120.

49. Laurence Stallings, *The Doughboys* (New York: Harper and Row, 1963), 34.

50. General Headquarters, American Expeditionary Forces, General Staff: First Section, Tables of Organization, Series A, January 14, 1918, corrected to June 26, 1918, dated August 1, 1918, Part I, Infantry Division, table 28.

51. Horatio Rogers, *World War I through My Sights* (San Rafael, Calif.: Presidio, 1975), 109.

52. Ibid., 53.

53. Sibley, *With the Yankee Division in France,* 107; Rogers, *World War I Through My Sights,* 109.

54. General Headquarters, American Expeditionary Forces, General Staff: First Section, Tables of Organization, Series A, January 14, 1918, corrected to June 26, 1918, dated August 1, 1918, Part I, Infantry Division, table 29.

55. Albert M. Ettinger and A. Churchill Ettinger, *A Doughboy with the Fighting 69th* (Shippensburg, Penn.: White Mane, 1992), 174.

56. Arthur H. Lynch, "Letter to the Editor," *Stars & Stripes*, October 11, 1918, 4.

57. Harries and Harries, *Last Days of Innocence,* 194.

58. See Keen, *Treatment of War Wounds,* 61–67. (For attributes and preparation of solution and as an effective alternative to the Dakin-Carrel Method outlined in chapter 4.)

59. Circular Letter No. 56, Para. V, February 27, 1918 (quoting from Circular No. 9, 7 February 1918), Headquarters 26th Division, Office of the Chief Surgeon. NA RG120.

60. Siler, ed., *Medical Department of the United States Army in the World War,* vol. 9, *Communicable and Other Diseases,* 203–20. See generally *Encyclopaedia Britannica,* 1959, s.v. "meningitis." (Later treated with either penicillin, sulpha drugs, or monovalent antimeningococcic serum ["rabbit serum"]).

61. *Encyclopaedia Britannica,* 1959, s.v. "scarlet fever."

62. Rod Paschall, *The Defeat of Imperial Germany, 1917–1918* (Chapel Hill, N.C.: Algonquin, 1989), 158–59.

63. A. A. Hoehling, *The Great Epidemic* (Boston: Little, Brown, 1961), 11.

64. Coffman, *War to End All Wars,* 81–82.

65. Hoehling, *Great Epidemic,* 31 and 107.

66. John Toland, *No Man's Land* (New York: Konecky, 1980), 436.

67. Hoehling, *Great Epidemic,* 24–28 and 34.

68. Coffman, *War to End All Wars,* 81.

69. Toland, *No Man's Land,* 527–28.

70. Hoehling, *Great Epidemic,* 31.

71. Coffman, *War to End All Wars*, 81–82; Hoehling, *Great Epidemic,* 27 ("cyanotic, blue in color from lung congestion").

72. Paul Braim, *The Test of Battle: The American Expeditionary Forces in the Meuse-Argonne Campaign* (Newark: Univ. of Delaware Press, 1988), 156.

73. Ibid.; Coffman, *War to End All Wars,* 82.

74. Coffman, *War To End All Wars*, 83.

75. Stallings, *Doughboys,* 323; Braim, *Test of Battle,* 113; Paschall, *Defeat of Imperial Germany, 1917–1918,* 183.

76. Derby, *"Wade in, Sanitary!"* 172–73.

77. Toland, *No Man's Land,* 429; Braim, *Test of Battle,* 155.

78. Paschall, *Defeat of Imperial Germany, 1917–1918,* 188.

79. Braim, *Test of Battle,* 126–27.

80. Coffman, *War to End All Wars,* 82.

81. Kennedy, *Over Here,* 189 (footnote119). But see Hoehling, *Great Epidemic,* 186 (25,000 army and 5,000 navy); Coffman, *War to End All Wars,* 84 (46,992 army and 5027 navy deaths from influenza). Worldwide, the situation was magnified. By the time it was over, it is estimated that between 21,000,000 and 27,000,000 people had died, including 150,000 in Great Britain, 400,000 in Germany, and 500,000 in the United States. See also Toland, *No Man's Land,* 527–28; Hoehling, *Great Epidemic,* 8 (21,000,000).

Appendix VI: Sick Call
(Treatment of Wounds)

POISON GAS

During the war, the most vulnerable people were the litter bearers and medics. They had to work under the most adverse conditions to bring the wounded to aid stations. These men braved shot and shell, as well as the wreaths of gas that often hung over the battlefield, especially in shell holes, where many of the wounded sought shelter. The gas mask was sometimes an impediment, since exertion made breathing more difficult with the mask on. Some chose not to wear the mask. These brave men went about their work oblivious to the deadly missiles about them. Removing and handling the clothing of mustard gas victims often led to the poisoning of the ambulance and field hospital personnel themselves.[1]

When the American medical units went to train with the French, their tutors were appalled at the lack of protection their students had been issued, and especially at their lack of any effective training. For years the French had been working out methods of treatment as well as suitable protective gear, such as non-permeable rubber gloves and coats with hoods.[2]

However, as the Americans became more experienced, they became more creative in solving problems. Poison gas was no exception. Given the rising number of gas cases and the need for quick treatment, they adopted an assembly-line method Henry Ford would have approved of. A treatment facility set up a line of stretchers covered with rubber blankets and tilted slightly head to foot on uneven sawhorses. All of a gas victim's clothing was removed and his valuables placed in "Dorothy bags" provided by the Red Cross. Douches containing an alkaline solution to irrigate the eyes, nose, and ears were suspended from wires above the stretchers. The gas victims were thoroughly washed by the enlisted attendants with soapy water poured from watering cans; the tainted water ran off quickly into wooden buckets. The deadly chemicals could then be disposed of. The patient was then dried, and sodium bicarbonate was sprinkled all over his body. This method proved very effective for the initial stage of treatment.[3]

By September 1918, the army had developed portable washing stations, much like the portable delousing ones. Each station consisted of two trucks and a dozen men, and it was always on call after a mustard gas attack. The first truck contained a 2,500-gallon water tank with water heaters. The other contained piping, tentage, and a supply of clean clothing. A crew could set up a rinsing station within minutes. These units had the capacity to handle twenty-four men at a time. Those who were badly burned were immediately evacuated to a hospital; the remainder stripped off their clothing and entered the facility. Helmets, shoes, and hands were dipped in limewater, and the men sprayed themselves with liquid soap. Approximately a minute and a half were expended in soaking, scrubbing, and rinsing. The men were hurried out to make way for the next batch and then were issued clean clothing. Attendants wore one-piece oilskin suits with headpieces, all of which was impermeable to gas.[4]

Because mustard gas was used with increasing frequency, Lieutenant Colonel Bevans issued guidelines for all medical officers in the 26th Division to assist them in the detection and defeat of this plague. The effects of the gas could be neutralized if the contents of four mess tins filled with chloride of lime was scattered over the affected area, in particular in a shell crater at its deepest part. Medical men doing so were directed to wear gloves so as to prevent burns, and furthermore they were to look particularly for evidence of the gas in liquid form, as it was often found toward the rear of the impact area.[5] As an alternative method of neutralizing the mustard gas, a vermorel solution, a mixture of sodium carbonate and sodium hyposulphite, was often sprayed over the affected area.[6]

All gasses caused serious effects if the exposure of the victim was lengthy or in a high concentration.[7] Worse, the symptoms of gas poisoning often did not show up for hours, sometimes a day or two. The soldier would go about his business, only gradually feeling the symptoms. When he perspired during exertion, such as a march, the sweat-soaked clothing brought the gas into contact with the skin and allowed the gas to begin its deadly work.[8] Quick action was called for when symptoms first appeared or a gas attack had taken place. The victim's clothing was stripped off and he was next given a hot soapy bath or shower.[9] New clothing had to be issued; battalion aide stations soon adopted the French procedure of maintaining a stock of clean uniforms at the site.[10] For victims of serious mustard gas poisoning, the medics applied zinc ointment to burns and castor oil to sore eyes.[11] Oxygen was frequently administered to gas casualties, with the exception of those exposed to chlorine gas.[12] Where a Haldane apparatus was unavailable and the administration of oxygen was indicated, the Gas Service devised a simple field expedient to produce it.[13]

The chief surgeon of the 26th Division was also a good case in point as to how seriously the question of gas treatment and defense were taken. In a circular letter dated February 27, 1918, he set forth guidelines for his medical officers in order to eliminate the apparent confusion of their roles with those of the officers of the Gas Service. While he urged cooperation, he clearly indicated that the treatment of gas poisoning victims was the responsibility of the Medical Department. Likewise, medical personnel were to help with the instruction of the troops in the precautions against gas as well as the proper use of gas masks. Special clothing as well as blankets used as gas curtains in dugouts were to be distributed by the medical supply officer to the various organizational surgeons. The Gas Service was responsible for the distribution of masks, sprayers, and klaxons. In turn, medical officers were expected to share their specialized knowledge with regard to gas and its effects with members of the Gas Service. In the event that his subordinate officers did not get the point and to eliminate any future turf disputes, the chief surgeon expressed his desire that medical officers *"accept rather than avoid responsibility with reference to the gas service."*[14]

As the fighting increased in intensity, medical officers found that not all "gas casualties" were in fact suffering the effects of the poison. Many soldiers were believed to be suffering from exhaustion or worse yet, malingering. However, it was often difficult for the battalion surgeon at an aid station to make that determination. Medical personnel were urged to "use proper judgment" in selecting gas casualties to be sent to the rear. If after four or five hours of observation, suspected cases developed no untoward symptoms, they were to be returned to duty. Some surgeons resorted to the stratagem of leaving suspected malingerers lying down through the meal hour, returning to the front line all of those who *"manifested a lively desire for dinner."* Doctors were urged not to ask questions that could suggest a response. Where phosgene was suspected, the patient was given a cigarette to smoke. The taste was distinctly bitter if the gas was present; the "tobacco test" became a simple and effective tool for diagnosis.[15] Lastly, it was recommended that all men who were to be treated for gas poisoning have their hair clipped short in order to facilitate the treatment.[16]

BULLETS, SHRAPNEL, AND FRAGMENTS

The eagerness of the doughboy was in stark contrast to the grim determination of the other Allied forces, jaded by three years of war. The policy makers in Washington were aware of the long casualty lists on both sides, and they had anticipated that all phases of the U.S. military effort would have to learn to cope with the particular nature of this war. This was true of the Medical Department, which sought to acquaint the nation's doctors with the latest techniques from the western front. War surgery and medicine had taken a quantum leap forward since the days of the Civil War. Accordingly, physicians like Dr. James Robb Church were sent by the army chief of staff to observe the methods employed by the French in coping with massive casualties and the horrendous wounds produced by high-velocity bullets and shells, not to mention poison gas. His book, *The Doctor's Part,* published in 1918, as a journal of his time as a military observer in 1916–1917, provided just such information and insights. Armed with letters of introduction from

Secretary of War Newton Baker and Theodore Roosevelt, Dr. Woods Hutchinson spent virtually all of 1917 either in Britain or on the western front observing British methods of treatment. The result was his book *The Doctor in War*, published in 1918. Likewise, Dr. W. W. Keen's book, *The Treatment of War Wounds*, published in 1917, was a collection of articles from contemporaneous medical journals (mainly British) dealing with the state of the art in war surgery. It provided would-be military surgeons some lifesaving insights and methods of dealing with surgical problems likely to be encountered on the battlefield or near it. Other doctors actually worked with the British, French, and Canadian forces prior to America's entry into the war, in spite of potential legal problems due to citizenship regulations.[17]

In all cases of wounds, one of the very first actions by the medic was the administration of an antitetanic serum as a preventive measure. Often a big purple "T" was painted on the wounded man's forehead indicating that he had been given the antitoxin.[18] During the division's stay in the Chemin des Dames, Lieutenant Colonel Bevans received reports that the procedure was not being followed in the central sector of the Yankee line, and he issued a reminder to all medical personnel.[19] Like that of gas gangrene, the threat of tetanus was very real, and the attitude was, "better safe than sorry." The mortality rate for soldiers who did not receive the serum was more than 70 percent.[20] Accordingly, doses of the serum were given at every stage of a wounded man's treatment, even following surgery. The serum was administered with a hypodermic needle, either intramuscularly, subcutaneously, and in cases where tetanus was definitely diagnosed, into the spinal cavity. Intra-venous injection was disapproved, due to the risk that the patient would go into anaphylactic shock. The classic symptom of tetanus was lockjaw (trismus), which was caused by the bacteria *Clostridium tetani*. However, military doctors did not wait for this to appear, since early diagnosis was critical to treatment and cure. Even the delay of a single hour could prove fatal. Nurses and ward attendants changing dressings were cautioned to look for "spasticity and increased reflex excitability of the muscles around the wound." In addition, they were to observe whether or not the muscles around the wound were more rigid than other muscles on the opposite side of the body, away from the wound. Any of these symptoms were to be reported immediately to the surgeon in charge of the case.

Some wounds were downright ghastly. Overall, the majority of wounds were inflicted by artillery fire, but rifle and machine-gun bullets did their share of damage.[21] Cranial wounds were very common, because of the extensive trench warfare. These wounds had a high mortality rate, because fragments of bone and metal often complicated the surgery.[22] Virtually all head wounds required investi-gation, however, there was debate as to when and how this was to be accomplished. Dr. Harvey Cushing, the famous Boston neurologist who spent considerable time with the 26th Division as a consultant, held the opinion that unless there was hemorrhaging, a patient with a head wound was best left alone and should be transported to the appropriate hospital in the rear, where an X-ray examination and full neurological information were available. Even a wait of day or two did not present a problem for him. He felt that the danger of infection, or worse, of doing more extensive damage, was not worth the risk. Some medical men even felt that where a bullet was lodged deeply in the brain, the best course was to leave it there and avoid the risk of infection.[23]

Abdominal wounds were the worst, because there was always the threat of peritonitis. The best results were achieved within six hours of the injury, but even then the mortality rate was high.[24] According to Keen, recovery rates dropped dramatically from 62.8 percent if the operation was performed within six hours, to 36.3 percent between six and twelve hours after, all the way down to 16.6 percent between twelve and sixteen hours after. As with head wounds, where there was no evidence or suspicion of hemorrhaging, the initial question for the medical personnel was whether or not to treat for shock and to stabilize him for his ride over a rough road. Where there was internal hemorrhaging the stomach might well be flaccid, as opposed to the marked muscular rigidity indicating the beginning of peritonitis. Several perforations from the same or multiple missiles were common. With multiple fragments, entry wounds were not always easy to locate in the bowel. Because of the ever-present danger of infection, all foreign bodies had to be removed. Starting with the cecum (the end of the large intestine), doctors were advised to work their way upward looking for perforations. These were to be wrapped in moist swabs and marked with tape, thus preventing the contents from spilling out. The colon and the posterior of the stomach were also to be examined. During 1917–1918, suture was preferred to resection, except where there was extensive damage to the mesentery membrane. Before closing, the surgeon was advised to "milk the gut" to prevent postoperative paralysis of the bowel and distention. The administration of morphine had to be watched, since too much could hide the abdominal symptoms. Quick transportation and timely operation were the keys to success.[25]

Chest wounds were also causes for concern. If the wound was small but open and let air move freely in and out, the most disturbing symptom was the sound of the patient's labored breathing, referred to as dyspnea. If that was the case, the wound was closed by strapping. However, if the wound was larger, the danger of infection loomed. The loose ends of bones were removed, and the wound closed by drawing the muscles and skin over it. If full closure was not possible, a drain was inserted and the cavity filled with antiseptic. In the case of intrathoracic hemorrhage, the medical personnel engaged in "watchful waiting." If there was no further hemorrhaging after seventy-two hours, the patient could be safely evacuated. Where the X-ray disclosed a foreign body or bodies in the chest, the patient was kept under observation for a day, unless his situation was critical. The object was then removed and the chest closed, after disinfection. If the patient was so critical as to affect heart rate and respiration, he was immediately evacuated, where possible, or operated on then and there, by rib resection and drainage.[26]

If the message to the doughboy was cautious enthusiasm, that went double for the military surgeon. Trained to save lives while operating under extraordinary stress, their temptation was great to perform an operation as soon as possible, and thus save a life. The experience of both the British and French was just the opposite.

There were just too many casualties, and decisions had to be made. Some wounded could safely wait, and some wounded *had to wait*. After weighing all the factors, from transport, the availability of qualified surgical intervention, to the gravity of the patient's condition, it was the doctor's decision whether or not to operate. However, this decision often placed great weight squarely upon the shoulders of the enlisted attendants. These young men, with virtually no previous medical training and learning on the job, were responsible for maintaining the patient's comfort, but more important, for treating him for shock and keeping him stabilized prior to surgery or transport to another hospital.

The field hospital was supposed to be cleared as rapidly as possible, especially under battle conditions, where room had to be made for new arrivals. In a Memorandum dated September 3, 1918, just prior to the St. Mihiel operation, Headquarters, 1st Corps reminded medical personnel that:

divisional hospitals must be as rapidly cleared as possible in order that they may be mobile at all times. Necessarily, a hospital for non-transportable wounded must be more or less immobilized, but it must also be evacuated as the condition of of the patients will permit so that it, too, may advance with the troops as the occasion requires.[27]

Recognizing that the field hospital, which was assigned the duty of treating the seriously wounded, had to make these decisions (i.e., immediate treatment or not), and wishing to care for all patients in a timely fashion, the American army instituted the practice of assigning surgical teams, including female nurses, together with X-ray equipment and technicians, to these hospitals to operate on cases considered non-transportable for medical reasons.[28] These cases were generally found among three classes: sucking chest wounds, perforating abdominal wounds, and severe hemorrhages. Since heart patients and spinal patients were believed to be able to stand transport before an operation better than after, they were to be sent on to the next facility.[29] Because medical personnel exercised discrimination with regard to evacuation and surgery, they learned much about the nature of wound shock. New treatments were applied, such as blood transfusions, the injection of stimulants like strychnine and vasoconstrictive drugs, and the raising of legs to improve circulation. In addition, field hospitals added shock wards and shock teams to combat this life-threatening condition and stabilize patients.[30]

"MENS SANIS": SHELL SHOCK[31]

This affliction was the direct result of intense, prolonged exposure to artillery fire or the stress of continuous combat. Shell shock manifested itself in a kind of paralysis (sometimes actual physical paralysis) and left the soldier unable to perform his duties. Some men also suffered from constipation.[32] A hollow, distant stare was a dead giveaway.[33] The condition was referred to at first as "war neurosis," but in 1915 the British adopted the term "shell shock." The term was frequently used on an informal basis, but for a variety of reasons, the British and Americans established a policy regarding its official use. A circular letter to all medical officers from the division surgeon of the 26th Division stated emphatically:

The term "shell shock" will not be used either by medical officers or enlisted men in handling cases of a psychoneurosis or in any suspicious cases. If the term "Psycho-Neurosis" cannot be mastered the term "Nervous" will be used. Have all members Medical Department instructed to use one or the other *and nothing else*.[34]

Where shell shock was suspected, medics and corpsmen were directed to write "N.Y.D. Nervous" on the patient's record or medical tag, meaning "not yet diagnosed, nervous." Battalion surgeons differed in their approaches toward those suffering from war neurosis or psychosis. Some sent virtually every man thought to be suffering from it to the rear, thus needlessly depleting the available infantrymen on the front line. Others were more practical, and they put them to work digging shelters and carrying litters. After carrying loaded litters more than 500 yards, exhausted, many asked to be sent back to the line.[35]

The Americans had the benefit of both British and French experiences in dealing with war neurosis. Dr. Thomas W. Salmon, a major in the Army Medical Corps, studied the British methods of treatment. He concluded that it was primarily a psychological disorder that resulted from either a trauma (e.g., a shell burst) or nervous exhaustion stemming from physical stress, lack of sleep, or stressful circumstances. As a result of his studies, he made certain basic recommendations. First of all, he suggested better screening both before induction and during training. Perhaps more important, he recommended that a psychiatrist be assigned to every division, and when that was not practical due to a shortage of such personnel, that certain medical officers undergo an intensive six-week course in how to recognize and treat the symptoms. In addition, the AEF organized a Neurology and Psychiatry Branch. For the most part, American patients were evaluated and treated close to their own units.[36]

Through the efforts of the surgeon general, William C. Gorgas, and others like Mary McMillan and Marguerite Sanderson, the U.S. Army Medical Department instituted an innovative program called the Division of Special Hospitals and Physical Reconstruction. Its mission was to look into physical and occupational therapy programs to help the wounded soldier recover and learn to be more self-sufficient in civilian life. At first, the small teams of young women encountered resistance from the predominately male mainstream hospital administration and staff. Many reconstruction aides were required to perform all kinds of menial tasks, like changing soiled bandages for overworked nurses and ward attendants, just to make themselves useful. Many were finally allowed to prove the worth of their skills. Reconstruction aides were divided into physiotherapists (physical) and occupational therapists. The former received training at places like Reed College in Portland, Oregon, prior to assignment overseas. Classes included anatomy, massage, and corrective gymnastics. On the other hand, occupational therapists were trained at places like Teacher's College at Columbia University. Their courses included weaving, woodwork, and basketry. However, as they were to find out, the patients themselves were interested in learning skills that would help them get and hold jobs, such as typing and mechanical drawing, and the aides changed emphasis to meet the need. Perhaps their most significant contribution was in the rehabilitation of men suffering from functional neuroses as a result of shell shock. Many of these men suffered such afflictions as partial paralysis, facial tics, tremors, and depression.[37]

What was learned much later was that some psychological damage is likely to manifest itself in virtually every soldier who has been exposed to prolonged periods of stress, particularly combat. "There is no such thing as getting used to combat."[38] Also, the symptoms do not always manifest themselves immediately but can show up years later. Author Robert Graves, himself a survivor of the trenches, described his condition in the postwar years:

Very thin, very nervous and with about four years' loss of sleep to make up. . . . I knew it would be years before I could face anything but a quiet country life. My disabilities were many: I could not use a telephone, I felt sick every time I traveled by train, and to see any more than two new people in a single day prevented me from sleeping.[39]

The American Psychiatric Association now recognizes the condition known to us as post-traumatic stress disorder.

ON DEADLY GROUND: GAS GANGRENE

Centuries of farming and the use of animal fertilizers have left a silent killer in the soil, like a time bomb awaiting the right time and place to explode. Massive artillery bombardment had denuded the landscape, particularly in places like Flanders, where the ground was churned into what the soldiers referred to as "sucking mud."[40] Couple those conditions with the staggering number of casualties, which all but overwhelmed the military's ability to evacuate and treat them, and you have the potential for a tragedy, within a tragedy, of enormous proportions. The silent killer was a bacteria, commonly referred to as gas bacillus or gas gangrene. Its scientific name was *Bacillus aerogenes capsulatus*, and it had been discovered by Welch and Nuttall in 1892. It went virtually unappreciated in the wartime planning due to the myth of the "clean" bullet wound. Prior to the First World War, a majority of the modern battles had been fought on a smaller scale, on uncultivated ground.[41]

Despite the often heroic efforts of litter bearers to remove casualties during and after battle, many wounded remained on the battlefield for days.[42] Their wounds could be relatively simple, or ghastly multiple, gaping wounds, where flesh and bone were rent and smashed, and all were mixed with bits of clothing, shell fragments, and the deadly ground. Both the French and British medical plans merely called for the application of antiseptic dressings in preparation for transportation of the wounded to the rear for more extensive treatment. First aid and dressing stations did what they could before sending the wounded down the line, but in many cases the damage was already done—often irreversibly. With every hour of delay, the odds increased that the bacillus had already begun its deadly, flesh-eating course. Wounds simply would not heal. Instead, they swelled with pus and putrefication. Surgeons cut away the necrotic flesh, in a procedure known as debridement,[43] only to find that the gangrene had spread overnight. Amputations, often successive and multiple, were common, and at first they were the only way to save a life. In fact, at some hospitals the rate of survival was only 20 percent. If the diseased wound was on the torso, death was virtually certain.[44] The doctors were at a complete loss, in spite of their efforts. There were no antibiotics and no effective disinfectants.[45] Sometimes luck was with the soldier; more often it was not.

Gas gangrene cases were often kept in separate wards, and those who treated them, particularly the nurses and aides, described their smell as overwhelming. Some could tell immediately upon entering a room whether or not gas gangrene was present.[46] Day after day, these ladies changed bandages and watched their charges slowly die as the bacteria ruthlessly consumed their flesh. Author Lyn Macdonald interviewed hundreds of doctors and nurses about their experiences. One, a British doctor serving on the western front, described gas gangrene and its effects:

> The wound was simply a mass of putrid muscle rotting with gas gangrene. . . . It was called that because the bacillus that grows in the wound creates gas. The whole thing balloons up. You can tap it under your fingers and it sounds hollow. . . . We would cut away as much of the diseased tissue as we could. On a leg or an arm we would remove the limb, but that didn't stop it. It just went on up.[47]

Not content to let this happen, Henry Dakin, a research chemist of British birth who had been working in New York,[48] and Alexis Carrel, worked tirelessly side by side to find an answer. In a hospital in the former Rond Royal Hotel at Compiegne, France,[49] they achieved remarkable success with the use of a hypochlorous acid solution; the wound was constantly soaked or flushed with it.[50] Later it became commonly known as the Dakin or Dakin-Carrel Solution. Its application to the wound burned somewhat, but when the alternative was considered, that was a small price to pay.[51] When he was confident that the procedure was effective, Carrel conducted clinics at Compiegne to educate other doctors. American physicians, anticipating their country's participation in the war, were introduced to the method at a special temporary hospital set up by the Rockefeller Institute in New York. By the time the country did actually get into the fight, most of its medical men were familiar with it.[52]

Prior to application of the solution, in addition to the debridement, the wound had to be thoroughly cleaned, and to the extent possible all debris and bone fragments removed. Also, any bleeding had to be stopped, since the solution had the effect of dissolving clots and could result in hemorrhage.[53]

The basic materials needed were a 500–1,000 cc glass container to hold the solution (approximately one meter above the wound), rubber tubing, an adjustable clamp for controlling the flow, rubber tube drains, glass connecting and distribution tubes, and cotton and gauze dressings. The idea was to make sure that the solution came in contact with all surfaces of the wound. The placement of the distribution tubes depended upon the nature of the wound, whether superficial or penetrating, and if the latter, whether anterior, posterior, or "through and through." For superficial wounds, a thin layer of gauze was placed over the wound and the distribution tubes secured to the wound edges. For penetrating wounds, the tube was inserted directly into the wound cavity to its full depth. If the cavity was collapsible, a small amount of gauze was packed into the wound to support the walls. Where the fluid was likely to flow back out, toweling was placed over the tube, and was sutured with silk so that the suture would not remain in the wound when the tube was removed. Some wounds had so many surfaces that multiple tubes with perforations had to be inserted so that all surfaces were exposed to the fluid. The entire wound was covered with a bandage. If the wound was on the hand, foot, or the stump of an amputation, the limb was immersed in the solution for ten to fifteen minutes every two hours. The surrounding skin was protected by petroleum jelly.[54]

At first, it was thought that constantly soaking the wound was best, but later the solution was administered in doses, by turning the adjustable clamp every two hours to release approximately 10 cc of fluid in order to keep the wound surfaces moist. Dressings were changed and wounds inspected daily. This procedure was followed until the wound was sterile, on average seven to nine days. Bacteria counts were checked every other day. Three negative counts in a row meant that the wound was sterile and could be closed. This sometime involved sutures, but for more gaping wounds the skin was drawn together and held in place with bandages or flannel strips secured with tape or laces.[55]

Since many American surgeons had volunteered to serve with the British and French medical services during the early stages of the war, when they joined the AEF, they were quite familiar with gas gangrene and the Dakin-Carrel Solution.[56] Moreover, due to the widespread acceptance of this method of treatment, the death rate from this cause was considerably reduced. However, the solution was only part of a successful course of treatment. Experience showed that the quicker a wounded man received aid, the better his chances for a successful recovery.[57] Conversely, a delay in treatment still increased the chances of death from gas gangrene. It is little wonder that American division surgeons pushed so hard to move hospitals as far forward as possible, and that they expressed such frustration during the training period with the French, who insisted on placing hospitals farther toward the rear.[58] The Americans would simply have to await their turn to implement their ideas.

NOTES

1. Robert B. Asprey, *At Belleau Wood* (Denton: North Texas Press, 1968), 18–19 and 291; Richard Derby, *"Wade In, Sanitary!"* (New York: G. P. Putnam's Sons, 1919), 30–32

(death of corpsman from exposure to mustard gas); Alistair Horne, *The Price of Glory: Verdun, 1916* (London: Penguin, 1993), 287.

2. James Lung Bevans, *Medical History of the 26th Division from Organization to June 24, 1918* (typescript, n.d.), 9–10; Derby, *"Wade In, Sanitary!"* 32.

3. Frederick E. Jones, *Historical Sketch of the Medical Department of the 26th Division* (typescript, n.d.), 24–25; War Department, *Report of the Surgeon General U.S. Army to the Secretary of War, Annual Reports, 1919* (Washington, D.C.: GPO, 1920), 3301; R. S. Porter, Memorandum to Commanding Officer, Field Hospital 102 and Field Hospital 101–104, 18 July 1918 (re standardized treatment of mustard gas cases). NA RG120.

4. *Stars & Stripes*, September 13, 1918, 1. USMA.

5. *Circular Letter No. 80, May 27, 1918, HQ 26th Division, Office of Division Surgeon.* A typical German 77 mm gas shell scattered the gas in a leaf-shaped area ten to fifteen meters long and eight meters wide; the gas often carried as much as twenty-five meters. Hundreds or thousands of gas shells in a concentrated area posed a considerable problem. NA RG120.

6. Circular Letter No. 56, February 27, 1918, A.E.F. Forces, HQ 26th Division, Office of the Chief Surgeon. NA RG120.

7. Haythornthwaite, *The World War One Source Book* (London: Arms and Armour, 1992, 1996), 90–92; Denis Winter, *Death's Men*, 122; Duane, *Dear Old "K,"* 84–88.

8. Asprey, *In Belleau Wood*, 278.

9. Richard Derby, *"Wade In, Sanitary!"* 31-32 and 73 (bathing gas victims in the Marne at Luzancy); John W. Thomason, *Fix Bayonets!* (New York: Scribners, 1970), 65–66.

10. Bevans, *Medical History*, 10.

11. Edward M. Coffman, *The War to End All Wars: The American Military Experience in World War I* (Madison: Univ. of Wisconsin Press, 1986), 221.

12. Harvey Cushing, *From a Surgeon's Journal* (Boston: Little, Brown, 1936), 127.

13. H. L. Gilchrist, Lt. Col., M.C., U.S. Army, Medical Director, Gas Service, A.E.F., *A Simple, Practical and Safe Method of Administration of Oxygen, (Illustrated), 27 March 1918.* The necessary materials included the following:

two pieces of half-inch rubber tubing about two inches in length

two pieces of quarter-inch glass tubing (one ten inches and the other three inches long)

one 1000 cc wide-mouthed bottle filled with water, closed with cork with two quarter-inch holes

one rubber double catheter

one roll adhesive tape

one oxygen tank

The glass tubing was inserted in the cork, with the longer piece used as the intake and the shorter piece as the exit tube. The rubber tubing was attached to the valve of the oxygen tank and to the long glass tube. The other rubber tube connected the shorter glass tube to the catheter, which was then inserted in both nasal passages. The valve was turned on, and the oxygen bubbled through the water, which in turn allowed the person administering it to monitor the amount, as reflected in the number and size of the bubbles produced. NA RG120.

14. Circular Letter No. 56, February 27, 1918, A.E.F. Forces., HQ 26th Division, Office of the Chief Surgeon, par. IV, 1–2. NA RG120.

15. Duane, *Dear Old "K,"* 87.

16. Memorandum to All Medical Officers, 16 August 1918, Office of the Division Surgeon 26th Division; Bevans, *Medical History of the 26th Division*, 16. NA RG120.

17. Cushing, *From a Surgeon's Journal*, 79 (reference to General Gorgas' recommendation, prior to U.S. entry into World War I, that two complete hospital units be recruited from the Medical Reserve Corps and sent to Neuilly, France, or used in the punitive expedition in Mexico).

18. Lettie Gavin, *American Women in World War I* (Niwot: Univ. Press of Colorado, 1997), 226–27.

19. Circular Letter No. 56, HQ, 26th Division, Office of the Chief Surgeon, February 27, 1918, para. II 1. NA RG120.

20. John J. Haller, Jr., *Farmcarts to Fords: A History of the American Ambulance, 1790–1925* (Carbondale: Southern Illinois Univ. Press, 1992), 186.

21. Woods Hutchinson, *The Doctor in War* (Boston: Houghton Mifflin, 1918), 40 (80 percent); Haller, *Farmcarts to Fords*, 185–86 (85 percent of wounds from high-explosive shells or grenades).

22. Winter, *Death's Men*, 193; Cushing, *From a Surgeon's Journal*, 73; Robert Graves, *Good-Bye To All That* New York: Doubleday, 1985), 11.

23. W. W. Keen, *The Treatment of War Wounds* (Philadelphia: Saunders, 1917), 100–109.

24. Derby, *"Wade In, Sanitary!"* 9–10; Cushing, *From a Surgeon's Journal*, 134 (a rate of recovery of fifty out of ninety was "not so bad").

25. Keen, *Treatment of War Wounds*, 115–21.

26. Derby, *"Wade In, Sanitary!"* 163–64; Keen, *Treatment of War Wounds*, 110–11.

27. Charles Lynch, ed., *The Medical Department of the United States Army in the World War*, vol. 8, *Field Operations* (Washington, D.C.: GPO, 1925), 74 (quoting from Memorandum).

28. Haller, *Farmcarts to Fords*, 188–89 and 192–93.

29. Lynch, ed., *Medical Department of the United States Army in the World War*, vol. 8, *Field Operations*, 73–74. See also Haller, *Farmcarts to Fords*, 189.

30. Haller, *Farmcarts to Fords*, 192.

31. Anthony Babington, *Shell-Shock* (London: Leo Cooper, 1997). Overall an excellent, authoritative, but readable study of this illness, from its earliest times to the present.

32. Winter, *Death's Men*, 92.

33. Ronald Schaffer, *America in the Great War: The Rise of the War Welfare State* (New York: Oxford Univ. Press, 1991), 199–200; Graves, *Good-Bye to All That*, 288.

34. Circular Letter No. 90, France, 4 Sept. 1918 NA RG120; *Stars & Stripes*, September 20, 1918, 6. (The chief surgeon, AEF referred to the term as "military slang" and not a "diagnosis or disability.")

35. Bevans, *Medical History*, 16.

36. Schaffer, *America in the Great War*, 204–5.

37. Gavin, *American Women in World War I*, 101–28.

38. John Keegan, *The Face of Battle* (London: Penguin, 1978), 335 (quote taken from American official report entitled "Combat Exhaustion").

39. Graves, *Good-Bye to All That*, 288.

40. Edward D. Churchill, *Surgeon to Soldiers* (Philadelphia: Lippincott, 1972), 271; Lyn Macdonald, *The Roses of No Man's Land* (New York: Macmillan, 1989), 24–25.

41. Churchill, *Surgeon to Soldiers*, 271–72.

42. Winter, *Death's Men*, 196.

43. Churchill, *Surgeon to Soldiers*, 271–72; James Robb Church, *The Doctor's Part*, (New York: Appleton, 1918), 110–11. Translated literally as "taking the bridle of the horse."

44. Macdonald, *Roses of No Man's Land*, 91.

45. Ibid., xii.

46. Ibid., xi and 91.

47. Ibid., 24.

48. W. Sterling Edwards, and Peter D. Edwards, *Alexis Carrel: Visionary Surgeon* (Springfield, Ill.: Charles C. Thomas, 1974), 68–69.

49. Macdonald, *Roses of No Man's Land*, 91. Dr. Alexis Carrel, was born Marie Joseph Auguste Carrel Billiard at Saint-Foy-des-Lyon, near Lyon, France, on June 28, 1873. Although not wealthy, his family was more than comfortable; however, his father died young, leaving his mother a widow with three small children to raise. The young man later began to use the name of his late father, Alexis, and he was known by that name for the balance of his life. Following graduation from medical school, he studied surgery, at first with an eye toward practice as a physician, but his true calling seemed to be the research laboratory. During his long and distinguished career, he improved and discovered surgical techniques. He did pioneer work in organ transplantation with animals and in vascular surgery. In fact, he pioneered many surgical procedures that are in use today, some of which bear his name. It is ironic that the world's foremost vascular surgeon worked within in miles of the front line in the First World War and that the techniques that he had developed for the repair of damaged blood vessels were not used to save countless lives and limbs until decades later, because the problems of infection and tissue rejection had not yet been solved. Much of the work took place at the Rockefeller Institute in New York. He was awarded the Nobel Prize for Physiology and Medicine in 1913. Dr. Carrel continued his medical research after the war and died in France on November 5, 1944. Edwards, *Alexis Carrel,* see generally regarding his life and work.

50. The hypochlorous solution itself was quite simple to make, and it had several variants. The most effective formula was made with boric acid in order to assure that the solution was ph-neutral. It was made by dissolving 140 grams of dry sodium carbonate (or 400 grams of washing soda) in twelve liters of tap water, and adding to that 200 grams of chloride of lime. After being shaken well the mixture precipitated, and after half an hour the clear liquid was siphoned off and filtered through a plug of cotton. Forty grams of boric acid were added *after* the filtration, and the solution was ready to use. However, before use, it was tested for neutrality; if a reddish color appeared indicating alkalinity, slightly more boric acid was added. It kept about a week. Edwards, *Alexis Carrel*, 69–70.

51. Macdonald, *Roses of No Man's Land*, 91.

52. Keen, *Treatment of War Wounds*, 40.

53. Ibid., 48–50.

54. Ibid., 46–48.

55. Ibid., 50–56.

56. Cushing, *From a Surgeon's Journal.*

57. Churchill, *Surgeon to Soldiers*, 271–74.

58. Bevans, *Medical History*, 8–9.

Appendix VII: Call to Quarters

In theory, each field hospital was supposed to carry tentage for both hospital wards and as shelter for the men. However, field hospitals moved frequently and often found themselves in locations previously occupied by other hospitals—in municipal buildings, churches, and schools. Medical Department policy at the time required that where available, priority be given to permanent structures over tentage. Since these locations tended to be in built-up areas, housing for personnel was, more often than not, in such billets as houses, barns, and nearby barracks. It was simpler that way.[1] In addition, especially during the early buildup phase, there were very few barracks available. The practice of billeting was relatively unknown to the American army. In France, a "town major" or billeting officer, would be appointed for a particular town or area. It would be his responsibility to make arrangements with the local authorities for sufficient housing for units assigned to his area. In towns, the ideal arrangement was the billeting of a company on both sides of one street. Company officers were to be located in the same block. The officers usually found cleaner, cozier billets, while the enlisted men wound up in stables with attendant smells and lice-ridden straw.[2]

Private first class Bartlett Bent arrived at his billet on September 8, 1918. His frustration with army life is palpable as he describes his new quarters: "At 2 o'clock we moved into a stable[;] a hell of a hole but sleep in it we must. Raining like sin and we all got soaked. I'm sure fed up tonight."[3] However, the next day, after the place was cleaned up and he ate an unusually good meal, his spirits soared: "beefsteak, french frys [sic], wine, melons—chocolate. Wonderful. How will I stand the shock."[4]

In January 1918, the billeting process became organized under the title American Requisition Service, which was attached to the Services of Supply. At this time, the

French gave the American army the same rights to billeting and quartering as they had, and the process gradually improved. Even so, the billeting officer still had to exercise the "utmost tact" in dealing with local officials, and his work often became a balancing act between military necessity and local custom.[5]

Each field hospital was allocated four kinds of tents: ward, hospital, small wall, and pyramidal tents. Each was constructed of 12.4-ounce cotton duck cloth.[6] These and the other tents were carried on the company trucks, and later, vehicles of the Provisional Truck Company.[7] The ward tent was by far the largest. Its dimensions were eleven feet high and thirty-six feet long at the ridge, and sixteen feet wide and fifty feet long at the base. There were three principal types of ward tents, two of European and one of American manufacture. The first was the marquee tent, built by the British, and the second was the Bessoneau tent, named for a popular French tent manufacturer.[8] Ten thousand Bessoneau tents were ordered by the army, and they started arriving around October 1, 1918, but by November 11, only 800 had been delivered. The marquee tent was in much greater use, since 3,000 had been delivered by the armistice, arriving at the rate of fifty per day.[9] Many tents were described as Bessoneau that were undoubtedly another style. In fact, Bessoneau tents themselves came in different sizes and types. The third style was the American-made Medical Department ward tent. Each field hospital company was allocated six of these tents, as well as six canvas covers for them when folded.[10] Since wood was scarce, the tents were provided with groundsheets to ameliorate the effects of the mud and dirt. Where available, electric lights were preferable, since the acetylene lamps had only a four-hour life and were easily extinguished by jars from the artillery shells that often rained down upon field hospitals, as well as the boom from friendly guns often placed nearby.[11]

In addition to the ward tents, each field hospital was allocated four complete hospital tents along with a large cover called a fly. The hospital tent was twelve feet high and a little more than fifteen feet wide at the base. It was over fourteen feet long at the ridge. On the other hand, wall tents came in two sizes, large and small. Each field hospital was also allocated anywhere from one to six small wall tents, which were eight and one-half feet high, nine feet along the ridge, and nearly nine feet wide at the base. This tent also came with a fly. It was used by the company officers.

Finally, for the shelter of enlisted personnel, each field hospital was allocated thirteen pyramidal tents, which were capable of holding the cots and personal gear of six men. This tent was eleven feet high and sixteen feet square at the base, tapering to eighteen inches square at the top. In addition, each soldier was issued a shelter half, a rectangular piece of canvas that when joined with another shelter half formed the well-known "pup" tent.[12] Even where the ubiquitous "Adrian" barrack or hut was available, the shelter half came in handy. Many of the wooden barracks erected were of poor construction and leaked like sieves. The men of the 104th Infantry found that the canvas came in very handy and used their shelter halves inside their barracks in order to stay dry.[13] In spite of the poor construction, barracks were preferable to tents since they could be better heated, lit, and ventilated.[14]

However, during the height of the influenza epidemic, even the chief surgeon sounded the praises of the humble pup tent, especially where barracks were overcrowded and the disease was most likely to spread.[15]

NOTES

1. *Manual for the Medical Department, 1916,* Art. XII, *"The Theater of Operations, General,"* par. 701(b), extract in Charles Lynch, ed., *The Medical Department of the United States Army in the World War,* vol. 8, *Field Operations* (Washington, D.C.: GPO, 1925), 1034. In fact, the Manual states that "suitable buildings are of great advantage. Such buildings should be utilized first, and only so much tentage put up as may be required."

2. Frank W. Weed, ed., *The Medical Department of the United States Army in the World War,* vol. 6, *Sanitation* (Washington, D.C.: GPO, 1926), 574–75.

3. Bartlett Bent, *Diary: England 1918–19,* diary entry for September 8, 1918. CHS.

4. Ibid., diary entry for September 9, 1918. CHS.

5. Weed, ed., *Medical Department of the United States Army in the World War,* vol. 6, *Sanitation,* 574–75.

6. U.S. Quartermaster Corps. *Specifications for Tentage* (Washington, D.C.: GPO, 1916). MHI.

7. Richard Derby, *"Wade in, Sanitary!"* (New York: G. P. Putnam's Sons, 1919), 100–101.

8. *Stars & Stripes,* February 8, 1918, 5 (advertisement). USMA.

9. Joseph H. Ford, ed., *The Medical Department of the United States Army in the World War,* vol. 2, *Administration American Expeditionary Forces* (Washington, D.C.: GPO, 1927), 260.

10. Edwin C. Wolfe, ed., *The Medical Department of the United States Army in the World War,* vol. 3, *Finance and Supply* (Washington, D.C.: GPO, 1928), 280–81.

11. Lynch, ed., *The Medical Department of the United States Army in the World War,* vol. 8, *Field Operations,* 171.

12. Jonathan Gawne, *Over There! The American Soldier in World War One* (London: Greenhill, 1997), 29 and 58–59.

13. James T. Duane, *Dear Old "K"* (Boston: Thomas Todd, 1922), 13; Frank Freidel, *Over There* (Philadelphia: Temple Univ. Press, 1990), 43. See also R. S. Porter, *101st Sanitary Train, 26th Division A.E.F., History, March 20th, 1919,* 345.

14. Lynch, ed., *The Medical Department of the United States Army in the World War,* vol. 8, *Field Operations,* 166.

15. *Stars & Stripes,* October 18, 1918, 8. USMA.

Appendix VIII: Assembly

Aside from the advances in weaponry, the single most important aspect of the First World War was the mobility of the respective armies.[1] Each nation was able to bring to the battle enormous quantities of material and men within a relatively short time frame. British shipping alone moved 10,000 Americans per day to France by the middle of 1918.[2] Railroads permitted the shifting of men from one front to another hundreds of miles apart. In the period following the Treaty of Brest-Litvosk, the Germans shifted whole divisions from the eastern front to the western front in time to launch the nearly successful spring offensive.[3] Steamships and trains had been in use for a century. However, it was the gasoline engine that opened the door to mechanized warfare.[4] Arguably, the truck proved the most important use of the gasoline engine in World War I. Instead of large, passive people-movers guided by anonymous drivers, trucks were driven by ordinary soldiers. The truck was the means by which the soldier was supplied or delivered to battle, and it was an ambulance that delivered him from the battle when he became wounded. The machine became the weapon, and as with the airplane and the tank, it became an extension of the individual soldier.[5] The gasoline engine was no longer a toy for the rich but a part of the lives of more than 2,000,000 American doughboys who served in France.

During the early years, much of the transportation was dependent upon animals. Artillery caissons and supply wagons were horse or mule drawn.[6] Originally, the table of organization and equipment (TOE) for field hospital companies called for one of the four companies to be supported by horse-drawn vehicles. The motorized units were initially allocated eleven trucks, which were later pooled into the Provisional Truck Company.[7] However, the sheer size and scope of the modern battlefield and the huge numbers of men involved forced a rethinking of the efficacy of the old models.[8] At the beginning of the war, the U.S. Army had only 3,000 trucks. It would ultimately need 85,000.[9] The AEF depended very heavily upon the French to transport rations from the rail line to the various units.[10] A credit to cooperation between the military and the automobile industry was the design and manufacture of the "Liberty" truck. The best design features were taken from various manufacturers, and parts were standardized.[11]

Despite its high initial cost, the truck was more practical than an animal, since it did not succumb to disease or require huge amounts of feed. Granted, tires were a problem due to the rough terrain, but a truck needed just one-tenth the storage space of a horse and saved one-third to one-half the transport time.[12] In the evacuation of sick and wounded, time was definitely an important factor in the recovery of a patient.[13] In addition to moving men and supplies to the front or to new stations, supply trucks often doubled as ambulances, taking the wounded to field hospitals and dressing stations in time of great urgency. Likewise, empty ambulances often moved supplies to the front, only to turn around with wounded, as the Provisional Truck Company did on the Heights of the Meuse at the Battle of St. Mihiel. Speed also meant that troops and supplies got to the front faster. Arguably, the most massive use of motor vehicles for supply and evacuation was by the French army during Verdun. During that campaign, the road from Bar-le-Duc to Verdun was virtually bumper to bumper, single file in each direction, twenty-four hours a day.[14] Col. James Robb Church was an American medical doctor and military observer, who spent two years on the Western Front in France; standing on a street corner in Bar-le-Duc in 1916, Dr. Church counted one vehicle every fifteen seconds, each way.[15]

From the time war broke out in Europe to the entry of the American army, two separate groups of volunteers carried out ambulance duties for the Allies, the American Ambulance Field Service (later shortened to the American Field Service, or AFS) and the Anglo-American Volunteer Motor Ambulance Corps, otherwise known as the Norton-Harjes Group, under the aegis of the Red Cross.[16] After America's entry, some of the units became integrated into the U.S. Army. Others remained in the French Service de Sanitaire.[17] Even so, many of those units were attached to American divisions, such as SSU 502, which was with the Yankees in the Pas Fini sector.[18] Early in the war, the volunteer ambulance organizations relied on vehicles of all descriptions, usually borrowed or donated.[19] Later, the American Field Service chose the Ford Model T, which proved to be a real workhorse close to the front. Its short wheelbase, which allowed it to maneuver in small spaces, gave it a funny appearance; the rear projected well beyond the body so as to accommodate stretchers.[20]

The beauty of the Ford "Tin Lizzie" was that it could be shipped in large numbers of ready-to-assemble engines and chassis, made of interchangeable parts. Nothing was wasted; the packing crates were used to build the outer body of the ambulance itself.[21] American field hospitals tried to maintain some Model Ts for the tough places and use the smoother-riding GMCs for transport to base hospitals in the rear.[22] After early reports from the British and French of patients dying en route to the hospital from asphyxiation due to the exhaust from gas heaters, ventilation holes were required in American Ford ambulances. A double row of one-inch auger holes was drilled at three-inch intervals in the panel behind the driver, another series just beneath the roof, and a third row in the tail board.[23] The table of organization allowed twelve motor ambulances per motorized ambulance company.[24]

NOTES

1. Rod Paschall, *The Defeat of Imperial Germany, 1917–1918* (Chapel Hill, N.C.: Algonquin, 1989), 11.

2. Carlo D'Este, *Patton: A Genius For War* (New York: HarperCollins, 1995), 230.

3. Paschall, *Defeat of Imperial Germany, 1917–1918*, 103.

4. Ibid., 106.

5. Arlen J. Hansen, *Gentlemen Volunteers* (New York: Arcade, 1996), 115.

6. Paschall, *Defeat of Imperial Germany, 1917–1918*, 93 and 103.

7. Tables of Organization, Series A, January 14, 1918, Corrected to June 26, 1918, Part I, Infantry Division, Maximum Strength, Table 28, column 8, "Sanitary Train."

8. John S. Haller, *Farmcarts to Fords: A History of the Military Ambulance, 1790–1925* (Carbondale: Southern Illinois Univ. Press, 1992), 102–3.

9. Paschall, *Defeat of Imperial Germany, 1917–1918*, 51.

10. Richard Derby, *"Wade in, Sanitary!"* (New York: G. P. Putnam's Sons, 1919), 2.

11. Jonathan Gawne, *Over There! The American Soldier in World War I* (London: Greenhill, 1997), 40.

12. Haller, *Farmcarts to Fords,* 107 and 166.

13. Ibid., 187; Derby, *"Wade in, Sanitary!"* 34–35.

14. Alistair Horne, *The Price of Glory: Verdun 1916* (London: Penguin, 1993), 147–48 and 349.

15. James Robb Church, *The Doctor's Part* (New York: Appleton, 1918), 134–35.

16. Hansen, *Gentlemen Volunteers*, xvi–xvii.

17. Ibid., 161–81.

18. Memorandum, Assistant Chief of Staff, G-4 Paris Group to Commanding General Second Division, July 3, 1918; Memorandum to Section Chiefs and M.S.O., para. V, HQ, 101st Sanitary Train, 5 July 1918. NA RG120.

19. Haller, *Farmcarts to Fords*, 164–65 and 168; Lyn Macdonald, *The Roses of No Man's Land* (New York: Macmillan, 1989), 63.

20. Hansen, *Gentlemen Volunteers,* 97–115 (excellent description of the attributes of the "Tin Lizzie").

21. Ibid., 108; Lyn Macdonald, *Roses of No Man's Land,* 10.

22. Derby, *"Wade in, Sanitary!"* 138–42. See also Bevans, *Medical History of the 26th Division from Organization to June 24, 1918* (typescript, n.d.),19; Frederick E. Jones, *Historical Sketch of the Medical Department of the 26th Division* (typescript, n.d.), 26. (The 26th Division maintained seventy-one motor ambulances, fifty-one GMCs (twelve of which belonged to the 162nd Ambulance Company), and twenty Fords. The latter belonged to an attached Service de Sanitaire unit, SSU 502). NA RG120.

23. *Stars & Stripes,* February 8, 1918, 4. USMA.

24. Tables of Organization, Series A, January 14, 1918, Corrected to June 26, 1918, Part I, Infantry Division, Maximum Strength, table 28.

Bibliography

Several books cited below are essential for the beginning researcher in order to obtain a basic overall grasp of the First World War, particularly American participation in it. The list is headed by *The Doughboys* (now sadly out of print) by Laurence Stallings, a rousing tribute to the American soldier. *The First World War,* by Martin Gilbert, *The War to End All Wars,* by Edward Coffman, and *The Defeat of Imperial Germany, 1917–1918,* by Rod Paschall are all very readable and well documented. I have relied heavily upon them in attempting to place the 103rd Field Hospital Company in the context of that conflict. Two histories of the 26th Division, *With the Yankee Division in France,* by Frank Sibley (a correspondent attached to the division), and *New England in France, 1917–1919,* by Emerson G. Taylor (a former division adjutant), although very partisan, provide the reader with an excellent picture of the division's role in the war and were of invaluable assistance me. *The World War One Source Book,* by Philip Haythornthwaite, is a very comprehensive summary of all aspects of the war and the participants, and I consulted it constantly, particularly in the area of weapons. In the decade following the war's end, the U.S. Army produced a comprehensive, fifteen-volume work entitled *The Medical Department of the United States Army in the World War.* This is an amazing resource, full of more information than one person could digest in a lifetime. Finally, I have long contended that we are a nation of packrats, and the ultimate source of original documents is the National Archives. Record Group 120 is a treasure trove.

BOOKS

Albertine, Connell. *The Yankee Doughboy.* Boston: Brandon Press, 1968.
Ashburn, P. H. *A History of the Medical Department of the United States Army.* Boston: Houghton Mifflin, 1929.
Asprey, Robert B. *At Belleau Wood.* Denton: North Texas Press, 1996.
———. *The German High Command at War: Hindenburg and Ludendorff Conduct World War I.* New York: Quill, 1991.
Babington, Anthony. *Shell-Shock.* London: Leo Cooper, 1997.

Baker, Chester E. *Doughboy's Diary*. Shippensburg, Penn.: Burd Street Press, 1998.

Benwell, Harry A. *History of the Yankee Division*. Boston: Cornhill, 1919.

Berry, Henry. *Make the Kaiser Dance*. Garden City, N.Y.: Doubleday, 1978.

Blumenson, Martin. *Patton: The Man behind the Legend, 1885–1945*. New York: Quill, 1985.

Braim, Paul. *The Test of Battle: The American Expeditionary Forces in the Meuse-Argonne Campaign*. Newark: Univ. of Delaware Press, 1988.

Bullard, Robert L. and Earl Reeves. *American Soldiers Also Fought*. New York: Maurice H. Louis, 1939.

Church, James Robb. *The Doctor's Part*. New York: Appleton, 1918.

Churchill, Edward D. *Surgeon to Soldiers*. Philadelphia: Lippincott, 1972.

Clark, George B. *Devil Dogs: Fighting Marines of World War I*. Novato, Calif.: Presido, 1999.

Coffman, Edward M. *The War to End All Wars: The American Military Experience in World War I*. Madison: Univ. of Wisconsin Press, 1986.

Cooper, John Milton, Jr. *The Warrior and the Priest*. Cambridge, Mass.: Belknap, 1983.

Cornewall-Jones, R. J. *The British Merchant Service*. London: Sampson Low, Marston, 1898.

Cushing, Harvey. *From a Surgeon's Journal*. Boston: Little, Brown, 1936.

Dallemagne, François. *Les Casernes Françaises*. Paris: Picard, 1990.

Derby, Richard. *"Wade in, Sanitary!"* New York: G. P. Putnam's Sons, 1919.

D'Este, Carlo. *Patton: A Genius for War*. New York: HarperCollins, 1995.

Duane, James T. *Dear Old "K."* Boston: Thomas Todd, 1922.

Edwards, William Sterling, and Peter D. Edwards. *Alexis Carrel: Visionary Surgeon*. Springfield, Ill.: Charles C. Thomas, 1974.

Eisenhower, John S. D. *Intervention! The United States and the Mexican Revolution, 1913–1917*. New York: W. W. Norton, 1993.

Ellis, John. *Eye Deep in Hell*. Baltimore: Johns Hopkins Univ. Press, 1989.

———. *The Social History of the Machine Gun*. New York: Random House, 1975.

Emmons, Frederick. *The Atlantic Liners*. New York: Bonanza, 1972.

Ettinger, Albert M., and A. Churchill. *A Doughboy with the Fighting 69th*. Shippensburg, Penn.: White Mane, 1992.

Farago, Ladislas. *Patton: Ordeal and Triumph*. New York: Obolensky, 1964.

Farwell, Byron. *Over There: The United States in the Great War, 1917–1918*. New York: W. W. Norton, 1999.

Fifield, James H. *The Regiment: A History of the 104th U.S. Infantry, A.E.F. 1917–1919*. Springfield, Mass.: Springfield Union, 1946.

Ford, Bert. *The Fighting Yankees Overseas*. Boston: McPhail, 1919.

Franks, Norman. *Who Downed the Aces in WWI?* London: Grub Street, 1996.

Freidel, Frank. *Over There*. Philadelphia: Temple Univ. Press, 1990.

Friends of the Armistice of Compiegne. *Armistice 1918*. Compiegne, France: Bourson, n.d.

Fromkin, David. *In the Time of the Americans*. New York: Knopf, 1995.

Fussell, Paul. *The Great War and Modern Memory*. London: Oxford Univ. Press, 1975.

Gallagher, Christopher J. *The Cellars of Marcelcave: A Yank Doctor in the BEF*. Edited by Mary E. Malloy. Shippensburg, Penn.: Burd Street Press, 1998.

Gavin, Lettie. *American Women in World War I*. Niwot: Univ. Press of Colorado, 1997.

George, Albert, and Edwin H. Cooper. *Pictorial History of the Twenty-Sixth Division United States Army*. Boston: Ball, 1920.

Gilbert, Martin. *The First World War*. New York: Henry Holt, 1994.

Graves, Robert. *Good-Bye to All That*. New York: Doubleday, 1985.

Greenwood, Paul. *The Second Battle of the Marne, 1918*. Shrewsbury, U.K.: Airlife, 1998.

Greiss, Thomas E., ed. *The Great War*. Wayne, N.J.: Avery, 1986.

Haller, John S., Jr. *Farmcarts to Fords: A History of the Military Ambulance, 1790–1925*. Carbondale: Southern Illinois Univ. Press, 1992.

Hamby, Alonzo L. *Man of the People: A Life of Harry S. Truman*. New York: Oxford Univ. Press, 1996.

Hansen, Arlen J. *Gentlemen Volunteers*. New York: Arcade, 1996.

Harbord, James G. *The American Army in France, 1917–1919*. Boston: Little, Brown, 1936.

Harries, Meirion, and Susie Harries. *The Last Days of Innocence: America at War, 1917–1918*. New York: Random House, 1997.

Harris, Harvey L. *The War As I Saw It: 1918 Letters of a Tank Corps Lieutenant*. St. Paul, Minn.: Pogo Press, 1998.

Herzog, Stanley J. *The Fightin' Yanks*. Stamford, Conn.: Cunningham, 1922.

Hinrichs, Ernest H. *Listening In*. Shippensburg, Penn.: White Mane, 1996.

Hoehling, A. A. *The Great Epidemic*. Boston: Little, Brown, 1961.

Holt, Tonie, and Valmai Holt. *Battlefields of the First World War*. London: Pavilion,1993.

Horne, Alistair. *The Price of Glory: Verdun, 1916*. London: Penguin, 1993.

Hudson, James J. *Hostile Skies*. Syracuse, N.Y.: Syracuse Univ. Press., 1996.

Hume, Edgar Erskine. *Victories of Army Medicine*. Philadelphia: Lippincott, 1943.

Hunt, John G. *The Inaugural Addresses of the Presidents*. New York: Gramercy, 1995.

Hutchinson, Woods. *The Doctor in War*. Boston: Houghton Mifflin, 1918.

Janis, Elsie. *The Big Show*. New York: Cosmopolitan, 1919.

Johnson, Douglas Wilson. *Battlefields of the World War*. New York: Oxford Univ. Press, 1921.

Johnson, Thomas M., and Fletcher Pratt. *The Lost Battalion*. Lincoln: Univ. of Nebraska Press (Bison), 2000.

Keegan, John. *The Face of Battle*. London: Penguin, 1976.

———. *The Price of Admiralty*. New York: Viking, 1988.

Keen, W. W. *The Treatment of War Wounds*. Philadelphia: Saunders, 1917.

Kennedy, David M. *Over Here: The First World War and American Society*. New York: Oxford Univ. Press, 1980.

Kennett, Lee. *Marching through Georgia*. New York: Harper, 1995.

Kludas, Arnold. *Great Passenger Ships of the World*, vol. 1: *1858–1912*. Cambridge: Patrick Stephens, 1975.

Langer, William L. *Gas and Flame in World War I*. New York: Knopf, 1965.

Macdonald, Lyn. *1914*. New York: Atheneum, 1988.

———. *1915: The Death of Innocence*. New York: Henry Holt, 1993.

———. *The Roses of No Man's Land*. New York: Macmillan, 1989.

———. *Somme*. New York: Dorset, 1983.

Mackin, Elton E. *Suddenly We Didn't Want to Die*. Novato, Calif.: Presidio, 1993.

Manchester, William. *American Caesar*. Boston: Little, Brown, 1978.

———. *The Last Lion: Winston Spencer Churchill, Visions of Glory 1874–1932*. New York: Dell, 1983.

Marshall, S.L.A. *The American Heritage History of World War I*. New York: Dell, 1964.

Massie, Robert K. *Dreadnought*. New York: Random House, 1991.

McCullough, David. *Truman*. New York: Simon and Schuster, 1992.

Montgomery, Bernard Law. *The Memoirs of Field Marshal Montgomery.* London: Collins, 1958.

Moorehead, Alan. *Gallipoli.* New York: Ballantine, 1958, 1996.

Nelson, John. *A Brief History of the Fighting Yankee Division A.E.F. on the Battlefront February 5, 1918–November 1918,* 3rd ed., Worcester: Worcester Evening Gazette, 1919.

Owen, Wilfred. *The Collected Poems of Wilfred Owen.* Edited by C. Day Lewis. New York: New Directions, 1965.

Parrish, Thomas. *Roosevelt and Marshall.* New York: William Morrow, 1989.

Paschall, Rod. *The Defeat of Imperial Germany, 1917–1918.* Chapel Hill, N.C.: Algonquin, 1989.

Patton, Robert H. *The Pattons.* New York: Crown, 1994.

Perret, Geoffrey. *A Country Made by War.* New York: Random House, 1989.

———. *Old Soldiers Never Die.* New York: Random House, 1996.

Pershing, John J. *My Experiences in the First World War.* New York: Da Capo, 1995.

Pottle, Frederick A. *Stretchers: The Story of a Hospital Unit on the Western Front.* New Haven, Conn.: Yale Univ. Press, 1929.

Remarque, Erich Maria. *All Quiet on the Western Front.* New York: Fawcett, 1967.

Renehan, Edward J., Jr. *The Lion's Pride: Theodore Roosevelt and His Family in Peace and War.* New York: Oxford Univ. Press. 1998.

Rogers, Horatio. *World War I through My Sights.* San Rafael, Calif.: Presidio, 1975.

Schaffer, Ronald. *America in the Great War: The Rise of the War Welfare State.* New York: Oxford Univ. Press, 1991.

Schneider, Dorothy, and Carl J. Schneider, *Into the Breach.* New York: Viking, 1991.

Sibley, Frank P. *With the Yankee Division in France.* Boston: Little, Brown, 1919.

Smith, Gene. *Until the Last Trumpet Sounds.* New York: John Wiley and Sons, 1998

Stallings, Laurence. *The Doughboys.* New York: Harper and Row, 1963.

Strickland, Daniel W. *Connecticut Fights: The Story of the 102nd Regiment.* New Haven, Conn.: Quinnipiack Press, 1930.

Taylor, Emerson G. *New England in France, 1917–1919: A History of the Twenty-Sixth Division U.S.A.* Boston: Houghton Mifflin, 1920.

Thomason, John W. *Fix Bayonets!* New York: Scribners, 1970, repr. Marine Corps Association, 1990.

Toland, John. *No Man's Land.* New York: Konecky, 1980.

Trumbo, Dalton. *Johnny Got His Gun.* New York: Citadel Press, 1994.

Tuchman, Barbara. *The Guns of August.* New York: Dell, 1962.

———. *The Zimmerman Telegram.* New York: Macmillan, 1958.

Tucker, Spencer C. *The Great War, 1914–1918.* Bloomington: Indiana Univ. Press, 1998.

Van Every, Dale. *The A.E.F. in Battle.* New York: Appleton, 1928.

Webster, Donovan. *Aftermath: The Remnants of War.* New York: Vintage, 1998.

Weintraub, Stanley. *A Stillness Heard Round the World.* New York: Oxford Univ. Press, 1985.

Winter, Denis. *Death's Men.* London: Penguin, 1979.

Young, Hugh. *A Surgeon's Autobiography.* New York: Harcourt, Brace, 1940.

REFERENCE WORKS

Chadwick, Alex. *Illustrated History of Baseball.* New York: Bison, 1988.

Encyclopaedia Britannica. Chicago: William Benton, 1959.

Esposito, Vincent J., ed., *West Point Atlas of American Wars*, vol. 2: 1900–1918. New York: Henry Holt, 1997.

Gawne, Jonathan. *Over There! The American Soldier in World War I*. London: Greenhill, 1997.

Gilbert, Martin. *Atlas of World War I*. New York: Oxford Univ. Press, 1994.

Greiss, Thomas E., ed., *Atlas for the Great War*. Wayne, N.J.: Avery, 1986.

Haythornthwaite, Philip J. *A Photohistory of World War One*. London: Arms and Armour, 1995.

——. *The World War One Source Book*. London: Arms and Armour, 1992, 1996.

Laffin, John. *Panorama of the Western Front*. London: Grange Books, 1996.

——. *A Western Front Companion: 1914–1918*. Gloucestershire, U.K.: Sutton, 1997.

Pope, Stephen, and Elizabeth-Anne Wheal, eds., *Dictionary of the First World War*. New York: St. Martin's, 1995.

Spiller, Roger, ed., *Dictionary of Military Biography*. Westport, Conn.: Greenwood, 1984.

Stringer, Harry R. *Heroes All!* Washington, D.C.: Fassett, 1919.

Waldron, William H. *The Infantry Soldier's Handbook*. New York: Lyons Press, 2000.

ARTICLES

"Annual Report" *Assembly*, June 10, 1931; June 11, 1936; July 1946.

Cartier, J. S. " The Old Front Line." *American Heritage*, November, 1993.

Lukacs, John. *1918. American Heritage*, November 1993.

——. *Yankee Doings* Vol. 25, no. 10 (November 1944) 10.

PRIMARY SOURCES

Books and Pamphlets

American Battle Monuments Commission. *American Armies and Battlefields in Europe: A History, Guide and Reference Book*. Washington, D.C.: GPO, 1938.

——. *American Memorials and Overseas Military Cemeteries*. Washington, D.C.: GPO, 1994.

——. *Flanders Field American Cemetery and Memorial*. Washington, D.C.: GPO, 1944.

——. *26th Division: Summary of Operations in the World War*. Washington, D.C.: GPO, 1944.

Haseltine, William E. *The Services of Supply of the American Expeditionary Forces: A Statistical Summary*. Washington, D.C.: GPO, 1919.

Historical Report of the Chief Engineer, Including All Operations of the Engineer Department, American Expeditionary Forces, 1917–1919. Washington, D.C.: GPO, 1919.

History of the 101st United States Engineers American Expeditionary Forces 1917–1918–1919. Cambridge, Mass.: Harvard Univ. Press, 1926.

Immortal Yankee Division 1917–1919. Boston: Young Men's Christian Association, 1919.

The Medical Department of the United States Army in the World War, 15 vols., Washington, D.C.: GPO, 1921–1929.

Putnam, Eben. *Report of the Commission on Massachusetts' Part in the World War*, vol. 1., *History*. Boston: Commonwealth of Massachusetts, 1931.

U.S. Army War College, Historical Division. *Order of Battle of United States Land Forces in the World War–A.E.F.:*

Divisions. Washington, D.C.: GPO, 1931.

General Headquarters, Armies, Army Corps, Services of Supply, and Separate Forces. Washington, D.C.: GPO, 1937.

The Genesis of the American First Army. Washington, D.C.: GPO, 1938.

U.S. Army Center of Military History. *Order of Battle of the United States Land Forces in the World War: American Expeditionary Forces, Divisions.* Washington, D.C.: GPO, 1988.

United States Army in the World War 1917–1919, 17 volumes. Washington, D.C.: GPO, 1968.

War Department. *Report of the Surgeon General U.S. Army to the Secretary of War, 1919,* 3 vols. Washington, D.C.: GPO, 1920.

Newspapers

Boston Globe, Boston Daily Globe, and *Boston Herald.* Microfilm copies at O'Neill Library, Boston College, Boston, Mass. (BCL)

Framingham Evening News. Framingham Historical Society, Framingham, Mass. (FHS)

Framingham News. Microfilm copies at Framingham Public Library, Framingham, Mass.(FPL)

Natick Bulletin. Microfilm copies at Morse Institute, Natick, Mass. (MI)

Stars & Stripes, 1918–1919. Microfilm copies at Cadet Library, United States Military Academy, West Point, N.Y. (USMA)

Worcester Evening Post and the *Worcester Telegram.* Microfilm copies at Worcester Public Library, Worcester, Mass. (WPL)

Manuscripts

Bevans, James Lung. *Medical History of the 26th Division from the Organization to June 24, 1918.* (typescript, n.d.). NA RG120.

History of the 304th (First Brigade) #314 Historical Branch. NA RG120.

Jones, Frederick E. *Historical Sketch of the Medical Department of the 26th Division.* (typescript, n.d., with "Introductory Note" by R. S. Porter, 8 August 1919). NA RG 120

Patton, George S. *Operations Report 304th (First Brigade) 18 Nov. 1918 A.E.F. together with G-3 Reports.* NA RG120.

Miscellaneous Orders and Reports of the 26th Division, Division Surgeon, 101st Sanitary Train, and the 103rd Field Hospital Company, 1917–1919, Record Group 120, National Archives and Records Administration, Washington, D.C.

Miscellaneous Orders and Reports of the 26th Division, Massachusetts National Guard Military Museum and Archives, Worcester, Massachusetts.

Journal of Field Orders (26th Division)—3 February 1918 through 25 April 1919.

Passenger List, RMS *Canada,* September 16, 1917.

Porter, R. S. *101st Sanitary Train, 26th Division A.E.F., History, March 20th, 1919.*
Roster Medical Department, 26th Division.

Miscellaneous Military Records. Adjutant General, Commonwealth of Massachusetts, Military Division, Boston, Massachusetts.
Miscellaneous Letters and Diaries. Connecticut Historical Society, Hartford.

Bent, Bartlett. *Diary: England 1918–19.*
Gunshannon, F. J. Notebook.
Hesselgrave, Charles E. *Narrative* (typescript).
Hudson, W. G. *The War Diary of W. G. Hudson 1917–1918.*
Neeld, Lawrence B. Letter, November 14, 1960.
Reynolds, John Edgar. Letters, September 15 and October 9, 1917.

Index

Ambly-sur-Meuse: 103rd Field Hospital at, 115, 117

American Expeditionary Forces (AEF):

Armies:

First Army: formation of, 74; headquarters at Ligny-en-Barrois, 96; St. Mihiel, 97; heavy casualties in Argonne, 112; Liggett assumes command, 124

Second Army: formation of, 124; Bullard assumes command, 124; area occupied by, 125

Third Army (Army of Occupation): formation of, 142

Corps:

1st Corps: Liggett assumes command, 77

5th Corps: George Cameron in command, 98; dissatisfaction of Pershing, 98

Divisions:

First Division ("Big Red One"): relief by 26th Division, 46; Cantigny, 54; Sedan, 125

Second Division: formation of, 54; Château-Thierry and Belleau Wood, 54–55; press coverage of the Marine Brigade (4th), 55; re-

lief by 26th Division, 75; enters Germany, 126

Third Division ("Rock of the Marne"): heroic stand at Marne River, 74

Sixth Division: relief of 26th Division, 129

Twenty-sixth Division ("Yankee"): formation of, 4–6; headquarters at Neufchâteau, 22; headquarters at Couvrelles, 39; division exercise canceled, 47; relief of 1st Division, 47; "bon secteur" (Toul), 55; headquarters at Boucq, 56; deplorable conditions, 55–56; Bois Brûlé (Apremont), 56; Seicheprey, 56–57; Hickey's Raid, 57, 60–61; Elsie Janis, 58–59, 77–78; move to Meaux, 75; counterattack near Vaux, 76; German prisoners, 76; Germans retreat from Château-Thierry, 76; attack stalls at Forêt de Fère, 76; division relieved, 77; part of 5th Corps, 98; relieves 2nd Division (French), 98; move to St. Remy Bois, 99; move to Verdun ("Neptune" sector), 112; terrible conditions in sector, 114; headquarters

About the Author

MICHAEL E. SHAY is a Superior Court Judge for the state of Connecticut. He has had a lifelong interest in history and genealogy and is currently working on two nonfiction works about the Yankee Division. He has lectured from time to time on Family Law.

CPSIA information can be obtained
at www.ICGtesting.com
Printed in the USA
BVHW030935031218
534172BV00046B/111/P